The Dalits and Dalit Awakening in India

Dr. Buta Singh

GYAN PUBLISHING HOUSE
NEW DELHI—110 002

THE DALITS AND DALIT AWAKENING IN INDIA
(Sociology)

ISBN: 81-212-0831-9

Published in 2004 in India by
Gyan Publishing House
5, Ansari Road
New Delhi-110002
Phones - 23282060, 23261060 Fax: 23285914
E-mail : gyanbook@vsnl. com
Visit our website at : www.gyanbooks.com

Lasertypesetting by: Varsha Graphics, Delhi
Printed by: Mehra Offset Press

Contents

Preface

Since the days of yore, the Dalits, very often despised as untouchables, had been suffering socially, culturally and economically. In fact our orthodox society always segregated them from the urban dwellings and existing norms and allotted menial works to them. It is thus evident that they were always at the beck and call of numerous societal functions. Their services could be commissioned for any kind of job even at an odd hour and it was not possible for them to refuse. Thus their social status remained pitiable throughout their life. They were just limping under the acute social pressure and their voice was stiffled without any consideration in their favour.

This pitiable condition of Dalits was seen and well-addressed by some eminent social and political philosophers like Mahatma Gandhi, Jagjivan Ram, B.R. Ambedkar and others and during their long career they have taken some ameliorative measures in order to raise their social status. Such measures include the launching of a long-drawn movement, reservation for jobs, constitutional safeguards, conversions, health and hygiene, inter-caste relations and entry into religious places.

In Adigranth, the verses of Guru Nanak Dev, Kabir and Ravidas are enshrined in connection with the low status of Dalits in our society. They have sincerely questioned their pitiable condition. Indeed Guru Nanak Dev is by the side of the lowest among the low caste. He ardently appeals to the Lord to cherish His grace on the poor. Sant Ravi Das talks of 'my city' where suffering and sorrow do not abide in it. He calls all fellow citizens as his loving friends. Similarly Sant Kabir showed a sense of unhappiness to differentiate between a Brahman and a low caste person. He elaborates his views thus: "If thou dost claim to be Brahmin by birth from a Brahmin woman . . . How are you Brahmin and we Surdas?"

As a student of political science and having some knowledge about socio-economic status of Dalits, I understand that this research work has been painstakingly undertaken following a toilsome job, with scholarly responsibility which have spread over a span of several years. It is evident that some kind of headway is a glaring phenomenon in this direction. There had been lot of opposition and criticism, mixed with non-violent satyagraha, which had to face difficult situations during all these years. However sincere efforts remained as the ongoing process with the hope that favourable dividends would touch their laps.

The theme has been weaved into ten Chapters having deep thrust on Dalits' status in ancient, medieval and modern India. The text deals with society and caste system in India, origin of Brahmins, social status of women, caste as the social group, profile of Buddha and Buddhism as a revolt against caste system, the age of foreign invasions, social structure of society in Medieval India, impact of Islam, Sikh ethics, Nath Panth and Nath Yogis, the Bhakti Movement as the voice of revolt, devotion and its implications and Raj Yoga and Gita and their effectiveness and perfection. Thus the theme elaborates a continued process of the alleviation of socio-economic status of the Dalits whose problems were magnified in regular writings, public meetings and legislative forum by those who always showed much concern for them.

Besides the theme depicts a survey of caste as a social group, religious influences, caste in the processes of evolution, primitive and foreign elements in Bombay castes and some typical castes like Vanis, Marathas, Lingayats and Kolis.

Thus it is evident that this comprehensive work is aimed at satisfying the academic urge of social scientists, politicians, parliamentarians, sociologists, anthropologists, planners, bureaucrats, teachers and students in India and abroad.

The next phase of untouchables has deep links with medieval India which depicts the exploits of Muhammad-bin-Qasim, Mahmud of Ghazni, Mohammad Ghori, accounts of Albiruni, Qutb-ud-din Aibak, Khilji dynasty, Muhammad Tughlaq and Firoz Tughlaq, the empire of Vijayanagar, Taimur, Lodi dynasty, advent of Mughal rule on Indian soil, viz., Babur, Humayun, Akbar and their successors.

The Bhakti movement has been considered as a strong voice of revolt. The tremendous contribution based upon the development and welfare of Dalits by Guru Nanak Dev, Guru Teg Bahadur, Guru Gobind Singh, Sant Kabir, Sant Ravi Das and others is highly commendable. Their theistic devotion had revolutionary effect on the functioning of Indian society.

In the end I must acknowledge the eminent scholars and their writings which have been used to fill up the relevant gaps in this volume. I appreciate their scholarship with the hope that their deep learning would be widely appreciated among the employees of the academic nurseries and institutions of higher learning.

Dr. Buta Singh

Acknowledgements

Foremost, I would like to offer my humble salutation to my Supervisor, Dr. Ram Avtar Sharma, whose guidance and goodwill rendered towards the endeavor are too large to be thanked. His optimism and dynamic attitude have been a source of constant inspiration.

I feel much beholden to Prof. Ramesh Chandra, Vice-Chancellor, Bundelkhand University for his academic motivation during my researches. A renowned scholar as he is, his sincere encouragement was a source of much inspiration to me.

It is my pleasant duty to thank Dr. Sangh Mittra, Deputy Directer, Indian Council of Historical Research, New Delhi for her valuable suggestions during the course of this investigation. Her contribution towards the completion of my thesis is too large to be stated. My gratitude towards her goes without saying.

I take this opportunity to acknowledge Dr. S.R. Bakshi for his unstinting cooperation since the beginning of my research endeavours. Words cannot express my heartfelt appreciation for his motivation.

I would also like to thank the Director of Dr. B.R. Ambedkar Institute of Social Science, Bundelkhand University, Jhansi for his constant source of encouragement in helping me achieve my objectives.

Lastly, I acknowledge my gratitude towards the Librarians and the staff members of Parliament House Library, Nehru Memorial Museum and Library, Teen Murti House, New Delhi, National Archives of India, Indian Council of Historical Research, Delhi University, Jawaharlal Nehru University, Jamia Millia Islamiam, Central Secretariat Library and all those who have helped me in manners unsaid and untold for the execution of my work.

Dr. Buta Singh

1

Origin of Caste and Caste System in India

From ancient times, India has been a country for the people of foreign origin, the outsiders, more correctly the invaders. Historians Anthropologists and Sociologists argue that, the Dravidians came to settle down on this land from some other parts of the world, even before Aryan-invasion. It is believed that the pre-Dravidian settlers were the natives the aborigines of India. It was a savage and primitive society. According to the continental drift theory the geographers and climatologists believe that the northern part of Australia was linked with the southern part of India another eastern part of Africa was enjoined with the western part of India sea coastal-Maharashtra, Kutch Gujarat and Sindh in Pakistan.

Prehistoric State

"The prehistoric stage of social development marks the starting point in the evolution of India's life and thought. The remotest part, as is generally held, represents the age when man lived in a state of nudity and barbarity. There was, however, a simple, democratic and dynamic state of primitive society which marched towards a civilized living only by slow stages. The natural simplicity, the hunger satisfying activity and indiscriminate sexuality were the modes of human relationship in primitive societies."[1]

Dravidians

"Even before Aryan settlers, Dravidians came to this land.[1] The Indo-Greeks, Sakas, Scythians, Parthians, Pallavas, Kushanas, Hunas, Christians, Jews, Zoroastrians, Muslims, Mughals and many small groups of tribes and races from time to time came in waves and settled down in this vast Indian sub-continent from the dawn of human civilization.

"A continuous synthesis is a part of our national life. At the very beginning the assimilation of the Aryan and Dravidian culture laid the very basis of Hindu civilisation."[2]

The Dravidians were an organised race and first attacked the aboriginal of India. They were basically nomads and wanted a settled life. The defeated race of natives or aboriginals joined the social life of the Dravidians and got mixed up in due course of time. But those who fled away in the thick-inaccessible forests and mountain areas remained aloof for centuries from the Dravidians, having uncivilized and barbarous life.

According to historian Stanley Wolpert the Dravidians reached a higher stage of development. They had a developed civilization as compared to the other races.

The Aryans have given various means to the natives. But the monumental excavations of Harappa and Mohen-jo-daro have "emphatically reversed the relative cultural status of India's Aryan conquerors and her pre-Aryan peoples. The pre-Aryan *Dasas* or Slaves whose darker skins differentiated them from "Aryan colour" were suddenly revealed as more advanced, sophisticated, and technologically precocious than the semi-barbaric hoard of Aryan invaders from the West whose only civilized advantage seem to have been some superior weaponry and the use of harnessed horses."[3]

Thus India's aborigines, the natives or the mixed race of the Dravidians reached a high stage of development in due course of time. The Dravidians were the first to attack and defeat the aboriginals of India. The Dravidians were basically nomads and wanted a settled life. The defeated aboriginals joined the social life of the Dravidians, some fled to forests and hills. Where they had settlements. In the words of Dr. B.R. Ambedkar, "the necessary blood-relationship, which occurred among the people of one race with another helped much in obliterating the distinctions between the natives and the Dravidians."

It seems all aborigines and natives were mixed up with the Dravidians in due course of time. The Indus valley civilization emerged and flourished in India, much before Aryan settlers in India.

The Aryan Race

The Aryan race made entry into the Indian sub-continent in groups. Gradually the Aryans could have their hold over the natives, the Dravidians. In the process of diffusion, centuries old confrontation and contact with the indigenous, people, the Aryan society underwent important changes in their way of life, social thinking, and culture. They became interested in permanent dwellings and establishment of tribal political system. In due course of time the *varna* system, which was initially social gradation, was on its way towards crystallization. In support of above viewpoint we may quote Romila Thapar's conclusions that "for some points of view the coming of the Aryans was a backward step, since the Harappan culture had been far more advanced than that of the Aryans who were as yet pre-urban."[4]

It is a fact that "when the Aryans entered India, they had outgrown the stage of tribal endogamy. Among them were only three divisions conforming to the three primitive functional divisions of priest, warrior and artisan. *Varna* in this trivarnic society indicated a particular social function and a distinct level of culture and way of life."[5]

The clash and conflicts between the Aryans and the Dravidians and aboriginals accentuated not only the social and cultural but even the occupational and functional division. In order to avoid a large scale intermixing of the natives amongst the invading race of Aryans a fourth caste, the *Shudras* came into being when they were conquered and enslaved or employed by the organised society of the Aryans, as a forced labour.

The conquered aborigines, or the broken-men, were deprived of all claim for a place in the divinely ordained social order and on the communal land. They were forced to live outside the village, and occupations regarded low and contemptible were assigned to them. They were the ancestors of the untouchables (now a distinct number of castes) and were known as the *Asprashyas* or the *Panchama.* They were attached to the Hindu society and yet they did not belong to it, having been assigned no place in the social hierarch of castes in the Chatur Varnya."[6]

In the process of conquest, compromise, and settlement customs all changed. Some native tribes who easily submitted to the Aryans and accepted their faith and belief, rituals and cultural pattern were graded higher and those who did not submit and accept their faith were tortured and kept as untouchables. Thus the trivarnic society became chaturvarnic. It was however, "a deliberate attempt to introduce gradations in rank according to place of origin."[7] These lower ranked people, or the Sudras "were apparently a conquered race."[8] The idea of caste struck its roots very deeply into Hindu social life. For Hindus the caste became a social and political package and for the Sudras and untouchables it became a curse, a licence of slavery and serfdom. In the words of Iyer : "Few topics within the sphere of Indian sociology present more difficulties than those connected with the origin and evolution of caste. Scholars have devoted considerable time to research and study of the subject, and have come to no conclusions. Various theories have been propounded by scholars. They can be roughly divided into two schools. The older school based its arguments on the sacred literature of the Hindus, and arrived at different conclusions; but all agree in ascribing to caste extreme antiquity, and regard the system as the artificial product of the Brahmanic hierarchy. Of late fresh lights has been thrown on the subject by the study of inscriptions, and by the patient investigations of Buddhist and Jain literature, the authors of which were directly opposed to the Brahmans, and gave quite a different account of early society. In fact there is the new school of theorists "who postdate the origin of caste to comparatively modern late times by looking for its origin in the nature of the elements composing the early Indian society and for its development in the working of social forces on these lines." Thus none of the theories so far advanced commands universal approval. Further, information on the early Hindu society is still meagre, and the discovery of any new fact will lead tot he revision of the best of the theories."[9] It was the Brahmanic or priestly class which created the Indian caste system (*Varna* System).

In the present social set up the eradication of caste system is very much desirable in the best interest of democratic traditions and national unity.

Rig Veda

The earliest work which the Aryans left to posterity is the Rig-veda. Aryan people believed in theistic and deterministic social system. In Aryan society family formed the basic unit. Monogamy was the fashion. The *Rishis* (the teachers) were all family men. Gradually the Aryans had domination over the aboriginals and the indigenous people, and Aryan culture underwent a major change. The pre-Aryan natives *(Shudras)* seems to be a conquered race. The defeated *Dasyas* became, slaves *(Dasas)* who in the beginning did not accept Vedic authority. The word *Shudra* was actually used for an inferior or lower race, Sshudra. Whosoever transgressed the rules of *varna* system was a rebel and an outcaste and finally crushed.

"Most of the tribal people, who believed in the institution of social collectivity, 'the Yajna' could not withstand the onslaught of domination by the aggressive Aryans." Dravidians compromised with them. Dasyus however fought with Aryans, and carried on an uneasing warfare against Aryans.[10]

According to Iyer : "The earliest reference to caste is found in the *Rig Veda,* in which mention is made of four castes which originated from Brahma, the Supreme. Being the Brahman came from his mouth, the Kshatriya from his arm, the Vaisya from his thighs and the Sudras from his feet.[11] This statement is somewhat allegorical. It means that the

Brahmans are the instructors of mankind, the Kshatriyas are the warriors and the Vaisyas and Sudras are the agriculturists and servants respectively. Similar references to the origin of caste are found in *Satapatha Brahmanas* (II-4-11), the *Taittiriya, Brahmana* (III-12-9, 3) *Vajaseneya, Samhita,* and the *Atharva Veda.* But from an examination of the legends contained in the *Brahmanas,* it is seen that the accounts vary.

From the beginning of the Vedic period to the middle of the *sutra* or Buddhist period, the fourfold division represented only classes, and this can be proved by the statements in the *Srauta-Sutra* of *Drahyana* and in the *Puranas* regarding the functions of priests and warriors.[12]

The Purusa-Sukta of the Rig Veda divides the entire society of Aryans and non-Aryans into four classes, known as *varnas* : The Brahmin, the Kshatriya, the Vaisya and the Sudra, created from Prajapati's mouth, arms, thighs and feet respectively.[13] *Rig Veda* says : "Brahmin was his mouth, Rajanya was made from his arm, Vaisya his thighs and Sudra sprang from his feet." (X, 9, 12).

Brahmans or priests were just like bureaucrats of today. They were virtually powerful. The Kshatriyas or warriors were the military personnel, the rulers. Vaishyas were merchants and cultivators, while the Sudras were menials and labourers. Below Sudras were certainly primitives and criminal tribes, and defeated as well as degraded broken men.

"The Brahmanic literature is a proof that the priestly class or the Brahmins were the intellectual and spiritual leaders. It was believed that learning and spiritual knowledge were esoteric virtues and their cultivation needed exclusive attention. Manual labour therefore became taboo for the Brahmins. It also became taboo for the Kshatriyas, with whom the Brahmins shared power and who were their rivals and equals. The aristocratic order of the Kshatriyas could not be sustained by more force. So the Brahmins framed elaborate rules laying down not only the status and grade of the various social and cultural groups but also prescribing distinct rituals and ceremonies for each."[14]

Max Muller states : "the three occupations of the Aryans in India were fighting, cultivating the soil and worshipping the gods. Those who fought the battles of the people would naturally acquire influence and rank and their leaders appear in the Veda as Rajas or kings. Those who did not, share in the fighting would occupy a more humble position; they were called 'Vaish', 'Vaishya' or householders and would no doubt have to contribute towards the maintenance of the Armies."[15]

In the ninth book of the *Rig Veda,* there is a famous passage referring to the various crafts. It is said that the organisation of castes is fully developed at the period of *Brahmanas,* and is codified in the laws of Manu. The four castes are fully established. The rites and duties of the *Brahmans* are in complete accord with modern descriptions, and the necessary purity of the race is fully inculcated. The caste is ignored by the persistent neglect of initiation.[16]

The orthodox Hindu, on the other hand, consider the caste system to be a divine institution, and that there have existed since the beginning four distinct orders of men, Brahman or priest, Rajanya, Kshatriya or noble, *Vaisya* or tiller of the soil, and *Sudra* or the servile class. There is a great difference between the first three and the last. The former are said to be the conquering Aryan and the latter the conquered *Sudra* or *Dasyu.* The Aryans are said to possess light colour, and the *Dasyus* dark colour. It is also said that before the end of the *Rigvedic* period, a belief in the divine origin of the four orders of men was firmly established, but there are no references to the sub-division of these order.[17]

"In the next period, the period of the *Yajur Veda* and the *Brahmanas,* are found the division of the Aryan society into four classes with distinct functions. The term denotes a social order, independently of any actual difference of colour, and we hear of the mixed *varnas,* the offspring of parents belonging to distant orders." Descent is the chief factor, though not the sole one. Tribal connection, religion, and occupation combine with descent to consolidate the social groups and keep them apart. "Throughout the Vedas" says Blunt, "there is not a single reference to connubial or commensal restrictions to any of the characteristics of the modern Hindu social system."[18]

Buddha attacked caste system. This will be discussed in the next chapter in detail. He said individual's merit may be taken into consideration and not the caste.

"In the *Jatakas,* a collection of folk-tales, there is an account of Hindu society in early Buddhist times. The colour distinction so prominent in the *vedas* has faded into the background, through its memory survives in the word *varna,* used for the social classes, namely, Kshatriya, Brahman, Vaisya and Sudra. Here the Kshatriya leads the lists. The lords spiritual have not assumed the pride of place at the expense of the lords temporal. The Brahman is held in status inferior to the Kshatriya nobility. The *varnas* have not yet developed to make them close corporations. Vaisyas and Sudras rise to the rank of Kshatriyas. Anybody can become a Brahman by becoming a priest. There is not endogamous restriction; a Brahman marries a Kshatriya widow, and according to one *Jataka,* Buddha himself, a Kshatriya, marries a poor cultivator's daughter. Marriage within the clan is considered preferable to marriage outside it. But social prejudice and social convention stand in the way of the latter. Below the *varnas* there are *hina jatyo,* low tribes, of barbers, potters or weavers—for example, a remnant of the *Dasya* tribes on the outskirts of civilization. The lowest of all are the Chandalas and other outcaste tribes."[19]

In the Vedic period and according to Manu, Vaisyas were basically herdsmen and after settling took to agriculture. During the Vedic period, *Visha* (a house or district) signified people in general, and its adjective *Vaisya* was afterwards applied to a householder. The *Vishas* or clans afterwards became the 'Vaisyas', the third classical caste. Before they entered India, the Aryans were pastoral people, their domestic animals being the horse, the cow and, perhaps, the sheep and the goat. The horse and the cow were specially venerated, and they were the chief means of transport. The *Vaisyas* must, therefore, have been herdsmen and shepherds who entered India, took to agriculture and settled down to the practice of cultivation. The word *Vaisya* signifies a man who occupies the soil, a cultivator or a merchant. According to Manu, God ordained them to tend cattle, give alms, offer sacrifice, to study, to cultivate, to trade, and learn the Vedas.[26]

The institution of caste created by *Rig Veda* is exclusively Indian phenomenon. It was just to maintain the gradation in Hindu society, to broaden the scope of enslavement and serfdom. It was purely an Aryan concept, nowhere found in the world. Brahmins have argued that the primary object of the caste system was to protect and maintain purity of blood. In the *Varna* system a calculated conspiracy was made to divide the society. "The persons who possessed knowledge of the sacred lore, officiated in religious ceremonies and received gifts were called Brahmins; those who fought, owned land and wielded political power were classed as Kshatriyas, the general mass of the people—the traders, the agriculturists, the craftsmen were grouped under the term *Vaisya,* and the persons, reserved for menial services were called *Sudras,* who generally belonged to the vanquished people."[21]

In the beginning this was mainly an occupational division, like trade guilds. But this division of class of labour turned into caste in due course of time. Rights from the pre-*Rig Vedic* age to the epic period the development of India's social thought and social condition, the Brahmanism continued to be a dominating force. The Brahmans, the Sutras the Puranas, all played the role of degrading and suppressing the self-employed class of artisans and agriculturists. The religious revivalism helped the Brahmanism to regain its power and position for nearly five thousand years.

The Rajnyas or the ruling class fully supported the Varna system and the percepts of Hindu Dharma and encouraged priestcraft to divide the society with the sword of scriptures. The unity and awakening in the Sudras was crushed

Since Vedic age the central purpose of all Brahmanical literature have been to keep supremacy of Brahmins over the sub-merged sections of society, the defeated non-Aryans, the artisans and the untouchables. This viewpoint can be examined by going through or perusing the available sources.

The Brahmanas

"The Brahmanas deal with the ritualistic aspect of Vedic social life. They have combined Vedic philosophy with rituals and sacrifices. Brahmanas accepted the divine authority of the Vedas for the guidance of social behaviour. The sacrifices were performed for gaining earthly profits and a prosperous life. The increasing dominance of the idea of sacrifices gave rise to the office of priesthood. The flexible class system gave way to the rigidity of the caste system. Varnas came to be distinguished from each other.

In the age of Brahmanas there was emphasis on sacrifice, supremacy of the priest, and the eternity of the Veda. The Varma System became more and more rigid. Sudra could not revolt against this Vedic-Brahmanic theory of social injustice, and were crushed for raising any voice. The Rig-Vedic division into the Aryan and non-Aryan *(Dasa)* was replaced by that of *Daivya* (godly) and *Asurya* (of Demons). The Brahmin was supreme and represented divine *Varna,* while the Sudra was the lowest in the social order and thus *Asur.* The Brahmins were 'Veritable Gods on earth'. The Sudras were inauspicious, condemned persons and 'were not to be seen' what to talk of touch.

The Brahmin was always higher than Kshatriya and Vaisya, while a Sudra was the servant and meant to serve all others, beaten, tortured and even killed. In order to maintain the continuity of religious tradition and the supremacy of Brahmins, the caste system or the *Varna vyavastha* was engineered as divine authority."[22]

The Upanishads

The *Aranyakas* and the *Upanishads* are the concluding parts of the Brahmanas. They provide the ritual system for the householders. In old age, a householder resorts to the forest and needs a substitute for the rituals which he has performed earlier as householder. The *Aranyakas* satisfy this need by encouraging meditation for those who wish to live in the woods. The hymns are the creations of poets, the Brahmanas are the works of the priests and Upanishads are the meditations of the philosophers. These are the strong philosophical protest against the rigid social thinking and religious performances of Brahmanas.

The *Upanishads* belong to the revealed literature *(Sruti)* and provide means for spiritual freedom. The *Upanishads* uphold the *Varnasrama Vyavastha* as an essential part of *Karma* doctrine. Man is required to perform his duties and serve the society. The duties depend on man's individual capacities, divided into four *varnas*. The *Upanishads,* however, could not entirely break the bonds of the caste system, but opened the gates of spirituality without any distinction of caste and sex. The Upanishads could not revolt against oppressive features of the priestly class which encouraged sacrifices and ritualism and maintained serious distinctions between man and man and *varna* system.

The sages of *Upanishads* emphasized more that the ascetic aspect of human life was important than society. In fact, the age of *Upanishads* failed to register any protest against growning sacrifices the Vedic rituals and orthodoxy. The priesthood ruined the moral values in society. The *Varna* system created inequality and the practice of untouchability. Though the Upanishadic concepts of *Atman* and Brahan (Soul and God) abolished distinctions between man and man spiritually and morally, but practically they could not eradicate inequalities and oppressive features in life.[23]

In fact, Upanishadic age witnessed more and more sacrifices priesthood, wequality, caste system and exploitation of *Sudras.*

The Kalpa-Sutras

The *Kalpa-Sutras* basically deal with Vedic sacrifices, household ceremonies and social laws. Literally 'Kalpa' means ritual. Therefore it was much of ritualism. They provide a good account of early social life in India. The complete *Kalpa-Sutras* comprise of the *Srautasutras* which deal with sacrifices known as *Srautyajanas.* The *Grihyasutas* conduct household ceremonies like marriages and *upanayana* and *Dharmasutras* deal with-rights and duties of different classes in society. In the age of *Sutras* the social life was the same as in the Vedic period. The first three castes were allowed to perform *Upanayana,* whereas the *Sudras* were denied the right to sacred thread ceremony. (Surprisingly, this practice has continued till today). This created two divisions the *'Dvijs'* or the *'Aryans'* and *Advijs'* or the non-Aryans. In the age of *Kalpa Sutras* the caste system became more rigid. There was great emphasis on the purity of the *Varnas.* It was the revival of tradition of Brahmanas. The Sudras became a distinct group of oppressed and suppressed class without any voice of revolt. In the social process, the Brahmin, Kshatriya and the Vaisya, known as *Dvijs* they became powerful and dominating class, who were allowed to have *Upanayana,* the study of *Vedas,* status in the society and above all social political power.

The *Smritis* recognized monarchy. A divine origin was attributed to the king. The clever and cunning class of Brahmins took powers from the King to define *Dharma* in order to suppress and enslave the *Sudras.*

Some *Sudras* were allowed to perform small domestic *Yajnas* and *Shraddha,* but recitation of Vedic mantras by them was strictly denied. A Sudra girl was also allowed to marry a *Dvij* without chanting *mantras.* The Sudras were neglected in social and cultural functions organised by the Brahmins, which were more religious and ritualistic. *Sudras* were only allowed to watch.

In social prestige and power sharing Kshatriya's are very close to the Brahmins. The *Sudras* suffered many disabilities, which continued for centuries. The population of *Sudras* was scattered over in various castes and sub-castes with gradations and they could never unite and revolt against the Brahmanical order.

In the age of *Sutras* the legal institutions were all based on *Dharma-Shastras,* which were definitely against *Sudras.* The power of legislation and codification was in the hands of the Brahmins, the dominating priestly class, who fully supported the Vedas. They enjoyed almost divinely status in society. Without *Upanayana,* which wasn't more than an oppressive signal, an individual of low Caste was doomed to social degradation, ignorance and poverty. This was the actual state of the *Sudras.* The egalitarian social system became a myth.

In the *karma* theory, the doctrine of transmigration is an essential part which has class relation with *Varna* social system. The soul transmigrates according to the acts of an individual. Therefore it gets the birth, for which it deserves. This was totally a misconception to prove that Sudras in their previous birth have not done good acts and have deviated from *Dharma.* Because of their past sins they were having a wretched life in the present times. The *Dharma Sutras* state explicitly that good acts leads to higher birth and evil deeds to a low one.

There was no social awakening in this age among the Sudras, the oppressed Dalit people.[24]

The Epic Age

The *Ramayana* and *Mahabharata* are the two great epics of the Hindus. They preach supremacy of Brahmanism and divinely order. The epics seem to have imposed the Varna system as originated by the gods themselves. The Kshatriyas are also placed in high position. The theory of *Karma* with transmigration of soul is combined with *Varnavyavastha* as the central doctrine of the epics. The author of the epics declare that various functions and duties of the *Varnas* are allotted to men in accordance with their nature which they inherit from their part. By doing service and *bhakti* to the gods they can attain *moksha.*

The *Ramayana* is a complete work which believes in divine government and the entire universe is governed by god's dispensation. All castes are supposed to perform their duties, which have been assigned to their *Karmas* of the past birth. The Ramayana has clearly accepted the authority of the *Varnasharm Dharma.* The *Mahabharata* also accepts the authority of the divine social order, *Karma* and transmigration. It believes that a man is born in high or low caste because of *Karma* in the previous birth. The central theme, which is identical with *Gita* is that one should perform his duties without caring for the reward *(Nishkam Karma). Mahabharata* has the complete faith in the divine origin of *Varna-vyavastha.* It resembles almost with the doctrine of *Purusha-Sukta* of *Rig Veda.*

Surprisingly, the Epics deny the right of *Upanayan* to Sudras, and re-establish the Brahmin supremacy which was challenged by the *Upanishads.* Epics thus revive the hold of priests on Sudras, who were treated as *asuras.* demons, *rakshasas,* etc.[25]

Social Deterioration of the Vaishyas

In the Buddhist period, as Dr. Dutt says, 'that Vaisyas and Sudras were not to be found as pure castes, nor did they represent groups anywhere. There is no mention anywhere of a member of any particular professional caste belonging to either *Dasya varna* or *Sudra varna.* The real distinction existed only during the Vedic period. Even during the early period of the Brahmanas, the distinction had almost vanished, and in later periods still more so. It was so in practice as well. In the early Buddhist period, mention is made of *Gahapat* or *Grahapati,* as a landowning and mercantile class which ranked below Kshatriyas and Brahmans. The word is synonymous with *Kudumbika* (house-holder) living in towns and villages.[26] Gradually the *Vaisyas* underwent a kind of social degradation, and the reasons are given below:

1. The rapid increase in number of the Kshatriyas, coupled with the expansion of the Aryan domination, and the advance from tribalisam towards feudalism and oligarchy;

2. The advancement and separation of the sacerdotal class from the common people, and their domination over them. The *Vaisya,* according to Taittiriya Samhita, lived only to be exploited by the Brahmans and Kshatriyas. Numerous passages attest to their interiority to the first two twice-born classes;
3. The abundant supply of slave labour in farming, pasturing and industrial arts, and the close association with certain branches of industry, together with a growing contempt for manual labour which brought the industries themselves low in the estimations of the higher classes. The separation of *Rathakaras* (chariot-makers), *Takshan* (carpenters) and *Kamaras* (workers in brass) from the Vaisya community is an instance in point. Thus the artisan classes became separated from the Vaisyas, among whom there were merchants and farmers. At the outset there was not distinction, and gradually a Vaisya farmer was looked upon as inferior in status to a Vaisya merchant. In the *Jataka* literature, it is said that merchants alone formed what might be called the Vaisya community, while other sank to the status of Sudras;
4. During the Vedic period all professions and industries were in the hands of the Aryans. But after the intermingling of the Aryan with non-Aryan races the industrial and economic life of the people became very much changed. A large number of occupations fell to the lot of lower classes;
5. When the colour bar and purity of blood came to be considered, the cultured and the ruling classes adopted a policy of segregation and refrained from inter-marriage and interdining with the non-Aryan peoples. The rank and file of the Vaisyas, owing to their number and association with the Sudras in various fields of activity, received a large admixture of non-Aryan blood. This also resulted in a lowering of the status of the Vaisyas.[27]

The Sudra

According to Senart and Wilson the Sudras were the originals and conquered by the Aryans; and forced to live as a servile class. They were also not allowed to mix up with the Aryan society.

"Senart points out that the division of the four castes appearing in the post-Vedic literature does not continue on the same lines. There were two groups, one composed of the three higher castes, the other of the Sudras, or the lowest. The higher caste constituted the fraternity to which admission was obtained only by the religious ceremony of initiation and investment of the sacred thread. The Sudras were excluded, and could take no part in sacrifice. The punishment for the commission of grave offence by a Brahman was degradation to a Sudra or outcaste. Dr. Wilson remarks : "They were the original inhabitants of the land, who conformed to the Brahmanic rules, and received certain privileges. They constituted the fourth caste, with the designation of Sudras. Manu has ordained that if Sudras are unable to maintain their families, they might subsist by handicrafts. The Sudras were ordained not to wear the sacred thread. They were regarded as a servile class whose duty it was to minister to the twice-born."[28]

It seems right from the Brahmanas to the Epic age, the Sudra's voice was suppressed. They were not allowed access to scriptures and other knowledge. Even Sudra ascetics and truth seekers were brutally liquidated.

The Chandalas

The *Chandalas* were the most despised of the Hindu society. They were not allowed to live within the walls of the town. The *Pukkasa* and *Chandalas* were also despised classes. They were excluded from the category of castes. In the *Dharmasastras* the occupation of a *Chandala* is to carry the dead bodies of men who have no relations or friends, and to execute criminals. In the fivefold division of society in the *Madhyadesa* (Middle country), Brahman, Kshatriya, Vaisya, Sudra, and Nishada are given. In the Buddhist *Jataka* literature also, the social divisions are on similar lines. The authors of *Dharmasastras*, relying on the Vedic texts as authority, excluded them from the fourfold division. The fifth caste was rejected, and the *Nishadas, Chandalas* and *Pukkasas* were under casteless classes (*Manu 4 et. seq*).[29]

But in the later Sanskrit works, like *'Raj Tarangini'* by Kalhan, *Chandalas* have been placed as martial or warriors. Here the word 'Chand' or 'Prachand' is used to depict one who is brave.[30]

Trade Guilds

During the Vedic period the number of professional classes went on steadily increasing, and their organisation bore a close analogy to the medieval guilds of Europe. The former were influential corporations in Buddhist times. Even Manu, yagnavalkya, Narada and other law-givers opined that they became dangerously powerful. They were the financiers of the age, and even Kings were their debtors. The numerous privileges, which they enjoyed were granted in return for their assistance in money. "They had their own family inheritance and apprentice laws with which the King could not interfere. They tried their own law suits, and could be taxed only with their approval. It is even laid down that the Kings must approve of whatever the guilds do for other problem, whether it be kind or cruel. Each guild was ruled by a president (*Sreshti*) and a council of four, who decided both domestic and business disputes. There was also a m erchant who exercised his authority over all the guilds in a particular city and in its neighbourhood." He was called *Mahasreshti.* Disobedience to the guild's orders was punished with fine or even expulsion. A wrong done by one member of a guild to another was treated as a wrong done to the whole community, and visited with severe punishment. A common fund was also raised for religious offerings, and also for promoting the common interests of the guild.

A guild is not a caste. There is no community of blood. Membership ceases on abandoning the trade or industry common to the guild. A caste is a homogeneous community, and membership is retained even when the occupation is given up. The functional castes have many things in common with the guilds. It is a primary rule among them that a member cannot deprive another of his privileges. So strong is the proprietary sense that the recognised rights of certain families are sometimes sold like a good-will, mortgaged and even given in dowry. An encroachment on another man's rights is severely dealt with, even to outcasting in some places. In fact, encroachment of any kind was vehemently resisted.

It is in these guilds that Dahlman[31] and other modern writers find the germs of modern functional castes. Corporations so powerful and well-organised must have exercised a considerable influence on the development of the Hindu social system. A survival of it is found at present in Bombay and Baroda.[32]

Caste Definition

The word 'caste' Dr. Wilson states, is not of Indian origin, but is derived from the Portuguese 'caste' signifying race, mould or quality. The Indian world for caste is 'Jat' or 'Jati' which has the original meaning of birth or production of a child, and hence denotes good birth or lineage, respectability and rank. 'Jatha' means well-born. Thus 'Jat' now signifies a caste as every Hindu is born into a caste determines this social position through life.

The two main ideas denoted by a caste are a community or persons following a common occupation, and a community whose members marry only among themselves. A third distinctive feature is that the members of a caste do not as a rule eat with outsiders with the exception of other Hindu castes of a much higher social position than their own.[33]

The coming of foreign races in Ihdia created many racial' political and social problems in the earliest period of history. The problem of Varna-system, formerly a mere division of labour became a tool of oppression and suppression in the hands of the dominating races very similar to Plato's idea of justice, which each man doing his proper duty in the state, *varnashramdharam* is a conceptual division of society into four categories according to the Hindu Classics chiefly the *Vedas* and *Dharma Shastras.* Notwithstanding the later innovations in face of existential realities *varnashramdhara* represented the harmonious inter-relationship of the four *varnas* or social order. The *Brahmin* was invested with spiritual and instructional duties; the Kshatriya was the guardian of temporal powers : the *Vaisya* was occupied with commercial pursuits : and the Sudra was meant to provide *menial* services to the first three *varnas.* In theory, the Hindu classics ensured a harmonious working of the society by prescribing the *right* and obligations of each of the *varnas*[34]. It seems Dr. Wilson's opinion is somewhat soft to the early Aryans.

In the opinion of Nehru, caste was probably neither Aryan nor Dravidian. It was an attempt at the social organisation of different races, a rationalisation of the facts as they existed at the time. It brought degradation in its train afterwards, and it is still a burden and a curse...Caste began with a hard and fast division between Aryans and non-Aryans, the latter again being divided into the Dravidians races and the aboriginal tribes."[35]

The word *caste* had been variously defined, and none of the definitions is satisfactory. These are given below :

1. Caste is defined "as an endogamous group or a collection of such groups bearing a common name and having the same traditional occupation, claiming a common descent from the same source, and commonly regarded as forming a single homogeneous community." (Sir E.A. Gait)
2. Sir Herbert Risley defines caste, "as a collection of families bearing a common name, claiming a common descent from a mythical ancestor, human or divine, professing to follow the same hereditary calling, and (are) regarded by those who are competent to give an opinion as forming a single homogeneous community. The name is always associated with a specific occupation."
3. Emile Senart has a more comprehensive definition. "Caste, according to him, is a close corporation, exclusive and in theory at any rate, rigorously hereditary; equipped with certain traditional and independent organizations including a chief and council;

meeting on occasion in assemblies of more or less plenary authority, and joining in the celebration of certain festivals; bound together by a common occupation; observing certain usages which relate more particularly to marriage, to food and to questions of occasional pollution; and ruling its members by the exercise of jurisdictions, the extent of which varies, but which succeeds, by the sanction of certain penalties and, above all, the power of final or revocable exclusion from the group, in making the authority of the community effectively felt."[36]

The test of caste is not intermarriage and interdining, but defilement by eating and touching what is unclean. On this consideration, *Sutras* show only the beginning of that formal theory of defilement which results in a pure man of the upper class being defiled by the shadow of an impure man and in the taboo of all contact with the impure. "According to Gautama (*Dharma Sutra* XVII,I), a Brahman may not eat food given by any of the reborn who are the worthy members of his caste, and in need of food to support his life, he may take food and other things even from a *Sudra.* Food forbidden is that defiled by hair or insects falling into it, and the touched by a woman in her menses, by a black bird (crow) or by its foot or given by an outcaste, a woman of bad character, a person accursed, an hermaphrodite, a police officer (*dandika)*, a carpenter, a miser, a jailer, a physician, a man who hunts without using a bow, i.e., a non-snarer of animals, a man who eats refuse or the food of a multitude, of an enemy." The list contains the taboo of food offered disrespectfully and of certain animals. "Apastamba (*Dharma Sutra,* 1, 6, 18, 11) allows the acceptance of gifts, including a house and land from the low caste *(Ugra),* though like the later law books his code stages that a priest may not eat in the house of any one of the three orders (*varnas)* below him, but he may eat the food of any caste except that of the *Sudras,* and eat even their food in times of distress. Forbidden by him is the food of an artisan, of people who let houses or lands, a spy, an unauthorised priest (a Buddhist), besides that of a surgeon, usurer and others. Caste is *varna* or *jati,* colour and kin, the former embracing the latter, as a social order including clans and families.[37]

Amongst the various theories on caste which have been formulated by scholars, the most important are given below :

1. According to Sir Denzil Ibbetson, occupation is the chief basis of the division of caste. Every separate occupation has produced a distinct caste, the status of which depends not either partially or entirely on its occupation. The fact that there may be several castes

pursuing the same occupation, as agriculture or weaving, does not invalidate this any way. If a caste changes its occupation, is may gradually change its status in a corresponding degree. Caste sometimes tends to rise or fall in social position with acquisition of land or other forms of wealth or dignity. Strictly speaking, a man inherits the social position of the caste in which he is born, and retains it, through life without the power of altering it. It is not the caste as a whole, or at least one of its important sections or sub-caste as a whole, or at least one of its important sections or sub-castes, which rises or falls in social position, and the process may extend over generations or centuries. This theory, though applicable to a large number of castes, does not cover the whole ground.[38]

2 Caste, according to Nesfield, is used to designate common occupation. It is the centre round which caste has grown up, and its social gradation corresponds precisely to the different periods of civilization during which their traditional occupation originated. The primitive tribes inhabiting the hills persue the occupation of hunting, and the pursuit of wild animals was the earliest stage in the development of human industry. Next in order comes the fishing caste, fishing being considered superior to hunting, because the water is a more sacred element than land among the Hindus. There is less apparent cruelty in capturing fish than in the slaughtering of animals. Above these come the pastoral castes. Above the pastoral castes are the agricultural castes and the various tribes included in them. Following the order in which these occupations are adopted during the progress of civilization, the others are mentioned. Above them are the various occupational castes. The higher group includes those castes whose occupations were coeval with the age of metallurgy, those who work in stone, wood metal, and make ornaments. At the top of the system stands the Kshatriyas, or the warrior class, whose duty it is to protect all the lower castes, and the Brahman who is their priest and spiritual guide.[39]

Dyer writes further : The gradation of society given above is in the scientific order of precedence, and it is likely that these divisions arose from the divisions of the principal social organisation of India in the village community.

According to this theory, the caste system springs from the regular evolution of social life, starting from the lowest level and following in its slow progression.[1] This theory cannot be reconciled with the relatively late date to which Nesfield refers to the constitution of society. He also affirms that the Brahman was the first born of castes, the model upon which all the other castes were subsequently formed, extending gradually from king or warrior to the tribes practising hunting and fishing whose rank is no higher than that of a savage. The Brahmans who formed themselves into the Levite guild set an example which was followed by others. It was he who invented for himself, the rule prohibiting marriage with a woman of another caste. There is a curious contradiction of later passages where he derives the regulation of marriage from the traditional usages of the tribe. The Vaisyas, according to him and the *Sudras* in particular, have never been anything except a kind of rubric intended to embrace a multitude of heterogeneous elements. [40]

Ibbetson's thesis is less complete and less forced than that of Nesfield, but is based on the same date. He summarises the various stages which are to be discerned in the history of caste:— (*i*) "The organisation of the tribe common to all primitive societies; (*ii*) the guilds founded on heredity of occupation; (*iii*) the exaltation peculiar to India of sacerdotal function; (*iv*) the exaltation of Levitical blood by the importance attributed to heredity; (*v*) the consolidation of the principle,—by the elaboration of a series of entirely artificial laws derived from Hindus beliefs, regulating marriage and fixing the limits within which it may be concentrated, declaring certain occupations and foods to be impure, and determining the conditions and extent of the relations permitted between the castes. It is seen that great importance is attached to the community of occupation and the constitution of the tribe." The status of the Brahman is reversed. They are represented as contributing to the spontaneous organisation of the country. The real weakness of the system consists in the inordinate importance attributed to community of occupation. If this really constituted the primitive bond of castes, the latter would have shown less tendency to split up and disintegrate.[41]

3. It is in race, that Risley unlike Nesfield, seeks the soul of castes. The conquerors take the daughters of the land as concubines, but give their own daughters in marriage only among themselves. Race is substituted as the generating principle. The nasal index is the formula for the proportions of the nose, and is the most unerring criterion of race. There seems reason of suppose that the contact of the Aryans with the indigenous people of India is mainly responsible for the growth of the caste system, and the main racial divisions may perhaps even be recognised, though their basis has to a great extent vanished. But when we come to individual castes and sub-castes, the scrutiny of their origin is based more on certain Puranic

stories. Risley bases his argument upon the use of the word *Varna* and meaning attributed to it. In this, he sees the natural enmity between the conquering and conquered races, the white and the black, as the germ of distinction. The endogamous laws are the foundation of the system. He arrives indirectly at the general acceptance of the orthodox Brahmine system, and believes in the dominance gradually acquired by the priesthood. The theory of mixed castes is, according to him, an invaluable proof of cross-breeding.[42] For Nesfield, caste is a matter of profession; for Risley, it is a matter of marriage

The Vedic Varna system is so deep rooted that it has given rise to social injustice and colossal vice like untouchability, slavery, degradation of womenfolk, uprooting from land, ancestral poverty, exploitation and under employment of vast majority of non-Aryan races. The scriptures and the Hindu social order legally handed over and concentrated the scare resources of power and privilege in the hands of the Aryans, the dominating communities and propagated false and baseiess theories of divine origin.

In Vedic literature, according to N.K. Dutt (1968) the *Dasas (Dasyus)* are "black skinned, noselers, of unintelligible speech, not sacrificing, worshipping no gods, following strange customs." Risely on the basis of ethnographic study describes them "of low strature, black skin, long head, broad nose...related to aborigines of Australia and linguistic affinity with Australian dialect."

Another French scholar Emile Senart obscrves "...they are definitely of inferior race, isolated by geographical conditions and by history,....but culturally they were by no means inferior."

Rig Veda (in its 104 hymn of the First Book) describes them...having 'castles and great wealth of natives whose womenfolk bathed in milk."

Dahlaman (1899) treating all the civilizations on equal footing regards Indian society as organised originally into three natural groups the priesthood, the nobility and the bourgeoise.

Nesfield (1885) defines caste as a "class of the community which disowns any connection with any other class and can neither intermarry, nor eat or drink...with any but the person of their own community."

Bonnerjee says that Aryan invaders were primarily responsible for the institution of caste. (p. 7)

Ibbestson emphasis on the exploitation of the position by the Brahmins which the supposes to have degraded all occupations except their own. He explains caste as arising from a combination of tribal origin, functional guilds and a Levitical religion."

Sarat Chander Roy (1937) accepts that caste is an outcome of interaction between the Indo-Aryan *Varna* system on one hand and the tribal system of pre-Dravidian and the occupational class system of the Dravidian on the other. These have been cemented by Indo-Aryan concept of Karma and a certain taboo-holiness.

According to G.S. Ghurye (1979) caste has arisen largely as a result of racial differences. Probably Aryans wanted to be the unquestioned supreme power for all time to come and strengthened their ideology through their viced literature. The institution of Manu finally placed the shackles of divinity. This is how the Vedas, the Dharamshastras found a religious status, beyond scientific scrutiny, logical questioning, critical evaluation and social challenge."[43]

Mixed Union of the Four Castes

From early times, by an ordinance of Manu, men of the higher castes or classes were permitted, after marrying a woman of their own caste, to have subsidiary wives from any of the classes below them. This custom seems to have been prevalent, and no definite rule was prescribed that the children of such unions should necessarily be illegitimate, and in many cases there is no doubt that their descendants ultimately became full members of the caste of the first ancestor. According to Manu, the children of a Brahman by a Kshatriya woman could attain Brahmanhood in the third generation, and those by a Vaisya woman in the fifth.[44] Such children could also inherit. According to the *Mahabharata,* (Chap. xivii) if a Brahman had four wives of different castes, the son by a Brahman wife took four shares, that by a Kshatriya wife three, that by a Vaisya wife two, and that by a Sudra wife one share. Manu gives a slightly different distribution, but also permits the son by a *Sudra* wife to have a share of the inheritances.[45] Thus the fact is clear that the son of a Brahman even by a *Sudra* woman had a certain status of legitimacy in his father's caste, as he could marry in it, and must therefore have been permitted to partake of the sacrificial food at marriage, and could also inherit a small share of the property. The detailed rules prescribed for the state legitimacy and inheritance shows that recognised unions of this kind between a man of higher class and a woman of lower class were once fairly frequent in spite of subsequent prohibitions. This must have led to mixture of blood in the different castes. There is still a survival of it in the practice of hypergamy.[46]

Tribe and Caste

Both *tribe* and *caste* are loosely applied to a social group. The tribe is defined as "the largest body of people, speaking about what they themselves regard as one language, and have a common language for themselves as well as a sense of solidarity which expresses itself in regarding other people as strangers," A tribe is not a close corporation. In its original form, it is an aggregate of persons who have or believe themselves to have a common origin. This together with common political interests, and mutual defence, holds them together. Sometimes, it admits of aliens who wish to throw in their lot with it especially women obtained by purchase or capture. It is not endogamous though circumstances tend to favour endogamy. It differs from caste inasmuch as the common name does not usually imply occupation. Its members occupy or profess to occupy a definite tract, but they do not necessarily marry among themselves. The modern tendency of such tribes is to be transformed into a caste.[47] In fact, a tribe is a prospective caste."[48] Thus a tribe took thousand of years to become a caste.

Class and Caste

The two names *caste* and *class* are often confounded with each other. They correspond neither in extent, in character, nor in natural tendencies. Each one among the castes which would belong to one and the same class is plainly distinguishable from its fellows. The class subserves political ambition. The caste obeys narrow scruples, traditional customs and local influence, which have generally no relation to class interests. More that all, the class clings to the safeguarding of an integrity which is the subject of deep concern and sensitiveness even with the humblest. It is distant echo of the class struggles handed down by legend with which tradition resounds. By the reaction of principles on facts, two institutions have become fused together. They are none-the-less essentially independent. The hierarchic division of the population into classes is universal. But the caste system is a unique institution. The Brahmanic ambition has taken advantage of it in order more securely to make its domination possible, but not obvious. A caste system is not necessarily the basis of theocracy. Its theory has confused the two sets of ideas. This is a fact of secondary importance. For the sake of historic development, they have to be carefully distinguished.[49]

In the Vedic literature the Brahmins are said to be the trustees and repositories to the civilization. Both Buddha and Mahavira and some other contemporary philosophers revolted against Brahmin supremacy and Vedic wisdom. Buddhism guided and shaped the human history and human thought discarding inhuman sacrifices too much ritualism, caste system and practice of untouchability.

Change in Traditional Occupation

With the entry of the British in India, the Trade Guilds changed to modern factory system, not owned by the capitalist class. There is a definite change in ancestral or traditional occupation of a particular castes, which is a signal of eradication of caste system. R.V. Russell observes :

"The abandonment of the traditional occupation has become a most marked feature of Hindu society as a result of the equal opportunity and freedom in the choice of occupations afforded by the British Government, coupled with the rapid progress of industry and the spread of education. So far it has had no very markedly disintegrating effect on the caste system, and the status of a caste is still mainly fixed by its traditional occupation but signs are not wanting of a coming change.[50]

Endogamous Group

As several castes have the same traditional occupation in other parts of the country, the distinctions of occupation therefore are not a sufficient basis for a classification of castes nor can a caste be simply defined as a body of persons who marry only among themselves or, as it termed, an endogamous ground; for almost every important caste is divided into a number of sub-castes which do not marry and frequently do not eat with each other. But it is distinctive and peculiar feature of a caste as a social institution that it splits up the people into a multitude of these divisions and bars their intermarriage and the real unit of the system and the basis of the fabric of Indian society is this endogamous group or sub caste.[51]

Sub-Castes

The sub-castes, however, connote no real difference of status or occupation. They are little known except within the caste itself and the they consist of groups within the caste which marry among themselves, and attend the communal feasts held on the occasions of marriages, funerals and meetings of the caste panchayats or committee for the judgement of offences against the caste rules and their expiation by a penalty feast."[52]

Caste from Chandragupta Maurya to Harsha

Megasthenes, who was an ambassador in the court of Chandragupta (Sandrokotus of the Greeks) in 300 B.C., wrote an account of the social system of his day in a work compiled by him, and this was preserved by Strabo, Arrian, and other writers. His classification of the people of his day into seven groups is somewhat confusing. He speaks of the philosophers, the hushandmen, the herdsmen and hunters, the traders and labourers, the fighting men, the overseers, the councillors, and the judge and administrators. From the above list, *Brahmans* and *Kshatriyas* are easily identified. The third and fourth groups include *Vaisyas* and *Sudras*. The fourth would include all the guilds of armourers and ship-builers of which Megasthenes speaks as possessing special privilege. The sixth and the seventh of Megasthenes' groups refer to professional classes. According to Strabo's version, "no one is allowed to marry out of his own caste or to follow more than one business. An exception is made in the case of the philosopher, who for his virtue is allowed this privilege." Arrian endorses this view. From the facts mentioned above may be inferred three important things, namely, prohibition of intercaste marriages, the importance of heredity, and the exemption of Brahmans from the above rules. Nevertheless there were violations. Chandragupta was of mixed descent. There were mixed marriages at a much later date, and perhaps there were exceptional instances as early as the fourth century B.C.[53]

Regarding the six centuries between 300 B.C. and 300 A.D., information bearing on the development of caste is rather scanty. Some attempts were made to prevent the intermixture of caste. During this period, there occurred the invasions of the Sakas, the Yavanas, the Pahlavas and the Kushans. These must have left their mark on the Hindu society, though very little is known, expect in the case of the Huns, about their intermixture with the population of the country.[54]

Quoting earlier researchers and writings of Blunt and Dutt as well as Institution of Manu, Iyer in the present study tries to fine out the growth of Varna system, which is complex from the very beginning. He observes : "*The institutes of Manus* and the chief *Puranas* in their present form are ascribed to the Golden Age of Sanskrit Literature under the early Gupta kings (330-450 A.D.). The Brahmanas and Kshatriyas,— the 'sacerdotal' and ruling and military castes respectively are shown as occupational. The *Vaisyas* and *Sudras* are not clearly defined. They are identical probably with trading, industrial and menial classes. The *Vratya* and *Vrishala* castes are the degenerate descendants of the twice-born classes who have neglected to perform their prescribed rites. Among them are included Khasa, Dravira, Yavana, Saka, Pahlava and China, and these names clearly show, what Manu's *Vratyas* and *Vrishalas* were. These must have been the names of the aboriginal tribes and races, that have partly or wholly merged in the then Hindu tribes and castes. Manu's *institutes* contain a fairly good account of the social system as it existed in his time. Many tribal castes must have sprung from foreign invaders, after their adoption of Hinduism. In this connection, it must be remembered that many of the invaders were barbarous, and their manners and customers would have become repugnant to the Hindus. It is very likely that these groups would have gradually become endogamous communities. Further, the real position of the Kshatriyas cannot be ascertained. It is said that Chandragupta Maurya was of mixed birth; the Andhra dynasty is usually regarded as of *Sudra* extraction. Harsha of Thanesvvar, the last great Hindu king, was a *Vaisya,* but ranked as a Kshatriya. It seems, therefore, that the ancient Kshatriyas, like the modern Rajputs, were a social class to which all rulers by virtue of their sovereignty were recognised as belonging. The Kshatriyas, like the modern Rajputs, may be regarded as an occupational caste following the Hindu ritual, and becoming rulers.[55]

Iyer further writes : In the early Buddhist period the Kshatriya was socially supreme. In Manu's account, the supremacy passed to the Brahman, it cannot be denied. In fact, as Blunt says, the causes may be found in the history of the time. From 200 B.C. to 500 A.D. India was subject to foreign invasions by powerful barbarian hordes, which led to the extirpation of the ancient Kshatriyas, who were also liable to be attacked from within. Buddhism, which was a Kshatriya religion, founded by a Kshatriya prince, was opposed to Brahmanism. The two religions went on side by side for ten centuries till at last Brahmanism gained the ascendency after the death of Harsha of Thanesvar in the middle of the seventh century A.D. It is also said that Parasurama extirpated the Kshatriyas. Thus the Kshatriya became extinct, and his power as ruler passed by right of sword to the foreign Sakas, Pahlavas and Kushans, each of whom in turn usurged the throne with the title of Kshatriya. Thus the kings and kinglets of India were often Hinduized foreigners who never attained to the rank and pre-eminence of the ancident Kshatriyas. This low position of the later Kshatriyas afforded an opportunity to the Brahman, who, in the meantime, increased his authority and consolidated his position. In the Vedic period he was an acolyte at sacrifices, and assistant to the head of the family who officiated as priest. During the period which ended with the advent of Buddha, in the midst of a people that was intensely religious, and still more intensely ritualist, he had become the hereditary priest, the sole master of religious ceremonial and doctrine, and as such had won for himself an almost unassailable supremacy.[56]

"Further, as philosopher and statesman, by sheer force of learning he had acquired considerable temporal power. The king's minister was a

Brahman—and was no more a figure head. Vasishta, the family priest of Trayyaruna, king of Kosala, acted as regent in his master's absence. Chanakya overthrew Nanda kings, put Chandragupta Maurya on the throne, and acted as his minister." The first Brahman dynasty after the Kanvas was the Shahya dynasty of Sindh in the tenth century. During the Buddhist period Brahman power suffered a little; Buddhism and the Kshatriya religion were revolts against Brahminism and its metaphysics. But Brahminism was never entirely destroyed. Under the Gupta dynasty the Brahmanic culture was widely diffused. The Brahman ascendancy, both temporal and spiritual revived. It increased during the troubled period which came with destruction of the old Arya nobility. The Brahman, 'the chief remaining link with the past, obtained the social hegemony, never again to lose it.'[57]

Dr. Ambedkar's Views on Caste

Dr Ambedkar observes : "The caste problem is a vast one both theoretically and practically. Practically, it is an institution that portends tremendous concequences. It is a local problem, but one capable of much wider mischief, for "as long as caste in India does exist, Hindus will hardly intermarry or have any social intercourse with outsiders; and if Hindus migrate to other regions on earth, Indian caste would become a world problem." Theoretically, it has defied a great many scholars who have taken upon themselves, as a labour of love, to dig into its origin. Such being the case, I cannot treat the problem in its entirety. Time, space and acumen, I am afraid, would all fail me, if I attempted to do otherwise than limit myself to a phase of it, namely, the genesis, mechanism and spread of the caste system. I will strictly observe this rule, and will dwell on extraneous matters only when it is necessary to clarify or support a point in my thesis.

To proceed with the subject. According to well-known ethnologists, the population of India is a mixture of Aryans, Dravidians, Mongolians and Scythians. All these stocks of people came into India from various directions and with various cultures, centuries ago, when they were in a tibal state. They all in turn elbowed their entry into the country by fighting with their predecessors, and after a stomachful of it settled down as peaceful neighbours. Through constant contact and mutual intercourse they evolved a common culture that superseded their distinctive cultures. It may be granted that there has not been a thorough amalgamation of the various stocks that make up the peoples of India, and to a traveller from within the boundaries of India, the East presents a marked contrast in physique and even in colour to the West, as does the South to the North. But amalgamation can never be the sole criterion of homogeneity as predicated of any people. Ethnically all people are heterogeneous. It is the unity of culture that is the basis of homogeneity. Taking this for granted, I venture to say that there is not country that can rival the Indian. Peninsula with respect to the unity of its culture. It has not only a geograhic unity, but it has over and above all a deeper and a much more fundamental unity-the indubitable cultural unity that covers the land from end to end. But it is because of thie homogeneity that caste becomes a problem so difficult to be explained. If the Hindu society were a mere federation of mutually exclusive units, the matter would be simple enough. But caste is a parcelling of an already homogeneous unit, and the explanation of the genesis of caste is the explanation of this process of parcelling."[58]

Senart, Nesfield, Risley and few others have already been quoted. However Dr. Ambedkar also quotes some scholars who have defined the caste system. He says : "Before launching into our field of enquiry, it is better to advise ourselves regarding the nature of a caste. I will therefore draw upon a few of the best students of caste for their definitions of it :—

1. Mr. Senart, a French authority, defines, a caste as "a close corporation, in theory at any rate rigorously hereditary: equipped with a certain traditional and independent organisation, including a chief and a council, meeting on occasion in assemblies of more or less plenary authority and joining together at certain festivals: bound together by common occupations, which relate more particularly to marriage and to food and to questions of ceremonial pollution, and ruling its members by the exercise of jurisdiction, the extent of which varies, but which succeeds in making the authority of the community more felt by the sanction of certain penalties and, above all, by final irrevocable exclusion from the group."
2. Mr. Nesfield defines a caste as "a class of the community which disowns any connection with any other class and can neither intermarry nor eat nor drink with any but persons of their own community."
3. According to Sir H. Risley, "a caste may be defined as a collection of families or groups of families bearing a common name which usually denotes or is associated with specific occupation, claiming common descent from a mythical ancestor, human or divine, professing to follow the same professional calling and are regarded by those who are competent to give an opinion as forming a single homogeneous community."

4. Dr. Ketkar defines caste as "a social group having two characteristics: (*i*) membership is confined to those who are born of members and includes all persons so born; (*ii*) the members are forbidden by an inexorable social law to marry outside the group."

Dr. Ambedkar[59] has reviewed the definitions of these scholars as under.[59] He observes : "To review these definitions is of great importance for our purpose. It will be noticed that taken individually, the definitions of three of the writers include too much or too little; none is complete or correct by itself and all have missed the central point in the mechanism of the caste as a isolated unit by itself, and not as a group within, and with definite relations to the system of caste as a whole. Yet collectively all of them are complementary to one another, each one those points common to all castes in each of the above definitions which are regarded as peculiarities of caste and evaluate them as such.

According to Dr. Ambedkar, Senart drew attention to the "idea of pollution" as a characteristic of caste. With regard to this point it may be safely said that it is by no means a peculiarity of caste as such. It usually originates in priestly ceremonialism and is a particular case of the general belief in purity. Consequently its necessary connection with caste may be completely denied without damaging the working of caste. The "idea of pollution" has been attached to the institution of caste, only because the caste that enjoys the highest rank is the priestly caste: while we know that priest and purity are old associates. We may therefore conclude that the "idea of pollution" is a characteristic of caste only in so far as caste has a religious flavour. Mr. Nesfield in his way dwells on the absence of messing with those outside the caste as one of its characteristics. In spite of the newness of the point we must say that Mr. Nesfield has mistaken the effect for the caste. Caste, being a self-enclosed unit naturally limits social intercourse, including messing, etc. to members within it. Consequently this absence of messing with outsiders is not due to positive prohibition, but is a natural result of caste, *i.e.*, exclusiveness. No doubt this absence of messing originally due to exclusiveness, acquired the prohibitory character of a religious injunction, but it may be regarded as a later growth. Sir H. Risley, makes no new point deserving of special attention."

Dr. Ambedkar analysing the views of Dr. Vatkar observe: "We now pass on to the definition of Dr. Ketkar who has done much for the elucidation of the subject. Not only is he a native, but he has also brought a critical acumen and an open mind to bear only his study of caste. His definitiion merits consideration, for he has defined caste in its relation to a system of castes, and has concentrated his attention only on those characteristics which are absolutely necessary for the existence of a caste within a system, rightly excluding all others as being secondary of derivative in character. With respect to his definition it must, however, be said that in it there is a slight confusion of thought, lucid and clear as otherwise it is. He who speaks of Prohibition of Intermarriage and Membership by Autogeny as the two characteristics of caste. I submit that these are but two aspects of one and the same thing, and not two different things as Dr. Ketkar[60] supposes them to be. If you prohibit intermarriage the result is that you limit membership to those born within the group. Thus the two are the obverse and the reverse sides of the same medal.

Further in the words of Dr. Ambedkar : "The critical evaluation of the various characteristics of caste leave no doubt that prohibition, or rather the absence of intermarriage—endogamy, to be concise—is the only one that can be called the essence of caste when rightly understood. But some may deny this on abstract anthropological grounds, for there exist endogamous groups without giving rise to the problem of Caste. In a general way this may be true, as endogamous societies, culturally different, making their abode in different localities more or less removed, and having little to do with each other are a physical reality. The Negroes and the Whites and the various tribal groups that go by name of American Indians in the United States may be cited as more or less appropriate illustrations in support of this view. But we must not confuse matters, for in India the situation is different. As pointed out before, the peoples of India form a homogeneous whole. The various races of India occupying definite territories have more or less fused into one another and do possess cultural unity, which is the only criterion of a homogeneous population. Given this homogeneity as a basis, caste becomes a problem altogether new in character and wholly absent in the situation constituted by the mere propinquity of endogamous social or tribal groups. Caste in India means an artificial chopping off of the population into fixed and definite units, each one prevented from fusing into another through the custom of endogamy. Thus the conclusion is inevitable that endogamy is the only characteristic that is peculiar to caste, and if we succeed in showing how endogamy is maintained, we shall practically have proved the genesis and also the mechanism of caste.

It may not be quite easy for you to anticipate why I regard endogamy as a key to the mystery of the caste system. Not to strain your imagination to much, I will proceed to give you my reasons for it. It may be relevant to say that the civilized society of today presents more survivals of primitive times that does the Indian society. Its religion is essentially primitive and its tribal code, in spite of the advance of time and civilization, operates in all its pristine vigour ever today. One of these primitive survivals, to which I wish particularly to draw your attention is the custom of exogamy. The prevalance of exogamy in the primitive world is a fact too well-known to need any explanation. With growth of history,[61] however, exogamy has lost its efficacy, and excepting the nearest blood-kins, there is usually no social bar restricting the field of marriage. But regarding the peoples of India the law of exogamy is a positive injection even today. Indian society still savours of the clan system, even though there are no clans; and this can be easily seen from the law of matrimony which centres round the principle of exogamy, for it is not that *Sapindas* (blood-kins) cannot marry, but a marrage even between *Sagotras* (of the same class) is regarded as a sacrilege.

It is therefore evident that endogamy is foreign to the people of India. The various *Gotras* of India are and have been exogamous ; so are the other groups with totemic organisation. It is no exaggeration to say that with people of India exogamy is a creed and none dare infringe it, so much so that, in spite of the endogamy of the castes within them, exogamy is strictly observed and that there are more rigorous penalties for violating exogamy. Than there are for violating endogamy. You will, therefoe readily see that with exogamy as the rule there could be no caste, for exogamy means fusion. But we have castes consequently in the final analysis creation or castes, so far as India is concerned, means the superposition of endogamy on exogamy. However, in an originally exogamous population an easy working out of endogamy (which is equivalent to the creation of caste) is a grave problem, and it is in the consideration of the means utilized for the preservation of endogamy against exogamy that we may hope to find the solution of our problem.

Thus the superposition of endogamy on exogamy means the cration caste. But this is not an easy affair. Let us take an imaginary group that desires to make itself into a caste and analyse what means it will have to adopt to make itself endogamous. If a group desires to make itself endogamous a formal injunction against intermarriage with outside groups will be of no avail, especially if prior to the introduction of endogamy, exogamy had been the rule in all matrimonial relations. Again, there is a tendency in all groups lying in close contact with one another to assimilate and amalgamate, and thus consolidate into a homogeneous society. If this tendency is to be strongly counteracted in the interest of caste formation, it is absolutely necessary to circumscribe a circle outside which people should not contract marriages."[62]

In this learned paper Dr. Ambedkar has futher examined the growth and spread of the caste system in India, that how did the institution of caste spread among the rest of the non-Brahmins. 'The question of the spread of the caste throughout India has suffered a worse fate than the question of genesis.'

According to common belief among scholars caste has either been imposed upon the docile population of India by a law-giver. Dr. Ambedkar believed Manu as tyrant law-giver who has not given the law of castes. Caste existed much befoe Manu. He has simply philosophised it, codified existing caste rules and preached caste *Dharma.*

In his opinion the theories of scholars are typical and mostly based on occupation, survivals of tribal organisation, rise of new belief, cross-breeding and migration. They have dealt with the problem why occupational group turned into on o(cupational caste. The earliest Hindu society in common with other societies was composed of following classes (*i*) The Brahmins, or the priestly class; (*ii*) the Kshatriya or the military class; (*iii*) The Vaishya, or the merchant class; (*iv*) The *Shudra (Sudra)* or the artisan and menial class.

In the opinion of Dr. Ambedkar : "This was essentially a class system. Individuals when qualified, could change their class, and therefore classes did change their personnel. In the history of Hindus, at some time, the priestly class socially detached itself from the rest of the body of the people and through a closed-door policy became a caste by itself. The other classes being subject to the law of social division of labour underwent differentiation, some into large others into very minute groups.

The *Vaisya* and *Shudra* classes were the original inchoate plasm, which formed the sources of the numerous castes of today. The Kshatriya were warriors and administrators and there is very little minute sub-division.

The Europeans have unnecessarily emphasised the colour in the caste system. Dr. Ketkar is correct that all princes whether Aryan or Dravidian were basically Aryas. Whether a family or a tribe was Aryan or Dravidian was a question which never troubled the Indian mind, until foreign scholars came and began to draw a line.

Inequality : Soul of Hinduism

The institution of caste created inequality. Hinduism did not attach importance to individual merit but to caste of an individual.

According to Dr. Ambedkar inequality is the sword of Hinduism. The morality of Hinduism is only social. It is immoral and inhuman to say the least. What is immoral and inhuman early becomes immoral, inhuman and infamous. This is what Hinduism has become.

The state of civilization of the Primitive Tribes in the Hindu social order "includes the entire period of human progress from savagery to barbarism and from barbarism to civilisation. The transition from one to other has been marked by some discovery or intention in some deparment of knowledge of art resulting in advancing the onward march of man."[63]

These aborigines of the Primitive Tribes, who were the forefathers of the present day workforce, the artisans, the agriculturists, the lower classes, invented fire and its use, discovered bow and arrow and other earlier tools (of wood, stone or metals), domesticated wild animals, kept domestic animals. Hunting, fishing and collection of food from forest were their main occupations. They were basically meat-eaters. They lived on trees and in caves, and had no hesitation in eating worms and insects, as well as dead animals and birds. The next group was of Criminal Tribes. They lived in forests as Primitive Tribes. They were barbarous and engaged in criminal activities. A few were engaged in agriculture and domestic industries but most of them took to nefarious practices. Besides, these two classes there were untouchables. They were the lowest among the Hindu social order. A vast majority of people were made slaves. The Breken man was almost a captive.

It is a naked truth that the Hindu social order for centuries denied human rights to these people. Right to education and knowledge was denied. The status was denied in the society. Physical, mental, economic growth was hampered. According to Dr. Ambedkar, "The Hindu social order[64] does not recognise the individual as a centre of social purpose. For the Hindu social order is based primarily on class or *varna*, and not on individual...The unit of the Hindu society is not the individual Brahmin or the individual Kshatriya or the individual *Vaishya* or the individual *Shudra* or the individual *Panchama.* Even the family is not regarded by the Hindu social order as the unit of society except for the purpose of marriage and inheritance. The unit of Hindu society is the class or *Varna* to use the Hindu technical name for class.

In the Hindu social order, there is no room for individual merit and no consideration of individual justice. If the individual has a privilege, it is not because it is due to him personally. The privilege goes with the class, and if he is found to enjoy it, it is because he belongs to that class."[65]

The caste Hindus excluded the *Sudras* from the mainstream of social, cultural and religious life. Their economic powers and activities were restricted. They were discouraged to adopt Vedic faith and denied education. There is no doubt that the practice of untouchability was promoted by the Aryan society to oppress and exploit the menial class in a planned and calculated manner. Thus the principle of 'graded inequality' became an order of Brahmanic social system.

The institution of Manu codified such laws which socially and economically condemned millions of innocent people for three thousand years. The institution of slavery in the form of caste system, followed by untouchability has no parallel in the history of the human race in the whole world.

References

1. Jatava, D.R. : *Evolution of Indian Social Thought,* p. 10.
2. Maity, S.K. : *Cultural Heritage of India,* p. 3.
3. Wolpert, Stanley: *A New History of India,* p. 14.
4. Thapar, Romila : *Ancient Indian History,* p. 34.
5. Jagjivan Ram : *Caste Challenge in India,* p. 9.
6. *Ibid.*, p.10.
7. Majumdar, R.C. : *Ancident India,* p.49.
8. Wheeler, J.T. : *Ancient and Hindu, India,* p.88.
9. Iyer, L.K.A. : *Mysore Tribes and Castes,* Vol. 1, pp. 128-29.
10. Jatava, D.R. *op. cit.*, p.15.
11. *Rig Veda,* X. 90, 11-12.
12. Wilson : *Rig Veda,* Intro. IL III, I, 20. (Quoted by Iyer, pp. 129-130.)
13. Prabhu, P.H. : *Hindu Social Organisation,* p.285.
14. Jagjivan Ram, *op. cit.*, pp. 10-11.
15. Quoted by Dr. Wilson, in *Indian Caste*, p. 209.
16. Iyer, *op. cit.* p.130.
17. Rapson, E.J. :*The Cambrige History of India,* Vol. I, *Ancient India,* pp. 54-55.
18. Iyer, *op. cit.* pp. 130-31.
19. Blunt, E.A.H. : *Caste in Northern India,* Chap. II, pp. 14-15. Dutt, N.K. : *Origin and Growth of Caste in India,* pp. 256-60. (Quoted by Iyer, p. *Op. cit.* p. 131.)
20. Iyer, *op. cit.* p. 136.
21. Radhakrishnan, S. : *Hindu View of Life,* p.10.
22. For details see Jatava, D.R., *op. cit.*, pp. 18-22.
23. *Ibid.*, pp. 22-26.
24. *Ibid.*, pp. 26-31.
25. See Jatava, D.R., *op. cit.*, pp. 22-38.
26. Dutt, N.K. : *Origin and Growth of Caste in India,* Chap. VI, pp. 269-70.
27. Dutt, N.K. : *Orgin and Growth of Caste in India,* Chap. III, pp. 97-101. (Quoted by Iyer, *op. cit,* p. 136-37.)
28. See for details Emile Senart, E. : *Caste in India.*

29. Iyer, *op. cit.*, p. 138.
30. Kalhan's *Raj Tarangini* gives detailed description on this issue.
31. Iyer, *op. cit.*, pp. 139-40.
32. Blunt, E.A.H. : *Caste in Northern India,* Chap.II, pp. 15-17. Dutt, N.K. : *Origin and Growth of Caste in India,* Chap. VI, pp. 273-74.
33. Wilson, Dr. : *Indian Caste,* p.12.
34. Srivastava, R.K. : *Gandhi and the Problem of Caste and Untouchability* (In Verinder Grover's Gandhi and Politics in India), p.54.
35. Nehru Jawaharlal : *Discovery of India,* pp. 84-85.
36. L.K.A. Iyer : *Lectures on Ethnography,* Chap. IV, pp. 75-77.
37. Rapson, E.J. : *Combridge History of India,* Vol. I, *Ancient India,* pp. 234-235.
38. Russell, R.V. : *The Tribes and Castes of the Central Provinces,* Vol. I, pp. 14-15.
39. *Ibid.*, pp. 14-15.
40. Emile Senart : *Caste in India,* pp. 158-62, 162.
41. Emile Senart : *op. cit.*, pp.169-72.
42. Iyer, *op. cit.*, p. 145.
43. See Jiloha, R.C. : *The Native Indian,* pp. 20-26.
44. Manu, pp. 10, 64, 65.
45. *Ibid.*, pp. 9, 149-57.
46. Iyer, *op. cit.*, p. 146.
47. *Notes and Queries of the Anthropological Institute,* p. 54.
48. Iyer, *op. cit.*, p. 147.
49. Senart, Emile : *op. cit.*, p. 152.
50. Russell, R.V. : *Tribes and Castes of the Central Provinces of India,* Vol. I, (Introduction), p. 9.
51. *Ibid.*, pp. 9-10.
52. *Ibid.*, p. 10.
53. Blunt, E.A.H. : *Caste System of Northern Indian,* Chap. II, pp. 17-21. also (Iyer, *op. cit.*, pp. 131-32).
54. *Ibid.*, pp. 17-21.
55. *Ibid.*. pp. 22 24. (Iyer, p. 133.)
56. Dutt, N.K. : *Origin and Growth of Caste in India,* Chap. VI, pp. 280-84. Iyer *op. cit.*, p. 134.
57. Blunt, E.A.H. : Caste System of Northern India, Chap. II. pp. 27-28. *Ibid,* p. 135.
58. Chanchreek, K.L. : *Social Justice and Political Safeguards for Depressed Classes.* (Dr. Ambedkar : *Caste in India,* p. 2)
59. *Ibid.*, p.3.
60. *Ibid.*, p.4.
61. *Ibid.*, p.5.
62. *Ibid.*, p.6.
63. Ambedkar, Dr. B.R. : *Writings and Speeches*, Vol. 3, pp. 87-89.
64. *Ibid.*, p. 99.
65. *Ibid.*, p. 99.

2

Society in India, and Remark on Caste System

The word *caste* is derived from the Portuguese, and is used in Europe to designate the different tribes or classes into which the people of India are divided[1]. The most ordinary classification, and at the same time the most ancient, divides them into four main castes. The first and most distinguished of all is that of *Brahmana,* or *Brahmins*; the second in rank is that of *Kshatriyas,* or *Rajahs;* the third the *Vaisyas,* or *Landholders* and *Merchants;* and the fourth the Sudras, or *Cultivators* and *Menials.* Each of the four main castes is subdivided into many others, the number of which it is difficult to determine because the subdivisions vary according to locality, and as sub-caste existing in one province is not necessarily found in another.

Amongst the Brahmins of the South of the Peninsula, for example, there are to be found, three or four principal divisions, and each of these again is subdivided into at least twenty others. The lines of demarcation between them are so well defined as to prevent any kind of union between one sub-caste and another, especially in the case of marriage.

The Kshatriyas and Vaisyas are also split up into many divisions and subdivisions. In Southern India neither Kshatriyas nor *Vaisyas* are very numerous; but there are considerable numbers of the former in Northern India. However, the Brahmins assert that the true Kshatriya caste no longer exists, and that those who pass for such are in reality a debased race.

Division of Sudras

The Sudra caste is divided into most sub-castes. Nobody in any of the provinces where I have lived has been able to inform me as to the exact number and names of them. It is a common saying, however, that there are 18 chief sub-castes, which are again split up into 108 lesser divisions.

The *Sudras* are the most numerous of the four main castes. They form, in fact, the mass of the population, and added to the Pariahs, or Outcastes, they represent at least nine-tenths of the inhabitants. When we consider that the Sudras possess almost a monopoly of the various forms of artisan employment and manual labour, and that in India no person can exercise two professions at a time, it is not surprising that the numerous individuals who form this main caste are distributed over so many distinct branches.

However, there are several classes of Sudras that exist only in certain provinces. Of all the provinces that I lived in, the Dravidian. or Tamil, country is the one where the ramifications of caste appeared to me most numerous. There are not nearly so many ramifications of caste in Mysore or the Deccan. Nowhere in these latter provinces have I come across castes corresponding to those which are known in the Tamil country under the name of *Moodelly, Agambady, Nattaman, Totiyar, Udaiyan, Valeyen, Upiliyen, Pallen,* and several others.

In some districts there are castes which are not to be met with elsewhere, and which may be distinguished by peculiarities of their own. We are not aware, for example, that the very remarkable caste of *Nairs,* whose women enjoy the privilege of possessing several husband is to be found anywhere but Travancore.[2] Amongst these same people, again, is another distinct caste called *Nambudiri,* which observes one abominable and revolting custom. The girls of this caste are usually married before the age of puberty; but if a girl who has arrived at an age when the signs of pouberty are apparent happens to die before having had intercourse with a man, caste custom rigorously demands that the inanimate corpse of the deceased shall be subjected to a monstrous connexion. For this purpose the girl's parents are obliged to procure by a present of money. Some wretched fellow willing to consummate such a disgusting form of marriage: for were the marriage not consummated the family would consider itself dishonoured.[3]

The Caste of Kullar

The caste of *Kullars,* or robbers who exercise their calling as an hereditary right, is found only in the Marava country, which borders on the coast, or fishing, districts. The rulers of the country are of the same caste. They regard a robber's occupation as discreditable neither to themselves nor to their fellow castemen, for the simple reason that they consider robbery a duty on a right sanctioned by descent. They are not ashamed of their *caste* or occupation, and if one were to ask of a *kullar* to what people he belonged he would coolly answer, 'I am a robber!' This caste is looked upon in the district of Madura, where it is widely diffused, as one of the most distinguished among the *Sudra.*

There exists in the same part of the country another caste, known as the *Totiyars,* in which brothers, uncles, nephews, and other near relations are all entitled to possess their wives in common.

In Eastern Mysore there is a caste called *Morsa-Okkala-Makkalu,* in which, when the mother of a family gives her eldest daughter in marriage, she is obliged to submit to the amputation of two joints of the middle finger and of the ring finger of the right hand. And if the bride's mother be dead, the bridegrooms' mother, or in default of her the mother of the nearest relative, must submit of this cruel mutilation[4].

Many other castes exist in various disticts which are distinguished by practices no less foolish than those above mentioned. Generally speaking, there are few castes which are not distinguished by some special custom quite apart from the peculiar religious usages and ceremonies which the community may prescribe to guarantee or sanction civil contracts. In the cut and colour of their clothes and in the style of wearing them in the peculiar shape of their jewels and in the manner in which they are displayed on various part of the person, the various castes have many rules, each possessing its own significance. Some observe rites of their own in their funeral and marriage ceremonies: others possess ornaments which they alone may use, or flags of certain colours, for various ceremonies, which no other caste may carry. Yet absured as some of these practices may appear, they arouse neither contempt no dislike in members of other castes which do not admit them. The most perfect toleration is the rule in such matters. As long as a caste conforms on the whole to the recognised rules of decorum, it is permitted to follow its own bent in its domestic affairs without interruption, and no other castes ever think of blaming or even criticizing it, although its practices may be in direct opposition to their own.

There are, nevertheless, some customs which, although scrupulously observed in the countries where they exist, are so strongly opposed to the rules of decency and decorum generally laid down that they are spoken of with disapprobation and sometimes with horror by the rest of the community. The following may be mentioned among practices of this nature. In the interior of Mysore, women are obliged to accompany the male inmates of the house whenever the latter retire for the calls of nature, and to cleanse them with water afterwards. This practice, which is usually viewed with disgust in other parts of the country, is here regarded as a sign of good breeding and is most carefully observed[5].

Use of Liquor

The use of intoxicating liquors, which is condemned by respectable people throughout almost the whole of India, is nevertheless permitted amongst the people who dwell in jungles and hill tracts of the West Coast. There the leading castes of Sudras, not excepting even the women and children, openly drink *arrack,* the brandy of the country, and *toddy,* the fermented juice of the palm. Each inhabitant in those parts has his *toddy*-dealer who regularly brings him a daily supply and takes in return an equivalent in gain at harvest time. The Brahmin inhabitants of these parts are forbidden a like indulgence under the penalty of exclusion from caste. But they supply the opium, the use of which, although universally interdicted elsewhere, is nevertheless considered much less objectionable than the use of intoxicating liquors.

The people of these damp and unhealthy districts have no doubt learnt by experience that a moderate use of spirits or opium is necessary for the preservation of health, and that it protects them, partially at any rate, against the ill-effects of the malaria amidst which they are obliged to live.

The various classes of *Sudras* who dwell in the hills of the Carnatic observe amongst their domestic regulations a practice as peculiar as it is disgusting. Both men and women pass their lives in a state of uncleanness and never wash their clothes. When once they have put on clothes fresh from the weavers they do not leave them off until the material actually drops from rottenness. One can imagine the filthy condition of these clothes they have been worn day and night for several months soaked with perspiration and soiled with dirt, especially in the case of women, who continually use them for wiping their hands, and who never change their garments until wear and tear have rendered them absolutely useless.

Yet this revolting habit is most religiously observed, and, if anybody were so rash as to wash but once in water the clothes with which he or she is covered exclusion from caste would be the inevitable consequence. This custom, however, may be due to the scarcity of water, for in this part of the country, there are only a few stagnant ponds, which would very soon be contaminated if all the inhabitants of a village were allowed to wash their garments in them.

Religious Customs

Many religious customs are followed only by certain sects, and are of purely local character. For instance, it is only in the districts of Western Mysore that I have observed Monday in each week kept nearly in the same way as Sunday is among Christians. On that day the villagers abstain from ordinary labour, and particularly from such as, like ploughing, requires the use of oxen and kine. Monday is consecrated to *Basava* (the Bull), and is set apart for the special worship of that deity. Hence it is a day of rest for their cattle rather than for themselves.

This practice, however, is not in vogue except in the districts where the *Lingayats,* or followers of Siva[6], predominate. This sect pays more particular homage to the Bull than the rest of the Hindus; and in the districts where it predominates, not only keeps up the strict observance of the day thus consecrated to the divinity, but forces other castes to follow its example.

Independently of the divisions and subdivisions common to all castes one may further observe in each caste close family alliances cemented by intermarriage. Hindus of good family avoid as far as possible intermarriage with families outside their own circle. They always aim at marrying their children into the families which are already allied to them and the nearer the relationship the more easily are marriages contracted. A widower is remarried to his deceased wife's sister, an uncle marries his niece, and a first cousin his first cousin. Persons so related possess an exclusive privilege of intermarrying, upon the ground of such relationship; and if they choose, they can prevent any other union to enforce their own preferential right, however old, unsuited, infirm, and poor they may be[7].

In this connexion, however, several strange and ridiculous distinctions are made. An uncle may marry the daughter of his sister, but in no case may he marry the daughter of his brother. A brother's children may marry a sister's children, but the children of two brothers or of two sisters may not intermarry. Among descendants from the same stock the male line always has the right of contracting marriage with the famale line; but the children of the same line may never intermarry.

The reason given for this custom is that children of the male line, as also those of the female line, continue from generation to generation to call themselves brothers and sisters for as long a time as it is publicly recognized that they spring from the same stock. A man would be marrying his sister, it would be said, if the children of either the male or the female line intermarried amongst themselves; whereas the children of the male line do not call the children of the female line brothers and sisters, and vice versa, but call each other by special names expressive of the relationship.

Thus a man can, and even must, marry the daughter of his sister, but never the daughter of his brother. A male first cousin marries a female first cousin, the daughter of his maternal aunt; but in no case may he marry the daughter of his paternal uncle.

Brahmin to the Pariah

This rule is universally and invariably observed by all castes, from the Brahmin to the Pariah. It is obligatory on the male line to unite itself with the female line. Agreeably to this a custom has arisen which so far as we know is peculiar to the Brahmins. They are all supposed to know the *gotram* or stock from which they spring: that is to say, they know who was the ancient *Muni* or devotee from whom they descend, and they always take care, in order to avoid intermarriage with a female descendant of this remote priestly ancestor, to marry into a *gotram* other than their own.

Hindus who cannot contract a suitable marriage amongst their own relations are nevertheless bound to marry in their own caste, an even in that subdivision of it to which they belong. In no case are they permitted to contract marriages with strangers. Furthermore, persons belonging to a caste in one part of the country cannot contract marriages with persons of the same caste in another part, even though they may be precisely the same castes under different names. Thus the Tamil *Yedeyers* and the Canares *Uppareru* would never consent to take wives from the Telugu *Gollavaru* and the Tamil *Pillay,* although the first two are, except for their names, identical with the second two.

The most distinguished of the four main castes into which the Hindus were originally separated by their first legislators is, as we have before remarked, that of the Brahmins. After them come to Kshatriyas, or *Rajahs.* Superiority of rank is at present warmly contested between the *Vaisyas,* or merchants, and the Sudras, or cultivators. The former appear to have almost entirely lost their superiority except in the Hindu books, where they are invariably placed before the *Sudras.* In ordinary life the latter hold themselves to be superior to the *Vaisyas,* and consider themselves privileged to mark their superiority in many respects.

With regard to the *Vaisya* caste an almost incredible but nevertheless well-attested peculiarity is everywhere observable. There is not a pretty woman to be found in the caste. We have never had much to do with the women of the *Vaisya* caste; we cannot therefore without injustic venture to add our testimony to that of others on this subject; but we may confess that the few Vaisya women seen from time to time were not such as to afford us an ocular refutation of the popular prejudice. However, *Vaisya* women are generally wealthy, and they manage to make up for their lack of beauty by their elegant attire.

Social Rank for Brahmins

Even the Brahmins do not hold the highest social rank undisputed. The *Panchals,* or five classes of artisans already mentioned, refuse, in some districts, to acknowledge Brahmin predominance, although these five classes themselves are considered to be of very low rank amongst the *Sudras* and are everywhere held in contempt. The Brahmin predominance is also sill more warmly contested by the Jains.

As to the particular subdivisions of each caste it is difficult to decide the order of hierarchy observed amongst them. Sub-castes which are despised in one district are often greatly esteemed in another, according as they conduct themselves with greater propriety or follow more important callings. Thus the caste to which the ruler of a country belongs, however low it may be considered elsewhere, ranks amongst the highest in the ruler's own dominions, and every member of it derives some reflection of dignity from its chief.

After all, public opinion is the surest guide of caste superiority amongst the *Sudras,* and a very slight acquaintance with the customs of a province and with the private life of its inhabitants will suffice for fixing the position which each caste has acquired by common consent.

In general it will be found that those castes are most honoured who are particular in keeping themselves pure by constant bathing and by abstaining from animal food, who are exact in the observance of marriage regulations, who keep their women shut up and punish them severely when they err, and who resolutely maintain the customs and privileges of their order.

Of all the Hindus the Brahmins strive most to keep up appearances of outward and inward purity by frequent ablutions and severe abstinence not only from meat or everything that has contained the principle of life, but also from several natural products of the earth which prejudice and superstition teach them to be impure and defiling. It is chiefly to the scrupulous observance of such customs that the Brahmins owe the predominance of their illustrious order, and the reverence and respect with which they are everywhere treated. Amongst the different classes of *Sudras,* those who permit widow remarriage are considered the most abject, and except the Pariahs, We know very few castes in which such marriages are allowed to take openly and with the sanction of the cast.[8]

The division into castes is the paramount distinction amongst the Hindus; but there is still another division that of sects. The two best known are those of Siva and Vishnu, which are again divided into a large number of others.

There are several castes, too, which may be distinguished by certain marks painted on the forehead or other parts of the body. The first three of the four main castes, that is to say the Brahmins, Kshatriyas, and *Vaisyas,* are distinguished by a thin cord hung across from the left shoulder to the right hip. But this cord is also worn by the Jains and even by the *Panchalas,* or five castes or artisans so one is apt to be deceived by it.

From what has been said it will appear that the name of a caste forms after all its best indication. It was thus that the tribes of Israel were distinguished. The names of several of the Hindu castes have a known meaning; but for the most part they date from such ancient times that it is impossible to find out their significance.

There is yet another division more general than any we have referred to yet, namely, that into Right-hand and Left-hand factions. This appears to be but a modern invention, since it is not mentioned in any of the ancient books of our country; and we have been assured that it is unknown in Northern India. Be that as it may, we do not believe that any idea of this baneful institution, as it exists at the present day, ever entered the heads of those wise lawgivers who considered they had found in caste distinctions the best guarantee for the observance of the laws which they prescribed for the people. This division into Right-hand and Left-hand factions, whoever invented it, has turned out to be the most direful disturber of the public peace. It has proved a perpetual source of riots, and the cause of endless animosity amongst the natives. Most castes belong either to the Left-hand or Right-hand faction. The former comprises the *Vaisyas* or trading classes, the *Panchalas* or artisan classes, and come of the low *Sudra* castes. It also contains the lowest caste, namely, the *Chucklers* or leather-workers, who are looked upon as its chief support.

To the Right-hand faction belong most of the higher castes of Sudras. The Pariahs are its chief support, as a proof of which they glory in the title *Valangai-Mougattar,* or friends of the Right-hand. In the disputes and conflicts which so often take place between the two factions, it is always the Pariahs who make the most disturbance and do the most damage.

Exclusive Privileges

The Brahmins, Rajahs, and several classes of *Sudras* are content to remain neutral, and take no part in these quarrels. They are often chosen as arbiters in the differences which the two factions have to settle between themselves.

The opposition between the two factions arises from certain exclusive privileges to which both lay claim. But as these alleged privileges are nowhere clearly defined and recognized, they result in confusion and uncertainty, and are with difficulty capable of settlement. In these circumstances one cannot hope to conciliate both parties; all that one can do is to endeavour to compromise matter as far as possible.

When one faction trespasses on the so-called rights of the other, tumults arise which spread gradually over large tracts of territory, afford opportunity for excesses of all kinds, generally end in bloody conflicts.

We have several times witnessed instances of these popular insurrections excited by the mutual pretensions of the two factions and pushed to such an extreme of fury that the presence of a military force has been insufficient to quell them, to allay the clamour, or to control the excesses in which the contending factions consider themselves entitled to indulge.

Occasionally, when the Magistrates fail to effect a reconciliation by peaceful means, it is necessary to resort to force in order to suppress the disturbances. We have sometimes seen these rioters stand up against several discharges of artillery without exhibiting any sign of submission. And when at last the armed force has succeeded in restoring order it is only for a time. At the very first opportunity the rioters are at work again, regardless of the punishment they have received, and quite ready to renew the conflict as obstinately as before. Such are the excesses to which the mild and peaceful Hindu abandons himself when his courage is aroused by religious and political fanaticism.

The rights and privileges for which the Hindus are ready to fight such sanguinary battles appear highly ridiculous, especially to a European. Perhaps the sole cause of the contest is the right to wear slippers or to pass through the streets in a palanquin or on horseback during marriage festivals. Sometimes it is the privilege of being escorted on certain occasions by armed retainers, sometimes that of having a trumpet sounded in front of a procession, or of being accompanied by native musicians at public ceremonies. Perhaps it is simply the particular kind of musical instrument suitable to such occasions that is in dispute; or perhaps it may be the right of carrying flags of certain colours or certain device during these ceremonies. Such at any rate are a few of the privileges for which Hindus are ready to cut each other's throats. It however does not frequently that one faction makes an attack on the rights, real or pretended of the other. Thereupon the trouble begins, and soon becomes general if it is not appeased at the very outset by prudent and vigorous measures on the part of the magistracy.

Thus we could quote numerous examples bearing on this fatal distinction between Right-hand and Left-hand; but what we have already said is enough to show the spirit which animates the Hindus in this matter. We once witnessed a dispute of this nature between the Pariahs and *Chucklers,* or leather-workers. There seemed reasons to fear such disastrous consequences throughout the whole district in question, that several of the peaceful inhabitants began to desert their villages and to carry away their goods and chattels to a place of safety, just as is done when the country is threatened by the near approach of a Mahratta army. However, matters did not reach this extremity. Naturally the principal inhabitants of the district offered to arbitrate in the matter and they succeeded by diplomacy and conciliation in smooting away the difficulties and in appeasing the two factions, who were only awaiting the signal to attack each other.

It is however difficult to guess the cause of this formidable commotion. It simply arose from the fact that a *Chuckler* had dared to appear at a public ceremony with red flowers stuck in his turban, a privilege which the Pariahs alleged to belong exclusively to the Right-hand faction[9].

References

1. The Sanskrit word is *Varna* = colour, thus showing that upon the difference of colour between the Aryan Brahmins and the aboriginal inhabitants the distinction of caste was originally founded.
2. It would be more correct to say West Coast. Moreover, although Nair women are commonly described as polyandrous they are not really so, for though they enjoy the privilege of changing their husbands, they do not entertain more than one husband *at a time.*
3. Whatever may have been the case in the days of the Abbe, these customs no longer exist. In regard to this, Mr. W. Logan, in his *Manual of Malabar,* writes thus: "T make tardy retribution — if it deserves such a name — to women who die unmarried, the corpse, it is said, cannot be burnt till a *tali* string (the Hindu equivalent of the wedding ring of Europe) is tied round the neck of the corpse, while lying on the funeral) pile, by a competent relative. Nambudiris are exceedingly reticent in regard to their funeral ceremonies and observances, and the Abbe Dubois account of what was related to him regarding other observances at this strange funeral-pile marriage requires confirmation.' Careful inquiries made of the leading members of the Nambudiri community and of others in Malabar who have an intimate knowledge of Nambudiri customs have convinced me that the Abbe must have misunderstood his informant in regard to the practice which he records here. What is done in such a case is merely to p perform the religious rites, usually associated with Hindu marriages, over the dead body of the woman before the corpse is cremated. By marriage here is merely the tying of the *tali* (the emblem of marriage) and not the act of consummation of marrigae."

6. Mr. L. Rice, in his *Mysore and Coorg,* remarks: 'Lingayats: The distinctive mark of this caste is the wearing on the person of a *Jangama lingam,* or portable *linga.* It is a small black stone about the size of an acorn, and is enshrined in a silver box of peculiar shape, which is worn suspended from the neck or tied round the arm. The followers of Basava (the founder of the sect, whose name literally means *Bull;* was in fact regarded as the incarnation of Nandi, the bull of Siva) are properly called *Lingavantas,* but Lingayats have become a well-known designation, though not used by themselves, the name Sivabhakta or Sivachar being one they generally assume.'—Ed.
7. This custom is gradually giving way now amongst the higher castes.—Ed.
8. Remarriage of virgin widows is one of the foremost planks in the platform of Social Reform, but it is opposed violently by the orthodox.—Ed.
9. These faction fights have gradually disappeared under the civilizing influences of education and good government; and if they ever occur at all, are confined to the lowest castes and never spread beyond the limits of a village. The distinctions between the two factions, however, still exist.—Ed.

3

Origin of the Brahmins

The real origin of the Brahmins is wrapped in mystery, and one can only put belief in myths. The story most generally accepted says that they were born from Brahma's head, which accounts for their name. One would suppose that as all castes were born from this same father they would be privileged to bear the same name; but as the Brahmins were the first-born, and issued from the noblest part of the common parent, they claimed special privileges from which all others were rigorously excluded. They have another theory to bear out the accepted belief that no one else is entitled to the illustrious name of Brahmin. They say that no one knows anything about Brahma's attributes and virtues beyond what they themselves choose to teach mankind, and that this knowledge in itself gives them the right to bear his name. Anyhow, their name is undoubtedly derived from Brahma's. The old writers call them 'Brahmanahas', or 'Brahmahas', which some of the Latin authors turned into 'Brachmanes'. The great difference between their caste and all others is that a Brahmin only becomes a Brahmin after the ceremony of the triple cord, which will be described hereafter. Until this essential ceremony has been performed the ranks only as a Sudra. By mere birth he is no different from the rest of his race; and it is for this reason that he is called *Dvija* (*Bis genitus,* or Twice-born). His first birth only gives him his manhood, whereas the second raises him to the exalted rank of Brahmin, and this by means of the ceremony of the triple cord. Indeed, two out of the seven famous penitents, who are supposed to have been the original founders of the various sects of Brahmins of the present day, did not originally belong to this caste at all; but by reason of the length and austerity of their term of penance, they were rewarded by having their state of penitent Kshatriyas changed to that of penitent Brahmins by the investiture of the triple-cord. These seven penitents, of *Rishis,* or *Munis,* of Hindu history are the most celebrated personage recognised by the people of India. Their names are Kasyapa, Atri, Bharadwaja, Gautama, Viswamitra, Jamadagni, and Vasishta. The last-named and Viswamitra are those who were considered worthy of being admitted into the high caste of Brahmins. These far-famed *Rishis* must be of great antiquity, for they existed even before the Vedas, which allude to them in several places. They were the favoured of gods, and more especially of Vishnu, who at the time of the Deluge made them embark on a vessel which he piloted, and thereby saved them from destruction. Even the gods were called to account for having offended these holy men, who did not hesitate to curse the deities who committed infamies.

The seven penitents, after setting a virtuous example on earth, were finally transferred to heaven, where they occupy a place amongst the most brilliant constellations. They are to be recognised in the seven starts that form the Great Bear, which, according to Hindu tradition, are neither more nor less than the seven famous *Rishis* themselves. They are, according to Hindu legend, the ancestors of the Brahmins in reality and not by metamorphosis, and it is believed that without ceasing to shine in the firmament they can, and occasionally do, revisit the earth to find out what is happening there.

Role of Astronomy

Astronomy has played an important part in the history of almost all idolatrous nations; and of all false creeds it certainly is the least unreasonable, and has survived the longest. The religious and political law-givers of these races were clever enough to perceive that the worship of the stars had taken a great hold upon mankind, and that the simplest and most effectual way of perpetuating the memory of their heroes would be to transform them into outward objects that were always before the eyes of the people. It was thus that the Greeks and Romans consecrated the memory of their divinities and demi-gods; and no doubt the Hindu law-givers were prompted to immortalize their seven *Rishis* by means of the brightest stars in the sky because they realized that a Hindu imagination is only appealed to through the visible, and therefore that was the best way to perpetuate the veneration due to these illustrious beings. But whatever may have been the claims of Brahmins to a celestial origin, it is a well-authenticated fact that neither their caste nor any other existed in the countries to the north-east of Bengal four or five centuries ago. About that time the inhabitants of those parts, thinking that it might be to their advantage to adopt the customs of their neighbours, began to clamour for Brahmins. Accordingly, some were made to order out of the youths of the country, who, after conforming to the customs and rites of the Brahmins, were incorporated into their caste by the investiture of the triple cord. The descendants of these ready-made Brahmins have ever since been considered on an equality with the rest. The southern Brahmins do not care to be reminded of the fact; yet they are obliged to admit it, as well as that two of the *Rishis* were originally Kshatrivas. An objection which people often put to them is that if nothing but the investiture of the triple cord can make Brahmins of them, then their wives, who do not go through the ceremony, really belong to the *Sudras;* and this means that all Brahmins are obliged to marry out of their caste and by so doing violate their most sacred principles. The reply they invariably make to this, as to other embarrassing questions, is that they are but following time-honoured customs and institutions.

One is certainly justified in expressing doubt on the subject of the Brahmins' origin, but we should be sorry to oppose our conjectures to their absurd fables. Far be it from us to start any theories. Our only desire is to collect materials which may help those who are trying to lift the veil which shrouds from view the cradle of the universe. It is practically admitted that India was inhabited very soon after the Deluge, which made a desert of the whole world. The fact that it was so close to the plains of Sennaar, where Noah's descendants remained stationary so long, as well as its good climate and the fertility of the country, soon led to its settlement. We will say nothing of the conquests of Hercules, Bacchus, and Osiris, as most learned men look upon them as fabulous beings, and who admit an element of truth in the tales carefully denuded them of all the extravagant details which tradition assigns to them[1]. The history of Sesostris, although equally full of impossibilities, has something more truthful and authenticated about it. The few ancient monuments which have been preserved make him out to have been the bravest, not to say the only, warrior that peaceful Egypt had to boast of for a period of more than sixteen centuries, and they also lead one to believe that he was the greatest of all conquerors, with an empire extending from the Danube to the Ganges. But his Indian conquests were as temporary and unstable as those of his illustrious rival, Alexander the Great, much later on in the world's history.[1]

The Arab Settlers

As to the settlements that the Arabs are supposed to have made in India, according to some authors, We think only superficial students will be found ready to believe in them. The fact that they are nomads, who have always lived a wandering life within reach of India, gives some appearance of reality to the theory. Some indeed believe that the caste system was borrowed from the since it still exists in Arabia; but, as a matter of fact, it is a custom common to all the ancient races of the earth.

Two famous mountains situated in Northern India, known as Great Meru (*Maha-Meru*) and Mount Mandara (*Mandara Parvata*), are frequently mentioned in their old books and in their prayers, liturgies, and civil and religious ceremonies. These mountains which we believe to be one and the same under slightly different names, are so far away that their precise whereabouts is unknown to the Brahmins of today[2]. And this is indeed surprising in a country where geographical science is confined to knowledge of the places situated between Benares and Cape Comorin. The Hindus themselves claim to be descended from the inhabitants of these distant northern regions, and they believe that it was there that the seven illustrious ancestors of the Brahmins were born, whose descendants have spread little by little throughout the length and breadth of the land. This opinion of the Hindus as to the origin of the Brahmins is confirmed by the Brahmins themselves, by the manner in which they treat one another.

The northern Brahmin considers himself nobler and of higher rank than his southern brother, inasmuch as, having originated closer to the cradle of the race, there is less room for doubt concerning the fact of his direct descent from the *Rishis*. Surely these seven Hindu penitents, or philosophers, must be the seven sons of *Japheth,* who, with their father at their head, led one-third of the human race towards the West, when men began to disperse after the flood. They did not all reach Europe. Some of them on their way turned northwards, under the guidance of Magog, second son of Japheth, and penetrated into Tartary as far as the Caucasian Range, in which vast tract of country they made several settlements.

Any one believing in the connexion betwen names and facts will be struck with the similarity existing between Magog's name and Gautama's commonly called Gotama. *Ma* or *maha,* signifies great, so that Gotama must mean the Great God or Mogog.[2]

Furthermore, pagan history adds weight to these conjectures of mine on the origin and antiquity of the Brahmins. Learned men allude to more than one Prometheus. According to the Greeks the most celebrated of them all is a son of Japheth. He created man out of the soil, and instilled life into him with the fire stolen from heaven. This bold enterprise irritated Jupiter, who punished him by chaining him to one of the Caucasian Mountains, where a vulture devoured his liver as fast as it renewed itself. Hercules killed the vulture, and thereby put the son of Japheth, out of his torture.

Why should not Brahma and Prometheus be one and the same person? The Hindu divinity is known also under the names of *Brema* and *Prume* in some of their tongues. All these names bear resemblance to prometheurs, or the god *Prome* of the Greeks. Brahma, like Prometheus, is looked upon as the creator of man, who is supposed to have issued from the various parts of Brahma's body. Brahma was also their great law giver, being the author of the Vedas, which he wrote with his own hand. He had more than once to appeal to Vishnu for help, just as Prometheus relied on Hercules to deliver him from his enemies.

This pretension on the part of the Hindu Prometheus to be regarded as the maker of man and therefore a god, has been handed down in some part to his eldest sons, the Brahmins, who humbly call themselves the *God Brahma,* or *the Gods of the Earth.* At certain times the people prostrate themselves before them in adoration, and offer up sacrifices to them.

Again, several authors, both sacred and profane, have tried to prove that th Prometheus who wished to pass as the creator of man was no other than Magog himself. It is hardly likely that so near the time of the Deluge the real Creator should have been so completely forgotten that a son of Noah was able to pass himself off as a god; but it is quite possible that his descendants defied him when the spirit of idolatry began to reign on earth. It was Magog who settled in Tartary with all those who elected to follow him, having decided to separate from Japheth's other children. From thence he or his descendants spread over India and other countries, which had rightly fallen to Shem's lot. This verified Noah's prophecy that Japheth's dominion would be far-reaching, and that his posterity would dwell in the tents of Shem (Gen. ix. 27). But admitting that Tartary or the neighbourhood of the Caucasus was the birthplace of the Brahmins, it is not easy to decide the precise date of their arrival in India. It appears certain, however, that they were already established there in a flourishing condition more than nine centuries before the Christian era, as that was about the time of Lycurgus's visit to them; and it is not likely that one of the wisest of the ancient philosophers would have undertaken such a long and tedious journey unless the reputation of the learned men he was going all that way to consult was an old and established fact.

Ancient Hindu Works

The ancient Hindu works teach us that the Brahmins of those times differed essentially in matters of principle and conduct from their brethren of today. The original *Brahmin* is described as a penitent and a philosopher, living apart from the world and its temptations and entirely engrossed in the pursuit of knowledge, leading a life of introspection and pratising a life of purity. At that period of their history the Brahmins were not such an intolerant and exclusive race that ponitents belonging to other castes could not be initiated by the *Diskha* ceremony,[3] or the investiture of the triple cord. There are many examples of this in their literature. The simple and blameless lives led by the primitive Brahmins, their contempt for wealth and honours, their disinterestedness, and, above all, their extreme sobriety, attracted the attention of the princes and the people. The greatest kings were not above rendering homage to them and treating them with more respect than they would have dared to demand for themselves from their own subjects. These philosophers, living secluded from the world with their wives and children, multiplied exceedingly.

Although the modern Brahmin has degenerated considerably, he still acts up to a great many of the customs and institutions of his ancestors. Like them, he prefers to live in retired places, far from the noisy haunts of man; and that is the reason why he settled in isolated villages, from which all natives belonging to other castes are excluded. There are numbers of these villages in the different provinces of the Indian peninsula, and they are known by the names *agraras* or *agrahara.*[4] Still more do the Brahmins resemble their ancestors in the way in which they fast frequently and wash themselves daily, and in all that concerns their sacrifices; but perhaps, most of all in their scrupulous abstinence, not only from meat and all forms of living food, but even from anything with which superstition or prejudice may have connected any idea of pollution.

The religious system of the Brahmins and the absurd theogony which they have prepagated in India seem to be the points on which they have gone most astray from the teachings of their predecessors. We cannot believe that the original lawgivers of the Hindus intended to introduce a creed so abominable and palpably absurd as that which at present exists amongst them. Their mythology originally consisted of allegories made intelligible by means of visible and material objects, so that religious knowledge should not die out of the minds of men who appeared to be little influenced by anything that failed to make a direct impression on their senses. But a coarse, ignorant, indolent, and superstitious race soon forgot the spirit of its creed, and ended by believing solely in the forms and emblems which had been employed; so that, before long, they quite lost sight of the spiritual beings of which these emblems were only symbolical. But we shall have occasion to refer to this question again, and so shall merely state here that the long tissue of fables on which the present religion of the Hindus is founded is not, to my mind, very ancient; at least, the greater part of it is not. Although some authors think differently, nothing will persuade us that their mythology is much older than that of the Greeks.[4]

The creeds of these two sects probably sprang from the common source of Brahminism, and are only corruptions of it. Some modern authors believe that originally Buddhism reigned supreme throughout India, on either side of the Ganges, and, perhaps, even throughout the whole of Asia from Siberia to Cape Comorin and the Malacca Straits, and from the Caspian Sea to the Gulf of Kamtchatka. In any case, Buddhism appears to have been as ancient as the cult of the Trimurti. In both Tibets, in Tartary, and in China, we know that Buddhism still predominates. According to the historian La Loubere, it was introduced into China from Siam in bygone ages and not, as is generally supposed, from Cape Comorin. In Burma, Siam, Laos, Cambodia, Cochin, China, Japan, Korea, and in most of the kingdoms beyond the Ganges, Buddhism is the recognized religion. The Sinhalese inhabitants of Ceylon are also Buddhists, and the cult was introduced to them by missionaries and colonists, who a long time ago came over from Burma to settle there. In fact, this religion, with the immortal *Grand Lama*[5] of Tibet as its sovereign pontiff, is still beyond dispute of all existing creeds the one that embraces the greatest number of adherents.

Besides these two predominant creeds, there exists a third about which, until recently, little was known. We refer to the religion of the Jains. This sect stands quite aloof, hating equally both Brahminists and Buddhists, as well as their doctrines. They maintain that both the Trimurti and Buddhism are abominable modern inventions and mere tavesties of the true and primitive religion of India, which has remained pure and unimpaired amongst them only. They also hold that they alone are the real descendants of the old Brahmin penitents, whose doctrines, customs and usages they protect from universal degradation and from the monstrous innovations of Brahmins and Buddhists alike.

The Hard Struggle

Brahminism underwent a hard struggle before it succeeded in establishing its dominion in India, owing to the opposition offered to it by the Jains; but after a long and bloody war the latter were crushed and had to submit to whatever conditions the Brahmins chose to dictate. The jealousy and animosity which these religious wars stirred up still prevail as strongly as ever, even after a lapse of two or three thousand years. Time, which generally softens the strongest hatreds and brings together the greatest enemies, has, in this case, failed to obliterate the traces of the ancient wrongs of which each sect mutually accuses the other. The daily prayer of a certain sect of Brahmins contains a curse levelled at the heads of the Jains, who retaliate by exclaiming, when they rise to pray, '*Brahma kshayam!*' 'May the Brahmin perish.' If either sect comes into power, it takes the opportunity of humiliating its adversaries and of punishing them without mercy whenever occasion offers.

But whatever may be the respective claims of Buddhists, Brahmins, and Jains with regard to the antiquity of their religions and the differences of doctrine that divide them, it appears highly probable that they all sprang originally from the same source. The images they worship bear a great likeness to one another and most of these seem to be merely allegorical emblems invented to help them to remember their original divinities. All their religious establishments are alike composed of priests, monks and hermits. All their sacrifices, and the ceremonies which accompany them, are nearly identical. And, lastly, there is the resemblance of the languages used by the priests in their religious services; that is to say, the Sanskrit of the Brahmins and Jains on this side of the Ganges, and the Pali, which is evidently derived from the Sanskrit, or the Buddhists beyond the Ganges. All these help to prove incontestably the affinity existing between the three religions.

Phases of Religion

These details of the lower phases of religion in India in the sixth century B.C. have great and essential similarity with the beliefs held, not only at the same time in the other centres of civilisation,—in China, Persia, and Egypt, in Italy and Greece,— but also among the savages of them and now. But there is a further and more striking resemblance. Sir Henry Maine has said: "Nothing is more remarkable than the extreme fewness of progressive societies—the difference between them and the stationary races is one of the greatest secrets enquiry has yet to penetrate."[1]

Whatever the secret, above and beyond the influence of economic conditions, may have been, it is a known fact that civilisation, of a kind at least, extended back in time, on the four great river basins of the Nile and the Euphrates, the Ganges and the Yellow River, not merely through centuries, but through thousands of years, if reckoned from today. Yet in each of those places—though there was real and progressive civilisation, and ideas and customs were no doubt constantly changing and growing—there was a certain dead level, if not a complete absence of what we should call philosophic thought. The animistic hypotheses, the soul-theories, of their savage ancestors seemed sufficient, even to the progressive races, to explain all that they saw or felt. men varied, but never dreamed or rejecting, the soul-theories. They did not even build up on the basis of them any large and general views, either of ethics, or of philosophy, or of religion. Then suddenly, and almost simultaneously, and almost certainly independently, there is evidence, about the sixth century B.C., in each of these widely separated centres of civilisation, of a leap forward in speculative thought, of a new birth in ethics, of a religion of conscience threatening to take the place of the old religion of custom and magic. In each of these countries similar causes, the same laws regulating the evolution of ideas, had taken just about the same number of centuries to evolve, out of similar conditions, a similar result. Is there a more stupendous marvel in the whole history of mankind? Does any more suggestive problem await the solution of the historian of human thought?

The solution will not be possible till we have a more accurate knowledge of the circumstances which led up, in each country, to the awakening. And in India one important factor in the preceding circumstances seems to me to have been, hitherto, too much neglected. The intense interest, from the world-history point of view, of the sixth century B.C.—the best dividing line, if there ever was any, between ancient history and modern, between the old order and the new—would be sufficient excuse, if one were needed, for a somewhat detailed consideration of this particular point.

In India, as elsewhere, the whole of the popular animistic notions mentioned in the last chapter, and no doubt others also, survived in full forces. But no one man believed in them all, or even knew of them all. In that part of the priestly literature which has come down to us a certain selected portion of these beliefs is taken, as it were, under priestly patronage, has received the stamp of respectability, has been given such social rank as the priests could confer. They seldom, perhaps never, stepped outside the charmed circle of animistic magic. But what they chose was probably, on the whole, of a better kind than what they left to itself. Even so the contents of the priestly books on ritual, though a rich mine of materials for a history of magic and superstition, are unspeakably *banal.* M. Sylvain Levi, the author of the most authoritative work on this subject, says in the introduction to his summary of the Brahmana theory of sacrifice:

"It is difficult to imagine anything more brutal and more material than the theology of the Brahmanas. Notions which usage afterwards gradually refined, and clothed with a garb of morality, take us aback by their savage realism."

Or again:

"Morality finds no place in this system. Sacrifice, which regulates the relation of man to the divinities, is a mechanical act, operating by its own spontaneous energy; and that, hidden in the bosom of nature, is only brought out by the magic art of the priest."[2]

To these writers, the sacrifice, if only rigidly carried out in each one of its details, is the source of all profit and advantage. The gods (who are quite unmoral, not immoral, though they are represented in these texts as having been guilty of falsehood, chicanery, and incest) are utterly unable to counteract the effect of such a sacrifice. Indeed they owe their own supremacy, their own position in heaven, to sacrifices they themselves had thus carried out to older gods. And it is by the same means that they continue to defeat the Asuras, that is the Titans, the rival gods, who would otherwise storm the gates of heaven.

Temples and Images

There were no temples, and probably no images. The altars were put up new for each sacrifice in a field or garden belonging to the sacrificer. The benefit to accure from the sacrifice went to him, and to him alone. He therefore had to pay for the performance; for the animals to be slaughtered, for the numerous work people employed, and for the fees for the priests.

"As to the fees, the rules are precise, and the propounders of them are unblushing. The priest performs the sacrifice for the fee alone, and it must consist of valuable garments, kine, horses, or gold ; —when each is to be given is carefully stated. Gold is coveted most, for 'this is immortality, the seed of Agni,' and therefore peculiarly agreeable to the pious priest."[6]

It would be unnecessary to go into the interminable detail of such sacrifices. They are expounded very fully and carefully in Professor Hillebrandt's standard works on the subject.[2] The expense must have been very great, even for the less complicated; and it is probable that this had something to do with the fact that a way was discovered to obtain the desired result without sacrifice.

The nearer we get to the time of Buddhism the greater is the importance we find attached to this second method, that of *tapas,*—self-mortification, or more exactly, self-torture. The word occurs, in this its technical sense, in the latest hymns included in the Rig Veda. It is literally "burning, glow" ; and had then already acquired the secondary sense of retirement into solitude in the forest, and the practise there of austerity, bodily self-mortification,—not at all with the idea of atonement or penance, but under the impression that self-torture of this kind would bring about magical results. Just as the sacrificer was supposed, by a sort of charm that his priests worked for him in the sacrifice, to compel the gods, and to attain ends he desired, so there was supposed to be a sort of charm in *tapas* by which a man could, through and by himself, attain to mystic and marvellous results. The distinction seems to have been that it was rather worldly success, cattle, children, and heaven, that were attained by sacrifice ; and mystic, extraordinary, superhuman faculties that were attained by *Tapas.*

Then, by a natural anthropomorphism, the gods too, in later works, were supposed—just as they had been supposed to offer sacrifice—to practise *tapas,* austerity. And it was not a mere distinction without a difference, it was a real advance in thought, when this sort of physical self-mastery, of the conquest of will over discomfort and pain, came to be placed above sacrifice. It had been by sacrifice that the gods had made the world. Now it came to be said, in different cosmological legends, that one god or another had brought forth the world by *tapas.*[7] And a Brahmana text declares:

"Heaven is established on the air, the air on the earth, the earth on the waters, the waters on truth, the truth on the mystic lore (of the sacrifice), and that on *Tapas.*"[8]

It will be noticed that *tapas* is here put in the most important place, higher than sacrifice which is, in its turn, higher than truth—a most suggestive order, as we shall see later on. We have no details in the books of this period of the particular practices in which the austerity, the self-mortification, consisted. It was no doubt of various kinds, and would tend, in course of time, to be elaborated. But we have a full statement of the stage it had reached in the Buddha's as set forth by a naked ascetic in a Diologue he had with Gotama. This professor of self-torture enumerates twenty-two methods of self-mortification in respect of food, and thirteen in respect of clothing, and among these the ascetic may make his choice. And he keeps his body under in other ways:

"He is a 'plucker-out-of-hair-and-beard' (destroying by a painful process the possibility of pride in mere beauty of appearance)—or he is 'stander-up' (rejecting the use of a seat)—or he is a 'croucher-down-on-the-heels' (moving about painfully by jumps)—or he is a 'bed-of-thorns-man' (putting thorns or iron spikes under the skin on which he sleeps)—or he sleeps on a plank, or on the bare ground, or always on the same side—or he is 'clad-in-dust' (smearing his naked body with oil and standing where dust clouds blow, he lets dust and dirt adhere to his body)."[9]

The Epic Era

Later on, in the epic for instance, the list grows longer, the penances harder, the self-torture more revolting. But from this time onwards, down to quite modern times, this *tapas* self-mortification, is a permanent idea and practice in the religious life of India. As is well known it is not confined to India. Tennyson, in the monologue of St. Simeon Stylites, has given us a powerful analysis of the sort of feelings that lay at the root of this superstition in the West. But the theological views that give the tone to the Christian saint's self-revelation are very different from those we find in India. The Indian way of looking at the whole conception is much more akin to the way Diogenes thought when he lived like a dog, in his tub-kenne. The Greek word *cynic* is indeed exactly analogous to the Indian expression *kukkura-vatiko,* "one who behaves like a dog." as applied (quite courteously) to the sophist, the naked ascetic, Seniya. There is no question here of penance for sin, or of an appeal to the mercy of an offended deity. It is the boast of superiority advanced by the man able, through strength of will, to keep his body under, and not only to despise comfort, but to welcome pain. By this it is not, of course, intended to imply that the Christian did not advance a similar claim. He did. But it was, in his case, overshadowed by other consideration which are absent in India.

Both in the East and the West the claim was often accepted. We hear a good deal in India of the reverence paid to the man who (to quote the words of a Buddhist poet).

"Bescorched, befrozen,
lone in fearsome woods,
Naked, without a
fire, afire within,
Struggled in awful silence toward the goal !"

Simeon, by the mere strength of popular acclaim, became a saint, even almost before he died. Dicgenes, and his parallel in India, Mahavira, founded important schools which have left their mark on history. And ought we, after all, to be surprised that those who despise earthly comfort, and subject themselves to voluntary torture, should be looked upon, with a kind of fearsome awe, as more holy, as better, than other men? There was some justice in the view. And until experience had shown the other side of the question—that attendant disadvantages, and the inadequate results of strength of will when applied to physical ends—it was inevitable that the self-mastery quite evident in such practices should appeal strongly to the minds of the people.

We find the other side put forward in india from two directions, one mainly philosophic, the other mainly ethical. The manner in which both these movements came about was perfectly natural, though it was much inclucenced by the custom alıeady referred to as peculiar, at that period of the world's history, to India', Students are often represented as beggining, just as students did in Europe in the Middle Ages[2]. And we hear of sophists, just as we do in the history of Greek thought. But the peculiarity was that, before the rise of Buddhism, it was a prevalent habit for wandering teachers also—and not only students—to beg. Such wandering teachers, who were not necessarily ascetics except in so far as they were celibates, are always represented as being held in high esteem by the people. In the monarchies the royal family, in the clans the community, put up (as we have seen above) public halls where such Wanderers (*Paraibbajaká)* could lodge, and where conversational discussions, open to everyone, were held on philosophic and religious questions. The career of such a wandering teacher seems to have been open to anyone, and even to women. And the most perfect freedom, both of thought and of expression, was permitted to them—a freedom probably unequalled in the history of the world.[10]

This curious state of things would only have been possible among people of a very fair degree both of average general intelligence and of gentle manners. And just as the Strolling Students in pre-Reformation times throughout Western Europe were both a sign of the coming change, and also helped largely to bring it about, so the conditions which made it possible for the Wanderers in Northern India to live as they did, in pursuit of what they thought to be truth, were the precursors of that movement of thought we now call Buddhism, which the Wanderers also so largely helped to bring about.

The early history of the Wanderers has yet to be written. We hear of a similar custom as already followed in one isolated case by a sacrificing priest. Uddálaka Áruni, of the Gotama family, of whom so many other legends have been preserved, is said to have wandered about the country offering a gold coin, as a lure for the timid, to anyone who, in a disputation on spiritual matters, could prove him wrong[11]. When defeated he becomes the pupil of his conqueror.

We may point out, in passing, that these "spiritual matters" are very characteristic of the Bráhmanas. When he is being defeated the problems put are such as this: Why are cratures born without teeth, then teeth grow, and when the creatures become old the the teeth decay? The answer of his opponent, the orthodox priest, is: The preliminary offerings of a sacrific have no formulas of invitation, therefore creaturers are born without teeth(!). The chief sacrifice has, therefore teeth, grow(!). The closing acts in the sacrifice have no such formulas, therefore in old age teeth decay (!). Other explanations, equally lucid and convincing, are given for the growth and decay of the procreative power, etc. Such are the deep mysteries Uddálaka Áruni is scoffed at (in the priestly manual which has preserved this interesting old story) for not knowing.

This is a foreshadowing of the well-known Buddhist story of the woman sophist who wandered from village of village offering to meet all the world in argument, and when beaten in a disputation, became the pupil of her Buddhist conqueror. In the centuries between the date of these two legends the whole system had grown up. But unfortunately there is so little about it in the priestly books that it is not easy to trace its progress.

The Priestly Works

In the priestly books it is taken for granted that every one entitled to do so is desirious to have the sacrifices performed for him. In actual life there were probably many who gi'ⁱed at the cost; and preferred, if they wanted magic, magic of other and cheaper kinds. In any case there was no central organisation of the priesthood; there were no permanent temples to their gods, and such sacred shrines as the people could frequent were the sacred trees or other objects of veneration belonging to the worship of the local gods, and quite apart from the cultus or the incluence of the priests. And the latter were divided against themselves. They vied with one another for sacrificial fees. The demand for their services was insufficient to maintain them all. Brahmins followed therefore all sorts of other occupations; and those of them not continually busied about the sacrifice were often inclined to views of life, and of religion, different from the views of those who were. We find Brahmins ranking *tapas,* self-torture, above sacrifice. We find Brahmins among those who reckoned insight above either, and who, whether as laymen or as Wanderers, joined the ranks of the other side. Unable therefore, whether, they wanted or not, to stay the progress of newer ideas the priests strove to turn the incoming tide into channels favourable to their Order. They formulated—though this was some time after the rise of Buddhism—the famous theory of the *Ás'ramas,* or Efforts, according to which no one could become either a Hermit or a Wanderer without having first passed many years as a student in the Brahmin schools, and lived after that the life of a married householder as regulated in the Brahmin law-books. It was a bold bid for supremacy. If successful it might have put a stop to the whole movement. But it remained a dead letter—probably always, centrainly during the period we are here considering. It is quiet true that the priestly manuals, especially those later that the Christian era, take it as a matter of course that the rule was observed. But they do not give us the actual facts of life in India. They give, and are only meant to give, what the priests thought the facts ought to be. And there is ample evidence even in the priestly literature itself of a gradual growth in the theory, of differing views about it, and of its loose hold on the people. I have elsewhere collected the evidence, which though most interesting, historically, and quite conclusive, is too long to set out there.' In the second place, the priests, already before the rise of Buddhism, had (as appendices to their sacred books on the sacrifice) short treatises setting out, as the highest truth, those forms of speculation which they held most compatible with their own mysteries. Their procedure, in this respect, was exactly parallel to their treatment of gods not included in their own pantheon, but too powerful and popular to be left alone. It is quite evident, from the outcome of the whole movement, that there must have been other ideas current besides those that the priests thus adapted and handed down in their text-books. And we have valuable evidence, in the lay literature of a later date, as to what these other ideas were, so that in this respect also, as in other matters, but still only a partial, record.

Certain forms of disease were supposed to be due to the fact that the soul had escaped out of the body; and charms are recorded for bringing it back. In dream sleep also the "soul' is away from the body. "Therefore they say : Let no one wake a man brusquely ; for that is a matter difficult to be cured for him if the soul find not its way back to him."

During the dream the soul, after leaving the body, wanders at its will, builds up a world according to its fancy, creates for itself chariots and houses lakes and rivers, manifold shapes, a gorgeous playground wherein it acts and enjoys and suffers, "either rejoicing with women, or laughing with its friends, or beholding horrible sights." Till at last, tired out,— just as a falcon after roaming hither and thither in the sky, tired, flaps its wings and is wafted to its nets,—so the soul returns from that playground of his to the body, when in deeop, fast sleep it wants no more, and dreams no more. it is charming and beautiful picture.

We are not told *how* the soul gets out of, and back into, the body. This is not surprising, for the opinions expressed as to how the soul got into its first body—whether at conception or at quickening or at birth—are contradictory. All views on this point were no doubt neither more nor less hazy then in India than they are now in the West. There are passages which suppose the soul to have existed, before birth, in some other body; and other passages which suppose it to have been inserted, at the origin of things, into its first body downwards, through the suture at the top of the skull, into the heart'. But there is a passage which affirms that the soul was inserted upwards, through the intestines and the belly, into the head. And we find a curious speculation, of which there are three variants, on the transfer of the soul by generation, through the seed.

But there is an almost entire unanimity of opinion in these upanishads that the soul will not obtain release from rebirth either by the performance of sacrifice in this birth or by practice of penance. It must be by a sort of theosophic or animistic insight, by the perception, the absolute knowledge and certainty, that one's own soul is identical with the Great Soul, the only permanent reality, the ultimate basis and cause of all phenomena.

The ideas had therefore just made, at the time when our history begins a complete circle. The hypothesis of a soul—a material, but very subtle sort of homunculus within the body—had been started to explain the life and motion, sleep and death, of human beings. By analogy, logically enough, it had been extended, ever more and more widely, to explain similar phenomena in the outside world. There must be a soul in the sun. How else could one explain its majestic march across the heavens, evidently purposeful, its rising and its setting, its beauty and light and glow? If its action was somewhat mysterious, who was to limit or define the motives of the soul of so glorious a creature? There was no argument about it. It was taken for granted; and any one who doubted was simply impious. These souls in nature—gods they called them—had, of course, no existence outside the brains of the men who made them. They were logical corollaries of the human soul. And the external souls, the gods, were therefore identical in origin and nature with the souls supposed to live inside human bodies. But the very men who made these external souls, the gods, looked upon them as objective realities, quite different from their own souls. They—the gods—were always changing—that is to say, men's ideas about them were always changing, moving, being modified. The long history of Indian mythology is the history of such changes, by no means always dependent on theological reasons. And with each change the objective reality of the external souls, the gods, their difference from the souls of men, seemed more clear and certain than ever.

Then came the reaction. The gods began, not in popular belief, but among thinkers to be more and more regarded as identical one with the other until at last, just before Buddhism, the hypothesis was started of a one primeval soul, the world-soul, the Highest soul, the Paramátman, from whom all the other gods and souls had proceeded. There was a deep truth in this daring speculation. But the souls inside men were held in it to be identical with god, the only original and true reality ; whereas, historically speaking, soul was the original idea, and the gods (and god) had grown out of it.

We have abundant evidence that this grand generalisation was neither due to the priests who adopted it, nor had its origin in the priestly schools. Precisely as regard the highest point of the generalisation, the very keystone on the arch, the priestly literature has preserved the names of the Rajput laymen who thought it out and taught it to the priests. And among the priests who had the greatest share in adopting, it, in procuring admission for it into their sacred books, is mentioned the very Uddálaka Áruni, the Gotama, whose defeat in argument on "spiritual matters" has been recorded above.

When this point had been reached, speculation on the basis of the soul theory could go no further. The only modification possible was in the ideas as to the nature and qualities of the souls, internal and external, and as to the relations between them. And to this point speculation reached, but later, and less clearly, in China also and in Greece. But it was in India, and in India only, that the further step was taken, by Gotama the rajput and his disciples, to abandon the soul theory altogether ; and to build up a new philosophy (whether right or wrong is not here the question) on other considerations in which soul or souls played no part at all.

That this thoroughgoing and far-reaching step was taken by laymen should not surprise us. To suppose that the Indians were more superstitious at that time than other folk, more under the thumb of their priests, is to misunderstand the evidence. On the contrary there was a well-marked lay feeling, a real sense of humour, a strong fund of common-sense, a wide-spread feeling, in all such matters, of courtesy and liberality. How otherwise can we explain the fact, already pointed out, of the most complete and unquestioned freedom, both of thought and expression, which the world had yet witnessed?

References

1. There can be no doubt that these mountains, and other mentioned as lying around them, belong to the great ranges of Central Asia, from which flow the great rivers that water Siberia, China, Tartary, and Hindustan.
2. Much of this extremely fanciful. Max Muller and other modern authorities should be consulted.

3. *Diksha* means consecration; (undergoing) a religious observance for a particular purpose; solemn preparation.
4. *Agrara* is merely a corruption of the word *agrahara,* which literally means 'land-grant to Brahmins.'
5. Like a second Phoenix the Grand Lama never dies. When he is about to divest himself of his earthly coil, the Bonzes choose a child of three or four into whose body they cause his soul to migrate, and this child is declared his successor. All faithful Buddhists believe implicity in this miraculous rebirth.—Dubois.
6. Hopkin: *Religious of India,* I92.
7. Satapatha-brahmana vi.I.I.I3, and often afterwards.
8. Aitareya Br. xi. 6.4.
9. Rh. D. : *Dialogues of the Buddha*, I, pp. 226-32.
10. Rh. D. : *Dialogues of the Buddha*, I. 244; and above, p.141.
11. Sat. Br. xi. 4. I.

4

Caste as a Social Group

History of the Bombay Ethnographical Survey

In May 1901 the Government of India issued orders for the commencement of the Ethnographical Survey of the Provinces : Bombay, Madras, Bengal, United Provinces, Punjab, Burma, Central-Provinces and Assam and proposed that the enquiries into the origin, social configuration, customs and occupations of the numerous castes and tribes should be spread over a period of four or five years. These enquiries were to follow closely the lines of certain questions approved by Messrs. Nesfield, Ibbetson and Risley at a Conference held in 1885. They were to be carried out by the Superintendents in addition to their ordinary official duties.

It was not found possible to allow more than a few thousand rupees annually to each province for the work of the Survey; and before the work was half done, i.e., in 1909, even this small financial provision was withdrawn. The Survey has since been practically dependent on the voluntary labours of the Superintendent-in-charge, with such assistance as he was able to secure without the expenditure of funds. This voluntary assistance has been forthcoming from three sources. Certain scholars such as D.R. Bhandarkar and B.A. Gupta have placed their knowledge at the disposal of the Superintendent and assisted the work of the Survey in the capacity of Honorary Assistants. A number of gentlemen have furnished valuable materials in the capacity of Honorary Correspondents. Finally, certain local committees organised by the Superintendent during the course of census operations in 1901 for the purposes of investigating and reporting on caste questions have supplied materials of considerable value and interest. With this assistance it has been possible to complete the Survey of the tribes and castes in the Presidency, excluding Sind, by the beginning of the present year. The work has involved the preparation of nearly 300 articles. These have been published in draft form and circulated for criticism before being finally embodied in the Survey record.

It may at once be admitted that the work could not possibly have been completed, even in this greatly extended period, had it not been for the very full materials available in the pages of the Bombay Gazetteers compiled by the late Sir James Campbell. Much of the work of the Survey has indeed consisted of the re-arrangement of these materials, which were drawn up originally on a district basis instead of dealing with tribes and castes as a whole. When compared with more recent information, the original district accounts have been found to be remarkably accurate in detail. With the assistance described, and in such leisure as was available to the Superintendent, in spite of the pre-occupation of more important official duties, a considerable amount of new information has been collected regarding the tribes and castes of the Bombay Presidency. The ensuing pages thus contain much new matter, though the main source of information has been found in the pages of the Bombay District Gazetteers, which contain accounts remarkable both for their fullness and accuracy.

Scope of the Work

At the time of issuing the first of the draft Monographs, of which the complete series is now published in these volumes, we indicated that the tribes and castes recorded in the Census Tables of 1901, and numbering over 500, would be dealt with in three classes:

Class 1, being those containing one hundred thousand members, were to be described as fully as possible;

Class 2, being those between one hundred thousand and five thousand, were to be dealt with in less detail;

Class 3, being those under five thousand, were for the most part to be described merely by rearranging the materials on the lines of the Ethnographical questions.

This scheme has been adhered to. The only important departure from the general scheme outlined by us in 1903 at the time of publishing the first Monograph, dealing with the Ahir, is the omission of the tribes and castes of Sind. This and the following volumes include only tribes and castes found in the Presidency Proper.

Special Features of the Survey

In the course of revising existing materials for the caste accounts a number of new caste divisions have been discovered, both in connection with the groups inside which marriage is essential, and the smaller divisions inside which marriage is forbidden. These are referred to in this work respectively as endogamous and exogamous groups. They are of special interest as the interior structure of a caste is frequently valuable evidence of its origin. It has also been found that certain caste names are synonyms. Castes have in such cases been re-grouped. In connection with castes of converts from Hinduism to Islam, useful information has been obtained from the marriage registers of the Kazis, showing the cases in which intermarriage between such castes is allowed. Many Musalman castes adhere to the Hindu practise of endogamy. Among those Musalman castes which intermarry are found armourers, butchers, farriers, elephant-drivers, and similar occupational groups which are probably descendants of the camp followers of the Mughal armies. It is interesting to note that contact with the Muhammadan armies has left its influence in the greater freedom with which intermarriage is allowed. The social prejudice which prevents members of many Muhammadan castes from marrying outside the caste is a relic of the previously existing Hindu custom, such castes being clearly traceable to a Hindu origin before conversion. They are found chiefly in areas where Musalman rule has stimulated conversion, either by example, as in Bijapur, or by force as in north Kanara, once under the dominion of Hyder and Tipu. A great deal of new information has been obtained regarding the interesting Lingayat community, which is found to be based partly on religious and partly on caste distinctions. The late Dr. J.F. Fleet, C.I.E., supplied some valuable notes for this article, which forms the basis of a new account of Lingayats contributed by the Superintendent to Dr. Hasting's Dictionary of Religion. The special interest of the community lies in the fact that it exhibits the process by which a religious movement, starting with the abolition of caste distinctions, develops slowly into a community of which the most recent converts adhere strictly to the non-intermarrying caste distinctions of their Hindu ancestors.

New Information

The Survey has brought to light a great deal of new information regarding totemistic divisions in the Deccan Southern Maratha Country. The identification of Maratha guardians or devaks with Kanarese *balis* is an indication of a similarity of origin between certain castes and tribes of the Presidency which has not hitherto been suspected. The subject is one which will repay very careful study.

Tribe and Caste

Broadly speaking, the term tribe is used in these pages for a unit based on common descent as opposed to the term caste which is applied to a social unit founded on common occupation, common residence, common language or common political control. A social unit based on religion is described as a sect.

Origin of Caste

A great deal of time and research has been devoted to attempts to arrive at an explanation of the origin of caste. I do not propose in the course of this brief introduction to recapitulate the various theories that have been put forward by numerous scholars to explain the origin and continuance of caste in India. It may, however, be remarked that, given the conditions which have prevailed in this country since the first Aryan invasion, a caste system involving the formation of a number of non-inter-marrying groups must from the first have been inevitable.

Racial Influence

From the dawn of history India has been subject to invasion by land and sea, and the invaders, who were themselves very probably of mixed origin, have seldom refrained from inter-marriage with the heterogeneous population already established in the country. In the Institutes of Manu we find an attempt to classify the resulting units of mixed descent under different names. The process of admixture of blood has continued to the present day. Probably its influence was especially marked during the series of post-Aryan invasions between the third century B.C. and the sixth century A.D. By this time Aryan, Dravidian, and mixed Aryo-Dravidian castes were numerous. Intermarriage with the invading tribes such as the Ahirs, Gujars and other Scythian units must have led to a great complexity of racial types, each naturally tending to preserve itself from further admixture of blood, by forming a marriage group excluded by the purer groups from intermarriage, and itself refusing to countenance unions with those who were members of groups regarded as inferior owing to greater impurity of blood.

The Influence of Occupation

To the influence of race, in itself of great importance, would shortly be added the effect of varying occupations as the tribal units passed from the pastoral to the agricultural state, and from that to the practice of arts and handicrafts. Thus true castes were formed; but occupation would not ordinarily obliterate the racial distinctions already referred to. The occupational group would contain various ethnic groups remaining endogamous. In this way, if we start with the idea of descent, we can show the population in tribes divided into groups (castes) following different occupations; or, starting from the occupation, we may show the caste including a number of different tribal groups. The Ahirs and Gujars, immigrant tribes of great importance, are now broken into many caste sections such as those found in the Shimpis, Sonars, Sutars, Chambhars, etc. We may therefore show Ahirs and Gujars with their occupational divisions as forming part of the tribe, or the castes as a whole, with Ahir and Gujar as sub-castes. In both cases, the sub-divisions are the endogamous units.

Tribe and caste, therefore, are different ways of looking at the same social groups, the tribal being the forerunner of the caste. Unfortunately, the question of the correct classification of such groups is further complicated by other influences besides those of decent and occupation. Of these the principal are religion and domicile.

Religious Influences

The effect of religious movements, such as Jainism, Lingayatism, Islam and Christianity on social grouping is specially interesting. Jains, found almost entirely in Gujarat and Bombay City, usually form an endogamous division of the occupational caste, though dining with the Hindu element may be permissible. Lingayatism is more complex. Starting with a repudiation of caste distinctions, Lingayats have passed through several phases, the earlier converts coming in time to separate themselves from those who joined later; and ultimately, as in the case of Jains, Lingayats merely form an endogamous division of the Hindu group from which they were converted. This development will be found treated at length in the article on Lingayats. Islam should not recognise caste; but the practice varies. There are Muhammadan castes that marry with other castes of the same faith. There are many that will only marry within their own caste, though of course not with the Hindu members. Even Christianity has been a source of caste division in places; for there are three caste divisions of Christians in Goanese territory, known as Brahman, Chardo and Sudra; and certain castes such as Bhandaris, Kolis and Kunbis contain Christian sections that only marry within such sections.

Domicile and Language

Most important in its effect on caste formation is the influence of domicile and language. A portion of a caste separated by migration from its parent body tends to develop certain differences in customs, occupation or interests. Owing to the common tendency to exaggerate the importance of such differences which is a specially Indian characteristic, marriage with the original body of the caste is frequently abandoned on account of these small differences. In the past, no doubt, the difficulty of communication accelerated this process. Marriages with caste fellows separated by a lengthy and tedious journey from a remote section of the caste would tend to be of rare occurrence, and eventually be looked on as in some way contrary to caste practice, this is to say, as unlawful. The result can be traced in numerous cases where the sub-castes have a territorial name. A reference to the articles on Brahmans and Vanis will show how numerous local groups of this nature are in Gujarat.

Mr. A.M.T. Jackson has drawn attention to the fact that a change of domicile on the part of a portion of a caste was peculiarly liable to create new sub-castes owing to the powers exercised by Hindu rulers over the caste organizations. As supreme authority, the king must decide questions of caste practice; and he might well do so in such a way as to create local practices at variance with the custom of sections of the caste under another jurisdiction. Here again the proneness of the people to attach undue importance to small points of difference would lead to intermarriage being abandoned between the sections of the caste under different political control. This is no doubt a good instance of the effect of domicile on caste fission. Mr. Jackson's theory will be found to derive much support from the close resemblance between the subdivisions of the two leading castes in Gujarat, the Brahmans and Vanis, which have many of the same territorial names, and from similar instances quoted in the following pages.

In the Deccan, where in Hindu times political control was more uniform than in Gujarat, castes have retained a greater measure of cohesion. This has been preserved under Muhammadan rule, even though the Deccan was then divided between five, and subsequently three, kingdoms. These territories, unlike the early Gujarat States, were ruled by Muhammadan kings, who did not interfere in caste disputes. That Bijapur, Ahmednagar and Golconda have not given their names to caste divisions is not therefore evidence against the validity of Mr. Jackson's political theory.

The Essence of Caste

It will be gathered from the foregoing remarks that caste is in reality a system of 'self-determination' based on the habit of attaching more importance to the differences between social groups than to that which they have in common. Social union is fostered and maintained by attaching importance to all that human beings, whatever their race, occupation or domicile, may have in common with each other. Social cleavage is inevitable when an exaggerated importance is attached to differences of race, occupation or domicile between one group of individuals and another. The barrier of religion may be expected to give rise to groups that will not intermarry, for it is based on fundamentals. But when to this is added an endless series of social fences erected on account of differences in origin, occupation or custom, it is inevitable that society should break into a number of self-contained elements to which there can scarcely be a limit. Too frequently the bar on inter-marriage and inter-dining, which is the essence of caste organization, is based on an assumed superiority of one group of individuals over another, so that, broadly speaking, the Indian caste system might be described as the most complete system of social exclusiveness that the world has ever witnessed. A common sentiment of Indian nationality might provide in time a sufficient motive for pulling down caste barriers. But in India habits and customs, readily formed, are adhered to with great tenacity. An inter-caste marriage law, now under discussion, does not promise to achieve any great measure of success. Recently inter-marriages have been recorded between endogamous castes such as Deshasth and Chitpavan Brahmans. These, however, are exceptional; and there is no present indication that caste barriers on inter-dining and inter-marriage are likely to be rapidly removed.

Survey Plan

The Survey, therefore, has had to deal with a number of groups which cannot accurately be described as being racial, occupational, sectarian or geographical though one or more of these influences has produced the group in each case. It is almost impossible in such circumstances to avoid cross divisions when drawing up a list of caste units, particularly in the case of Lingayats. The aim of the Survey has been to show in each case the groups that form endogamous units, combined for convenience of description under the heading of a major group which must in some cases be religious, e.g., Lingayats, sometimes occupational, e.g., Vanis, and in rarer instances tribal, as for instance Bhils, Kolis, Kathis, etc.

Caste in Process of Evolution

It is of interest to note that when, owing to the influence of the four main causes of caste evolution already described, a group divides into sub-castes the process occasionally has two distinct stages. To commence with, a group that formerly allowed inter-marriage freely between all its members develops a section that for racial, functional or similar reasons hold itself superior in status to the rest of the group. This is shown by the former declining to allow their daughters to marry the sons of the other caste members, but accepting brides for their own sons from the main body of the caste. In Punjab a great many castes are thus related to each other to the present day, and completely endogamous castes are of rare occurrence. In the Bombay Presidency the practice is less common; but it is found among Rajputs, Marathas, Lingayats and even among the lowest castes. Marathas, who were once one with Kunbis, will still marry Kunbi girls in some parts of the Presidency. Lingayat Panchamsalis are divided into Jangams and Banjigs, of which the former will marry the daughters of the later after a process of initiation, though in no circumstances would they allow their own daughters to marry Banjigs. Two such groups, of which the lower is known technically as hypergamous, will usually tend to develop into completely separate castes in course of time. The marriage of girls from the lower section is abandoned as soon as the breach between the social status of the two sections is sufficiently wide. In the writer's experience, one of the lowest castes of the Presidency, the Mahars, developed an embryo new caste recently in this way, owing to a number of Mahars having learnt to drive motor vehicles. The added wealth and prestige that this occupation brought with it showed itself in a "Driver" section, which was disinclined to continue free inter-marriage with the caste as a whole. It only requires time in such circumstances for the caste to develop a completely endogamous "Driver" division.

Primitive and Foreign Elements in Bombay Castes

In the course of the work of the Survey, it has been possible to accumulate some interesting facts bearing on the extent to which primitive, e.g., pre-Aryan as well as foreign or immigrant elements can be traced in the castes of the Presidency excluding Sind. The result of investigations in the southern portion of the Presidency, where castes are clearly organized on primitive lines, has brought to light a regular system of totemistic divisions of special interest and significance. These divisions are known locally as *balis* and are named after animals such as the hog, deer, the elephant, the monkey, the tortoise, certain fish, and trees or plants such as the banyan, pipal, screw pine, plantain, etc. There is a division named after the white ant's nest. These *balis* are exogamous, and display the usual totemistic features, i.e., members worship the tree, plant, animal or other object, giving its name to the *bali,* on special occasions such as marriage or the occupation of a new house. They will not cut or injure it in any way, and in no circumstances may those who have a common *bali* be allowed to inter-marry. Children appear originally to have inherited the mother's totem. Later this system has been modified into one of tracing the totem through the male parent.

Further north in the Presidency we find that many castes show traces of having originally possessed a similar organization. There is a remarkable resemblance traceable between the guardians or *devaks* of the Maratha castes in the Decan and the *bali* of North Kanara. The same trees as, for instance, the *nagchampa* (Mesua ferrea) and screw pine

(Pandanus odoratissimus) are found as *devaks* and as *balis*. In the article of Marathas information will be found regarding these *devaks*. Being regularly worshipped, carefully preserved, and governing inter-marriages, they appear to possess the leading characteristics of totems. It is reasonable to assume that the *devak* with its suggestive resemblance to the *bali* is strong evidence of the primitive origin of at least an important element in the castes in which it is found. From this assumption very interesting results may follow. It is not possible within the limits of this brief survey to develop the argument to its logical conclusion; but clearly Marthas contain a much stronger pre-Aryan element than has hitherto been supposed.

We are on more difficult ground when we endeavour to trace the remains of foreign elements in the caste formations of the Presidency. The late Sir James Campbell attached much importance to the survival of the names of post-Aryan invading tribes such as Yavans, Parthians, Ahirs, Gujars and Yadavs, or of the early ruling Indian dynasties, e.g., Maurya, Kadamba, Chalukhya, among the castes of the Presidency. It has been seen that Ahir and Gujar divisions are still found in many castes. Maurya, Kadamba and Chalukhya survive in the form of surnames, i.e., More, Kadam and Cholke, among Marathas, Kunbis, Mahars and Kolis. But it is unsafe to attach much significance to names in India. They probably bear little more signification than the term "Shivajis" which was formerly applied by the English to numerous castes enlisted under the banner of the Maratha hero, that is to say, they indicate subservience to a common leader or dynasty, but do not connote common descent. The Ahir and Gujar elements stand on a somewhat different footing to the surnames; but it is impossible at the present day to arrive at the exact relation which such sub-castes bear to the original Ahir and Gujar tribes. The subject has been very ably treated by D.R. Bhandarkar in his study of the foreign elements in Hindu society, where both Nagar Brahman and Sisod Rajput have been shown to have been Gujars originally. It is certain that inter-marriage with local elements has largely obscured the extent to which Ahir and Gujar have contributed to modern caste formations, even in cases where the name survives.

The general impression conveyed by the Survey is that the original foreign element in many of the castes has been greatly obscured by inter-marriage with the indigenous population. Even the Parsis, the most exclusive of immigrant castes, have admittedly mixed with the jungle tribes of Gujarat and the issue, until recently, has been admitted to the Parsi community. Ultimately we may perhaps be prepared to the conclusion that the tribes and castes of the Presidency have far more in common as regards their origin than has hitherto been admitted.

Irregular Unions

The pages of the Survey contain much evidence in support of this contention. There is scarcely a caste that is not found to possess a section known as Akaramashe, Bande, Shinde, Dasa, Kale, etc., signifying that there has been irregular union either with women of a lower caste or with men of a higher one. The institutes of Manu allow seven generations of marriage within the caste to restore the full status to the issue of such a union. The evidence available tends to show that a much less drastic test was imposed in recent times. The Abyssinian Angria married a Maratha girl; and history equally records instances of Koli chieftains who have been allowed a similar privilege, the children being doubtless classed as Marathis in both instances. For many year Maratha Kunbi women have served in Brahman houses in the Konkan, the issue being classed as Shinde under Marathas.

Some Typical Castes

It is my intention on some future occasion to deal in a separate work with the full results of the Ethnographical Survey. Within the limits of an introductory note space can be found only for a few points of special interest; and these have necessarily been very summarily treated. To illustrate the difficulties in which the classification of the people of the Presidency by tribe and caste is involved. I will describe briefly a few typical groups representing important units of the population—Vanis, Marathis, Lingayats, Bhils and Kolis.

Vanis

The Vani, Banya or Banjig is a trader corresponding to the Vaishya of the fourtold classification of Manu. As Vaishyas they claim a twice-born status; but here their common interest ceases, for they are divided into a large number of groups that will not intermarry. Of these in Gujarat, the following divisions are common to Brahman and Vani:

1. Agarval
2. Desaval
3. Gujar
4. Harsola
5. Jharola
6. Khadayata
7. Kapol
8. Mevada

10. Nagar
11. Nandora
12. Osval
13. Palival
14. Porvad
15. Shrimali
16. Sorathia
17. Vayada

9. Modh

These being mainly geographical in origin, tend to bear out Mr. Jackson's theory of caste fission to which reference has already been made. These numerous groups contain Jain and Hindu divisions, known as *Shravak* and *Meshri,* that will not intermarry. They have also divisions known as Visa (20), Dasa (10), Panch (5), Adhich (2½), representing an increasing admixture of some lower element.

In the Deccan the Vani caste is more homogeneous, only a few divisions being found, owing no doubt to the fact that political control has been more uniform in that area than in Gujarat.

Further South, the Vani is known as a Binjig, and is generally a Lingayat. As such, he will not many with Hindu or Jain Vanis.

Marathas

Marathas are the chief unit in the Deccan and Konkan, probably deriving their name from Maharashtra, i.e., the Deccan, and representing a tribe with some Northern elements but largely aboriginal. There is probably no substantial difference in origin between the landholding and warrior section, i.e., Marathis Proper, the cultivators, i.e., Maratha Kunbis, and the numerous local occupational castes such as Maratha Vanis, Sonars, Sutars, Parits, etc. Intermarriage is not ordinarily allowed between these groups, although, in remote parts, Marathas Proper will take girls in marriage from the Kunbi or Kulvadi caste. They will not marry their girls to boys of the Kulvadi caste. The Kunbi, again, is at times recruited from the Koli who settles down to agriculture and acquires a "Kunbi" or cultivator status. The rise of the Maratha power in the seventeenth century induced the fighting classes (land holders) to claim for themselves Kshatriya rank, and to discourage widow remarriage. It is chiefly on this ground that they claim to be superior to the Kunbis. But by descent the Maratha appears to be one with the Maratha Kunbi and, certain other occupational castes in the Deccan.

Lingayats

Lingayats are a religious body dating from the eleventh century, when they separated from the Hindu fold by denying the authority of the Brahman, rejecting the scriptures, and abandoning Hindu ceremonies and pilgrimages. Largely recruited from Jain traders or Banjigs, these with their priests, known as Jangams, formed originally one body ignoring caste distinctions. Later converts, however, were in course of time relegated to an inferior social status thus giving rise to endogamous groups resembling the ordinary Hindu caste in exclusiveness, though adopting the special religious rites of Lingayatism. Hindus and Lingayats do not intermarry, even if they have a common caste name and occupation. The original rejection of caste distinctions has thus, it will be seen, given place to the formation of castes containing Lingayats bearing the same relation to Hindus in such castes as the Jains in the Vani divisions of Gujarat bear to the Hindu members.

Bhils and Kolis

Bhils and Kolis are aboriginal tribes which probably do not differ at all in origin. They are doubtless the former inhabitants of the greater part of the Presidency, now largely confined to hilly or jungle tracts of country. The common bond between Bhils is one of descent, as is the case with Kolis. Changes of occupation and a certain admixture of foreign blood has led to the formation of a number of divisions in each case. Among Kolis we find divisions with the names of Ahir, Bhil, Dhangar and Maratha. Ahirs and divisions with Maratha names are found among the Bhils. Other primitive tribes besides Kolis, such as Berads, have Bhil divisions. It has been seen that the Koli, by taking to cultivation, may rise to the position of a Maratha Kunbi. For the most part Bhils and Kolis remain good examples of purely tribal stocks. Inter-marriage with inferior Rajputs has in places produced mixed castes from both sources.

Caste Disputes

During the progress of the Survey the Superintendent has automatically become a tribunal for settling disputes regarding caste precedence. The circulation of the draft monographs led to the formulation of claims such, for instance, as those of Panchals to be classed as Vishva Brahmans, of Sonars to be described as Daivadnya Brahmans, and of Vadvals to be admitted to rank as Panchkalshis, or Somvanshi Kshatriyas. Interesting documents have been produced bearing on these disputed points. Manbhavs have been proved to be entirely distinct from the degraded caste of Mangs with which they were formerly supposed to be connected. The Savashe Brahmans have established their appeal against their former classification as degraded Deshasth Brahmans and have been reclassed as Sahavasi Brahmans. If in the decisions arrived at on these and similar points, the Superintendent's views fail to meet with general acceptance, it may at least be agreed in support of them that the evidence on both sides has been very carefully examined in arriving at these results.

II

We have heard some persons, sensible enough in other respects, but imbued with all the prejudices that they have brought with them from Europe, pronounce what appears to me an altogether erroneous judgement in the matter of caste divisions amongst the Hindus. In their opinion, caste is not only useless to the body politic, it is also ridiculous, and even calculated to bring trouble and disorder on the people. For my part, having lived many years on friendly terms with the Hindus, we have been able to study their national life and character closely, and we have arrived at a quite opposite decision on this subject of caste. We believe caste division to be in many respects the *chef-d' oeuvre,* the happiest effort, of Hindu legislation. We are persuaded that it is simply and solely due to the distribution of the people into castes that India did not lapse into a state of barbarism, and that she perserved and perfected the arts and sciences of civilisation whilst most other nations of the earth remained in a state of barbarism. We do not consider caste to be free from many great drawbacks; but we believe that the resulting advantages, in the case of a nation constituted like the Hindus, more than outweigh the resulting evils.

To establish the justice of this contention we have only to glance at the condition of the various races of men who live in the same latitude as the Hindus, and to consider the past and present status of those among them whose natural deposition and character have not been influenced for good by the purifying doctrines to Revealed Religion. We can judge what the Hindus would have been like, and they not been held within the pale of social duty by caste regulations, if we glance at neighbouring nations west of the Peninsula and east of it beyond the Ganges as far as China. In China itself a temperate climate and a form of government peculiarly adapted to a people unlike any other in the world have produced the same effect as the distinction of caste among the Hindus.

After much careful thought we can discover no other reason except caste which accounts for the Hindus not having fallen into the same state of barbarism as their neighbours and as almost all nations inhabiting as their neighbours and as almost all nations inhabiting the torrid zone. Caste assigns to each individual his own profession or calling; and the handing down of this system from father to son, from generation to generation, makes it impossible for any person or his descendants to change the condition of life which the law assigns to him for any other. Such an institution was probably the only means that the most clear-sighted prudence could devise for maintaining a state of civilisation amongst a people endowed with the peculiar characteristics of the Hindus.

Duty and Rules of Caste

We can picture what would become of the Hindus if they were not kept within the bounds of duty by the rules and penalties of caste, by looking at the position of the Pariahs, or outcastes of India, who, checked by no moral restraint, abandon themselves to their natural propensities.

Anybody who has studied the conduct and character of the people of this class—which, by the way, is the largest of any of India—will agree with me that a state consisting entirely of such inhabitants could not long endure, and could not fail to lapse before long into a condition of barbarism. For my own part, being perfectly familiar with this class, and acquainted with its natural predilections and sentiments, we are persuaded that a nation of Pariahs left to themselves would speedily become worse than the hordes of cannibals who wander in the vast waste of Africa, and would soon take to devouring each other.[1]

We are no less convinced that if the Hindus were not kept within the limits of duty and obedience by the system of caste, and by the penal regulations attached to each phase of it, they would soon become just what the Pariahs are, and probably something still worse. The whole country would necessarily fall into a state of hopeless anarchy, and, before the present generation disappeared, this nation, so polished under present conditions, would have to be reckoned amongst the most uncivilised of the world. The legislators of India, whoever they may have been, were far too wise and too well acquainted with the natural character of the people for whom they prescribed laws to leave it to the discretion or fancy of each individual to cultivate what knowledge he pleased, or exercise, as seemed best to him, any of the various professions, arts, or industries which are necessary for the prevention and well-being of a State.

They set out from that cardinal principle common to all ancient legislators, that no person should be useless to the commonwealth. At the same time they recognised that they were dealing with a people who were indolent and careless by nature, and whose propensity to be apathetic was so aggravated by the climate in which they lived, that unless every individual had a profession or employment rigidly imposed upon him, the social fabric could not hold together and must quickly fall into the most deplorable state of anarchy. These ancient lawgivers, therefore, being well aware of the danger caused by religious and political innovations and being anxious to establish durable and inviolable rules for the different castes comprising the Hindu nation, saw no surer way of attaining their object than by combining in an unmistakable manner those two great foundations of orderly government, religion and politics. Accordingly there is not one of their ancient usages, not one of their observances, which has not some religious principle or object attached to it. Everything, indeed, is governed by superstition and has religion for its motive. The style of greeting, the mode of dressing, the cut of clothes, the shape of ornaments and their manner of adjustment, the various details of the toilette, the architecture of houses, the corners where the hearth is placed and where the cooking pots must stand, the manner of going to bed and of sleeping, the forms of civility and politeness that must be observed: all these are severely regulated.

During the many years that we studied Hindu customs we cannot say that we ever observed a single one, however unimportant and simple, and, we may add, however filthy and disgusting, which did not rest on some religious principle or other. Nothing is left to chance; everything is laid down by rule, and the foundation of all their customs is purely and simple religion. It is for this reason that the Hindus hold all their customs and usages to be inviolable, for, being essentially religious, they consider them as sacred as religion itself.

And, be it noted, this plan of dividing the people into castes is not confined to the lawgivers of India. The wisest and most famous of all lawgivers, Moses, availed himself of the same institution, as being the one which offered him the best means of governing the intractable and rebellious people of whom he had been appointed the patriarch.

Division of People

The division of the people into castes existed also amongst the Egyptians. With them, as with the Hindus, the law assigned an occupation to each individual, which was handed down from father to son. It was forbidden to any man to have two professions, or to change his own. Each caste had a special quarter assigned to it, and people of a different caste were prohibited from settling there. Nevertheless there was this difference between the Egyptians and the Hindus: with the former all castes and all professions were held in eastern; all employments, even of the meanest kind, were alike regarded as honourable; and, although the priestly and military castes possessed peculiar privileges, nobody would have considered it anything but criminal to despise the classes whose work, whatever it happened to be, contributed to the general good. With the Hindus, on the other hand, there are professions and callings to which prejudice attaches such degradation that those who follow them are universally despised by those castes which in the public estimation exercise higher functions.

If must here be remarked, however, that the four great professions without which a civilised nation could not exist, namely, the army, agriculture, commerce, and weaving, are held everywhere in the highest esteem. All castes, from the Brahmin to the Pariah, are permitted to follow the first three, and the fourth can be followed by all the principal classes of Sudra.[2]

These same caste distinctions observable amongst Hindus exist likewise, with some differences, amongst the Arabs and Tartars. Probably, indeed, they were common to the majority of ancient nations. Cecrops, it will be remembered, separated the people of Athens into four tribes or classes, while their great lawgiver, Solon, upheld this distinction and strengthened it in several ways. Numa Pompilius, again, could devise no better way of putting an end to the racial hatred between Sabines and Romans that by separating the body of the people into different castes and classes. The result of his policy was just what he had desired. Both Sabines and Romans, once amalgamated in this manner, forgot their national differences and thought only of those of their class or caste.

Those who instituted the caste system could not but perceive that with nations in an embryonic stage the more class distinctions there are the more order and symmetry there must be, and the more easy it is to exercise control and preserve order. This, indeed, is the result which caste classification amongst the Hindus has achieved. The shame which would reflect on a whole caste if the faults of one of its individual members went unpunished guarantees that the caste will execute justice, defend its own honour, and keep all its members within the bounds of duty. For, be it noted, every caste has its own laws and regulations; or rather, we may say, its own customs, in accordance with which the severest justice is meted out, just as it was by the patriarchs of old.

Punishment for Adultery

Thus in several castes adultery is punishable by death.[3] Girls or widows who succumb to temptation are made to suffer the same penalty as those who have seduced them. The largest temple of the town of Conjeeveram, in the Carnatic, an immense building, was constructed, so it is said, by a rich Brahmin who had been convicted of having had illicit intercourse with a low-caste Pariah woman. He was, however, sentenced to this severe penalty, not so much on account of the immorality of his action, seeing that in the opinion of the Brahmins it was not immoral at all, but on account of the low-caste person who had been the partner of his inconsistence. There are various kinds of delinquencies in connexion with which a caste may take proceedings, not only against the principal offenders, but against those who have taken any part whatever in them. Thus it is caste authority which, by means of its wise rules and prerogatives, preserves good order, suppresses vice, and saves Hindus from sinking into a state of barbarism.

It may also be said that caste regulations counteract to a great extent the evil effects which would otherwise be produced on the national character by a religion that encourages the most unlicensed depravity of morals, as well in the decorations of its temples as in its dogmas and ritual.

In India, where the princes and the aristocracy live in the extreme indolence, attaching little importance to making their dependants happy and taking small pains to inculcate in them a sense of right and wrong, there are no other means of attaining these desirable ends and preserving good order by authoritative rulings of the caste system. The worst of it is, these powers are not sufficiently wide, or rather they are too often relaxed. Many castes exercise them with severity in cases that are for the most part frivolous, but display an easy and culpable indulgence towards real and serious delinquencies. On the other hand, caste authority is often a check against abuses which the despotic rulers of the country are too apt to indulge in. Sometimes one may see, as the result of a caste order, the tradesmen and merchants of a whole district closing their shops, the labourers abandoning their fields, or the artisans leaving their workshops, all because of some petty extortion suffered by some member of their caste; and the aggrieved people will remain obstaintely in this state of opposition until the injury has been atoned for and those responsible for it punished.

Purity of Descent

Another advantage resulting from the caste system is the hereditary continuation of families and that purity of descent which is a peculiarity of the Hindus, and which consists in never mixing the blood of one family or caste with that of another. Marriages are confined to parties belonging to the same family, or at any rate the same caste. In India, at any rate, there can be no room for the reproach, so often deserved in European countries, that families have deteriorated by alliances with persons of low or unknown extraction. A HIndu of high caste can, without citing his title or producing his genealogical tree, trace his descent back for more than two thousand years without fear of contradiction. He can also, without any other passport than that of his high caste, and in spite of his poverty, present himself anywhere; and he would be more courted for a marriage alliance than any richer man of less pure descent. Nevertheless, it is not to be denied that there are some districts where the people are not quite so particular about their marriages, though such luxity is blamed and held up to shame as an outrage on propriety, while those guilty of it take very good care to conceal it as much as possible from the public.

Further, one would be justified in asserting that it is to caste distinctions that India owes the preservation of her arts and industries.

For the same reason she would have reached a high standard of perfection in them had not the avarice of her rulers prevented it. It was chiefly to attain the object that the Egyptians were divided into castes, and that their laws assigned the particular place which each individual should occupy in the commonwealth. Their lawgivers no doubt considered that by this means all arts and industries would continue to improve from generation to generation, for men must needs do well that which they have always been in the habit of seeing done and which they have been constantly practising from their youth.

This perfection in arts and manufactures would undoubtedly have been attained by so industrious a people as the Hindus, if, as I have before remarked, the cupidity of their rulers had not acted as a check. As a matter of fact, no sooner has an artisan gained the reputation of excelling in his craft than he is at once carried off by order of the sovereign, taken to the palace, and there confined for the rest of his life, forced to toil without remission and with little or no reward. Under these circumstances, which are common to all parts of India under the government of native princes, it is hardly surprising that every art and industry is extinguished and all healthy competition deadened. This is the chief and almost the only reason why progress in the arts has been so slow among the Hindus, and why in this respect they are now far behind other nations who did not become civilised for many centuries after themselves.

Their workmen certainly lack neither industry nor skill. In European settlements, where they are paid according to their merit, many native artisans are to be met with whose work would do credit to the best artisans of the West. Moreover they feel no necessity to use the many European tools, whose nomenclature alone requires special study. One or two axes, as many saws and planes, all of them so rudely fashioned that a European workman would be able to do nothing with them—these are almost the only instruments that are to be seen in the hands of Hindu carpenters. The working materials of a journeyman goldsmith usually comprise a tiny anvil, a crucible, two or three small hammers, and as many files. With such simple tools the patient Hindu, thanks to his industry, can produce specimens of work which are often not to be distinguished from those imported at great expense from foreign countries. To what a standard of excellence would these men have attained if they had been from the earliest times subjected to good masters!

Hindus in Industry

In order to form a just idea of what the Hindus would have done with their arts and manufactures if their natural industry had been properly encouraged, we have only to visit the workshop of one of their weavers or of one of their printers on cloth and carefully examine the instruments with which they produce those superb muslins, those superfine clothes, those beautiful coloured piece-goods, which are everywhere admired, and which in Europe occupy a high place among the principal articles of adornment. In manufacturing these magnificent stuffs the artisan uses his feet almost as much as his hands. Furthermore, the weaving loom, and the whole apparatus for spinning the thread before it is woven, as well as the rest of the tools which he uses for the work, are so simple and so few that altogether they would hardly comprise a load for one man. Indeed it is by no means a rare sight to see one of these weavers changing his abode, and carrying on his back all that is necessary for setting to work the moment he arrives at his new home.

Their printed calicoes, which are not less admired than their muslins, are manufactured in an equally simple manner. Three or four bamboos to stretch the cloth, as many brushes for applying the colours, with a few pieces of potsherd to contain them, and a hollow stone for pounding them: these are pretty well all their stock in trade.

We will venture to express one other remark on the political advantages resulting from caste distinctions. In India parental authority is but little respected: and parents, overcome doubtless by that apathetic indifference which characterises Hindus generally, are at little pains, as we shall show later on, to inspire those feelings of filial reverence which constitute family happiness by enchaining the affections of the children to the authors of the existence. Outward affection appears to exist between brothers and sisters, but in reality it is neither very strong nor very sincere. It quickly vanishes after the death of their parents, and subsequently, we may say, they only come together to fight and to quarrel. Thus, as the ties of blood relationship formed so insecure a bond between different members of a community, and guaranteed no such mutual assistance and support as were needed, it became necessary to bring families together in large caste communities, the individual members of which had a common interest in protecting, supporting, and defending each other. It was thus that the links of the Hindu social chain were so strongly and ingeniously forged that nothing was able to break them.

Ancient Law-givers

This was the object which the ancient lawgivers of India attained by establishing the caste system, and they thereby acquired a title to honour unexampled in the history of the world. Their work has stood the test of thousands of years, and has survived the lapse of time and the many revolutions to which this portion of the globe has been subjected. The Hindus have often passed beneath the yoke of foreign invaders, whose religions, laws, and customs have been very different from their own; yet all efforts to impose foreign institutions on the people of India have been futile, and foreign occupation has never dealt more than a feeble blow against Indian custom. Above all, and before all, it was the caste system which protected them. Its authority was extensive enough to include sentences of death, as we have before remarked. The story is told, and the truth of it is incontestable, that a man of the Rajput caste was a few years ago compelled by the people of his own caste and by the principal inhabitants of his place of abode to execute, with his own hand, a sentence of death passed on his daughter. This unhappy girl had been discovered in the arms of a youth, who would have suffered the same penalty had he not evaded it by sudden flight.

Nevertheless, although the penalty of death may be inflicted by some castes under certain circumstances, this form of punishment is seldom resorted to nowadays. Whenever it is thought to be indispensable, it is the father or the brother who is expected to execute it, in secrecy. Generally speaking, however recourse it had by preference to the imposition of a fine and to various ignominious corporal punishments. As regards these latter, we may note as examples the punishments inflicted on women who have forfeited their honour, such as shaving their heads, compelling them to ride through the public streets mounted on asses and with their faces turned towards the tail, forcing them to stand a long time with the basket of mud on their heads before the assembled caste people, throwing into their faces the ordure of cattle, breaking the cotton thread of those possessing the right to wear it, and excommunicating the guilty from their caste.[4]

Of all kinds of punishment the hardest and most unbearable for a Hindu is that which cuts him off and expels him from his caste. Those whose duty it is to inflict it are the *gurus,* of whom we shall have more to say in a subsequent chapter, and, in default of them, the caste headmen. These latter are usually to be found in every district, and it is to them that all doubtful or difficult questions affecting the caste system are referred. They call in, in order to help them to decide such questions, a few elders who are versed in the intricacies of the matters in dispute.

This expulsion from caste, which follows, either an infringement of caste usages or some public offence calculated if left unpunished to bring dishonour on the whole community, is a kind of social excommunication, which deprives the unhappy person who suffers it of all intercourse with his fellow-creatures. It renders him, as it were, dead to the world, and leaves him nothing in common with the rest of society. In losing his caste he loses not only his relations and friends, but often his wife and his children, who would rather leave him to his fate that share his disgrace with him. Nobody dare eat with him or even given him a drop of water. If he has marriageable daughters nobody asks them in marriage, and in like manner his sons are refused wives. He has to take it for granted that wherever he goes he will be avoided, pointed at with scorn, and regarded as an outcaste.

If after losing caste a Hindu could obtain admission into an inferior caste, his punishment would in some degree be tolerable; but even this humiliating compensation is denied to him. A simple Sudra with any notions of honour and propriety would never associate or even speak with a Brahmin degraded in his manner. It is necessary, therefore, for an outcaste to seek asylum in the lowest caste of Pariahs if he fails to obtain restoration to his own; or else he is obliged to associate with persons of doubtful caste. There are always people of this kind, especially in the quarters inhabited by Europeans; and unhappy is the man who puts trust in them! A caste Hindu is often a thief and a bad character, but a Hindu without caste is almost always a rogue.

Expulsion from Caste

Expulsion from caste is generally put in force without much formality. Sometimes it is due merely to personal hatred or caprice. Thus, when persons refuse, without any apparent justification, to attend the funeral or marriage ceremonies of their relations or friends, or when they happen not to invite the latter on similar occasions, the individuals thus slighted never fail to take proceeding in order to obtain satisfaction for the insult offered to them and the arbitrators called in to decide the case usually pass a decree of excommunication. When a case is thus settled by arbitration, however, a sentence of excommunication does not bring upon the guilty person the same disgrace and the same penalties which are the lot of those whose offence offers no room for compromise.

Otherwise it matters little whether the offence be deliberate, whether it be serious or trivial, in determining that a person shall pay this degrading penalty. A Pariah who concealed his origin, mixed with other Hindus, entered their houses and ate with them without being recognized, would render those who had thus been brought into contact with him liable to ignominious expulsion from their caste. At the same time a Pariah guilty of such a daring act would inevitably be murdered on the spot, if his entertainers recognised him.

A Sudra, too, who indulged in illicit intercourse with Pariah woman would be rigorously expelled from caste if his offence became known.

A number of Brahmins assembled together for some family ceremony once admitted to their feast, without being aware of it, a Sudra who had gained admittance on the false assertion that he belonged to their caste. On the circumstance being discovered, these Brahmins were one and all outcasted, and were unable to obtain reinstatement until they had gone through all kinds of formalities and been subjected to considerable expense.

We have witnessed amongst the *Gollavarus,* or shepherds, an instance of even greater severity. A marriage had been arranged, and in the presence of the family concerned, certain ceremonies which were equivalent to betrothal amongst ourselves had taken place. Before the actual celebration of the marriage, which was fixed for a considerable time afterwards, the bridegroom died. The parents of the girl, who was very young and pretty, thereupon married her to another man. This was in direct violation of the custom of the caste, which condemns to perpetual widowhood girls thus betrothed, even when, as in this case, the future bridegroom dies before marriage has been consummated. The consequence was that all the persons who had taken part in the second ceremony were expelled from caste, and nobody would contract marriage or have any intercourse whatever with them. A long time afterwards we met several of them, well advanced in age, who had been for this reason alone unable to obtain husbands or wives, as the case might be.

Let us relate another instance. Eleven Brahmains travelling in company were obliged to cross a district devastated by war. They arrived hungry and tired in a village, which contrary to their expectations, they found deserted. They had with them a small quantity of rice, but they could find no other pots to boil it in than some which had been left in the house of the village washerman. To touch these would constitute in the case of Brahmins an almost ineffaceable defilement. Nevertheless, suffering from hunger as they were, they swore mutual secrecy, and after washing and scouring the pots a hundred times they prepared their food in them. The rice was served and the repast consumed by all but one, who refused to partake of it, and who had no sooner returned home than he proceeded to denounce the ten others to the chief Brahmins of the village. The news of such a scandal spread quickly, and gave rise to a great commotion amongst all classes of the i inhabitants. An assembly was held. The delinquents were summoned and forced to appear. Warned beforehand, however, of the proceeding that were to be instituted against them, they took counsel together and agreed to answer unanimously, when called upon to explain, that it was the accuser himself who had committed the heinous sin and who had imputed it to them falsely and maliciously. The testimony of ten persons was calculated to carry more weight than that of one. The accused were consequently acquitted, while the accuser alone was ignominiously expelled from caste by the headmen, who, though they were perfectly sure of his innocence, were indignant at his treacherous disclosure.

From what has been said, it will no longer be surprising to learn that Hindus are as much, nay, even more, attached to their caste than the gentry of Europe are to their rank. Prone to using the most disgustingly abusive language in their quarrels, they nevertheless easily forgive and forget such insulting epithets; but if one should say of another that he is *a man without caste,* the insult would never be forgiven or forgotten.

This strict and universal observance of caste and caste usages forms practically their whole social law. A very great number of people are to be found amongst them, to whom death would appear far more desirable than life, if, for example, the latter were sustained by eating cow's flesh or any food prepared by Pariahs and outcastes.

It is this same caste feeling which gives rise to the contempt and aversion which they display towards all foreign nations, and especially towards Europeans, who, being as a rule but slightly acquainted with the customs and prejudices of the country, are constantly violating them. Owing to such conduct the Hindus look upon them as barbarians totally ignorant of all principles of honour and good breeding.

In several cases, at least, restoration to caste is an impossibility. But when the sentence of excommunication has been passed merely by relations, the culprit conciliates the principal members of his family and prostrates himself in a humble posture, and with signs of repentance, before his assembled castemen. He then listens without complaint to the rebukes which are showered upon him, receives the blows to which he is oftentimes condemned, and pays the fine which it is thought fit to impose upon him. Finally, after having solemnly promised to wipe out by good conduct the taint resulting from his degrading punishment, he sheds tears of repentance, performs the *sashtanga* before the assembly, and then serves a feast to the persons present. When all this is finished he looked upon as reinstated. The *sashtanga*, by the way, is a sign or salute expressing humility, which is not only recognized amongst the Hindus and other Asiatic nations, but was in use amongst more ancient peoples. Instances of it are quoted in Scripture, where this extraordinary mark of respect is known as *adoration*, even when it is paid to simple mortals. (*Vide* Genesis

xviii. 2; xix. 1; xxxiii. 3; xlii. 6; xliii. 26; 1. 18, &c., &c.) In the same way the Egyptians, Chaldeans, and other nations mentioned in Holy Writ were acquainted with this method of reverent salutation and observed it under the same circumstances as the Hindus. As we shall often have occasion in this work to mention the *sashtanga* we will give here a definition of it. The person who performed it lies prostrate, his face on the ground and his arms extended beyond his head. It is called *sashtanga* from *the prostration of the six members,* because, when it is performs the feet, the knees, the stomach, the chest, the forehead, and the arms must touch the earth. It is thus that prostrations are made before persons of high degree, such as princes and priests. Children sometimes prostrate themselves thus before their fathers. It is by no means rare to see Sudras of different classes performing *sanshtanga* before Brahmins; and it often happens that princes, before engaging an enemy, thus prostrate themselves before their armies drawn up in battle array[5].

When expulsion from caste is the result of some heinous offence, the guilty person who is readmitted into caste has to submit to one of other of the following ordeals: his tongue is slightly burnt with a piece of heated gold; he is branded indelibly on different parts of his body with red-hot iron; he is made to walk barefooted over red-hot embers; or he is compelled to crawl several times under the belly of a cow. Finally, to complete his purification, he is made to drink the *pancha-gavia.* These words, of which a more detailed explanation will be given later on, signify literally *the five things or substances* derived from the body of a cow; namely, milk, curds, ghee (clarified butter), dung and urine, which are mixed together. The last-named, urine, is looked upon as the most efficacious for purifying any kind of uncleanness. We have often seen superstitious Hindus following the cows to pasture, waiting for the moment when they could collect the precious liquid in vessels of brass, and carrying it away while still warm to their houses. We have also seen them waiting to catch it in the hollow of their hands, drinking some of it and rubbing their faces and heads with the rest. Rubbing it in this way is supposed to wash away all external uncleanness; and drinking it to cleanse all internal impurity. When this disgusting ceremony of the *pancha-gavia* is over, the person who has been reinstated is expected to give a great feast to the Brahmins who have collected from all parts to witness it. Presents of more or less value are also expected by them, and not until these are forthcoming does the guilty person obtain all his rights and privileges again.

Heinous Offences

There are certain offences so heinous in the sight of Hindus, however, as to leave no hope of reinstatement to those who commit them. Such, for example, would be the crime of a Brahmin who had openly cohabited with a Pariah woman. Were the woman of any other caste, we believe that it would be possible for a guilty person, by getting rid of her and by repudiating any children he had had by her, to obtain pardon, after performing many purifying ceremonies and expending much money. But hopeless would be the case of the man who under any circumstances had eaten of cow's flesh. There would be no hope of pardon for him, even supposing he had committed such an awful sacrilege under compulsion.

It would be possible to cite several instances of strange and inflexible severity in the punishment of caste offences. When the last Mussulman Prince reigned in Mysore and sought to proselytize the whole Peninsula, he began by having several Brahmins forcibly circumcised, compelling them afterwards to eat cow's flesh as an unequivocal token of their renunciation of caste. Subsequently the people were freed from the yoke of this tyrant, and many of those who had been compelled to embrace the Mahomedan religion made every possible effort, and offered very large sums, to be readmitted to Hinduism. Assemblies were held in different parts of the country to thoroughly consider their cases. It was everywhere decided that it was quite possible to purify the uncleanness of circumcision and of intercourse with Mussulmans. But the crime of eating cow's flesh, even under compulsion, was unanimously declared to be irredeemable and not to be effaced either by presents, or by fire, or by the *pancha-gavia.*

A similar decision was given in the case of Sudras who found themselves in the same position, and who, after trying all possible means, were not more successful. One and all, therefore, were obliged to remain Mahomedans.

A Hindu, of whatever caste, who has once had the misfortune to be excommunicated, can never altogether get rid of the stain of his disgrace. If he ever gets into trouble his excommunication is always thrown in his teeth.

Apparently there is no existing institution older than the caste system of the Hindus. Greek and Latin authors who have written about India concur in thinking that it has been in force from time immemorial; and certainly the unswerving observance of its rules seems to me an almost incontestable proof of its antiquity[6]. Under a solemn and unceasing obligation as the Hindus are to respect its usages, new and strange customs are things unheard of in their country. And person who attempted to introduce such innovations would excite universal resentment and opposition, and would be branded as a dangerous person. The task, however, would be such a difficult one that we can hardly believe that any proposal of the kind would ever enter an intelligent person's head. Everything is always done in exactly the same way; even the minutest details are invested with a solemn importance of their own, because a Hindu is convinced that it is only by paying rigorous attention to small details that more momentous concerns are safeguarded. Indeed, there is not another nation on earth which can pride itself on having so long preserved intact its social customs and regulations.

The Hindu legislators of old had the good sense to give stability to these customs and regulations by associating with them many outward ceremonies, which; by fixing them in the minds of the people, ensured their more faithful observance. These ceremonies are invariably observed, and have never been allowed to degenerate into mere forms that can be neglected without grave consequences. Failure to perform a single one of them, however unimportant it might appear, would never go unpunished.

One may remark how very similar some of these ceremonies are to those which were performed long ago amongst other nations. Thus the Hindu precepts about cleanness and uncleanness, as also the means employed for preserving the one and effacing the other, are similar in many respects to those of the ancient Hebrews. The rule about marrying in one's caste, and even in one's family, was specifically imposed upon the Jews in the laws which Moses gave them from God. This rule, too, was in force a long time before that, for it appears to have been general amongst the Chaldeans. We find also in Holy Writ that Abraham espoused his niece, and that the holy patriarch sent into a far country for a maiden of his own family as a wife for his son Isaac. Again, Isaac and his wife Rebecca found it difficult to pardon their son Esau for marrying amongst strangers, that is, amongst the Canaanites; and they sent their son Jacob away into a distant land to seek a wife from amongst their own people.

In the same way to-day, Hindus residing in a foreign country will journey hundreds of leagues to their native land in search of wives for their sons.

Again, as to the caste system, Moses, as is well known, established it amongst the Hebrews in accordance with the commands of God. This holy lawgiver had, during his long sojourn in Egypt, observed the system as established in that country, and had doubtless recognised the good that resulted from it. Apparently, in executing the divine order with respect to it he simply adapted and perfected the system which was in force in Egypt.

The Indian caste system is of still older origin. The Hindu sacred writings record that the author of it was the God Brahma, to whom they attribute the creation of the world, and who is said to have established this system when he peopled the earth. The Brahmins were the product of his brain; the Kshatriyas or Rajahs issued from his shoulders; the Vaisyas from his belly; and the Sudras from his feet.

It is easy to understand the allegorical signification of his legend, in which one can distinctly trace the relative degrees of subordination of the different castes. The Brahmins, destined to fulfil the high functions of spiritual priesthood and to show the way of salvation to their fellowmen, issue from the head of the Creator; the Kshatriyas, endowed with physical force and destined to undergo the fatigues of war, have their origin in the shoulders and arms of Brahma, the Vaisyas, whose duty it is to provide the food, the clothing, and other bodily necessities of man, are born in the belly of the god; and the Sudras, whose lot is servitude and rude labour in the fields, issue from his feet.

It is a fact that amongst the immense number of classes of which the Sudra caste is composed, it is impossible to give precedence to any one class in particular; the natives themselves not being agreed on the point, and the social scale varying in different parts of the country. There are certain classes, however, who, owing to the depth of degradation into which they have fallen, are looked upon as almost another race of beings, altogether outside the pale of society; and they are perfectly ready to acknowledge their own comparative inferiority. The best known and most numerous of these castes is the *Parayer,* as it is called in Tamil, the word from which the European name Pariah is derived.[7]

Their contempt and aversion for these social outcastes are as extreme, on the one hand, as are the respect and veneration which they pay, on the other, to those whom their superstitions have invested with god-like attributes. Throughout the whole of India the Pariahs are looked upon as slaves by other castes, and are treated, with great harshness. Hardly anywhere are they allowed to cultivate the soil for their own benefit, but are obliged to hire themselves out to the other castes, who in return for a minimum wage exact the hardest tasks from them.

This class is the most numerous of all, and in conjunction with that of the *Chucklers,* or cobblers, represents at least a quarter of the population. It is painful to think that its members, though so degraded, are yet the most useful of all. On them the whole agricultural work of the country devolves,[8] and they have also other tasks to perform which are still harder and more indispensable.

However, notwithstanding the miserable condition of these wretched Pariahs, they are never heard to murmur, or to complain of their low estate. Still less do they ever dream of trying to improve their lot, by combining together and forcing the other classes to treat them with common respect which one man owes to another. The idea that he was born to be in subjection to the other castes is so ingrained in his mind that it never occurs to the Pariah to think that his fate is anything but irrevocable. Nothing will ever persuade him that men are all made of the same clay, or that he has the right to insist on better treatment than that which is meted out to him.[9]

They live in hopeless poverty, and the greater number lack sufficient means to procure even the coarsest clothing. They go about almost naked, or at best clothed in the most hideous rags.

They live from hand to mouth the whole year round, and rarely know one day how they will procure food for the next. When they happen to have any money, for invariably spend it at once, and make a point of doing no work as long as they have anything left to live on.

In a few districts they are allowed to cultivate the soil on their own account, but in such cases they are almost always the poorest of their class. Pariahs who hire themselves out as labourers earn, at any rate, enough to live on; and their food, though often of the coarest description, is sufficient to satisfy the cravings of hunger. But those who are their own masters, and cultivate land for themselves, are so indolent and careless that their harvests, even in the most favourable seasons, are only sufficient to feed them for half the year.

The contempt and aversion with which the other castes—and particularly the Brahmins—regard these unfortunate people are carried to such an excess that in many places their presence, or even their footprints, are considered sufficient to defile the whole neighbourhood. They are forbidden to cross a street in which Brahmins are living. Should they be so ill-advised as to do so, the latter would have the right, not to strike them themselves, because they could not do so without defilement, or even touch them with the end of a long stick, but to order them to be severely beaten by other people. A Pariah who had the audacity to enter a Brahmin's house might possibly be murdered on the spot. A revolting crime of this sort has been actually perpetrated in States under the rule of native princes without a voice being raised in expostulation.[10]

Any one who has been touched, whether inadvertently or purposely, by a Pariah is defiled by that single act, and may hold no communication with any person whatsoever until he has been purified by bathing, or by other ceremonies more or less important according to the status and customs of his caste. It would be contamination to eat with any members of this class; to touch food prepared by them, or even to drink water which they have drawn; to use an earthen vessel which they have held in their hands; to set foot inside one of their houses, or to allow them to enter houses other than their own. Each of these acts would contaminate the person affected by it, and before being readmitted to his own caste such a person would have to go through many exacting and expensive formalities. Should it be proved that any one had had any connexion with a Pariah woman he would be treated with even greater severity. Nevertheless, the disgust which these Pariahs inspire is not so intense in some parts of the country as in others. The feeling is most strongly developed in the southern and western districts of the Peninsula; in the north it is less apparent. In the northern part of Mysore the other classes of Sudras allow Pariahs to approach them, and even permit them to enter that part of the house which is used for cattle. Indeed, in some places custom is so far relaxed that a Pariah may venture to put his head and one foot, but one foot only, inside the room occupied by the master of the house. It is said that still further north the difference between this and other Sudra caste gradually diminishes, until at last it disappears altogether.

Origin of Degraded Class

The origin of this degraded class can be traced to a very early period, as it is mentioned in the most ancient Puranas. The Pariahs were most probably composed in the first instance, of all the disreputable individuals of different classes of society, who on account of various offences, had forfeited their right to associate with respectable men. They formed a class apart, and having nothing to fear and less to lose, they gave themselves up, without restraint, to their natural tendencies towards vice and excess, in which they continue to live at the present day.

In very early days, however, the separation between Pariahs and the other castes does not appear to have been so marked as at present. Though relegated to the lowest grade in social scale, they were not then placed absolutely outside and beyond it, the line of demarcation between them and the Sudras being almost imperceptible. Indeed, they are even to this day considered to be the direct descendants of the better class of agricultural labourers. The Tamil *Vellalers* and the *Okkala-makkalu-*

kanarey do not disdain to call them their children. But one thing is quite certain, that if these classes share a common origin with the Pariahs and acknowledge the same, their actions by no means corroborate their words, and their treatment of the Pariahs leaves much to be desired.

Europeans are obliged to have Pariahs for their servants, because no native of any other caste would condescend to do such menial work as is exacted by their masters. For instance, it would be very difficult to find amongst the Sudras anyone who would demean himself by blacking or greasing boots and shoes, emptying and cleansing chamber utensils, brushing and arranging hair, &c.; and certainly no one could be found who for any consideration whatever would consent to cook food for them, as this would necessitate touching beef, which is constantly to be seen on the tables of Europeans, who thereby show an open disregard of the feelings and prejudices of the people amongst whom they live. Foreigners are therefore obliged to have recourse to Pariahs to perform this important domestic service. If the kind of food which they do not scruple to eat lowers Europeans in the eyes of the superstitions native, much more are they lowered by the social status of the people by whom they are served. For it is a fact recognised by all Hindus that none but a Pariah would dare to eat food prepared by Pariahs.

It is undeniable that this want of consideration on the part of Europeans—or rather the necessity to which they are reduced of employing Pariahs as servants—renders them most obnoxious to other classes of natives, and greatly diminishes the general respect for the white man. It being impossible to procure servants of a better caste, foreigners have of necessity to put up with members of this inferior class, who are dishonest, incapable of any attachment to their masters, and unworthy of confidence... Sudras who become servants of Europeans are almost invariably vicious and unprincipled, as devoid of all feeling of honour as they are wanting in resource; in fact, they are the scum of their class and of society at large. No respectable or self-respecting Sudra would ever consent to enter a service where he would be in danger of being mistaken for a Pariah, or would have to consort with Pariahs. Amongst other reasons which contribute largely to the dislike that natives of the better class entertain for domestic service under Europeans, is the feeling that their masters keep them at such a great distance and are generally haughty and even cruel in their demeanour towards them. But above all things they dread being kicked by a European, not because this particular form of ill-treatment is physically more painful than any other, but because they have a horror of being defiled by contact with anything so unclean as a leather boot or shoe. Pariahs, accustomed from their childhood to slavery, put up patiently with affronts of this kind which other natives, who have more pride and self-respect, are unable to endure.

Under other circumstances, it should be remarked, domestic service in India is by no means regarded as degrading. The servant has his meals with his master, the maid with her mistress, and both go through life on an almost equal footing. The conduct of Europeans being in this respect so totally different, natives who have any sense of decency or self-respect feel the greatest repugnance to taking service with them. One cannot wonder therefore that only the very dregs of the population will undertake the work.

The Pariahs

But to return to the Pariahs. One is bound to confess that the evil reputation which is borne by this class is in many respects well deserved, by reason of the low conduct and habits of its members. A great many of these unfortunate people bind themselves for life, with their wives and children, to the ryots, or agricultural classes, who set them to the hardest labour and treat them with the greatest harshness. The village scavengers, who are obliged to clean out the public latrines, to sweep the streets, and to remove all rubbish, invariably belong to this class. These men, known in the south by the name of *totis,* are, however, generally somewhat more humanely treated than the other Pariahs, because, in addition to the dirty work above mentioned, they are employed in letting the water into the tanks and channels for irrigating the rice fields; and on this account they are treated with some consideration by the rest of the villagers. Amongst the Pariahs who are not agricultural slaves there are some who groom and feed the horses of private individuals, or those used in the army, some are in charge of elephants; others tend cattle; others are messengers and carriers, while others, again, do ordinary manual work. Within recent times Pariahs have been allowed to enlist in the European and Native armies, and some of them have risen to high rank, for in point of courage and bravery they are in no way inferior to any other caste. Yet their bringing up puts them at a great disadvantage in acquiring other qualifications necessary for the making of a good soldier, for they are induced with difficulty to conform to military discipline, and are absolutely deficient in all sense of honour.

Pariahs, being thus convinced that they have nothing to lose or gain in public estimation, abandon themselves without shame or restraint to vice of all kinds, and the greatest lawlessness prevails amongst them, for which they do not feel the least shame. One might almost say that, in the matter of vice, they outstrip all others in brutality, as the Brahmins do in malice. Their habits of uncleanliness are disgusting. Their huts, a mass of filth and alive with insects and vermin, are, if possible, even more loathsome than their persons. Their harsh and forbidding features clearly reveal their character, but even these are an insufficient indication of the coarseness of their minds and manners. They are much addicted to drunkenness, a vice peculiary abhorrent to other Hindus. They intoxicate themselves usually with the juice of the palm-tree, called toddy, which they drink after it has fermented, and it is then more spirituous. In spite of its horrible stench they imbibe it as if the nauseous liquid were nectar. Drunken quarrels are of frequent occurrence amongst them, and their wives are often sufferers, the unhappy creatures being nearly beaten to death, even when in a state of pregnancy. It is to this brutality and violence of their husbands that I attribute the frequent miscarriages to which Pariah wives are subject, and which are much more common amongst them than amongst women of any other caste.

What chiefly disgusts other natives is the revolting nature of the food which the Pariahs eat. Attracted by the smell, they will collect in crowds round any carrion, and contend for the spoil with dogs, jackals, crows and other carnivorous animals. They then divide the semiputrid flesh, and carry it away to thier huts, where they devour it, often without rice or anything else to disguise the flavour. That the animal should have died of disease is of no consequence to them, and they sometimes secretly poison cows or buffaloes that they may subsequently feast on the foul, putrefying remains. The carcases of animal that die in a village belong by right to be *toti* or scavenger, who sells the flesh at a very low price to the other Pariahs in the neighbourhood. When it is impossible to consume in one day the stock of meat thus obtained they dry the remainder in the sun, and keep it in their huts until they run short of other food. There are few Pariah houses where one does not see festoons of these horrible fragments hanging up; and though the Pariahs themselves do not seem to be affected by the smell, travellers passing near their villages quickly perceive it and can tell at once the caste of the people living there. This horrible food is, no doubt, the cause of the greater part of the contagious diseases which decimate them, and from which their neighbours are free.

Is it to be wondered at, after what has just been stated, that other castes should hold this in abhorrence? Can they be blamed for refusing to hold any communication with such savages, or for obliging them to keep themselves aloof and to live in separate hamlets? It is true that with regard to these Pariahs the other Hindus are apt to carry their views to excess;

but as we have directly pointed out, and shall often have to point out again, the natural instinct of the natives of India seems to run to extremes in all cases.

The condition of the Pariahs, which is not really slavery as it is known amongst us, resembles to a certain extent that of the serfs of France and other countries of Northern Europe in olden times. This state of bondage is at its worst along the coast of Malabar, as are several other customs peculiar to the country.[12] The reason is that Malabar, owing to its position, has generally escaped the invasions and revolutions which have so often devastated the rest of India, and has thus managed to preserve unaltered many ancient institutions, which in other parts have fallen into disuse.

The Slavery

Of these the two most remarkable are proprietary rights and slavery. These two systems are apparently inseparable one from the other: and, indeed, one may well say, *no land without lord.* All the Pariahs born in the country are serfs for life, from father to son, and are part and parcel of the land on which they are born. The land-owner can sell them alongwith the soil, and can dispose of them when and how he pleases. This proprietary right and this system of serfdom have existed from the remotest times, and exist still amongst the Nairs, the Coorgs, and the Tulus, the three aboriginal tribes of the Malabar coast. This is, we believe, the only province in India where proprietary right has been preserved intact until the present day. Everywhere else the soil belongs to the ruler and the cultivator is merely his tenant. The lands which he tills are given to him or taken away from him according to the will of the Government for the time being. On the Malabar coast, however, the lands belong to those who have inherited them from their forefathers, and these in their turn possess the right of handing them down to their descendants. Here the lands may be alienated, sold, given away, or disposed of according to the will of the owners. In a word, the *jus utendi et abutendi,* which is the basis of proprietary right, belongs entirely to them. Every landed proprietor in that country possesses a community, of Pariahs to cultivate his fields, who are actually his slaves and form an integral part of his property. All children born of these Pariahs are serfs by birth, just as their parents were; and their masters has the right, if he chooses, to sell or dispose of parents and children in any way that he pleases. If one of these Pariahs escapes and takes services under another master, his real master can recover him anywhere as his own property. If a proprietor happens to possess more slaves than he requires for cultivating his land, he sells some of other landlords who are less fortunate than himself. It is by no means uncommon to see a debtor, who is unable to pay his debts in a hard cash, satisfy his creditors by handing over to them a number of his Pariah slaves. The price of these is not exorbitant. A male still young enough to work will fetch three rupees and a hundred *seers* of rice, which is about the value of a bullock.

But the landed proprietors do not usually sell their slaves except in cases of great emergency; and even then they can only sell them within the borders of their own country. In no case have they a right to export them for sale to foreigners.

Each land-owner is in the province of Malabar lives in a house that is isolated in the middle of his estate. Here he dwells, surrounded by his community of Pariah serfs, who are always remarkably submissive to him. Some land-owners possess over a hundred of them. They treat them usually in the most humane manner. They give them only such work as their age or strength permits; feed them on the same rice that they themselves eat; give them in marriage when they come of age; and every year provide them with clothing, four or five yards of cloth for the women and a coarse woollen blanket for the men.

In Malabar it is only the Pariahs who are thus condemned to perpetual slavery; but then there are no free men amongst them. All are born slaves from generation to generation. They have not even a right to buy their own freedom; and if they wish to secure their independence they can only do so by escaping secretly from the country. All the same, I have not heard that they often resort to this extremity. They are accustomed from father to son to the state of servitude; they are kindly treated by their masters; they eat the same food as they do; they are never forced to do tasks beyond their strength; and thus they have no notion of what freedom or independence means, and are happily resigned to their lot. They look upon their master as their father, and consider themselves to belong to his family. As a matter of fact, their physical condition, which is the only thing that appeals to their senses, is much better than that of their brethern who are free. At any rate, the Pariah slave of Malabar is certain of a living, the supreme requirement of nature, whereas the free Pariah of other provinces, lives for half his time in actual want of the meanest subsistence, and is often exposed to death from starvation.

References

1. This is true only of Southern India, where the Pariahs number 5,000,000.

They form one-seventh of the total population of the Madras Presidency. Of late years the degraded condition of these outcastes has attracted much attention, and a great deal is now being done to elevate them morally and materially.

2. This statement is not quite correct, for in Southern India, at any rate, some classes of Pariahs are most expert weavers, and are honoured as such throughout the country.
3. This of course is no longer allowed by law.
4. The infliction of such punishments might nowadays be followed by prosecution in the Civil and Criminal Courts.
5. Here and elsewhere the Abbé makes the mistake of interpreting *sanshtanga* to mean *'the six angas'*, or 'parts of the body.' *Sanshtanga* (Saashtanga) really means *with the eight parts of the body,* which are the two hands, the two feet, two knees, forehead, and breast.
6. Dr. Muir, in *Old Sanskrit Texts,* Vol. I. p. 159, reviewing the texts which he had cited on this subject, says:— 'First, we have the set of account in which the four castes are said to have sprung from progenitors who were separately created; but in regard to the manner of their creation we find the greatest diversity of statement. The most common story is that the castes issued from the mouth, arms, thighs, and feet of Purusha, or Brahma. The oldest extant passage in which this idea occurs, and from which all the later myths of a similar tenor have no doubt been borrowed, is to be founded in the Purusha Sukta; but it is doubtful whether in the form in which it is there represented, this representation is anything more than an allegory. In some of the texts from the Bhagavata Purana traces of the same allegorical character may be perceived; but in Manu and the Puranas the mystical import of the Vedic text disappears, and the figurative narration is hardened into a literal statement of fact. In the chapters of the Vishnu, Vayu, and Markandeya Puranas where castes are described as coeval with creation, and as having been naturally distinguished by different *gunas*, or qualities, involving varieties of moral character, we are nevertheless allowed to infer that those qualities exerted no influence on the classes in which they were inherent, as the condition of the whole race during the Krita age is described as one of uniform perfection and happiness; while the actual separation into castes did not take place, according to the Vayu Purana, until men had become deteriorated in the Treta age.

'Second in various passage from the Brahmanas epic poems, and Puranas, the creation of mankind is described without the least allusion to any separate production of the progenitors of the four castes. And whilst in the chapters where they relate the distinct formations of the castes, the Puranas assign different natural dispositions to each class, they elsewhere represent all mankind as being at the creation uniformly distinguished by the quality of passion. In one text men are said to be the offspring of Vivasat; in another his son Mami is said to be their progenitor, whilst in a third they are said to be descended from a female of the same name. The passage which declares Manu to have been the father of the human race explicitly affirms that men of all the four castes were descended from him. In another remarkable text the Mahabharata categorically asserts that originally there was no distinction of classes, the existing distribution have arisen out of difference of character and occupation. In these circumstance, we may fairly conclude that the separate origination of the four castes was far from being an article of belief universally received by India antiquity.'

The following is the categorical assertion in the Mahabharata (Santi parva) above referred to. It occurs in the course of a discussion on caste between Bhrigu and Bharadwaja. Bhrigu, replying to a question put by Bharadwaja, says: "The colour (*varna*) of the Brahmins was white; that of the Kshatriyas red; that of the Vaisyas yellow, and that of the Sudras black.' Bharadwaja here rejoins, 'If the caste (*varna*) of the four classes is distinguished by their colour (*varna*), then a confusion of all the castes is observable...' Bhrigu replies, "There is no difference of castes: this world, having been at first created by Brahma entirely Brahmanic, became (afterwards) separated into castes in consequence of works. Those Brahmins (lit. twice-born men) who were fond of sensual pleasure, fiery, irascible, prone to violence, who had forsaken their duty and were red limbed, fell into the condition of Kshatriyas. Those Brahmins who were addicted to mischief and falsehood, who derived their livelihood from kine, who were yellow, who subsisted by agriculture, and who neglected to practise their duties, entered into the state of Vaisyas. Those Brahmins who were covetous, who lived by all kinds of work, who were black and had fallen from purity, sank into the condition of Sudras'.

7. *Parayen* means one that beats the drum (*parai*).

8. This is the case only in certain districts of Southern India, such as Chingleput and Tanjore. An appreciable percentage of the Pariahs has now migrated to the towns, where they serve as domestic servants in European and Eurasian households.—Ed.

9. The Christian missionaries in India have done and are doing much to elevate the condition and character of this class. In Madras city there are now Pariah associations, and also a journal specially representing Pariah interests.

10. Even to this day a Pariah is not allowed to pass a Brahmin street in a village, though nobody can prevent, or prevents, his approaching or passing by a Brahmin's house in towns. The Pariahs, on their part, will under no circumstances allow a Brahmin to pass through their *parcherries* (collections of Pariah huts), as they firmly believe that it will lead to their ruin.

11. The Abbe is too sweeping in many of his statements about Pariahs. For

instance, in these days at any rate, the Pariah Sepoys in the Madras army are extremely well disciplined, especially the corps of Sappers.

12. It is a well known fact that things in this respect have, greatly, changed a great deal for the better since the Abbe wrote.

5

Buddhism: A Revolt Against Caste System

Crusade Against Caste Prejudices

In the 6th century B.C., Buddhism besides a quite new reason based reformative religious order, was a crusade against caste prejudices and a revolt against Brahmanism. It was a movement against superstitions, social odds, including untouchability and all sorts of human exploitation as well as animal sacrifices in the *Yajnans.* He vehemently criticised and condemned Vedic literature which preached caste system and human exploitation in the name of divinely order of *Varna* system. He did not compel people to join his Dharma, but showed a path of salvation, telling people that life was full of pains and suffering and all worldly pleasures and attachments were worthless and a hindrance in the way of Nirvana.

No Caste: No Inequality

Buddha abandoned *Varnasharm Dharma* and established a new order when there was socio-political chaos and the tribal republics were only for name sake. The society was guided by the Vedic traditions and *Shudras* exploited by the *Trivarnic* social order and Hindu aristocracy. In such an atmosphere Buddha said, "No caste, no Brahmin inequality, no superiority, all are equal.[1]"

Buddha's new social traditions and democratic norms, as well as humanistic religious order demolished the boundaries of the Brahmanism. The social distinctions and caste barriers were all abolished with the spread of Buddhism. It was during the period of Brahmanism that Buddhism was born. Brahmanism preached inequality, Buddhism preached equality... Hinduism believes in *chaturvarna,* and caste system, Buddhism has no place for the caste system and *chaturvarna.*[2] Thus Buddha was the first teacher who showed a path of humanity and opposed caste. His philosophy is totally based on reason and logic.

Buddhism: A Liberal Religious Order

Buddha said nobody was born high or low, one's nobility lies in his deeds. He denied that only Brahmins were the custodians of knowledge and learning. He strongly opposed the Brahmanic orthodoxy which resulted in opposing and exploitation of the *Shudras.*

According to E. Benz: "The problem of exploitation of man by man is solved in Buddhism by absolute condemnation of all forms of greed: of greed for possession, for power and for the pleasures of the senses..."[3]

Thapar observes: "Buddhism was very liberal and accommodating. It did not believe in caste system or in the supremacy of the priestly class. It treated all men as equal recognising dignity of man as man. Caste according to Buddha was no obstacle to the highest truth... By abolishing caste distinctions and introducing democratic principles, Buddha raised the status of the lower caste people, the degraded ones.[4]"

Shudra in Indo-Aryan Society

In pre-Buddhist India, the "*Shudras* of the Indo-Aryan society in course of time became so degraded as a consequence of the severity of the Brahmanical laws that they really came to occupy a very low status in public life. Two consequences followed from this. One consequence was a change in the connotation of the word *Shudra.* The word *Shudra* lost its original meaning of being the name of a particular community and became a general name for a low-class people without civilisation, without culture, without respect and without position."[5]

Buddha a social reformer and founder of a new order revolted against Indo-Aryan social structure and treated the Shudras as human beings and provided them equal status in the society. For him a Brahmin and a Buddhist Shraman were equal.

Hinduism Stands for Division of Society

Buddhism flourished in India between 500 B.C. to 500 A.D. It had declined between 500 A.D. and 1000 A.D. and through this period there is revival of Brahmanism and many other related cults. Most of the Puranic writings were made after the decline of Buddhism. Buddhism is based on scientific principles, reasoning and logic challenged the Hinduism, totally "negating the concept of division of society on hierarchical basis of caste system. Buddhist percepts posed a threat to the social position of Aryans, and they opposed Buddhism tooth and nail saying that Buddhist percepts literally followed would not hold the world together; but would lead nations to subjection, to inaction and to beggary."[6]

Buddha's Teachings

According to R.C. Dutt, "the Ideals or virtues like charity, love and unselfishness were the percepts conveyed by Buddha which were unchallenged holy message of equality of men proclaimed to the caste-stricken society was benevolent and his teaching moral lessons to the world's together and not to integrate it."[7] Even today India is known throughout the world because of Buddha's message of peace, non-violence, social unity, universal brotherhood and service to the humanity.

Buddhism was patronised by the ruling classes, as he himself was a Kshatriya prince, when he was alive. Even after his *nirvana* some dynasties helped in spreading the message of Buddha. "The extension of Buddhism was also influenced by the fact that the casteless and the democratic religion was adopted by post Alexandrine rulers in the Greeco-Bactrian period.[8]

In Magadha, Chandragupta Maurya (320 B.C.—291 B.C.) established his empire in 4th century B.C. sharing power with Seclucus, on the ruins left by Greek invaders. His Prime Minister Kautilya has written *Arthasastra* which throws enough light on the prevailing caste system and social life of the Hindus.[9]

Megasthenes (302 B.C. to 298 B.C.) who was a Greek Ambassador in the Court of Chandragupta Maurya has given an interesting account of existing caste system and social life of the people in his famous book *Indica*. His classification is mostly based on occupational basis.

Fa-Hein, a Chinese pilgrim who visited India during the reign of Chandragupta—Vikramaditya (405 A.D.—411 A.D.) has written on the status of the Shudra's, who were a degraded class, like slaves. People were poor but religious, he alwys opined.

Another Chinese traveller and Buddhist Scholar Hieun Tsang (630 A.D.—645 A.D.) who visited India in search of Buddhist scriptures and places of worship had provided an elaborate account of the social conditions of the people. All these acounts are authentic proof of social structure of that age.[10]

Shudras Crushed After Buddha's Nirvana

The Shudras who got an upper hand and sympathetic attitude during the emergence and rise of Buddhism for about 1000 years or so, again were deprived of their human rights, enjoyed by the so-called trivarnic society, the dominating communities. The social awakening and unity among Shudra was crushed. They were physically and mentally shackled in a manner that it was not possible for them to came out of the slavery and serfdom. They were disintegrated and divided in hundreds of castes and sub-castes on the basis of petty occupations one below the other that they could never dare to think of their social welfare and development. The so-called village republics were turned into open settlements of slavery. The degradation of Shudras and extraordinary powers of Brahmins appeared in full form in Puranic age.

This age painted an imaginary or mythological picture of society keeping the Shudras as servants and slaves.

Buddhism : A Rational Doctrine

Buddhism allowed all lower castes to join hands in performing religious celebrations, who were so far denied right to worship and knowledge. The great work of levelling and uniting the oppressed and sub-merged sections of society were fulfilled during the Buddhist era and the Brahmin tyranny was exposed and the myth of scriptures exploded. His teaching of non-violence, equality and social justice attracted a vast majority of people to follow his new faith. Shudras and untouchables welcomed his philosophy and doctrine in a big way.

Since long "the oppressed, expropriated and humiliated native people who got dehumanised as low castes were eagerly waiting to get liberty from the crushing bondage of divine slavery. They all sang the welcome songs of the institution and doctrine that brought forth the Kingdom of mental, spiritual and material liberty. Jumping they came out of the reign of terror through the prison holes of caste system to settle in a reign of peace and happiness in the free settlements of sanghas. From the reign of blinding darkness of orthodoxy, superstitions and magical performances of spirituality; from a domain of stagnant and vegetative religion of irrational belief they entered into the religion of rational doctrine."[11] It was thus a great social transformation in the lives of the untouchables. They got a voice of rebel in Buddha.

Nehru on Sramana Culture

In the words of Nehru "A great deal has been done by scholars and philosophers to trace the development of philosophic and metaphysical thought in India of the past; much has also been done to fix the chronology of historic events and draw in broad outline political maps of those periods. But not much has so far been done to investigate the social and economic conditions of those days, how people lived, carried on their work, what they produced and how, and the way trade functioned."[12]

"An earlier account, which definitely takes us back to the pre-Buddhist period in India, is continued in the collection of the Jataka tales. These Jatakas were given their present shape sometime after the Buddha."[13]

"The Jatakas deal with the period when the final amalgamation of the two principal races of India, the Dravidians and the Aryans, was taking place."[14]

Jatakas tells that the Brahmanic tradition was loosing ground in the society. Sramana culture enjoyed great respect. There are references of revolt against priestly class and unjust and tyrannical Kings, who were killed and subjected to torture by their rivals.

"The village assemblies enjoyed a measure of autonomy."[15] It was pre-dominantly an agricultural civilisation and the basic unit was the self-governing village.[16]

But Nehru perhaps is too an idealist, as the Indian village had been the worst human settlements where Shudras and untouchables were exploited in day today life and treated like slaves in the pre-independence day.

Buddha : A Social Rebel

We see much social awakening during Buddha's times. He was a great thinker and rebel. He was a tribal Kshatriya of Shakya clan, and married in Koliyas, and both belonged to the solar race. He denied the authority of the Vedas and founded his own sect and organisation (Sramana Sangha) of celibate monks and priests.[17]

"Buddha had the courage to attack popular religion, superstition, ceremonial and priestcraft, and all the vested interests that clung to them. He condemned also the metaphysical and theological outlook, miracles, revelations, and dealings with the supernatural. His appeal was to logic, reason, and experience; his emphasis was on ethics, and his methods was one of psychological analysis, a psychology without a soul. His whole approach comes like. The breath of the fresh wind from the mountains after the stale air of metaphysical speculation."[18]

Buddha opposed all forms of social injustice, including varna system and practice of untouchability. He loved humanity and encouraged universal brotherhood. Buddha not only opposed Vedic ritualism and animal sacrifices vigorously, but also condemned vehemently the priestly class for their orthodoxy; as he believed in the welfare of human beings. For him all men were equal irrespective of caste, colour and race. He said there is no difference in a true Brahmana and a Buddhist monk (Sramana). He initiated monks in his sangha from all varnas or castes. The caste has no meaning for him, but the merits of an individual.[19] Even Buddha is reported to have been proud of being born in as a Kshatriya. This clearly shows that Brahmanism lost its glory in him in due course of time.

As Nehru rightly says : "Buddha did not attack caste directly, yet in his own order he did not recognise it, and there is no doubt that his whole attitude and activity weakened the caste system. Probably caste was very fluid is his age and for some centuries later. It is obvious that a caste-ridden community could not indulge in foreign trade or other foreign adventures... It is interesting to observe this process of absorption which worked at both ends. New caste were formed at the bottom of the scale, and any successful invading element became transformed soon into Kshatriyas or the ruling class."[20] But according to Dr. Jatava, Buddha's order was against caste and an old beliegs.

When we peep into the pages of the history, we learn that nearly 2550 years ago Buddha emerged as a saviour of the Shudras who were oppressed and overlooked by the Brahmanical order. Buddha embraced the outcastes and submerged sections of the society, and initiated them into his Dhamma. He asked them to join him, and his Dhamma and Sangha (Buddham Sharnam Gachchami, Dhammam Sharnam Gachchami, Sangham Sharnam Gachchami).

In the words of Jagjivan Ram: In the 6th century B.C. Lord Buddha raised his powerful voice against the institution of caste and practice of untouchability. He was such a great noble man that he embraced the untouchable classes and initiated the womenfolk in his Sangha, as the right of knowledge was earlier denied to them.

In the history of Indian religions, Lord Buddha occupies an unique place. He was one of the great philosophers, teachers and seekers of truth of his age and even today the order which he founded throughout the world for ethical and social values, non-violence, love of humanity and universalism. His conception of religion was purely ethical. He did not bother about caste system when he initiated a person into the Buddhist Sangha. He gave instruction to his disciples: "Go into all lands, preach his gospel of humanity and non-violence. Tell them that the poor and the lowly, high and the rich, all are one and all castes unite in this religion as the rivers in the sea."

Buddhism not only awakened the socially degraded people but also enlightened the Brahmans who blindly followed the scriptures, believed in ritualism and orthodoxy. Buddhism in the long run became a uniting force and a symbol of revolt against all the oppressive features of the Hindu social order, and a champion of the suppressed and lowest sections of society."

"Buddha had done the utmost to remove the stigma of the ages on the Aryan society. He revolted against caste system and untouchability and promoted social justice, equality and purity in life."[21]

He purified the Brahmans and put them on right path, who were all ignorant in believed in superstitions and magical powers, and have forgotten the human values.

"Born as Kshatriyas in the Shakya clan and closely related to the Kohiyas, Buddha created stir in the Vedic society, the priestly class, as a crusader. He created awakening amongst the suppressed and the oppressed class. He unfurled the banner of social revolt against Hindu orthodoxy, sacrifices and social evils. He gave a severe blow to the Aryan caste system and dedicated himself for the course of the untouchables."[22] Other contemporary philosophers and thinkers were also against Vedic Valves and caste system.

For the first time in the social and religious history of India great teacher and reformer, "Buddha explained the evolution of society through dialectical method. He lived in a tribal society which was at the threshold of 'class' and 'class societies' of Kosala and Magadha. Buddha revolted against Vedanta (Upanishada) philosophy and rejected the authority of Vedas and their infallibility. He said the world has evolved but not created as it is not revealed. He said there must be a cause and effect. He thus used the dialectical methods to study the evolution of society."[23]

As stated earlier, Buddha as rebel and reformer believed in equality and social justice for him a true Brahman and a Buddhist monk were equal. Brahman means a learned scholarly person, not illiterate and superstitions person, born in priestly caste. He denied existence of God, soul and condemned scriptures.

"Buddhist ethics believed in the non-existence of permanent self (an-atta). It rejects the doctrine of retributive *karma,* in which personal rewards and punishments are meted out from birth to birth. It stresses that the consequence of *karma* are born from generation to generation in the entire world collectively. This aspect of Buddhist ethical doctrine, "wherein *karma* is reinstalled as a tremendous impersonal and cumulative moral force of the collectively, wherein the evil thought, word or deed of a single individual is calculated to disrupt the entire fabric of society, just as his good thought, word or deed relieves and uplifts generations of suffering mankind, is a strong protest to the pernicious, retributive theory of *karma.* Its stress on earnest and diligent striving for the disciplined life, on self-transcending love and charity, demolishing the boundaries of the transient ego, is the supreme challenge to the arid intellectualism, scepticism, individualism and social fatalism of the age.

Buddhism, on this basis, developed its own thought of democratic social relationship. The Buddhist view of society was set "against

Brahminism's picture of a divine social order established for all time, in which every individual had his immutable place. Practically, this view perpetuated the social, political and economic privileges of the dominant Hindu aristocracy. Buddha...upset the whole concept of caste by insisting that the distinctions were arbitrary and secular, not divinely ordained. repudiating the special claims of the Brahmins, he propounded an evolutionary conception of the world and society. The Buddha abandoned varnasrama dharma and asked people to enter a new society based on spiritual relationship, to participate in a spiritual fraternity, believing that "man is not fundamentally a material being driven by the instincts of production and reproduction."

The Buddha was the inaugurator of a "Social critique." "He was opposed to the political and social alienation of man that implied in the caste system and particularl) in the dominance of the Brahmins; in so far as he was positively opposed to the theistic beliefs of his time it was because he saw that they were a principal support of the Brahmanical system..."[24] His social critique embodied both a critical analysis of human condition and a way of changing it. It was concerned with the liberation of man from his unhappy condition, a condition that was socially conceived in varna system and individually in *dukkha,* existential suffering. It emphasised the need of doing away with the evil consequences of human ego and greed. The Buddhist social organisation was based on the respect and equality of all human beings—*karuna* and *maitri,* being the principal support to it. The Buddha instead upon the principle that "the measure of man must be worth, not birth."[25]

The theory of merit or worth for judging one's ability and knowledge and not birth or caste, was a great revolution in the field of social thought. Buddha emphasised that do not believe scriptures real truth, believe logic or reasoning for knowing the truth.

His views were very liberal. He opened the doors of his Dhamma (religion) and Sangha (religious order) for everybody irrespective of caste, colour, race or status. He embraced Shudras and admitted the socially condemned males and females is his Dhamma and showed them the right path, the path of salvation. He acquired a central position amongst teachers and reformers of his age and became immortal.

The physical, mental, economic and social exploitation of man by man was vehemently opposed by Buddha. He developed such a moral and religious culture which liquidated the desire for personal gain and worldly pleasures. He promoted equality and social consciousness, whereas in Brahmanical order social status was largely linked with each varna or caste.

Buddha was probably the first teacher who openly voiced against social injustice and untouchability which were the main themes of the Hindu social order. He discarded social gradation on the basis of caste.

Contemporary Religious Heads

According to Majjhim Nikaya, Chulsaropam Sutta, there were six religious—social heads operating in Maghadha region, who were all against Vedic ritualism, prior to Buddha's order. Buddha is asked: "O Sramana Gautama! Who are those six leaders called Sanghi, Gani, Ganacharya, Prasigddha, Yasaswai and Tirthankara revered by the Bahujanassa (masses). They were Purana Kashyap, Makkhali Gosala, Ajit Keshkambali, Pakudh Kachhayan, Sanjay Belathiputta and Nigantha Nataputta. ("Yeme Bho Gotama Samana Brahmana/Sanghino Ganino Ganacharita Trata/Yaja Saswino Tithukara Sadhu Sammata Bahujanassa Seyyttudang/Purana Kassapa Makkhaligosala, Ajita Keshkambala, Pakulho Kachhayana, Sanjayd Belatthputta, Nigantho Nattaputta")[26]

Buddha experienced the socio-religious, politico-cultural aggression from the much organised and advanced Brahmanism who stood as a guard to Vedic social order. Buddha strove to find out the path of liberty, and freedom from bondage, servitude, slavery and poverty. He discarded and condemned the divine theory of caste system and embraced untouchables and even hard criminals and prostitutes, slaves and exploited people in his Sangha. His religion and social thought of individual freedom, love, knowledge, as well as ideals of equality and fraternity attracted the attention of ruling class and the common masses. It was a beginning of a casteless, and classless society and, a Dalit renaissance, a non-violent peaceful movement of emancipation of millions of untouchables, Shudras and exploited class.[27]

Buddha attacked caste rigidities in his own way he first condemned the Vedic social ideology and organised the masses for a social revolt through his religious order. In Jatakas numerous castes have been mentioned. They were mostly occupational. In Jatakas the Brahman supremacy has been openly challenged, wherein they have been mentioned as physicians, beggars, magicious, fruit sellers and farmers. Some of them were tenderers of animals and used to sell their daughters.

The occupational castes were Karmar (farm labour), Kumbhkar (Potter), Tantuvai (weavers, Swarnakar (Goldsmith), Manikar and Rajaka. Slavery existed during Buddhist age. Every caste has its own Dasas. the Chandalas were the most exploited class, they were the lowest beings.[28]

According to Matanga Jataka,[29] the sixteen thousand Brahmins were ex-communicated because of eating abandoned foods of the Chandalas. Chandala lived outside the village. They generally used to burn dead bodies of other castes. His seeing was enough to pollute a man. Brahmanism hatred them and used to run-away from their air-touch. Pukkas, Nisada, Benu, Charmakar and Dusadhas were all degraded people.

The Buddhist period is an age of social transformation and a period of awakening. A period of struggle between master and the slaves. Though caste system could not be vanished altogether, but social awakening and religious order of Buddha changed the entire social structure.[30] As told earlier for Buddha caste had no meaning. He attached importance and emphasised on individuals merit, not his birth. His period is of new social and religious values based on equality and humanity.

Buddha was against all the oppressive features of the early Hindu society. He opposed all their barbaric activities against animals in the name of Yajnas. He symbolised the hopes and aspirations of the oppressed Shudras and untouchables.

Most of the Buddhists monks and Bhikkus were from the non-Brahmin communities. A large number of householders from Shakyas, joined his order. According to G.C. Pandey the Buddhist monks by becoming the members of Buddhist Sangha, "tried to rise above the bondage of physical drives and the egoistic limitations of family and property. By respecting the life and property of others, they signified that they were not anti-social. If they gave up the world of common social and economic relations, it was only for the fuller pursuit of Truth, which transcends the sphere of bodily appetites and egoism. They sought to transcend, not disrupt, social life. Indeed, having embraced secular society, they themselves entered a new society based on spiritual relations. They became true spiritual sons of the Teachers whom they followed and participated in a spiritual fraternity, believing that man is not fundamentally a material being driven by the instincts of production and reproduction.[31]

The gospel of Buddha was a significant factor in the process of social change without which the higher evolution, that took place in India's social thought, during the years which followed the decadence of Brahmanism, would not have been possible. New concepts of social relationship and ethical conduct arose, which inspired the Indian society to establish democratic, secular and fraternal relations among its people. It was a major change in social life that posterity could not ignore. "Buddhism was at one time the religion of the majority of the people of India. It continued to be the religion of the masses for hundreds of years.

It attacked Brahmanism on all sides as no religion had brought so much change before. Brahmanism was the wane if not on the wane, it was certainly on the defensive."

It is, for other reasons, however, that Buddhism could not consolidate its followers into a separate and distinct community of people. In fact, Buddhism, in its movement for change, awakened and strengthened the hitherto suppressed forces of social dynamism against the long continued forces of social determinism and theological fatalism. The struggle between these two forces, which was hidden, became more evident with the rise of heterodox systems, especially the Buddhist movement, which made it clear that the world was not a creation, but a process wherein the dynamic forces would never die, though their movement might be slow in the historical perspective.[32] Buddhism attracted all the ruling chiefs, affluent people and the suppressed people in his Dhamna. It stood firmly against age old caste system.

Jain Agamas on Caste

The Panhavagaranaim (Prasana-Vyakaranani) which is counted as the tenth Anga of the Svetambara Agama discusses the position of the professional (Shudra) communities like boar-killers, fish catchers, fowlers, hunters and the like. It also discusses the social position of several untouchables and criminal tribes which have been mentioned as cruel tribes, such as Sakas, Yavanas, Sabras, Barbaras, Kayas, Murundas, Udas, Bhadakas, Tittikas, Pakkanikas, Kulaksas, Gaudas, Simhalas Parasas, Kroncas, Andhras, Dravidas Bilvas, Pulindas, Acrosos, Dumbas, Pokkanas, Gandhaharakas, Valhikas, Jallas, Romas, Masas, Bakusas, Malavas, Cuncukas, Culikas, Kankanakas, Medas, Pahlavas, Mahuras, Abharika, Anakkas, Cinas, Lelinkas, Khasas, Hasikas Neharas, Maharastras, Arabas, Davilakas, Kuhanas, Vekayas, Hunas, Romakas, Roravas, Marukas and Ciratas (Kiratas).

According to the Jaina scholars the list of tribes and peoples of ancient India of Mahavira and Buddha period is a sufficient proof that Broken men who conquered non-Aryans and Dravidians existed in India in the post Christian age and were hated by the Brahmins. Some of the castes have lost their real identity, but still their origin can be traced easily amongst the untouchables, Shudras and the ex-criminal tribes who were the aboriginal and the natives.[33]

In Buddha and Mahavira's times they existed in one form or the other and in due course of time mixed up with other Dravidian and Aryan castes. These were certainly ancient non-Aryan races, and their socio-economic condition was not so good. They were hated and exploited by the people of the Aryan race. In Jaina literature the Shudras and lower classes, the forest dwellers and untouchables were identified as Demons, Nagas, Garudas and Supannas.

After the decline of the Buddhism, the Bhikkus and Buddhists were mercilessly tortured by the priestly class in several ways—social, economic, cultural and even political.

During the revival of Brahmanism, specially in the reign of Pushyamitra Shunga both Koliyas and Shakyas, the community of tribal Kshatriya's Buddha belonged, was subjected to torture and barbarous attacks. So much so that Koliyas and Shakyas who were related to each other, in due course of time lost their glory and identity and became Dalit Shudra caste.[34]

History tells that all the Kshatriyas rulers of Buddha and Mahavira period revolted against Brahmanic rituals and caste system and oppressing features. Prasenjit of Kosala was from a lower caste. He was not even well treated by the Shakyas and the Koliyas, who refused to give their daughter to him. It means casteism was practised in those days and kings of lower classes were disrespected. Under the influence of Buddha Prasenji neglected the Brahmins. Whose status was not more than beggars. In Buddha's Sangha all monks were equal, the followers of his order were socially of high status, whether they came from ordinary low classes. In this way Buddha tried to establish an egalitarian society, a classless and casteless new social order.

Buddha accepted a large number of Brahmins in his Sangha. Brahmins never expressed any sign of reaction and disrespect to him when he was alive. Only a few orthodox priests argued with him in vain. Buddha's learning, treatment and coolness satisfied them. No doubt, the Brahmins too came forward to follow this ideals. In fact he was not against any caste including Brahmins. He only opposed superstitions, blind following, inhuman behaviour to men and animals. Buddha extended support to the degraded humanity and freed them from the Brahmanic divine slavery in big way. He strongly condemned and criticised the *varna* system through his preachings and initiating the lower classes in his Dhamma and Sangha, he declared that his order was the only hope to save them from the tyranny of the Brahmanism and the vested interests in the name of Vedic Dharma. He maintained that every human being has liberty to know, to utter, to organise and argue freely, this helped him in the abolition of caste system, untouchability and bonded Buddhism opened new channels of equality in society, labour.

For one thousand years the oppressed and exploited *Shudras* were treated well in the society and their socio-economic position was sound. There was much political and cultural awakening in them. After *nirvana* (salvation) of Buddha, the Shakyas and Koliyas and few other Kshatriya tribes, were socially harassed and religiously tortured by the Brahmins under the leadership of Shungas, the Bahujan Masses became awakened and united became socio-economically weak in due canvas of time. The epic age destroyed truth and reality.

I

Evidently, the Buddha belongs in the company of the *shramanas,* the non-brahman teachers who were critical of the Brahmanical sacrificial system and who rejected the religious and social claims of the Brahmans. How the Buddha's teaching differed from the other non-Brahman schools of thought is considered later. Meanwhile, there are other questions to be answered. We have to enquire about the characteristic concerns of the Buddha, the nature of his public activity, what kind of people he met with and what his relations with them were, how he was regarded by others, and so on. In this way, as the pattern of the Buddha's life is examined, and some sort of a profile emerges, it may be possible to determine a little more closely how he is to be characterized: that is, as religious innovator, or reformer, or as philosopher, or what.

First, we have to note that for the earliest Buddhists it was the word of Buddha rather than the life of the Buddha which seems to have been of paramount importance. It was the discourses which were remembered, rehearsed at his death, and carefully preserved and transmitted in the community of his followers. His life-story was not in itself a matter of such intrinsic interest apparently, since the canon of scripture of the Theravadin school, which is representative of early or 'primitive' Buddhism (though not necessarily exclusively representative) contains no continuous narrative of his life. It was not until later in Buddhist history that full-length biographies of the Buddha were produced, such as the Sanskrit work of perhaps (at the earliest) the second century BC, entitled *The Great Event (Mahavastu)* or the more elaborate work, by the Sanskrit poet of the second century AD, Ashvaghosha, entitled *The Acts of the Buddha (Buddhacarita).* Because of this apparent pre-occupation of the earliest followers of the Buddha with his doctrines rather than his life, the idea has been suggested by some Buddhists that possibly the doctrine is all that matters. It is the doctrine, they urge, which has eternal validity; the disciples' concern is to accept it, apprehend it and practise it; the Buddha-figure is simply the personification of a spiritual principle. 'The existence of Gotama as an individual', writes Edward Conze, 'is, in any case a matter of little importance to Buddhist faith."[1] To some extent this attitude may have been provoked by the suggestions of Western scholars (at a time when it was fashionable to question the historical existence of any cult hero) that the Buddha who is described in even the earliest Buddhist literature is pure invention. H.H. Wilson, for instance, argued that the Buddha's life as it has come down in the traditions, is nothing more than an allegorical version of the Sankhya philosophy; others, such as E. Senart and H. Kern, suggested that the Buddha was a solar symbol and the story of his life a solar myth.[2] The Indian scholar, T.R.V. Murti, while not denying the historical existence of Gotama, regards it as unimportant for the Mahayana form of Buddhist religion—that is, the form which he regards as the most fully developed and most adequate as a religion. "The Mahayana religion escapes the predicament of having to depend on any particular historical person as the founder."[3]

Wave of Scepticism

It is worth noting, in passing, that the late-nineteenth-century wave of scepticism about the historicity of the Buddha has now receded. As Andre Bareau has said, nowadays, as a result of greater knowledge of the philological and archaeological sources, scientific study admits that in the case of the Buddha there really existed an historical personage the principal traits of whose life and personality can be known.[4] It is important to notice, too, that while the Buddha's earliest disciples seem to have had no interest in recounting the entire life of the Buddha *seriatim,* they were nevertheless concerned to record carefully what they appear to have considered the most important events, events relating to certain crucial or significant moments in the pattern of the Buddha's life, such as his renunciation of the life of a prince, his enlightenment, the inauguration of his public activity as a teacher, and his decease.

These four events provide a convenient framework within which to examine the personality and role of the Buddha; they indicate four historically important aspects of the Buddha's relation to the life of his time: (i) his particular social and cultural milieu; (2) the experience of spiritual unrest, and subsequent enlightenment which he underwent; (3) the nature of his public activity; and (4) the significance of the ceremonies connected with his decease. The man who was to become known as the Buddha (and who until his enlightenment at Bodh-Gaya is properly known as the *Bodhisattva,* or one who has the essence of Buddhahood, or enlightenment) was, says the tradition, the son of Suddhodana, the leading citizen of Kapilavastu. This was a busy town on the north-west to south-cast trade route which ran along the foot of the Himalayan mountains, amid the thick forests at the extreme northern edge of the Gangetic plain. It lay due north of Banaras, and a few miles within the border of what is now Nepal. The town was the capital of the Shakyas, a people who had, as we have seen, an aristocratic republican form of government. Their territory probably extended about fifty miles from east to west, and about thirty or forty from north to south, from the foot of the Himalayas. Apart from Kapilavastu, the capital, the region contained a number of market towns. The Buddha-to-be belonged to the clan of the Gotamas, and it is by this name that he is often known, as if it were a surname. His given, or personal name was Siddhartha. Later Buddhist literature magnifies the position of his father to that of a very great king and depicts the life-style of the young prince as one of extreme grandeur, luxury and wealth. It is more probable that his father was the elected head of an aristocratic hereditary ruling class, having some of the rank, status and prestige of the ruler of a small kingdom, but nothing more. As might be expected, the Buddhist sources provide a certain amount of information about the Shakyas, although it is mostly of the kind that has to be pieced together from scattered references. With regard to the ancestry of the Shakyas, for example, there is an interesting allusion to the progenitors of their tribe having had their dwelling 'on the slopes of the Himalayas'. In the present form of the story, as it is told in the Pali canon, although it is explained that these progenitors *went* to the Himalayas when they were banished from the court of their father, a legendary Indian raja of ancient times, named Okkaka, the explanation could well be a device to account for the fact that the ancestors of what was now a north Indian tribe had at an earlier period lived in the Himalayas, if this were a strongly established tradition among them. It would, in fact, be more in accordance with the natural course of migration for a Himalayan tribe to have moved southwards towards the sun and the plains than vice versa, for, in general, this has been the predominant direction in which migration of peoples occurred throughout North India and continental South-East Asia. The *Ambattha Sutta,* in which the story occurs, suggests that the Shakyas were a non-Brahman tribe. The Brahman Ambattha, in conversation with the Buddha, referring to the division of society into those who were brahmans and those who were not, reminded the Buddha that it was the duty of the latter to serve the former, and to honour them. The Shakyas, he complained, appeared to be lacking in this sense of respect for

Brahmans. 'Once, Gotama, I had to go to Kapilavastu on some business or other . . . and went into the Shakya's Congress Hall *(Santhagara-sala). Now* at that time there were a number of Shakyas, old and young, seated in the hall on grand seats, making merry and joking together, nudging one another with their fingers; and for a truth, methinks, it was I myself that was the subject of their jokes; and not one of them even offered me a seat. That, Gotama, is neither fitting, nor is it seemly, that the Shakyas, menials as they are, mere menials, should neither venerate, nor value, nor esteem, nor give gifts to, nor pay honour to Brahmans."

Status of Brahmans

Such lack of respect for Brahmans which is attributed to the Shakyas in this tale may possibly reflect the attitude of the developed Buddhist community towards the Brahmans. It is also possible that this was known by the Buddhists to have been the attitude of the Shakya people. If the Shakyas were Himalayan hill people who had migrated to the edge of the plains, it is likely that they would have been of a sturdy independent spirit, and well disposed to reject the social pretensions of the Aryan Brahman class. That they were of such a spirit is suggested by one or two other casual references. Their sturdy spirit is shown too in their relations with the neighbouring great monarchy of Koshala (see Chapter 3, pp. 45 f.). The king of Koshala, Pasenadi, a great admirer of the Buddha, and benefactor of the Buddhist Order, wished to strengthen his relationship with the Shakyas. He sent to the Shakyan elders a polite request that he might be allowed to marry one of their daughters. They, however, considered that such a marriage would be degrading to them; it would, they said, destroy the purity of their race and be contrary to their tradition. But they could not afford to risk the anger of this very powerful neighbouring king, so they sent him the illegitimate daughter of one of the chiefs, born of a slave-woman, passing her off as pure Shakyan. The attitude of the Shakyans is referred to in the course of the story, (the *Bhadda-Salu Jataka)* in the words of king Pasenadi's messengers: "These Shakyas are desperately proud, in matters of birth!" Another interesting fact about the Shakyas is that they were fond of sports, and especially archery. They had an established school of archery, run by a family who specialized in this sport. It is said, too, that the Buddha, as a young man, had to prove his prowess as an archer before any Shakyan nobleman would consider him as a future son-in-law. While Kapilavastu, the capital of the Shakyan republic, was not one of the recognized six great cities *(mahanagara)* of the time, it was certainly a place of importance and some affluence. It is described as a city where there were crowds of people and plenty of food, a place whose streets were full of traffic, in the form of elephants, horses, chariots, carts and pedestrians, and where, with their hubbub and jingle and clatter, was mingled the sound of street musicians, singers and traders. The general pattern of Indian cities of this period has already been described (see Chapter 3, pp. 45 f.), and Kapilavastu would, no doubt have conformed generally to this pattern. The Buddhist sources mention the council hall, the *Santhagara-sala,* which stood at the centre of the town, and where public business, administrative and judicial, was carried out. Mention is made, too, of the massive ramparts surrounding the city, said to have been eighteen cubits high. It was as the leading citizen of such a city, and as one who carried the responsibility for presiding over the affairs of the small state of which Kapilavastu was the capital, that we have to see the father of the Bodhisattva. It is appropriate to think, not so much in terms of the idle ostentation of the court of some great oriental emperor, as of the material comfort and wellbeing of a cultured upper-class townsman in a prosperous commercial and administrative centre: of urbanity and sophistication, rather than of luxurious imperial grandeur.

The background of the Buddha's youth and early manhood is represented, therefore, as having been one of urban life, comfortable and easy by the standards of the time, and made more so by the privileges that went with superior social class; Shakyan society was certainly not classless, as the story of king Pasenadi's bride makes clear. The fact that the Shakyan state was not a monarchy may be significant in connection with the problem which was raised in Chapter 4, namely, which came first—individualism, monarchy, or urbanism? Gotama's milieu, to the time of his manhood, was that of urban life, but it did not include experience of a developed monarchical society. The problem which he seems to have felt most keenly and which set him on his spiritual quest, was that of the suffering of *the individual.* This suggests that it was primarily urban life which precipitated individualism, rather than monarchy, or, at any rate, that this is how it was understood by the early Buddhist community. Moreover, it was a concern with the pain and the unsatisfactoriness of ordinary, common mortal existence which stirred Gotama; this can be seen as both a consequence of his upbringing and a determining factor in the shape of the solution which lie discovered for the ills of human existence. For the milieu in which he probably grew up is that of a traditional ruling class, one occupied with the practical aspects of public life, with the smooth functioning of the machinery of society and perhaps at least some general concern with, and feeling of responsibility for, human welfare.

It is meaningless to say, as some have done[3] that the Buddha, a child of his time, was heir to the Hindu religious tradition. In the first place, it is an anachronism to ascribe a Hindu religious tradition to this early period; the characteristic set of beliefs and practices which came to be known as 'Hindu' (the word itself being a product of the Muslim period) was yet to be developed. Moreover, it is difficult to see how the Buddha can be described as an heir to the Brahman religious tradition. One who did not believe in God, nor in theories of creation, and who did not accept the authority of the Veda, was about as much an heir to the Hindu tradition as Karl Marx was a Zionist.

It has been suggested that if Gotama was indebted to any earlier figure in the cultural history of India, the most likely candidate is Kapila, to whom is attributed the atheistic Sankhya doctrine. It is very likely, writes R.C. Majumdar, that Gotama, since he came from Kapilavasta, 'had some knowledge of the Sankhya doctrine'.

Teaching of Buddha

The affinity between the teaching of the Buddha and the Sankhya philosophy was hinted at by Ashvaghosha (the Buddhist writer mentioned on page 87) in his full-length biography of the Buddha, the *Buddhacarita.* Those who hold the view that the Buddha was influenced by Sankhya attitudes point to the fact that one of the teachers to whom he resorted in the course of his wanderings, before his own 'awakenment' at Bodh-Gaya, was Alara (or Arada) Kalama. Alara's philosophy seems to have borne some slight resemblance to the Sankhya system, although there seem also to have been significant differences. The fact that Gotama stayed only a short while with Alara and then left him, because he was not satisfied with his teaching, could mean that Gotama found Alara either insufficiently Sankhyan in his views, or too much so. A modern Indian writer takes the view that it would be a serious error to overlook the major similarity between the Sankhya system and Buddhism—the atheistic position which—is common to them: "since the Sankhya was undoubtedly much older than the rise of Buddhism, we are left with the strong presumption that at least for his atheism the Buddha was directly indebted to the Sankhya, though he evidently differed much from Kapila in his main interest." But this is to assume that Gotama was incapable by himself of arriving at an atheistic view, or adopting an atheistic premise as his starting-point. The likelihood that Gotama, living in Kapilavastu, might have been familiar with the Sankhya view, has to be taken in conjunction with the suggestion of Dandekar that the origin of the Sankhya is to be found in a 'pre-Vedic, non-Aryan thought complex'. So it is an open possibility that Gotama's atheism also had its origin in the pre-Vedic, non-Aryan, non-Brahmanical culture of north-eastern India in general, and of the Shakya people in particular.

The notion that Gotama was a 'religious' man evidently needs careful scrutiny. That he has come to be so regarded may be partly because of the assimilation of Buddhism with theistic systems of belief and practice as a 'religion', and partly because of the ill-founded idea that the inhabitants of India are, and always have been, more religiously inclined than the peoples of the West. In this way the Buddha has been subsumed under the general category of religious teachers or leaders. The Buddha's teaching, and the life of the early Buddhists is often regarded as an answer to personal spiritual *malaise,* a doctrine of personal salvation. The possibility which is being raised here is that it was something other than this. It has to be admitted, however, that the story of Gotama's enlightenment does, on the face of it, look very like a personal salvation story of a purely religious kind. But this may be because the modern understanding of 'religion' is being projected back into the time of the Buddha and made the criterion of his experience. We need to enquire what is said in the tradition of early Buddhism about the whole complex of events leading to the enlightenment at Bodh-Gaya.

Gautama's Enlightenment

According to tradition, Gotama was twenty-nine years of age when the decisive events occurred which led to his enlightenment. Various accounts are available, and they differ considerably, especially with regard to the circumstances of the renunciation. According to the later, more elaborate accounts, written in Sanskrit, the Bodhisattva, while he was out driving his chariot, was confronted successively by a very old man, then by a very sick man, and finally by a corpse being carried out to the burning *ghat.* These sights disturbed him profoundly, for they raised questions which he had apparently not considered before. Finally, the sight of a holy man stirred in him the desire to live the ascetic life and strive for spiritual enlightenment.

On the other hand, an early Pali text gives an account which suggests that it was as a result of long reflection upon the human condition that Gotama decided to devote himself to a disciplined quest for spiritual satisfaction. In this account of the matter, Buddha, some years after the event, makes known to his followers the two possible ends to which men may devote their lives, in terms of his own earlier experience. He identifies these two ends as the noble or holy quest *(ariya-pariyesana)* and the ignoble or unholy quest. Briefly, the human situation is seen as one in which, because of belief in self (*atta* or *atman*), men are vulnerable to the process of ageing, decay and dying, and hence to sorrow. The word translated as sorrow *(dukkha) in* fact carries a much deeper and stronger connotation than the English word, and implies a sense of the utter unsatisfactoriness, weariness and pain of mortal existence. The ignoble quest, to which many devote their lives, consists in seeking after things which are liable to ageing, decay and death, the very conditions from which deliverance is needed.

'And what, monks, is the noble quest? That someone, being liable to birth because of self, and knowing the peril in whatever is liable to birth, seeks the unborn, the uttermost security from bonds—*nibbana.' The* same formula is then repeated for each of the other conditions of mortal existence. The noble quest is that in which someone, who because of self is vulnerable to ageing, decaying, dying, stain and sorrow, and who knows the peril in whatever is liable to the same things, seeks the unageing, the undecaying, the undying, the stainless, the unsorrowing—that which is itself freedom from all constraints: *nibbana.* The Buddha then goes on to say that when he was still the Bodhisattva, it was considerations such as these which stirred him, and made him ask 'Why do I seek what is liable to birth . . . to ageing . . . to decay . . . to death . . . to stain ... to sorrow? Being myself liable to birth, to ageing, to decay, to death, to stain, to sorrow, I should seek the unborn, the unageing, the undecaying, the undying, the stainless, the unsorrowing.'

It is understandable, as E.J. Thomas pointed out, that this kind of account of personal experience and reflection should have been developed into the story of encounters with an old man, a sick man, and a corpse; it is less understandable, on the other hand, how, if these encounters had been real events the story subsequently 'have been converted into this abstract form'. On the day on which he saw these three manifestations of the human condition, so the tradition asserts, another event took place—the birth of Bodhisattva's son. On hearing the news, he pronounced his son's name, 'Rahula'. The commentators suggest the presence of a purn; the word 'rahula' means, they say, 'a bond', and so the Bodhisattva's utterance had a double meaning: 'Rahula is born. A bond is born.' Thus, it is very interesting to notice that of the six conditions of human existence mentioned in the Buddha's discourse—birth, ageing, decay, dying, stain and sorrow—four illustrative examples have been found in what are represented as the events surrounding the great renunciation. Finally, there is the further curious incident concerning a Shakya maiden named Kisagotami. It is said that from her balcony she saw Gotama returning home in his chariot after the news of his son's birth had been announced to him. She saw Gotama's 'beauty and glory' and 'she was filled with joy and delight', and began to sing: 'Happy is the mother, happy is the father, happy is the wife who has such a husband!' The word which she used for 'happy' *(nibbuta)* meant also 'cool' or 'healthy'. The Bodhisattva, upon hearing her song took the word to mean 'cool', and, says the tradition, 'with aversion in his heart for lusts, he thought, "When the fire of passion is cooled, the heart is happy; when the fire of illusion, pride, false views and all the lusts and pains are extinguished it is happy".' In gratitude for the lesson she had taught him, the story continues, he sent the maiden a very costly pearl necklace. 'She thought that prince Siddhattha (Gotama) was in love with her, and had sent her a present, and she was filled with delight.' But a few hours later, in the quietness of the night, awakening to the sight of the dancers who had been entertaining him, and were now asleep in all kinds of disgusting and unseemly postures, he renounced the life of sensual pleasures, and took the crucial step of leaving his home, to set out on the life of the homeless wanderer, in search of spiritual peace.

Perhaps both the abstract analysis of the human situation, and the picturesque account, with its various personal illustrations, of the kind of 'fetters' or constraints from which Gotama felt he had to escape, indicate in their contrasting ways the nature of his quest. The abstract version emphasizes that it is 'the self', the *atman,* which is the ultimate root of the human experience of sorrow. It is because of the idea of 'self' that men are vulnerable to birth, ageing, decay, death, stain, and sorrow; it is this notion of 'self' which causes men to experience life as sorrowful. The stories of Gotama's encounters with old age, disease, death, birth and the taint of passion may have been the kind of characteristic experiences which brought a young man to see that it is the unending search for the satisfaction of the desires of the individual which leads to spiritual disenchantment. It was from this condition, from these constraints, that he sought some way of deliverance.

We return, therefore, to the point which was made earlier, that it was the ultimate unsatisfactoriness, the sorrowfulness of life, which set Gotama on his spiritual quest. How this quest was fulfilled, what was the nature of the 'salvation' which he found, we shall consider in detail in the next chapter. What we now have to take account of is the typical environment, the locale for his public activity after the enlightenment, after the great discovery had been made.

If we are correct in thinking that the problems of human life with which the Buddha was primarily concerned were the kind of problems which arise with the development of individualism, and if this was a feature which was more characteristic of urban than of rural life, then it is reasonable to expect that those in greatest need of his teaching, of his prescription for freedom and peace, would be found in the urban centres rather than in the countryside. It was, in fact, precisely there, in the cities, that most of the Buddha's public activity took place.

The Bodh-Gaya

The profound experience he underwent at Bodh-Gaya was his awakening to the truth; it was itself an end of all the constraints of which he had previously been aware, and it was therefore described as *vimutti,* release, or *nibbana,* the state of 'coolness' or 'health after fever'. The tradition represents him as at first uncertain whether this truth which he had apprehended could ever be conveyed to other men. 'This *dhamma,* attained to by me is deep, difficult to see, difficult to understand, tranquil, excellent, beyond dialectic, subtle, intelligible to the learned. But this is a creation delighting in sensual pleasure, rejoicing in sensual pleasure ... [and for them] this were a matter difficult to see. . .' The Buddha recalls that, as he was pondering and deciding against the attempt to communicate his discovery of truth to the generality of men, it occurred to the god Brahma that the world would be lost, would be destroyed, if the Buddha now refrained from teaching his doctrines *(dhamma).* He thereupon manifested himself to the Buddha in the way we have already seen. The intention of this story may have been to show that even the gods were dependent on the eternal *dhamma* which the Buddha had perceived, and were therefore subordinate both to the *dhamma* and to him who was its bearer. The story has the effect, too, of showing that the relationship between the Buddha and the gods of popular belief was one of tolerant co-existence.

Now that he was persuaded that he should attempt to communicate the truth to others, the Buddha began to consider how this might most effectively be done. It is significant that the place he then made for was Varanasi, or Banaras, which, as we have seen, was at that time the intellectual and philosophical metropolis of northern India . To some extent, this significant fact is concealed by the ostensible reason given for his choice of Banaras—that he knew that he would meet there a group of five men whom he had known earlier, when he and they had been seeking spiritual satisfaction. It was to them that he now hoped to make known the truth. What has to be noticed is that their spiritual quest had led them to Banaras: it is almost as though, in ancient India, it was the case that all religious and philosophical seekers must at some time or other find their way to that ancient and holy centre of worship and philosophy. There, in a park a little way outside the city, he found them; and there he expounded to them in systematic, developed order, the *dhamma,* the truth by which release from the problems and constraints of mortal existence might bc gained.

The account of this exposition is the famous *Dhamma-cakka-ppavattana Sutta*—the discourse (or *Sutta*) concerning the putting into motion of the wheel of *dhamma.* The Buddha remained with the five at Banaras and, a few days later, after another session of teaching, the five achieved the state of wisdom, dispassion, and release from all the bonds of empirical mortal existence, a state known technically in Buddhism as *arahant*-ship, a term which will be explained later. It is appropriate to call the occasion 'a session of teaching', for this is the nearest, in the writer's view, that one can get to a satisfactory description of the method used by the Buddha. To say that he preached a sermon (although this terminology has been used by Western writers to describe the Buddha's activity) would be rather misleading, for, to Western ears at least, it suggests a wholly passive role for the hearers, and for the preacher a position which is sometimes described as 'six feet above contradiction'. This was not so in the kind of teaching-sessions which are recorded in early Buddhist literature. The hearers frequently interject, or raise questions, or supply answers to questions addressed to them by the Buddha, and sometimes the Buddha engages them in what is almost a catechism. Even 'discourses' suggests something rather stilted, formal, and humourless, and it is clear that they were far from being addresses of that sort. It was, in fact, almost always a session of teaching, with the Buddha suiting his words to the occasion, and taking advantage of incidents happening at the time, adapting himself to the mood or condition of the hearers and allowing them to take a good deal of the initiative. In some ways these sessions might suggest, as the closest parallel, an academic seminar or tutorial, but the resemblance is only partial. On occasions the Buddha was addressing very large numbers of people, and apart from the fact that one is unlikely to meet tutors of his quality, there seems, in addition, to have been something of what today would be called a 'charismatic' quality about his teaching.

At Banaras

At Banaras Buddha stayed throughout the rainy season which then followed: that is to say, for about four months. His teaching won further adherents. The first was Yasa, a young man who, according to the Pali sources, came to Buddha by night, feeling distress and disgust at the sordid sight presented by his own attendants who were asleep in unseemly postures. This disgust at the physically sordid aspects of human life was only the occasion for his flight from home; other, earlier experiences had conditioned him for it. He is represented as having been, like Gotama, one who had enjoyed a comfortable life; his father was one of the most wealthy financiers of Banaras. The Buddha, seeing his distressed state, called him and said 'Come, Yasa, here you will find neither distress nor danger.' There followed a session of teaching, as with the five, and at the end of it Yasa, too, apprehended the truth which the Buddha had been expounding and achieved the state of release, or *arahant*-ship. His father, alarmed by his absence, had followed the marks of Yasa's slippers, and now he, too, arrived on the scene. Not seeing Yasa at first, but only Buddha, the father engaged him in conversation. After a time the father also came under the power of the Buddha's words, and there and then declared himself a follower. He is remembered in Buddhist tradition as the first lay-follower, or *upasaka.* The next day Yasa's mother and another woman became the first female lay-followers, when the Buddha, in response to an invitation from Yasa's father, visited the family at home and had a meal with them. Four of Yasa's companions, sons of leading families in Banaras, also became disciples of the Buddha. These, with the five former associates of the Buddha who had been the first to receive his teaching, now constituted the nucleus of what was to become the *Sangha,* or assembly of disciples, sometimes called the Buddhist Order. Later, fifty more citizens of Banaras, who had heard the Buddha's teaching, became *arahants* and entered the Order. So there came into being at Banaras a community of disciples of some size. Its members, having understood the doctrine taught by the Buddha, were sent out in different directions to teach the *dhamma* to others. The result is represented as having been a great number of further candidates who were, from this time onwards, ordained into the Order by the monks, rather than by Buddha himself.

At the end of the rainy season the Buddha set out from Banaras eastwards, towards another of the six great cities of the time, Rajagriha, the Magadhan capital. On the way he visited the site of his enlightenment, staying there for a while and making converts to his doctrine. At Rajagriha more converts were made, including Sariputta and Moggallana, who later became, with Ananda, the most prominent members of the Order. The then king of Magadha, Bimbisara, became interested in the Buddha's teaching; he, too, was convinced of its value, and became a lay-follower.

No consecutive narrative of the public activity of the Buddha was constructed by the early Buddhists, but from the account of the travels and teaching which is contained in the Pali canon, it is possible to suggest, as Malalasekere has done, an outline for at least the first twenty years. Then comes a period of a further twenty-five years when it is impossible to trace any consecutive chronology, until the last few weeks of the Buddha's life, when there is the very detailed account of the last journey in the *Maha Parinibbana Sutta,* the *Sutta* concerning the great event of the entry by the Buddha into complete nirvana *(pari-nibbana).*

What is significant, however, from the evidence contained in the vast collection of discourses of the Buddha in the Pali canon, is the large proportion of these which were delivered in two major cities, Rajagriha and Shravasti. In almost all cases the discourse is introduced by a short note, indicating the place where it was delivered, and the occasion. From the evidence of these contextual notes it is possible to see that the Buddha lived more in the city of Shravasti than anywhere else. Until the later part of his life, when it lost its pride of place to Rajagriha, Shravasti, the capital of Koshala, was the most important city of the Gangetic plain, commercially and politically. The Buddha first went there at the invitation of a rich merchant named Anathapindika, whom he met at Rajagriha on the visit which has just been described. Anathapindika was visiting Rajagriha on business, and like so many others in the city, came to hear of the new doctrine which was being taught by the Shakyas age. He, too, was converted and became a lay-follower. He invited the Buddha to spend the next rainy season at Shravasti, and when the invitation was accepted, he set off back to the Koshalan capital. Having arrived, he bought a piece of land on the outskirts of the city, at considerable cost, and had a suitable *vihara,* or retreat-house, built in readiness for occupation by the Buddha and his company.

From the time when the Buddha and his companions first went to live in Shravasti it became virtually their headquarters. Twenty-five rainy seasons were spent there by the Buddha; the remaining twenty were spent in various other towns and cities, mainly Rajagriha. Of the discourses of the Buddha which go to make up the *Sutta-Pitaka,* 871 are said to have been delivered in Shravasti. Of 498 canonical *Jataka* stories, the telling of which is attributed to the Buddha, 416 are said to have been told in Shravasti.

Kapilvastu

Kapilavastu, the Buddha's home city, was visited by him more than once in the course of the years. On the first visit, in the year of his enlightenment, Gotama's little son, Rahula, was ordained as a novice. Thirteen years later, when he had come of age, Rahula was given *upasampada,* or higher ordination, this time in the city of Shravasti.

Rajagriha, the other major city with which the Buddha's work was most closely associated, was the capital of the Magadhan kingdom, which was increasing in power and prestige throughout the Buddha's lifetime. The expansion of the city beyond its old bounds during this period was a sign of its increasing population. Its king, Bimbisara, remained a firm friend and supporter of the Buddha throughout his life. He entertained Buddha and his companions and presented them with a place of residence. Even during the years when Shravasti was mainly his headquarters, Buddha seems to have paid frequent visits to Rajagriha. Many important discourses are connected with the Magadhan capital, and it was from here that Buddha set out on his last journey. By that time there were in Rajagriha eighteen large monasteries for members of the Buddhist Order. This concentration of Buddhist houses in a large capital city shows the kind of milieu in which early Buddhism flourished and was most at home.

The Buddha's Last Journey

The Buddha's last journey is described in some detail in one of the longest of the Pali texts, the *Sutta of the Great Decease (Maha Parinibbana Sutta).* The events which are related cover a period of some months, and the narrative has many facets, each having its special value to this or that reader or hearer. What is unmistakable is the portrait of the Buddha which emerges: the portrait of the discoverer, initiator and exponent of a social, psychological and political philosophy, who takes his place among the great leaders and rulers of the world (a *Chakravartin,* or *world-ruler).*

The narrative of the *Sutta* begins in the city of Rajagriha. Bimbisara, the Buddha's helper and admirer, is no longer king of Magadha; he has been succeeded by his son, Ajatashatru. We are told that he was about to launch an attack on one of the remaining republican federations, the Vajjians, whose territory was to the north of Magadha, across the Ganges. He is represented, rather curiously, as sending a messenger to the Buddha, who at that time was in Rajagriha, to ask his advice on the matter. 'Tell him', the king instructs his Brahman messenger, 'that Ajatashatru, the king of Magadha . . . has resolved, "I will strike at these Vajjians, mighty and powerful though they be, I will root out these Vajjians, I will destroy these Vajjians, I will bring these Vajjians to utter ruin!" The messenger is instructed to listen carefully to what the Buddha has to say by way of comment, and to come and repeat it to the king. The Buddha's comment turns out to be rather cryptic. He declares that so long as the Vajjians continue to observe their traditions properly, and to meet regularly in their republican assembly, seeking agreement in all matters, so long as they honour their elders, and maintain their customary rites and ceremonies as a republic, no harm can come to them; their prosperity is assured. The Brahman messenger takes the meaning of the prediction to be that the Vajjians cannot be overcome in battle; they will be overcome only by diplomacy and internal dissension. Having drawn this conclusion, he hurries back to his royal master.

Buddha then repeats to his companions word for word what he had said concerning the Vajjians, but applying his prediction, now, to the Buddhist *Sangha.* So long as the *Sangha* members continue to observe their traditions properly, and to meet regularly in their assembly, seeking agreement in all matters, and so on, no harm can come to the *Sangha:* it can only prosper. The crucial fact in the interpretation of this utterance of the Buddha is that the Vajjians were destroyed very shortly after this incident. According to tradition, spies and infiltrators succeeded in sowing the seeds of suspicion among the leaders and elders of the ruling assembly, and soon there was a rich crop of dissension and internal conflict which Ajatashatru was able to turn to his advantage. The Vajjian republic was conquered, and absorbed into the Magadhan monarchy. So, by the time this prediction of Buddha was being repeated and transmitted in the oral tradition of the monks, it was known that, as a fact of history, the Vajjians had *not* succeeded in meeting the conditions required for their survival. It would have been clear to the monks who passed on these words of Buddha that there must be some other, more permanent value in this utterance than simply an oblique prediction of the ruin of a people who were now only of historical interest. The point of the discourse lay in the application to the Buddhist *Sanghas* of the same conditions for survival. The old republican *sangha.*or assemblies had now almost all disappeared, victims of historical circumstances in the form of expanding monarchical power. If that were a matter for regret, it had to be remembered that the *sangha* tradition was nevertheless being perpetuated and preserved in a new form—in the life of the Buddhist community, the new *Sangha;* we shall take up this point again later, when we come to examine the life of the *Sangha* (Chapter 8). Meanwhile, what emerges from this opening section of the *Sutta of the Great Decease is* the evident and real interest of Buddha in forms of social and political structure.

Soon after the incident concerning the Vajjians, according to the narrative, Buddha and his companions left Rajagriha and began travelling northwards. They reached the southern shore of Ganges at a place which at that time was called Pataligama, but which a century or so later was to be known as Pataliputra, when it became the new capital city of the expanding kingdom of Magadha; today it is Patna, the chief city of Bihar State. At this place Buddha talked through the night with some local people who had assembled specially at the rest-house for travellers, where the Buddha was staying. These were lay-followers, who, while acknowledging the outstanding value of Buddha's teaching, still continued their household life. In Buddha's view, they too had an important place in the scheme of things, and it was for this reason that he undertook to instruct them in detail in the matters of social morality, pointing out to them the various advantages of moral uprightness and integrity. The morning after he had spoken with these householders, the Buddha observed that some ministers of the Magadhan state were supervising the construction of a new fortress at Pataligama. He then, it is said, uttered a prediction concerning this new stronghold. 'As far, Ananda, as Aryan people resort, as far as merchants travel, this will become the chief city, Pataliputra, a centre for the interchange of all kinds of wares. But three dangers will hang over Pataliputra, that of fire, that of water and that of dissension among friends.' The event referred to, the transfer of the royal capital of Magadha to Pataliputra, took place probably during the reign of Ajatashatru's son; the significance of the reference for our present purpose lies—in the fact that Buddha is represented as being keenly interested in a matter of this sort—the founding and growth of what was to become a great city.

After crossing the Ganges, and passing through two smaller towns, the Buddha and his companions came to the city of Vaishali, the capital of the Licchavi republic. Here Buddha accepted the invitation of Ambapali, the chief courtesan of the city, to take a meal at her house after she had heard him teaching and been gladdened by his words. The chief citizens of Licchavi, hearing of the acceptance from Ambapali herself, asked her to be so good as to give way in deference to them, so that they might entertain the Buddha. But although they offered her a large sum of money, on this occasion her favour was not to be bought. 'My lords', she replied 'were you to offer all Vaishali with its subject territory, I would not give up so honourable a feast!'

At Vaishali

Buddha remained in Vaishali for some time. It was a place which he had visited several times before in his travels, and for which he seems to have had a special liking. It contained a number of splendid shrines dedicated to popular local deities, and Buddha particularly enjoyed their beauty. 'How delightful a spot, Ananda, is Vaishali. How charming the

Udena Shrine, and the Gotamaka Shrine, and the Shrine of the Seven Mangoes, and the Shrine of Many Sons, and the Sarandada Shrine, and the Chapala Shrine.' The Sutta tells that after this visit, when the time came for him to leave the city, knowing that it would be the last time he would see Vaishali before he died, the Buddha turned and took a long, full look at the city, and then continued on his journey.

The place in which his entry into final *nibbana* occurred was a small insignificant village called Kushinara. A little while before, it had become clear to the Buddha's companions that the end of his mortal existence was now very near; not only was he eighty years of age, but he had become physically very weak. They had asked what ceremonies would be appropriate after his death, and had been instructed that the remains of a Tathagata, or Buddha, should be treated in the same way as it was customary to treat the remains of a *Chakravartin*, a universal emperor. They were to be wrapped in cloth, and soaked in oil, placed on a funeral pyre made of all kinds of fragrant wood, and burned; the relics were then to be enshrined in a great memorial cairn, or stupa, built at the centre of a crossroads. This was how the funeral rites of a *Chakravartin* were carried out; the memorial cairn would be built at some important crossing of routes, in a major city.

Buddha's Weakened Condition

The Buddha's companions were surprised when they realized, from their master's severely weakened condition, that it was in Kushinara that his life was to end. Ananda expressed their feeling: 'Let not the Exalted One die in this little wattle-and-daub town, in this town in the midst of the jungle, in this branch township. For, lord, there are other great cities, such as Champa, Rajagriha, Shravasti, Shaketa, Kaushambi and Banaras. Let the Exalted One die in one of them. There are many wealthy nobles and heads of houses, believers in the Tathagata, who will pay due honour to the remains of the Tathagata.'

Perhaps Ananda really did feel such dismay at the prospect of the Buddha's life ending in Kushinara and of the cremation of his remains having to be carried out in so remote a spot. Perhaps Buddhists of a later age were embarrassed by, or at least surprised at, the lowliness of the place where, as a matter of historical fact, the death of the Buddha had occurred. The word which is used here to describe Kushinara as a town 'in the midst of the jungle' *(ujjangala)* may mean what in India would be called a jungly' place: that is, as the commentator Buddhaghosa understood it, a lawless, heathen, pagan sort of place; or it may mean simply a barren, waste place. In either case, Ananda's objection seems to indicate that the appropriate place for the Buddha to end his life would be a great city, an urbane and civilized place, the kind of place with which he was most properly associated.

An attempt to remove the objection and the embarrassment is made by the insertion at this point in the narrative of a tale of the ancient splendours of Kushinara in some former age when it was the capital city of a great emperor, Maha Sudassana. In those days the royal city, Kushavasti (as it was then known) 'was mighty and prosperous and full of people, crowded with men and provided with all things for food'. This description of the former glories of Kushinara is elsewhere expanded into a full-length discourse, contained in a separate *Sutta,* called the *Maha Sudassana Sulta,* and it is found also as a Jataka story. The account of the city which is given in these longer versions is highly idealistic; even if no such city ever quite existed in Indian history, the description allows us to see what was obviously the Buddhist notion of an ideal city.

The Urbanity of the Buddha

Whether appropriately or inappropriately, then, it was in this little town in the jungle that the Buddha's life ended. There his body was cremated, and the relics were divided, a portion being given to each of eight legitimate claimants: the king of Magadha, the people of Vaishali, the people of Kapilavastu, the people of Kushinara, three other tribes, and a Brahman named Vethadipaka. In each of the respective towns or cities to which the relics were taken a memorial cairn was built. Over the vessel in which the remains had been collected another cairn was built, and yet another over the remaining embers. According to the tradition, therefore, ten *stupas,* or places where the Buddha was remembered and honoured, came into being immediately after his death. Some of these were in great cities—Rajagriha, Vaishali, and Kapilavastu—and so the dishonour which Ananda felt was incurred in the Buddha's life ending outside a great city, where no worthy memorial could be maintained, was removed.

II

Etymologically, the Sanskrit/Pali word *buddha* means "one who has awakened"; in the context of Indian religions it is used as an honorific title for an individual who is enlightened. This metaphor indicates the change in consciousness that, according to Buddhism, is always characteristic of enlightenment. It suggests the otherness and splendor associated with those named by this epithet in various Buddhist traditions. *Buddha* is also related etymologically to the Sanskrit/Pali term *buddhi,* which signifies "intelligence" and "understanding." A person who has awakened can thus be said to be "one who knows."

Within the traditional Buddhist context *buddha* is an appellative term or title—that is, a term or title that is inclusive in character. As with all titles of office (e.g., king), the term *buddha* denotes not merely the individual incumbent but also a larger conceptual framework. As an appellative, *buddha* describes a person by placing him or her within a class, instead of isolating and analyzing individual attributes. It emphasises the paradigm that is exhibited, rather than distinctive qualities or characterisatics.

The designation of *buddha* has had wide circulation among various religious traditions of India. It has been applied, for example, by Jains to their founder, Mahavira. The definition of the inclusive category has varied, however, and *buddha* has been used to describe a broad spectrum of persons, from those who are simply learned to those rare individuals who have had transforming and liberating insight into the nature of reality. Buddhists have, in general, employed the term in this second, stronger sense.

Buddhists adopted the term *buddha* from the religious discourse of ancient India and gave it a special imprint, just as they have done with much of their vocabulary. It seems, however, that the early Buddhists may not have immediately applied the term to the person—the historical Gautama whom they recognized as the founder of their community. In the accounts of the first two Buddhist councils (one held just after Gautama's death, the other several decades later) Gautama is spoken of as *bhagavan* ("lord," a common title of respect) and *sastr* ("teacher"), not as *buddha*. However, once the term *buddha* was adopted, it not only became the primary designation for Gautama but also assumed a central role within the basic structure of Buddhist thought and practice.

We will begin our discussion by focusing on the question of the historical Buddha and what—if anything we know about him and his ministry. This issue has not been of particular importance for traditional Buddhists—at least not in the way that it is formulated here. But it has been of major significance for modern scholars of Buddhism, and it has become of great interest to many contemporary Buddhists and others who have been influenced by modern Western notions of history.

We will then turn to the term *buddha* as it has been employed within the various traditions that constitute classical Buddhism. As an appellative term utilized in classical Buddhist contexts, *buddha* has had three distinct, yet interwoven, levels of meaning. It has referred, first of all, to what we will call "the Buddha"—otherwise known as the Gautama Buddha or the Buddha Sakyamuni (sage of the Sakyas). Most Buddhists recognize Gautama as the *buddha* of our own cosmic era and/or cosmic space, and they honour him as the founder of the existing Buddhist community. As a perfectly enlightened being, Gautama is understood to have perfected various virtues (paramitas) over the course of numerous lives. [See Paramitas.] These prodigious efforts prepared Gautama to awake fully to the true nature of reality just as other Buddhas had awakened before him. The preparation also gave him—as it did other Buddhas—the inclination and ability to share with others what he had discovered for himself. Following his Enlightenment, Gautama became a teacher who "set in motion the wheel of Dharma" and oversaw the founding of the Buddhist community of monks, nuns, laymen, and laywomen.

The second level of meaning associated with *buddha* as an appellative term has to do with "other Buddhas." Many Buddhas of different times and places are named in Buddhist literature. Moreover, anyone who attains release *(moksa, nirvana)* from this world of recurring rebirths (samsara) can be called—in some contexts at least—a Buddha. Buddhas, then, are potentially as "in numerable as the sands of the river Ganges." But all Buddhas are not equal: they possess different capabilities according to their aspirations and accomplishments. The enlightened insight of some is greater than that of others. Some attain enlightenment only for themselves (e.g., *pratyekabuddha*), others for the benefit and welfare of many (e.g., *samyaksambuddha*). Some accomplish their mission through their earthly careers, others through the creation of celestial Buddha fields into which their devotees seek rebirth. Finally, the term *buddha* as an appellative has a third level of meaning that we will designate as Buddhahood—a level that provides its widest conceptual context. This level is constituted by the recognition that the Buddha and other Buddhas are, in a very profound sense, identical with ultimate reality itself. Consequently, Buddhists have given the more personal and active connotations associated with the Buddha and other Buddhas to their characterizations of absolute reality as *dharma* (salvific truth), *sunyata* (emptiness), *tathata* (suchness), and the like. At the same time, the term Buddhahood has on occasion given a somewhat depersonalized cast to the notions of the Buddha and other Buddhas. For example, early Buddhists, who were closest to the historical Buddha, were reluctant to depict Gautama in anthropomorphic forms and seem to have intentionally avoided biographical structures and iconic imagery. They used impersonal and symbolic representation to express their perception that Buddha whose teachings they had preserved was fully homologous with reality itself. In some later traditions the pervading significance of this third level of meaning was expressed through the affirmation that the Buddha's impersonal and ineffable *dharmakaya* (*dharma* body) was the source and truth of the other, more personalized manifestations of Buddhahood.

The scholars who inaugurated the critical study of Buddhism in the late nineteenth and early twentieth centuries were deeply concerned with the question of the "historical Buddha." But their views on the subject differed radically. The field was largely divided between a group of myth-oriented scholars, such as Emile Senart, Heinrich Kern, and Ananda Coomaraswamy, and a group of more historically oriented philologists, such as Hermann Oldenberg and T.W. and C.A.F. Rhys Davids. The myth-oriented interpreters placed emphasis on the study of Sanskrit sources and on the importance of those elements in the sacred biography that pointed in the direction of solar mythology; for these scholars, the historical Buddha was, at most, a reformer who provided an occasion for historicizing a classic solar myth.

In contrast, the historically oriented philologists emphasized the texts written in Pali, as well as those elements in these texts that they could use to create (or reconstruct, in their view) an acceptable "historical" life of the Buddha. From the perspective of these scholars, the mythic elements—and other supposedly irrational elements as well—were later additions to a true historical memory, additions that brought about the demise of the original Buddhism of the Buddha. Such pious frauds were to be identified and discounted by critical scholarship.

More recently, scholars have recognized the inadequacy of the older mythic and historical approaches. Most scholars working in the field at present are convinced of the existence of the historical Gautama. The general consensus was well expressed by the great Belgian Buddhologist Etienne Lamotte, who noted that "Buddhism would remain inexplicable if one did not place at its beginning a strong personality who was its founder" (Lamotte, 1958, p. 707). But at the same time scholars are aware that the available tests provide little information about the details of Gautama's life.

The difficulties involved in saying anything significant about the historical Buddha are illustrated by the lack of certainty concerning the dates of his birth and death. Since different Buddhist traditions recognize different dates, and since external evidence is slight and inconclusive, scholars have ventured diverging opinions.

Buddhist Texts

Two chronologies found in Buddhist texts are important for any attempt to calculate the date of the historical Buddha. A "long chronology," presented in the Sri Lankan chronicles, the Dipavamsa and the Mahavamsa, places the birth of the historical Buddha 298 years before the coronation of King Asoka, his death 218 years before that event. If we accept the date given in the chronicles for the coronation of Asoka (326 BCE), that would locate the Buddha's birth date in 624 BCE and his death in 544. These dates have been traditionally accepted in Sri Lanka and Southeast Asia and were the basis for the celebration of the 2500th anniversary of the Buddha's death, or *parinirvana,* in 1956. However, most modern scholars who accept the long chronology believe, on the basis of Greek evidence, that Asoka's coronation took place around 268 or 267 BCE and that the Buddha's birth and death should therefore be dated circa 566 and circa 486, respectively. These later dates are favoured by the majority of Buddhologists in Europe, America, and India.

A "short chronology" is attested to by Indian sources and their Chinese and Tibetan translations. These sources place the birth of the Buddha 180 years before the coronation of Asoka and his death 100 years before that event. If the presumably reliable Greek testimony concerning Asoka's coronation is applied, the birth date of the Buddha is 448 and the date of his death, or parinirvana, is 368. This short chronology is accepted by many Japanese Buddhologists and was spiritedly defended by the German scholar Heinz Bechert in 1982.

Although there seems to be little chance of resolving the long chronology/short chronology question in any kind of definitive manner, we can say with some certainty that the historical Buddha lived sometime during the period from the sixth through the fourth centuries BCE. This was a time of radical thought and speculation, as manifested in the pre-Socratic philosophical tradition and the mystery cults in Greece, the prophets and prophetic schools of the Near East, Confucius and Laotzu in China, the Upanisadic sages and the communities of ascetic wanderers (sramanas) in India, and the emergence of "founded" religions such as Jainism and Buddhism. These intellectual and religious movements were fostered by the formation of cosmopolitan empires, such as those associated with Alexander in the Hellenistic world, with the Ch'in and Han dynasties in China, with Darius and Cyrus in Persia, and with the Maurya dynasty in India. Urban centres were established and soon became the focal points around which a new kind of life was organized. A significant number of people, cut off from the old sources of order and meaning, were open to different ways of expressing their religious concerns and were quite ready to support those engaged in new forms of religious and intellectual endeavour.

The historical Buddha responded to this kind of situation in northeastern India. He was a renouncer and an ascetic, although the style of renunciation and asceticism he practiced and recommended was, it seems, mild by Indian standards. He shared with other renunciants an ultimately somber view of the world and its pleasures, and he practiced and recommended a mode of religious life in which individual participation in a specifically religious community was of primary importance. He experimented with the practices of renunciants—begging, wandering, celibacy, techniques of self-restraint (yoga), and the like—and he organized a community in which discipline played a central role. Judging from the movement he inspired, he was not only an innovator but also a charismatic personality. Through the course of his ministry he gathered around him a group of wandering mendicants and nuns, as well as men and women who continued to live the life of householders.

Can we go beyond this very generalized portrait of the historical Buddha toward a fuller biography? Lamotte has advised caution, observing in his *Histoire* that writing the life of the historical Gautama is "a hopeless enterprise" (p. 16). There are, however, a few details that, though they do not add up to a biography, do suggest that there is a historical core to the later biographical traditions. These details are presented in almost identical form in the literature of diverse Buddhist schools, a reasonable indication that they date from before the fourth to third centuries BCE, when independent and separate traditions first began to develop.

Some of these details are so specific and arbitrary or unexpected that it seems unlikely that they were fabricated. These include the details that Gautama was of the Kshatriya caste, that he was born in the Sakya clan (a more distinguished pedigree could have been created), that he was married and had a child, that he entered the ascetic life without the permission of his father, that his first attempts to share the insights that he had gained through his Enlightenment met with failure, that his leadership of the community he had established was seriously challenged by his more ascetically inclined cousin, and that he died in a remote place after eating a tainted meal. But these details are so few and disconnected that our knowledge of the historical Buddha remains shadowy and unsatisfying. In order to identify a more meaningful image of Gautama and his career we must turn to Buddha who is explicitly affirmed in the memory and practice of the Buddhist community.

The general history of religions strongly suggests that the death of a founder results in the loss of a charismatic focus. This loss must be dealt with if the founded group is to survive. In his classic article "Master and Disciple: Two Religio-Sociological Studies," Joachim Wach suggests that "the image" of the beloved founder could produce a unity sufficient for the group to continue (*Journal of Religion* 42, 1962, p. 5).

Each founded religion has developed original ways of preserving the image of their master: Christians with the Gospels and later artistic expressions, Muslims with *hadith* and Mi'raj stories of Muhammad's journeys to heaven, and so on. Buddhists, it seems, have addressed this crisis with the assumption—explicitly stated in the words of a fifth-century CE Mahayana text known as the *Saptasatika-prajnaparamita*—that "a Buddha is not easily made known by words" (Rome, 1923, p. 126). This recognition has not proved to be a restraint but has instead inspired Buddhists to preserve the image of Gautama through the creation and explication of epithets, through a variety of "biographical" accounts, and through a tradition of visual representation in monumental architecture and art. The image of the founder became, in Joachim Wach's phrase, "an objective centre of crystalization" for a variety of opinions concerning the nature and significance of his person.

Image of Buddha

The creative preservation of the image of the Buddha was closely related to evolving patterns of worship—including pilgrimage, contemplation, and ritual—in the Buddhist community. This reminds us that the various ways of portraying the Buddha are the result of innumerable personal efforts to discern him with immediacy, as well as the product of the desire to preserve and share that image.

Certainly one of the earliest and most ubiquitous forms in which Buddhists have expressed and generated their image of Gautama Buddha was through the medium of epithets. For example, in the *Majjhima Nikaya* (London, 1948, Vol. 1, p. 386), a householder named Upali, after becoming the Buddha's follower, acclaims him with one hundred epithets. The Sanskrit version of this text adds that Upali spoke these epithets spontaneously, as an expression of his faith and respect. Over the centuries the enumerations of these and other epithets focused on the extraordinary aspects of the Buddha's person, on his marvelous nature. In so doing they became a foundation for Buddhist devotional literature, their enunciation a support of devotional and contemplative practice.

Countless epithets have been applied to the Buddha over the centuries, but *buddha* itself has been a particular favourite for explanation.

Even hearing the word *buddha* can cause people to rejoice because, as the Theravada commentary on the *Samyutta Nikaya* says, "It is very rare indeed to hear the word *buddha* in this world" (London, 1929, Vol. 1, p. 312). The Patisambhida, a late addition to the Theravada canon, explored the significance of the word *buddha* by saying that "it is a name derived from the final liberation of the Enlightened Ones, the Blessed Ones, together with the omniscient knowledge at the root of the Enlightenment Tree; this name "buddha" is a designation based on realization" (The *Path of Purification,* translated by Nyanamoli, Colombo, 1964, p. 213). Sun Ch'o, a fourth-century Chinese writer, explicated the *buddha* epithet in a rather different mode, reminiscent of a Taoist sage: "'Buddha' means 'one who embodies the Way'. . . . It is the one who reacts to the stimuli (of the world) in all pervading accordance (with the needs of all beings); the one who abstains from activity and who is yet universally active" (quoted in Erik Zurcher's *The Buddhist Conquest of China,* Leiden, 1959, p. 133).

Views of Tagore

In the words of a Rabindranath Tagore, the way of the Buddha is 'the elimination of all limits of love', it is 'the sublimation of self in a truth which is love itself'. Tagore has, in these words, identified the essence of what has come to be called Buddhism. For Buddhism is not, as so many Westerners have imagined, a private cult of escape from the real world. The word 'imagined' is used deliberately because such a view of Buddhism can proceed only from the exercise of the imagination, not from knowledge of the Buddha's teaching, or of the nature of the Buddhist community, the *Sangha,* or of Buddhist history. To speak of Buddhism as something concerned with the private salvation of the individual soul is to ignore entirely the basic Buddhist repudiation of the notion of the individual soul. The teaching of the Buddha was not concerned with the private destiny of the individual, but with something much wider, the whole realm of sentient being, the whole of consciousness. This inevitably entailed a concern with social and political matters, and these receive a large share of attention in the teaching of Buddha as it is represented in the Pali texts. Moreover, as we have seen, the context of Buddha's own spiritual quest was the increasing individualism which accompanied the growth of cities and monarchies, and the problems attendant upon this growth. To attempt to understand Buddhism apart from its social dimension is futile. Individualism places limits on love, and if Buddhism is an attempt to deal with what it sees as the disease of individualism, and is primarily a method of eliminating these limits, as Tagore realized, then it will entail a concern with the social and political dimension.

The primary form which this process takes is the life of the Buddhist community, the *Sangha.* The members of this community were in India called *bhikkhus* (Pali) or *bhikshus* (Sanskrit). In Western languages they are most usually referred to as 'monks' or the equivalent, and the *aramas,* or local institutions which provide the physical setting for their common life are often referred to as 'monasteries'. But this terminology, borrowed from European practice, is misleading. The word 'monk', derived from the word *monachus,* 'originally meant a religious hermit or solitary'; later on it came to mean 'a member of a community or brotherhood living apart from the world'. In neither of these senses can the word be applied appropriately to a member of the Buddhist *Sangha.*

The word *bhikkhu* means, literally, a 'sharesman', that is, one who receives a share of something. The Buddhist *bhikkhus* were, in fact, a special case of what had been a common feature of Indian civilization from a very early period. In general, as Sukumar Dutt has pointed out, the almsman or sharesman in India is 'differentiated from an ordinary beggar by the sacramental character of his begging. His begging is not just a means of subsistence but an outward token'—an outward token of his renunciation of private or personal sources of livelihood or ownership of wealth, and his dependence instead on the 'common wealth', the public resources of the society in which he lives. Certainly, the Buddhist 'sharesman', has not contracted out of society. The life he leads and the goal he seeks is not for his own private benefit, for this would be directly contrary to the Buddhist repudiation of individualism. By being what he is and by following the life he does, society will benefit. The nature of the role-relationship between the *bhikkhu* and the householders clearly demonstrates that the Buddhist professional is integrally involved in society.

The 'share' which the *bhikkhu* received and which gave him his name was, primarily, the portion of food which was set aside for him by those householders who supported him. But it was more than this that he received; the share of food was representative of other things—the robes he wore, the shelter in which he lived, and the other material necessities of life, all of which were provided by the lay-people of the neighbourhood. His acceptance of these things from the 'common wealth' so to speak, was a symbol of his own renunciation of private property. In return the Buddhist *bhikkhus* had important contributions to make to the common life of society, as we shall see. These were not material or economic contributions but they were sufficiently important for the *bhikkhus* to be able to accept the material support which they were offered as something which was their proper 'share'. If what they received is sometimes referred to as 'alms', it must be remembered that these were offered in a spirit of deference and gratitude; the *bhikkhus* were not, and are not, 'beggars' in any sense of the word. The *bhikkhu* was certainly *not*, therefore, someone who lived apart from the world, like the Christian monk. One of the important achievements of early Buddhism was that it developed a new context for the spiritual quest. Traditionally in India, the search for salvation from the evils of human existence meant a life of solitude. For the Buddhist it meant a life in the community. For a time, however, in the earliest period of Buddhist history, the old idea seems to have survived. So strong a hold did the Indian tradition of solitude have that even among Buddhists there were those who tried to practise the Buddha's teaching by the old method and, as an ancient text puts it, 'fare lonely as rhinoceros'. But it was among the Buddhists that there soon emerged, for the first time in Indian history, an ordered community of those who were seeking for salvation from the human malaise as they saw it.

The reasons for having an ordered community, organized in local settlements, in close touch with the neighbourhood, are to be found in the nature of the new wisdom itself. The *occasion* for the actual coming into existence of such organized local settlements was, as it happens, a phenomenon peculiar to ancient India. We shall look at each of these aspects in turn.

The reason for the Buddhist community life is inherent in the nature of the Buddha's teaching. We have seen that this teaching consists of diagnosis and prescription: diagnosis of the human malaise as consisting essentially of the disease of individualism, and prescription for its cure as consisting primarily of the undermining or erosion of the notion that individuality is something permanent and of great importance. It is in the life of the *Sangha* that the prescription can most effectively be applied. Here is the community of being which comes into existence when the walls of individuality are completely and permanently broken down. And here, too, are found the optimum conditions for those who are seeking to achieve that state of life and consciousness where individuality is no more, but who have not yet arrived at that state.

Meditation Process

The process of meditation which is prescribed in the early texts gives something of a glimpse of the community of consciousness which was aimed at in the *Sangha*. The method was one which began from the recognition that, in its normal state, the mind, and particularly the surface of the mind, is constantly being fretted and distracted; it is in a state of continual upheaval, like the surface of the sea, tossed into countless waves by the buffeting of the wind. The first stage of meditation, or the first *jhana,* to give it its technical name, is the calming of the mind by detaching it from the bombardment of the senses, and from discursive thinking. This makes possible the second stage in the process, namely concentration: that is, the concentration of the consciousness upon one point. When this has been achieved, and only then, the next stage can begin, the stage of experiencing clarity and equanimity. Consciousness, thus purified and calmed, is then able to expand, and the experience becomes that of 'unbounded space'. The final stages of the process do not concern us here. What is of interest at this point is the sequence: a narrowing down of consciousness, followed by expansion. The underlying theory seems to be that when consciousness, normally restless, wild or even uncontrollable, is brought to a single point, it can then be dealt with effectively (like the bringing under control and harnessing of a wild horse). Thus controlled, by concentration, it then begins to exhibit the pure qualities which are always waiting to be manifested, namely joy and equanimity. In this way the concentration of consciousness produces, of itself, a subsequent broadening out into unbounded dimensions of the inherent qualities which are now given their rightful place.

Now, it is evident that the process of meditation carried on by more than one 'individual' will begin, in each case, from a state where each is conscious of a multiplicity of sense objects and desires, and that it will lead to a state where all are sharing in the same consciousness of joy and equanimity, which is infinite and the same for all. When the impurities have been removed, then there can be a fusion. Incidentally, this raises the question of the Buddhist view of the fundamental moral nature of man. In Buddhist philosophy, human nature is seen as fundamentally good rather than evil. The discipline which the life of the *bhikkhu* entails is likened by the Buddha to the process of refining gold. Stage by stage impurities are purged away: first the coarse dust and sand, gravel and grit; then the finer grit, then the trifling impurities like the very fine sand and dust. At last 'the gold-dust alone remains', and this is placed in the crucible and melted together, until it can be run out of the crucible. 'Then that gold is melted, molten, flawless, done with, its impurities strained off. It is pliable, workable, glistening, no longer brittle; it is capable of perfect workmanship. . . . Just in the same way in a monk who is given to developing the higher consciousness there are gross impurities of deed, word and thought.' These, too, are gradually purged out, first the coarser impurities, and then the finer, subtler impurities, until there comes a time when all this dross has been removed and the basic pure state of consciousness is reached. According to the Buddha, this level of permanently pure consciousness is achieved when all the common distinctions and ways of differentiating human beings have been purged away—such considerations, for example, as family pride, national pride and personal reputation. 'We note here', writes a modern Buddhist, commenting on this passage, 'how our preoccupations with thoughts concerning our race or state are considered harmful to the concept of a common humanity.'

This can be seen in connection with the ownership of property. One who becomes a member of the *Sangha* ceases to own any private property whatsoever. This has been a feature of *Sangha* life from the earliest times. Even those few articles of personal use, the robe, the alms-bowl and one or two other requisites, were in theory vested in the *Sangha*, and made available for the use of its members.

Rights of Bhikkhu

However, it is interesting to notice that while the *Sangha* was, from a juristic point of view, the corporate person in whom property was vested, and while no *bhikkhu* had legal property rights, nevertheless, as K.N. Jayatilleke pointed out, 'some rights such as the right to life, to free speech, to personal freedom, etc., cluster round the notion of individual personality'. He acknowledged that this would seem to be an inconsistency, for the doctrine of *anatta* would appear to be incompatible with the notion of personal responsibility. But since the psycho-physical processes of human life maintain a relative and temporary 'individuality', it is useful to distinguish one of these relatively individual series of processes from another, and to refer to each by the term 'person'. Where the Buddhist analysis differs from most other views of human nature is in denying any absolute and permanent substratum, 'soul', or 'person', in these temporary psycho-physical processes. In the Buddhist view of things it seems that the concept of individuality which is primarily and most emphatically denied is that of the private-property-owning individual. This is a practical, institutional expression of the basic doctrine that greed or grasping *(tanha) is* the root of human ills.

The *Sangha,* therefore, provides the environment in which a new dimension of consciousness becomes possible as a result of the denial, not only in theory but also in practice, of the idea of absolute and permanent individuality.

In the earliest period of Buddhist history the *Sangha* seems to have existed as a wandering sect, a movement with which a man identified himself with the minimum of formal ceremony, 'a unitary organization of monks hailing from all quarters irrespective of regional provenance'. If European terms are to be used at all, such a wandering brotherhood was more like an order of friars than of monks. But this very fluid stage of its history seems to have been brief and transitional. The nature of the doctrine combined with historical circumstances soon resulted in the development of settled, local communities of *bhikkhus*. We have already seen that it was necessary in the conditions which prevail in the monsoon period in India for wandering sects of all kinds to seek shelter during the rainy season. But where Jains, Brahmanical wanderers, and other such schools neither required nor (in the case of the Jains) allowed any specially set apart 'retreat-houses' or lodgings in which all the members of the school in a given locality were to reside together for the period of the rains, in the case of the Buddhists it was precisely this which came to be prescribed. 'The Buddhist idea of rain-retreat seems to have been not to live [just] anywhere, or alone and companionless, or in promiscuous company, but to settle in a congregation of fellow-monks.' The fact that this was the practice of no other sect of *shramanas* may be connected with the other feature which was unique to the Buddhist order—their adherence to the doctrine of *anatta,* or non-individuality. Perhaps the local settled communities were bound to have come into existence, the Buddhist view of life being what it was. Nevertheless, it happened that historically it was a particular feature of Indian life which precipitated the matter, and provided the actual occasion for the formation of local communities.

It is noteworthy that these were not established in remote places, in the depths of the forest and far from the busy centres of travel and trade and government; this was the environment which Brahmanical ascetics sought, but not the Buddhists. The latter, on the contrary, established their typical settlements on the edge of a town or city, partly, as we have already seen, because it was from among the growing urban population of the time that the Buddhists found most of their recruits, and partly, too, because the size of the Buddhist communities required a substantial number of householders near enough to provide the necessary economic support. This, therefore, soon became the normal location for a Buddhist *arama,* as the local institutional settlement was called, although there was a minority of *bhikkhus,* of more conservative disposition, who preferred to have their dwellings in forest glades, and who were known by the general designation, *Aranyakas* (forest-dwellers). They were in this way conforming to the more traditional Indian view of the proper setting for a life of meditation; but the majority of Buddhist *bhikkhus* was characterized by the more radical attitude, one which was more consistent with the special nature of Buddhist ideas, and which recognised that close proximity to the important centres of the world's business was where the communities belonged.

One point which is frequently emphasized in the early tradition is that the Buddha had firmly rejected the notion of authoritarian rule in the new community which he had brought into existence. The Buddhist *Sangha,* whatever else it might resemble, would not resemble a monarchy. The Buddha himself was not in any sense a personal ruler, nor was any member of the community to think of himself in this way after the Buddha's death: 'Surely, Ananda, should there be anyone who harbours the thought, "It is I who will lead the brotherhood", or, "The Order is dependent upon me", it is he who should lay down instructions in any matter concerning the Order. Now the Tathagata [the Buddha], Ananda, thinks not that it is he who should lead the brotherhood, or that Order is dependent on him. Why then should he leave instructions in any matter concerning the Order?' The implication for the members is clear: 'Therefore, O Ananda, be ye lamps unto yourselves . . . Hold fast to the *Dhamma* as a lamp.'

In this respect the Buddhist community was perpetuating the tradition of the tribal republican *sanghas,* which, 'knew nothing of personal rule' as S. Dutt points out; 'they deliberated and acted together, were communistic in their property relationships, republican in their conduct of affairs and had the tribal council as their organ of Government.'

As another recent and more specialist study of the tribal republics of this period observes 'each member of the assembly was called a *raju* (ruler), but none had the individual power to mould the decisions of the assembly.'

It is clear that the Buddhist community inherited certain forms and methods of organization from the tribal republics. The question which was raised earlier must now be considered more fully, namely, whether the Buddhist *Sangha* was simply a reproduction of the old tribal collective or *sangha,* or whether it was a conscious and deliberate improvement on the older model, which was in the Buddha's day disappearing before the advance of the great monarchies, Koshala and Magadha. Was the Buddhist *Sangha* organized in imitation of the older political *sanghas* for no other reason than that the Buddhists were politically behind the times, or was it done, perhaps, in order to preserve something which was felt to be of value but which could be preserved in no other way (just as private enthusiasts in Britain today get together to preserve as a going concern some local steam railway) ? On the other hand, was the Buddhist community organized as a new-style *Sangha,* one in which the defects which had. made the old political model obsolete were corrected; was it a new and improved version which was being put forward as a serious contribution to political experimentation and development? Was it a version which would remedy, too, the weaknesses and disadvantages apparent in the monarchical system (just as, to continue the analogy, a reorganized and rationalized railway system of diesel locomotion might be seen as the most effective solution to the traffic and transportation problems of a country which is being slowly stifled by private motor cars)?

The answer to the first part of the question is relatively straightforward. The pattern which is represented as being laid down by the Buddha for the regulation of the affairs of the new community was one which has been loosely described as 'democratic'. Democracy is an ancient word, but as it is now understood, it is, of course, a political concept which emerged somewhat later in history and implies the existence of certain political institutions. The *Buddha-Sangha* has been described as democratic largely because there was no monarchical head, no authoritarian chain of command and responsibility, and because a recognized procedure existed for decision-making by the whole community corporately. Certainly every member of the *Sangha* was regarded as having equality of rights in any deliberations concerning the life of the community. K.N. Jayatilleke has argued that 'even the cosmic perspective is for the Buddhist democratic, for any man of his own free will may aspire to and attain to the status of a Buddha', and that democracy was of the essence of the early community. The *Sangha* has been described, also, as a 'system of government formed by the *Bhikkhus,* for the *Bhikkhus* and of the *Bhikkhus*', and therefore a democracy. But the principles of government in the *Sangha* differed from those of a modern democratic state in one important respect, which needs to be carefully considered.

The ideal for the government of the new community is described by Buddha, as we have seen, in connection with the Vajjian confederacy. 'So long, O *bhikkhus,* as the brethren foregather oft, and frequent the formal meetings of their *Sangha, so long as they meet together in concord, and carry out in concord the duties of the Sangha . . . so* long may the brethren be expected not to decline but to prosper.' It is expressly stated that 'concord' or unanimity is essential for the proper functioning of the *Sangha,* otherwise its life will decline. The corpus of rulings on its life and organization and the conduct and discipline of its members, known as the *Vinaya-pitaka*, contains similar injunctions for the community. The principle which seems to have been regarded as of supreme importance was that of the maintenance of unity of view within each *local* company or *sangha.* For as soon as permanent local settlements had been developed each of these was regarded as a *sangha* in itself, a complete microcosm, so to speak, of the whole *Sangha.* And while it was accepted that differences of opinion were likely to develop, what was regarded as of greatest importance was that each local fellowship, which provided the actual, day-to-day experience of common life, was to be a unity, undivided by any controversial issues. If controversy did arise—and it was recognized that it could and would—the method laid down for dealing with the situation was that the dissenting group should remove itself and form a new settlement. This 'law of schism', as it was called, was a matter of discussion at the second Buddhist Council, held at Vaishali a century after the Buddha's death; it was very important that this procedure should be agreed upon because the maintenance of the essential principle of unity in the *sangha* depended on it. It was recognized that honest differences of opinion had to be allowed for, but not at the expense of the structural unity of the local *sangha.* As Sukumar Dutt has put it, the unitary character of the local *sangha* was 'the basic principle of its functioning'. All other considerations were subordinate to this basic principle of local structural unity.

Constitution of Sangha

In view of what was said earlier concerning the *sangha* as the necessary context for living the new life of non-individualism, it will be easily understood why unity was so important. It is this aspect of the *sangha's* constitution, therefore, which, in the final analysis, distinguishes it from a democratic body. A democratic organization is one in which the majority opinion is honoured and prevails. The advantage of this method is that, if it can be followed consistently, the formation of schismatic, dissenting groups is avoided; but the price is the subordination of minority views. The Buddhist method is one which allows minority views to be held, and not disregarded, but the price to be paid is the multiplication of bodies with different points of view. The Buddhists, like others, had to choose between the two principles; that the choice was a very difficult one to make is seen from the fact that the matter was not settled until a hundred years after the Buddha's decease. However, once a principle has been agreed upon, allowances can be made for the fact that certain advantages accruing from the opposite decision have been surrendered. In this case, what was surrendered was ideological solidarity. Other political and religious institutions faced with a similar choice have sometimes chosen the totalitarian way: formal organizational unity has been maintained at the expense of the rights of self-expression on the part of minority groups. The history of Catholicism in Europe, which is as much a matter of politics as of religion, demonstrates what ensues when total institutional unity is evaluated more highly than arrangements for the tolerance of dissent. Any group which threatens the formal unity of the total organization has to be regarded as something alien to the true nature of the organization itself; it is a sect, rather than true church. In the Buddhist case, the inevitability of sectarian differences has been acknowledged, with the result that Buddhism has not experienced the internecine wars of religion that have characterized some other traditions, where dissent or 'heresy' has been something to be stamped out.

This should not be taken to imply that the Buddhist *Sangha* recognized no canons or orthodoxy. The matter is represented as having been explicitly dealt with by the Buddha himself, who set out certain criteria by which authentic Buddhist doctrine could be recognized.

In the matter of the relationship between the *sangha* of the Vajjian confederacy and the Buddhist *sangha,* it emerges that the latter was modelled very closely on the former. It is not properly described as democratic in the modem sense; its characteristics were those of the old tribal republic, in which unanimity among the assembled elders was the supreme requirement. Now, it is clear that where this was the underlying principle of government, lack of unanimity would produce dysfunction of the system and possibly its breakdown, more quickly than any other single factor; the Buddha implied as much in the observations he made on the prospects for the Vajjian confederacy's continued well-being. Events showed that the Vajjian system was fallible. The reason adduced for this, in the Buddhist view, was the disease of individualism, which had now spread to the tribal republics, and was proving too much for the strength of republican solidarity. J.P. Sharma sees the collapse of the tribal republics, which took place soon after the Buddha's decease, as due to the intrusion of individualism. The old understanding was that no individual member of the republican assembly had the power to mould the decisions of the assembly; nevertheless, by the time that Buddha was called upon to give an opinion on the prospects of the republican *sanghas,* a situation had developed in which it is probable, says Sharma, 'that some councilors or leaders of the republic either wished to rise above the rest and become virtual rulers . . . or that some preferred to betray the republic for their selfish interests, thus becoming lieutenants of a king. The latter could offer these betrayers substantial rewards either in the form of material gains or by entrusting them with important state offices which they could not expect while the republic continued and prospered.' The downfall of the republics was thus closely connected with the spread of monarchy and of the spirit of individualism, or, as Sharma describes it, of 'personal ambition'.

The Buddhist *sangha* might be seen, then, in the context of fifth century BC, as the prototype social organization of the future. But there were serious difficulties in the way of such a prescription for the welfare of human society. Between the prototype, even as it could be seen in existence here and there, and the transformation of the whole of human society into a universal *sangha,* there was, so to speak, a large practicability gap. To organize what was still a relatively small sect or cult-association as a republican *sangha* was one thing; to propose that this form of politico-social organisation could, by means of the therapy which Buddhism offered, become once again the norm for Indian society as a whole was quite another. Such a proposal would, in the circumstances of the time have been entirely impracticable, for a number of reasons. There is evidence to suggest that they were fully appreciated by Buddha or at least in early Buddhist tradition, and that an interim scheme was envisaged which would make the best of the existing situation and encourage the development of a political and social climate more favourable to the full adoption of Buddhist attitudes and principles.

The two major reasons against the idea of the whole of contemporary Indian society becoming a universal Buddhist *sangha* were, first, the existence of powerful monarchies, and second, the unreadiness of the mass of the people for participation in the kind of society envisaged in Buddhist teaching. The Buddhist mission society, if one may call it that, appears to have had both of these problems in view, and to have developed appropriate policies in each case.

The common people, or, more precisely, 'the ordinary man', is referred to by a word which occurs with relative frequency throughout the Pali literature—puthujjana. The basic meaning of *puthu* is 'widespread' and this meaning is carried into the usage of the word composed from it by the addition of *jana,* a person or a man. The word has thus been translated appropriately into English as 'the ordinary man', 'the common man' or 'the average man'. From the various occurrences of the word in the early literature, it appears that Buddha used it to refer to the generality of man distinct from brahmans and recluses. It has to be remembered that Buddha gives the word·'brahman' a new meaning, apart from its technical caste connotation. The priestly class who had in the Buddha's day appropriated the term had no special, innate right to it, according to Buddha. A brahman is a brahman by character, and not merely by some hereditary right. In the conversations of Buddha with brahmans the latter are often represented as being led by the course of the argument to admit this point. Perhaps some real brahmans of Buddha's day did so, in fact. In any case it is clear that this was the Buddhist view of the matter. So 'brahmans and shramanas' becomes a phrase virtually equivalent in meaning to those who, from a Buddhist point of view, are genuinely in pursuit of the truth and of a righteous life. The generality of men who are thus distinguished from them are, in effect, the mass of mankind who are not members of the Buddhist community.

It is possible to construct from the references in the Pali texts a fairly detailed picture of the average man, or, literally, man as he is commonly found, from the point of view of the Buddha, or of the early Buddhists.

The ordinary man, we are told, 'is addicted to pleasure', and is at the mercy of his senses. He is enthralled by the eye with objects that charm, by the tongue with savours that charm, etc. He follows his natural desires, 'uncontrolled in the six-fold sense sphere, and eats his fill with ravenous delight among the five sensual pleasures'. He welcomes personal fame and praise but resents obscurity and blame. He is easily provoked to deeds of a morally unwholesome kind; he will murder his own father or his mother, inflict wounds on a saintly man, and cause dissension within the Buddhist *sangha.* He is greedy and lustful. On the other hand, he resents any ill fortune; when afflicted with pain he is distressed and overcome with bewilderment about it; he finds that those things on which he sets his hopes frequently turn out to be a disappointment; he dislikes the sight of disease, or old age or death; when old age comes upon him he mourns and pines and is tormented by sorrow, and finally he goes to Purgatory. All this is because he is lacking in wisdom, and in knowledge of the truth. Not only does he adhere to popular superstitions, but he knows not, he sees not things as they really are, he takes no account of those who are holy, those who are true, he does not comprehend which things should and which things should not be attended to; he knows nothing of the origination of compounded things, and so is not set free from the power of ill; he fails to reflect adequately and to understand the experiences of life for what they really are.

The fact that he is described in the singular should not be allowed to disguise from us that this is the Buddha's view of the mass of mankind. Such being the case, J.P. Sharma is justified in his conclusion that the Buddhist *Sangha, like* the Greek oligarchies, was based on a belief in the 'unwisdom of the multitude'.

Such belief did not lead, however, in the Buddhist case at least, to an attitude of cynicism towards the multitude. Far from it: the common people have an important part in the Buddhist scheme of things, for their present condition is not accepted as permanent or final. Indeed, between them and the Sangha there exists an important relationship, not of reciprocity exactly, but of complementariness. This relationship is set out formally in an early Buddhist text, the *Sigala* homily, which remains today one of the best-known portions of Buddhist literature among the Buddhists of Ceylon and South East Asia.

The *Sigala* homily is presented as being the extended answer given by the Buddha to a question from a young householder regarding his moral duties. The comprehensive nature of the advice which the Buddha gives him with regard to domestic and social relationships would by itself be sufficient to dispose of any assertion that the early Buddhist community's concerns were entirely 'otherworldly', 'spiritual' or 'selfish'. As a Buddhist of a later age, commenting on it, said 'nothing in the duties of a householder is left unmentioned'. It was, added the same writer, for the householder what the *Vinaya,* or code of discipline, was for the members of the *Sangha.*

Division of Duties

The duties are set out in an orderly way, intended, no doubt, as T.W. Rhys Davids observed, to assist the memory. Six sets of reciprocal role expectations, or duties, are enumerated: first, those between parents and children; next, between pupils and teachers; husband and wife; followed by friends and companions; masters and servants; and finally householders and members of the *Sangha.* In each category, five duties are enumerated, with the exception of the *Sangha's* duties to householders, and in this case there are six.

Children are to support their parents, who once supported them; they are to perform the proper family duties, to maintain the family line; to uphold the family tradition; (meaning, perhaps, not dissipating the family property and maintaining the family honour); and they are to show themselves worthy of their heritage. Parents are to restrain their child from wrongdoing, to inspire him to virtue; to train him for a profession, to contract a suitable marriage for him; and in due time to make over to him his inheritance.

Pupils are to serve their teachers by showing respect to them, by waiting upon them, by showing eagerness to learn, by supplying their needs, and by paying attention when they are being taught. Teachers in return are to give their pupils moral training, they are to inspire in them a love of learning, they are to instruct them in every subject, are to speak well of their pupils, and to protect them from any danger.

A husband is to cherish his wife by treating her with respect, by being kind to her, by being faithful, by allowing her her proper due rights, and by providing her with suitable ornaments. In return, a wife is to show her love for her husband by maintaining a well-ordered household, by being hospitable to their relatives and friends, by being faithful, by being thrifty, and by being diligent.

A man should recognize his obligations to his friends by making them gifts, by courtesy and benevolence towards them, by treating them as his equals, and by keeping his word to them. In return he may expect that they will take care of him or of his interests when he is unable to do so himself (for example, says the commentator, if he falls down in the street after too much drinking, his friend will stay with him until he sobers up, so that his clothes are not stolen), they will provide him with refuge when he needs it, they will stand by him in times of trouble, and will be kind to his family.

A good master (i.e., employer) is one who may be relied upon to show consideration towards his employees by allotting each one work suited to his capacity, by supplying them with good food and pay, by providing care for them when they are sick, by sharing with them any unusual delicacies which he receives, and by granting them regular time off from work. In return, employees or servants should show their affection for their master by being out of bed betimes and not going to bed until he has done so, by being contented with the fair treatment they receive, by doing their work cheerfully and thoroughly, and by speaking well of their master to others.

Finally, the reciprocal duties of householders and members of the *Sangha* are set out. A good householder ministers to the *bhikkhus* by showing affection for them in his actions, in his speech, and in his thoughts, by giving them a warm welcome and ample hospitality and by providing generally for their material needs. In return, the members of the *Sangha* are to show their affection for the householder by restraining him from evil courses of action, by exhorting him to do what is honourable, by entertaining kindly feelings towards him, by imparting knowledge to him, by dealing with his difficulties and doubts, and by revealing to him the way to heaven. The last is the sixth duty. Every other class of citizen named has been given five duties, but for the *bhikkhu* there is this one extra, which thus stands by itself in a position of special emphasis.

'We can realize', commented T.W. Rhys Davids, 'how happy would have been the village or the clan on the banks of the Ganges, where the people were full of kindly spirit of fellow-feeling, the noble spirit of Justice, which breathes through these naive and simple sayings.' Those who have been acquainted with the life of a country like Burma, where Buddhist culture was still a living force will know that this is true, for the reality has existed. There is evidence that in India something approaching such a state of society existed wherever Buddhist culture or civilization was able to establish itself.

Here the crux of the matter is reached: the ability of Buddhism to establish and maintain itself. The 'practicability gap' which was mentioned a little earlier, between the Buddhist vision for human society and the realization of it in any actual society, was not quickly or easily bridged. There were, and are, certain essential conditions to be fulfilled before a Buddhist form of civilization can come into being anywhere. These necessary conditions have two primary focal points: (i) the *Sangha*, and (2) the governing power. In India at the time of the Buddha, the latter meant, of course, the monarchy. These will now be considered in a little more detail. In the first place, it was essential that the *Sangha* should function within the wider society in the kind of way that was outlined in the Sangha homily. The duties there envisaged for the *bhikkhu* in his relations with the householder require constant, day-to-day contacts between the two. That is why the word 'monk', if it means a man who lives apart from the world, is in the strict sense inappropriate as a translation of *bhikkhu*. The *bhikkku* has to exhort the householder, restrain him when necessary, instruct him, clear up his doubts, and constantly direct his attention to the path he should follow in order to reach 'heaven'. This he would do most effectively if he himself was following that path and was providing an example and an inspiration to the householder, who otherwise, as we have seen, was all too prone to aim at the short-term goal of sensual pleasure. From the point of view of an anthropological analysis of Buddhism in modern Ceylon, Obeyesekere points out a principle which is inherent in early Buddhism also. The life of the *bhikkhu,* who has given up the comforts of household life as something which he no longer needs, has an important social function. His life 'exemplifies in exaggerated form the inhibition of natural drives, and such inhibition is a prerequisite for the conduct of all social life'. The effect of the example of an ascetic life was pointed out by Durkheim in terms which exactly fit the Buddhist situation: 'it is . . . a good thing that the ascetic ideal be incarnated eminently in certain persons, whose specialty, so to speak, it is to represent, almost with excess, this aspect of the ritual life, for they are like so many models, inciting to effort. Such is the historic role of the great ascetics. When their deeds and acts are analysed in detail, one asks himself what useful end they can have. He is struck by the fact that there is something excessive in the disdain they profess for all that ordinarily impassions men. But these exaggerations are necessary to sustain among the believers a sufficient disgust for an easy life and common pleasures. It is necessary that an elite put the end too high, if the crowd is not to put it too low. It is necessary that some exaggerate, if the average is to remain at a fitting level.'

Whether these words of Durkheim are true for any other system or not, they are certainly true of early Buddhism. A passage from a canonical text reflects exactly the kind of attitude on the part of the lay-follower that Durkheim has depicted. 'As long as they live, the *Arahants* . . . are abstainers from the slaying of creatures; ... they are modest, show kindness, they abide friendly and compassionate to all creatures, to all beings. So also do I abide this night and day . . . abstaining from such actions, showing kindness to all beings. As long as they live the *Arahants* . . . abstain from stealing . . . they abide in purity free from theft. So also do I myself also abide. . . .' The same formula is repeated for each of the eight precepts which were observed by those lay-followers or *upasakas* who were aiming at a somewhat higher level of moral attainment, in imitation of the example of the *bhikkhus,* and especially of the *Arahants,* who were regarded as having fully conquered selfish passions. 'As long as they live the *Arahants* dwell observing chastity ... abstaining from falsehood ... abstaining from fermented liquor, which gives occasion to sloth ... living on one meal a day ... refraining from going to exhibitions of dancing ... from the use of luxurious beds.... So also do I abide. I also this night and day do likewise. By this observance I imitate the *Arahants* . . . and I shall have kept the sabbath.'

The particular occasion for the recital of these words was, as the last sentence indicates, the lay disciple's observance of a higher standard of moral discipline during the night and day of the sabbath, a practice which is still followed in Buddhist countries today. The householder who, once or twice a month, undertook this somewhat stricter rule of life would naturally be more disposed to follow the normally required five basic precepts more carefully than if he were not disciplining himself from time to time at a more advanced level. And from his example other householders might also be encouraged to take the Buddhist moral code more seriously. There was thus a widening circle from each local Buddhist *sangha,* a radiation of heightened morality, whose influence would, as time went by, penetrate more and more deeply into the surrounding society.

In this way, what was referred to above as the unreadiness of the mass of people to participate in, and make a success of, the kind of society envisaged in Buddhist teaching, would gradually diminish. Meanwhile, however, there would still be many who were not likely to respond to these influences, and whose attitudes and actions would have socially destructive effects if they were not held in check. In other words, there was the problem of how to deal with potentially violent or anti-social elements, even though it was only for an interim period while the Buddhist prescription became more widely effective in raising the level of moral life and eliminating social conflict and violence. There were, moreover, the monarchies, decreasing in numbers as the larger swallowed up the smaller, but not decreasing in the extent or degree of their power. These would constitute the most serious obstacle of all in the way of any hopes for the gradual establishment of a universal republic with the Buddhist *sangha* as its heart.

It may be useful at this point to remind ourselves that the Buddha, when he had achieved Buddhahood, does not appear to have abandoned the interest, which his family tradition and milieu had given him, in public affairs and the concerns of government. We may remind ourselves, too, that it was perfectly natural that the public world should come within the scope of the Buddhist prescription. This was not due merely to the need to guarantee the *Sangha* with political freedom and a sound economic basis, necessary pre-conditions for its untramelled existence and security though these were. It was due equally to the fact that the private world of the individual, as the 'real' or important world, was denied legitimacy in Buddhist doctrine. Salvation was the movement away from this private, separate and ultimately false existence to a wider, non-egotistical sphere of being. Here, then, we have three very important reasons why there developed in early Buddhism so strong a concern with the wise and beneficent government of human society: the Buddha's own background, the need to ensure optimum conditions for the Buddhist prescription for society to take effect, and—most important—the fact that by its very nature, unique among the ideologies of the time in its denial of the individual soul, Buddhism could never be a 'private' salvation, 'the flight of the alone to the Alone' or any other kind of world-rejecting escapism; by its very nature its concerns were with the public world.

The *Sangha* was to provide the growth point, or, rather, a multiplicity of growth points, from which would spread the new pattern of humanity, the social restructuring of human life, which had as its aim the elimination of individualism with all its human ill effects. While this process was going on, it would be folly to disregard the large areas of society which were as yet untouched by the influence of the *Sangha,* for unchecked individualism and violence in these areas would threaten the peaceful growth of the *Sangha,* and of what may be called the Buddhistically oriented areas of society. Social stability appears to have been recognized by the Buddha as a necessary condition for the success of social and moral reconstruction. In the existing situation in north India in the fifth century BC the surest guarantee of social stability appeared to be in the direction of a strong and benevolent monarchy. Moreover, a really enlightened monarchy, sympathetic to Buddhism, might have the further important, positive function of providing those conditions and of helping to create those attitudes among the people which would facilitate the widespread acceptance of the Buddhist prescription. This appears to have been the logic underlying the attitude of the Buddha towards the contemporary monarchs of Koshala and Magadha, as it is represented in the Pali canon.

Buddha and Royal Courts

Throughout his life, as we have seen, Buddha was closely associated with the royal courts of his day. Pasenadi, the king of Koshala, and Bimbisara, the king of Magadha, were his life-long personal friends and supporters. Pasenadi, it is said, frequently visited Buddha to have discussions with him. It may be recalled that it was in Pasenadi's capital, Shravasti, that the majority of the Buddha's discourses were delivered. Bimbisara, from the time when he first entertained Buddha, in his palace at Rajagriha, until his death thirty-seven years later, was a firm supporter of the Buddhist *Sangha,* and himself a disciple or *upasaka,* practising the layman's higher eight-fold morality six times a month. It may be recalled, too, that by this time Koshala and Magadha between them covered most of the territory of the lower Gangetic plain, that is, roughly the whole extent of the plain between the Himalaya and the Chotanagpur plateau, from modern Lucknow eastwards to Bhagalpur. The Buddha can hardly be said to have been out of contact with the important centres of political power of his day. He may justly be described as a social and political theorist, and indeed this aspect of his historical significance has been so generally ignored that it needs heavy emphasis. But he was not only a theorist; in addition to the familiarity with the concerns of government, which his upbringing in Kapilavastu would have given him, he was in constant touch with current problems of government, through the two kings who were his supporters and disciples. Nor was this indirect involvement simply a matter of *ad hoc* problem-solving; the early Buddhist literature represents the Buddha as one who frequently had something to say on matters of policy.

It is not surprising, therefore, to find one of the most outstanding of historians of Indian political thought, U.N. Ghoshal, observing that 'the most important contribution of the early Buddhist canonists to the store of our ancient political thought consists in their "total" application of the principle of righteousness to the branches of the king's internal and foreign administration.'

The unwisdom of the multitude, the need for social and economic stability as a prerequisite of the prescription to overcome this unwisdom, the emergence of powerful monarchically ruled states—these things together provide an explanation of why the Buddha, who seems to have regarded the republican *sangha* as the ideal form of government, nevertheless gave a large place in his teaching to the important role of the righteous monarch. A number of the Jataka stories contain descriptions of the ideal king, and exhortations concerning good government. The realm of the wise king is one which is free from all oppression, not ruled arbitrarily but with equity, where good men are honoured and where the king and his officials exhibit qualities of selflessness, rectitude, mercy, political wisdom and a sense of equal respect for all beings, including different classes of society, townsmen, countrymen, religious teachers, and even birds and beasts. The importance of the personal righteousness of the king is strongly emphasized. A figure of speech frequently used is the bull who leads the herd aright: 'so should a king to righteous ways be true; the common folk injustice will eschew, and through the realm shall holy peace ensue. "When kings are righteous, the ministers of kings are righteous. When ministers are righteous, brahmans and householders also are righteous. Thus townsfolk and villagers are righteous. This being so, moon and sun go right in their courses. This being so, constellations and stars do likewise; days and nights, months and fortnights, seasons and years go on their courses regularly; winds blow regularly and in due season. Thus the *devas* are not annoyed and the sky-*deva* bestows sufficient rain. Rains falling seasonably, the crops ripen in due season. *Bhikkhus,* when crops ripen in due season, men who live on those crops are long-lived, well-favoured, strong and free from sickness."

Figs, oil, honey, molasses, root-crops, fruits all taste sweeter and better in a country where the king rules righteously, according to another Jataka story.

Welfare of People

The economic welfare of the people should, in the Buddhist view, be a special concern of the wise king, who is exhorted to take positive, specific measures which will benefit the country, together with or in addition to the effects of his own personal righteousness. In the *Kutadanta Sutta* we are told of a great king who, conscious of his good fortune hitherto, thought it advisable to offer a great sacrifice, and thereby ensure the continuance of his prosperity. His chaplain, however, tried to dissuade him, and pointed out that there would be greater wisdom in taking preventive action against possible occurrences of crime. This could be done, suggested the chaplain, by removing the economic causes of discontent. To farmers the king should issue a subsidy of food and of seed-corn. To merchants and tradesmen he should make available sources of capital which they could invest in their businesses. To those in government service he should give adequate wages and supplies of food. If this were to be done there would be no danger of subversion of the state by malcontents, but on the contrary, 'the king's revenue will go up; the country will be quiet and at peace; and the populace, pleased one with another and happy, dancing their children in their arms, will dwell with open doors.' The king followed his chaplain's advice and all happened as the chaplain had predicted. It will be noticed that the advice given by this 'chaplain' is of a kind that would be offered by a Buddhist rather than by a brahman. Sacrifice is a waste of time; the king should concern himself instead with ensuring full employment in the country. The same principle is emphasized in another well-known *Sutta,* which tells the story of the city of Kushinara in its former days of prosperity, under the Great King of Glory.

On the other hand, another *Sutta*[71] tells of a king who failed to make provision for the poor, and of the serious consequences in the life of the state. This king, we are told, instead of going to a holy man to ask advice concerning the proper duty of a king, as his prosperous and wise predecessors had done, followed his own devices. 'By his own ideas he governed his people; and they so governed, differently from what they had been, did not prosper as they used to under former kings. The one thing he had failed to do, apparently, was to make provision to remedy the condition of the poor in his realm. 'And because this was not done, poverty became widespread.' This led to cases of theft. At first the king had dealt with the offenders by making them grants of money, on the grounds that they had stolen because they were poor men and this was the best way to remedy the situation. But in a short time this suggested itself to others as an easy way of making money, and the incidence of theft increased rapidly. The king thereupon changed his policy, and began cutting off the heads of those who were caught stealing. But this violent measure only engendered further violence. Thieves now began to say among themselves, Let us also resort to violence: 'Let us also now have sharp swords made ready for ourselves, and [as for] them, from whom we take what is not given us—what they call theft—let us put a final stop to them, inflict on them the uttermost penalty, and cut their heads off.' And so, we are told, 'they got themselves sharp swords, and came forth to sack village and town and city, and to work highway robbery. And them whom they robbed they made an end of, cutting off their heads.' Such also, was the sad end of the state itself, whose ruler had failed to make adequate and wise provision for the relief of poverty. From stealing and violence there followed murder, lying, evil-speaking, adultery, false opinions, incest, and perverted lust, until the physical condition of the people deteriorated to the point where their life span was only a fraction of what it had once been. In these and similar early Buddhist stories, a great responsibility is laid upon the sovereign ruler of the state to act righteously, as far as his own life and conduct of affairs is concerned, and wisely, too, in terms of a social and economic ethic concerning which, it is emphasized, he needs to take advice from 'brahmans'. In the Buddhist literature, as we have seen, 'brahmans' are classed with *shramanas* and are recognized as such by their character and holy life, not by any hereditary right from having been born of a priestly family. The advice the righteous king needs to take, in other words, is that which, ideally, he will be offered by the Buddhist *sangha*.

There is a significant difference between the ethics of the state, with which the early Buddhist tradition was concerned, and the Brahmanical idea of the moral responsibilities of the king. As U.N. Ghoshal has observed, the Brahmanical royal ethic was the king's own personal *dharma* or duty, 'conceived in sufficiently elastic terms to provide for the needs of the kingdom and to permit in *Manu* and still more in the *Mahabharata* (after Bhishma) the wholesale incorporation of the

Arthasastra categories'. On the other hand, 'the Buddhist *dharma* in its relation to the king involves the application of the universal ethics of Buddhism to the state administration.' The king, in Brahmanical theory, is working out his own personal *moksha*, or salvation, by doing his proper duty, or *dharma*, as a king, just as any other man works out his salvation by doing his own proper duty. The performance of one's personal *dharma is* the dominating principle in the Brahmanical theory. But in the Buddhist view, the king is the agent or instrument through which the eternal, universal *Dharma is* made effective.

The point is made explicitly in a collection of sayings concerning kings found in the Pali *Anguttara-Nikaya*. The Buddha is represented as saying to the members of the *Sangha*, '*Bhikkhus*, the king who rolls the wheel of state, a *Dhamma-man*, a *Dhamma-king*, rolls indeed no unroyal wheel.' One of the *bhikkhus* then asks, 'But who, Lord, is the king of the King?' The answer given by the Buddha is 'It is *Dhamma,O bhikkhu!*' The Buddhist king—the *Dhamma-king* or *Dharma-raja*—that is, the kind of king whose rule is envisaged as necessary for the implementing of the Buddhist scheme for society, is the king who rules in subordination to one power only—that of the eternal, universal *Dharma (Dhamma)*. It is this which gives his rule a unique quality; in so far as he rules in accordance with universal *Dharma*, his rule itself has a quality of universalism; it is not appropriate to any one locality or region or period of time. The corollary of this would appear to be that neighbouring *Dhamma-kings* will find themselves ruling by the same eternal universalist principles and therefore in harmony with one another. The notion of a single universal *Dharmaraja is* already to be found in the early Buddhist tradition, as the idea of the one universal monarch, the *Chakravartin*. In Sanskrit literature *Dharma-raja is* another name for the Buddha.

Pali Buddhist Literature

It is significant that in Pali Buddhist literature also there is, in many of the references to the *Chakravartin*, a clear and conscious parallelism between this universal world-ruler and the Tathagata, or Buddha. Beside or behind the *Chakravartin* there stands the Buddha: the two are so closely linked that they almost appear to be one and the same in different roles. There was a strong tradition that Gotama's Buddhahood was seen as an *alternative* to his being a *Chakravartin*. But there is also a suggestion, in many passages, that Buddha is in every respect virtually identical with the *Chakravartin*. '*Bhikkhus*, these two persons born into the world are born to the profit and happiness of many, to the profit. happiness and welfare of many folk. What two? A Tathagata, an *arahant* who is a fully

Enlightened One (Buddha), and a world-ruling monarch . . . *Bhikkhus,* these two persons born into the world are born as extraordinary men. What two? A Tathagata . . . and a world-ruling monarch. *Bhikkhus,* the death of two persons is regretted by many folk. Of what two? A Tathagata . . . and a world-ruling monarch. *Bhikkhus,* these two are worthy of a relic-shrine *[stupa].* What two? A Tathagat a . . . and a world-ruling monarch.' Ghoshal interprets the parallel drawn here and elsewhere in Buddhist canonical texts between the Buddha and the World-ruler as meaning that the World-ruler 'is the temporal counterpart of the spiritual World-teacher, resembling him not only in his outward bodily form (the so-called thirty-two bodily signs of the superman) and the extraordinary incidents of his birth, death, cremation and commemoration, but also in the jointly unique role as universal benefactors.'

It is this close resemblance, amounting to virtual identity, between the World-ruler and the World-teacher which has the effect, by implication, of distinguishing the Buddhist conception of an emperor or world-ruler from the Brahmanical conception of the emperor, as the latter is set out, for instance, in the *Arthasastra* of Kautilya. The political philosophy which this treatise embodies, and with which political practice corresponded fairly closely, is that might is right, or that what is expedient is right. The Buddhist political philosophy was founded, as K.N. Jayatilleke pointed out, on the principle that 'the wheel of might turns in dependence on the wheel of righteousness.' The conflict between the two philosophies was one which, as we shall shortly see, was experienced as a conflict of conscience by the emperor Ashoka.

Certain clear inter-relationships can thus be seen within the structure of society envisaged in early Buddhist tradition and practice. Three major elements can be distinguished: the *Sangha,* the king, and the mass of the people. Three relationships can also be distinguished.

The *Sangha,* as the realization in practice, or visible embodiment, of the new wisdom, stood in a special relationship to the king which was a continuation of the relationship which had existed between the Buddha in his day and the kings of Koshala and Magadha. This relationship was in principle of the same kind as that between the World-teacher and the World-ruler.

In the other direction the *Sangha* was related to the mass of the people. The community of the *Sangha* arose out of the common people who both provided its recruits and ministered to its needs. Moreover, what the community of the *Sangha* was now, all humanity was eventually to become; proleptically, the common people were members of the *Sangha.*

Meanwhile, it was necessary that until all should have fully apprehended the Buddha-Dhamma and have entered into the wider realm of consciousness to which life in the *Sangha* led, there should be a centre of political power to bring an interim unity into what would otherwise be the chaos of multiple units, to maintain law and order and promote the common welfare. From the people, in the Buddhist view, the king derived his authority rather than from any divine source; in their name and for their good he exercised it.

IV

Buddhist Philosophy

Scholars are generally agreed that the beginnings of Buddhist thought as propounded by Siddhartha Gautama, the Buddha, comprised no more than a collection of ethico-religious principles, lacking the form or content of what could be called a philosophy. It was only with the appearance of Abhidharma (Pali, Abhidhamma) scholarship that Buddhism began to face philosophical questions and take up apologetic problems through the exegesis of canonical texts. Yet, true though this be, we should not forget Max Weber's statement that "like Jainism, but even more clearly, Buddhism presents itself as a product of the time of urban development, of urban kingship, and the city nobles" (*The Religion of India: The Sociology of Hinduism and Buddhism.* Glencoe, III, 1962, p. 204). It would have been impossible for Buddha to appeal to the people of his time, many of whom were deeply interested in philosophical issues inherited from the Upanisadic philosophy (such as Yajnavalkya's lofty speculations on *atman* mysticism), had he not raised his new message to the revolutionary heights of a spiritual philosophy able to hold sway over the numerous traditional and contemporary trends of religious thought in India.

The notorious silence of the Buddha regarding the meta-physical problems—in particular, (1) whether or not the universe is eternal; (2) whether or not the universe is finite; (3) whether or not the *jiva* (spirit or principle of life) belongs to the body; and (4) whether or not a *tathagata* (i.e., a Buddha), once released from worldly life, continues to exist, exists and does not exist at the same time, or is neither existent nor nonexistent—does not mean that he was either indifferent to philosophical problems or ignorant of them. Quite the contrary, his teaching presupposes a critical standpoint *vis-a-vis* metaphysical reasoning that enabled him to comprehend and analyse the antinomies implicit in the assertions of the various contemporary traditions. We find Buddha forging a "middle path" between the antinormic extremes of theoretical and practical reason by shifting the focus to the question of the efficacy of ideas to deliver the self from the ceaseless transmigratory repetition of karmic misery through death and sin.

It is in this context that the Buddha offers his teaching on the Four Noble Truths (Skt. *catvary aryasatyani;* Pali, *cattari ariyasaccani*). It was from a similar focus on soteriological efficacy that in early Buddhism there sprang the main doctrinal themes of the five aggregates (Skt. *skandhas;* Pali, *khandhas*) or existential components of being human, of the dependent co-arising (Skt., *pratitya-samutpada;* Pali, *paticca-samuppada*) of all being-in-the-world, or in later Mahayana Buddhism the notion of which were worked out in Madhyamika and Yogacara thinking. In turn, the Madhyamika and Yogaçara schools in India provided the framework for later philosophical syntheses of doctrine in China, Tibet, Japan, and elsewhere.

Early Buddhist Thought: The Four Noble Truths

It is recorded that in his first sermon after his enlightenment, directed to the five men who had shared his ascetic practices, Buddha proclaimed a Middle Path toward absolute truth that avoided the extremes of hedonism on the one hand and asceticism on the other. In their stead he proclaimed the Four Noble Truths as the only effective way to purify insight and terminate suffering. Here we find the simplest statement on the content of enlightenment and the means to attain it. The early scriptures depict Buddha as constantly preaching these truths. During his last journey and in the face of death, the eighty-year-old Buddha repeats the same doctrine to the people of a village he passes through.

We cannot now share the certitude of early believers that the extant texts (the Pali Nikayas and Chinese Agamas) on the Four Noble Truths represent the actual content of Buddha's first sermon. It is impossible to distinguish cleary his own words from those of later disciples. Yet the tradition witnesses to the fact that from the time he started preaching until the end of his life, Buddha himself took the Four Truths as the central core and axis of his doctrine.

The Four Noble Truths express the content of the Buddha's religious experience of conversion and enlightenment. They are the Truth about Suffering (illness), the Truth about the Origin of Suffering (its cause), the Truth about the Surcease of Suffering (its annihilation), and the Truth about the Way to End Suffering (the Noble Eightfold Path).

Recently, some scholars have begun to question whether the doctrine of the Four Noble Truths can in fact be attributed to the Buddha himself.

They argue that the medical format in which these truths are expressed first appears in Buddhist and other writings only around the beginning of the common era. But Greek philosophy can shed some unexpected light on the question, for it has been ascertained that Greek medicine of the time of Plato and Aristotle, or even as much as a century before them, was heavily influenced by Indian medical science. The section on mental illness in Plato's *Timaeus* describes the pathological elements as the illness, the cause of illness, the removal of that cause, and the method of treatment. In Aristotle's *Metaphysics* (Z, 1032bl5-30), specific mention is made and detailed explanations are offered on the technique of treating cases according to the four elements of the illness, its cause, the removal of that cause, and the method of so doing.

Nowhere in Buddhist writings, or in any other Indian sources, is it made clear just how the Four Truths relate to one another as categories of medical science or how they constitute an effective method of treatment. Yet all of this appears very clearly in Plato and Aristotle. If one can conclude that these Greek ideas corne from an earlier Indian source, it becomes credible that they may have been known and respected by the Buddha and his disciples. Moreover, there seems to be a connection between medical science and skepticism, particularly in Greek antiquity. If we can assume the same connection in the Buddha's India, then the fact that some of the most intellectual followers of the Buddha, Sariputta and Mogallana, before becoming followers of the Buddha were disciples of the famous skeptic Sanjaya Belatthiputta suggests the possibility that medical terminology was prevalent in the group surrounding the young Gautama. This may be quite significant in that Sariputta played a central role in the formative history of Buddhist thinking.

One must, however, note that the medical usage of these terms differs from their soteriological use. The concern with "suffering" in primitive Buddhism points to the basic problem of human finitude, not simply to dissatisfaction resulting from frustrated passions or unpleasantness involved with sensations of pain. Any modem interpretation of the truths of suffering, its cause, the removal of that cause, and the path leading to such must begin in an awareness of the radical existential thrust of these concepts. Suffering must be seen against the background of impermanence, for Buddhism describes suffering as: "All things are impermanent *[anitya],* all things are suffering and sorrow *[duhkha],* all the elements of being are no-self *[anatman].*"

Here impermanence does not simply indicate the objective fact of the perpetual change and disappearance of external things. First and foremost, impermanence signifies the problem of my own existence, my being-unto-death. Deep insight into and resignation to my own impermanence does not mean that I have accepted any particular fact about external conditions, but that I am resigned in all things and all circumstances to my own existence as impermanent. It is the turning around of the outward-looking eye of the self carried along by everyday desires to focus upon that self as it really is. The self and its feelings undergo a crystallization in the process, for everything previously experienced congeals within an awareness of that self as impermanent. It is within the framework of this experience that suffering comes to awareness.

Origin of Suffering

Thus the suffering signified by the phrase "All things are impermanent, all things are suffering" is not the psycho-physical sensation of pain or dissatisfaction with the course of events. These are instances of suffering defined by some object whereby one is inflicted. For this kind of suffering the fundamental issue is how to dispose of this object through the proper technical means.

Likewise, to look for "the origin of suffering" does not mean to investigate the cause of an illness from its symptoms. Rather it means that the self crystallizes in suffering, congealing into a definite structure with suffering as its focus. In that crystallization the opposition between subject and object tends to be clarified in its true nature as the attachment of the subject to objects. This is what the commentaries mean when they take the origin of suffering to be the self-regenerating, unquenchable thirst of desire.

One must completely understand suffering and annihilate its origin. It is like the suffering that appears in a dream: once one realizes that one has been dreaming, the suffering is completely understood and one is brought to a new awareness that the dream was the cause of the suffering. Indeed, the awareness of the dream as dream entails an awakening from the dream. The Buddha is the awakened one, and through his awakening he must rouse and awaken those who still go on sleeping.

From the above we can summarize the Four Noble Truths in the propositions that (1) the arising of suffering is itself the surcease of suffering and (2) the noble truths involve a communication of I and Thou on the way to awakening, whereby that surcease implies that one's own awakening awakens others. Often the path is conceived as simply the means or method to reach the goal of surcease or awakening. But while that is appropriate when speaking in medical or technical terms, it does not express the dynamic structure of the existential categories proper to religion.

It is reported that the skeptical Sariputta, before he became a follower of the Buddha, once met Assaji, one of the five original disciples of the Buddha, and asked him about the essentials of the Buddha's doctrine. The disciple, however, excused himself, saying that he was not yet sufficiently versed in the doctrine. But he added, "Those things that arise from a cause, of these the Buddha had told the cause and that which is their surcease—the great recluse has such a doctrine." Upon hearing these words, Sariputta immediately attained the insight that "the arising of suffering turns into the surcease of suffering." In other words, he realized that the condensation of all suffering into its cause or ground triggers an immediate turnabout into its annihilation.

There is one radical difference between the skepticism of ancient Greece or India and modern skepticism. In the former, the suspension of all judgment provoked by the awareness of the relativity of all human knowing is accompanied by a decision to abandon all attachment. It is in this abandonment that the heart is brought to the peace of detachment. Here skepticism is a doctrine of religious liberation through renunciation, although for Sariputta it lacked an ultimate foundation on which to ground this liberation and peace. It was not until Sariputta met Assaji that he recognized in this lack of foundation the final bondage to be overcome in order to arrive at true liberation. Thus a single phrase was sufficient to lead him to grasp the promise of conversion: "The darkness of ignorance turns around and light is born." It should, however, be remembered that this conversion was only the first step on Sariputta's road to complete awakening, which was to be realized later in his continued master-disciple relationship with Buddha.

Four Noble Truths

By understanding the doctrine of the Four Noble Truths as an existential path wherein one's own awakening awakens others, we gain access to the fundamental spirit of early Buddhism. Undoubtedly, through the religious community they shared the Buddha and his disciples went on to deepen their insight into the meaning of the identity of the arising of suffering with the surcease of suffering. The more philosophical speculations of the Abhidharma scholars also stemmed from their insight into the communal aspects of the Four Truths. Certainly, many Buddhist tenets trace their origin back to that spiritual communion. Such early doctrines as the five aggregates and the six sense organs, as well as such central philosophical notions as dependent co-arising, were first taken up as religious symbols within the community, developing in Buddhist doctrinal history from that beginning.

In the later enfolding of Buddhism within its various historical circumstances and in its various communities, we find the same emergence of the Buddha's original thrust recurring again and again. Both the cognitive and the ethical value of each of the Buddha's teachings derive from their overall religious significance. The interrelationships between the individual teachings are like the various constellations of the evening sky brightening before our view. Just as the whole configuration of the stars gently revolves as one star after the other rises up from the horizon of space, so the different teachings throughout the history of Buddhism present themselves to our awareness. Although it remains the same from beginning to end, yet it is always giving rise to something new, for this is how the teaching that one's own awakening awakens others developed and deepened within the Buddhist community. Since Dharma-teaching is a work of compassion (love), we can see how it must always be concretized in the world, for it evinces a cosmic love that embraces all equally and reaches to the totality of being in all its dimensions and configurations.

This existential thrust of early Buddhism did not then exclude philosophical understanding. Rather, it led directly to the Abhidharma schools and their attempts to express its content in a clear and consistent philosophy. [*See also* Four Noble Truths *and* Eightfold Path.]

Abhidharma Philosophy

The rise of the Abhidharma schools some centuries before the beginning of the common era signaled a shift from the popular style of the earlier scriptures to a more systematic and theoretical understanding of the content of the Buddha's teaching, deemed necessary in order to preserve its meaning against misinterpretations. Although at first the term *abhi-dharma,* which literally meant "in regard to the doctrine," referred to commentarial explanations of the scriptures, in time the Abhidharma masters began to rearrange the teachings systematically and offer their own interpretations of their meaning. The Abhidharma then became known as the "superior *(abhi)* doctrine *(dharma)"* and constituted a separate, third collection of the canon, along with the Scripture (Sutra) and Discipline (Vinaya) collections.

The Abhidharma thinkers began by composing lists of technical terms *(matrka)* aimed at defining the basic truths of Buddhism. They sought to identify the "essences" *(svabhava)* of all things, which then were regarded as absolutely real and true, since they were incapable of any further analysis. For example, the belief in selfhood was rejected because no self *(atman)* could be identified underlying the continuity of human living. But the five constituent factors *(dharma)* or aggregates *(skandha)*—material form (rupa), sensation *(vedana),* conceptualization *(samjna),* karmic impulse *(samskara),* and consciousness (vijnana)—were detected as being the real factors behind the mistaken belief in self and were accordingly pronounced to be real and true. Abhidharma is a philosophy of realism and conceptualism, for its principal thinkers, by and large, held that such real factors were correctly and truly expressed in well-analyzed concepts. [See also Dharma, article on Buddhist Dharma and Dharmas and Soul, article on Buddhist Concepts.]

The Abhidharma thinkers, however, did not undertake their theoretical task from a mere desire for logical consistency or academic learning. Their main interest was soteriological, for they thought that detachment from passion *(klesa)* resulted from the attainment of the correct view *(sarnagdrsti).* They discoursed at length on the sixteen aspects of the Four Noble Truths and on the many stages of meditation necessary to reach cessation (nirvana). The tradition they initiated continues in the Theravada tradition today.

Yet, in the eyes of the founders of the Mahayana tradition, the Abhidharma thinkers' basically intellectualist approach tended to substitute conceptual and propositional truth in place of the existential thrust of the primitive Buddhist teachings. The basic doctrine of dependent co-arising was shunted to the periphery and treated under the heading of karmic maturation, for in a world of absolutely true and real dharma factors the stress is upon the ontological status of things, not upon their interdependence.

It was in direct response to this Abhidharma realism and conceptualism, particularly that of the Sarvastivada school, that the Prajnaparamita scriptures were composed from 50 BCE to 150 CE. These scriptures, written in an anti-intellectual and paradoxical style, recommended as "the perfection of wisdom" a nondiscriminative understanding *(prajna)* that rejected all Abhidharma "attachment" to views and declared all things to be empty of essence. [See Prajna.] These scriptures declared that the truth of wisdom is found not in correct views, but in the embodiment of wisdom in practices of compassion. [See Karuna.]

But these Prajnaparamita scriptures were composed in a direct and paradoxical style and did not design to engage the Abhidharma masters in philosophical dialogue. Indeed, it is probable that the Prajnaparamita adherents were not trained monks like the Abhidharma masters but rather laymen committed to the Buddha's doctrine. It was the Madhyamika philosophy of Nagarjuna (fl. c. 200) that took these wisdom insights and expressed them in philosophic terms. [See also Sarvastivada and Sautrantika.]

Madhyamika Philosophy

Nagarjuna's Madhyamika philosophy laid the foundation for all subsequent Mahayana thinking. He took over and continued the Prajnaparamita; a theme of emptiness (*Sunyata*) and argued consistently against the Abhidharma ideas of real essences *(dharmas).* [See Sunyam and Sunyata.]

However, the main feature of Madhyamika philosophy is not simply its insistence upon emptiness. Rather, the unique achievement of Nagarjuna lies in his identification of emptiness with dependent co-arising. The primitive teaching of dependent co-arising *(pratitya-samutpada)* had fallen into a rigid formulation within the Abhidharma ontology as the operation of *karman.* Nagarjuna reclaimed it as expressing the dependent co-arising of all essenceless reality. Things co-arise dependently because they are empty of any fixed essence and that which is empty is precisely the essenceless being of dependent co-arising. All being is empty of essence, for emptiness is embodied in dependently co-arising being. [See Pratitya-samutpada.]

Although Madhyamika is permeated with "a hundred negations and a thousand denials," it is not nihilism (nastivada). Rather, it thematizes the essenceless being of dependent co-arising. Nagarjuna aimed not only at a deconstruction of Abhidharma realism, but also at a construction of a dialectic of dependently co-arising being that might embody awareness of emptiness. His insistence on emptiness is not the nihilistic ravings of a madman but an attempt to think being within the context of emptiness and emptiness within the context of being. In Madhyamika, reality *(dharmata)* and suchness *(tathata)* signify dependently co-arising being understood through the negation of emptiness. Stated conversely, they signify emptiness embodied in essenceless being. The Middle Path is this understanding of emptiness as concretized in the empty, concrete being of dependent co-arising. *[See also* Tathata.]

The identity of emptiness and dependent co-arising flows into the complementary Madhyamika theme of the double truth *(satya-dvaya),* a teaching the Nagarjuna was probably the first to treat as central. The truth essences. It is a grasping at such imagined essences *(svabhava),* as if a named image signified the reality of a corresponding essence over against the knower.

The second point is the presentation of the character of that which is dependently co-arisen, that is, the basic other-dependent pattern of consciousness *(paratantra-. laksana),* which identifies within consciousness the ground of dependent co-arising. Consciousness is a synergy of different operations and functions. The storehouse consciousness *(alaya-vijnana)* functions as a store of conceptually and verbally unmediated karmic experience acting in tandem with the active consciousnesses *(pravrtti-vijnana)* that do mediate those experiences in words and ideas. *(See* Alaya-vijnana.] Thus, there is a mutual dependency between base experience and thinking upon that experience, for each depends on the other. Furthermore, consciousness is other-dependent because it appears as image *(nimitta)* and insight *(darsana).* Images are presented by the senses but do not of themselves issue in meaning, for imagination is not constructive of meaning. It is only insight into those images that constructs meaning.

In the absence of such insight, images remain uninterpreted pictures imagined to depict of themselves the essences of things seen and imagined. But without the image no insight can occur. Here the notion of dependent co-arising is understood as the basic structure of all consciousness and grounded critically within an understanding of conscious understanding as other-dependent. In virtue of this other-dependent pattern, consciousness not only devolves into its illusory, imagined pattern but also is open to and capable of being converted into wisdom, into the fully perfected pattern *(parinisanna-laksana)* of consciousness, which is precisely the absence of the imagined pattern within the other-dependent pattern. It is the absence of imputing essences to things presented in images. It is the realization that all dependently co-arising things are empty of essence.

In these first two points Asanga has reinterpreted and critically grounded the notions of emptiness and dependent co-arising within consciousness. But he does not stop with this, for his third point is a presentation of the meaning of what has been declared in the scriptures. Here Asanga makes a unique contribution to Buddhist philosophy in presenting a hermeneutic based on the theme of the three patterns of consciousness, for once consciousness has been converted *(asraya-paravrtti)* from the imagined pattern to that of full perfection, it becomes capable of skillfully embodying the wisdom of ultimate meaning within worldly and conventional language. The validity of such conventional truth is found then in its faithfulness to the scriptures and its logical consistency. Thus, both Asanga and Vasubandhu composed works on logic, explicating the genesis and validity of conventional truth.

All words and ideas are dependent on others, for they are nothing but constructs of consciousness *(vijnaptimatra).* But once recognized as such, once they no longer threaten to usurp the place of silent realization, they have a valid, if limited truth. Thus, in evolving their critical theory of consciousness Asanga and Vasubandhu allow scope for valid doctrinal discourse and meaningful theoretical thinking within an understanding of the other-dependent and empty structure of consciousness *[See* Yogacara *and the biographies of Asanga and Vasubandhu.]*

Epistemology and Logic

Epistemological and logical issues had not been neglected in Buddhist thought. Within the Abhidharma circle such questions had indeed been discussed. Nagarjuna, Asanga, and Vasubandhu all dealt with logic and treated the question of the valid means of knowing *(pramana).* These endeavors were brought to the fore by the Yogacara affirmation of a critical understanding of consciousness. If thinking is valid as other-dependent, if conventional truth is indeed truth, then questions of epistemology and logic become crucial prolegomena for all philosophical discussion. Thus such thinkers as Dignaga (480-540) and Dharmakirti (seventh century) developed a "Buddhist" epistemology and logic.

Inasmuch as these thinkers inherited the Yogacara affirmation of the validity of other-dependent knowing and the synergistic structure of understanding, they are also known as Yogacarins. But inasmuch as they do not employ either scriptural authorities or the Yogacara doctrinal language, never mentioning such central terms as the storehouse consciousness or the three patterns of understanding, they are distinguished as Vijnaptimatra thinkers of the logical tradition *(nyayanusarino vijnanavadinah).* Yet, although they avoid such terminology, they do reflect the basic Yogacara teachings on consciousness.

The interdependent, synergistic functioning of consciousness is described by Dignaga in terms of the two means of knowing: direct perception and inference. Direct perception *(pratyaksa) is* unmediated, pure sensation, prior to words and before any imagining. It presents the "own mark" *(svalaksatna)* of the sensed thing. Since the Yogacarins had identified the source of illusion as imagining through verbal fabrication, so Dignaga identified true and sure knowing as the pure perception that precedes such fabrication. By contrast, inference *(anumana)* is the verbal mental construction that by naming things establishes their classes and gains insight into their relationships, presenting their of ultimate meaning *(paramartha-satya) is* always ineffable and beyond any conceptual knowing, and yet it must be expressed in the truth of worldly convention *(samvrti-satya)* in order to be understandable to common worldlings. Conventional truth is language attempting, but always failing, to express the ineffable. It is thus described as a clouding over and occluding of truth. When recognized as such, it can point beyond to that ultimate meaning that it clouds and occludes.

Madhyamika takes its stand upon the identity of emptiness and dependent co-arising and weaves the theme of the double truth within that context. Ultimate meaning is the truth of emptiness, while conventional meaning is the truth of dependent co-arising, appearing to the awakened as totally inadequate and false, but to the unawakened as propositional truth in the world.

Yet, although the Prajnaparar..ita scriptures and the Madhyamika philosophy are in no sense nihilistic, they did occasion distress among Buddhists who could not follow their initial deconstructionist mode of thinking. Not all practitioners were concerned with the dangers of Abhidharma realism, for most had probably never had the inclination to engage themselves in its intricate scholasticism. It is thus not surprising that the more affirmative Tathagatagarbha mystic trend of thought should have arisen to counter the perceived negativism of Prajnaparamita and Madhyamika. The notion of emptiness was found to be unacceptable (or at least, incomplete), for the Buddha declared that "the Buddha nature exists in every sentient being." In contrast to the supposed negativism of Madhyamika, the Tathagatagarbha texts all present Buddha nature, the realm of the seed *(garbha)* of awakening (becoming a *tathagata),* as the only truly existent being. [*See* Tathagatagarbha.]

Rather than Nagarjuna's identification of emptiness and dependent co-arising, the reality of empirical, everyday being *(sat-tva) is* identified with the ultimately true Dharma Realm *(dharmadhatu).* All things are not empty, for the Buddha nature is really real and existent, as evidenced in the attribution to it of the four perfect qualities of eternity, constancy, purity, and immutability, attributes that Nagarjuna would have immediately rejected as illusory fabrications. The one real reality is this Buddha nature. This really existent seed of Buddha nature is empty of all defilements, which are unreal and illusory, but not empty of the Buddha attributes, which are not really distinct from it. All defilements are adventitious *(agantuka)* and do not pertain to the original essence of that seed. The scope of emptiness and non-being is restricted to the defiled coverings over that underlying seed and its intrinsic attributes. Emptiness is no longer all-inclusive, for after negating all the defilements as illusions, there remains left over *(avasista)* the eternal, immutable, already pure reality of the Buddha nature. The Tathagatagarbha tradition represents a Buddhist philosophy of original being and stands in sharp contrast to Prajnaparamita and Madhyamika thought.

However, the Tathagatagarbha tradition in India was not a fully articulated philosophical alternative to Madhyamika. It is represented by only one *sastra* (treatise) and was never criticized by Madhyamika thinkers. But its presentations of the theme of the original, really existent Buddha nature served as a basis for much philosophical thinking in later developments, especially in China, where it was reinterpreted in terms of the dependent co-arising of the awakening in the world.

In the Indian context, however, the Tathagatagarbha tradition failed to account for the genesis of defilement, for all defilement was swept away by it as unreal and illusory. Even Madhyamika in its thematization of dependent co-arising had not focused upon the genesis of illusion, being content to demonstrate the logical falsity of all views. But without some explanation of the genesis of illusion it was difficult to ground doctrinal discourse within the dependent co-arising world of ignorance and illusion. The rejection of Abhidharma theory by Madhyamika and the bypassing of any theory by Tathagatagarbha left scant room for any rational presentation of doctrine and seemed to undermine even the possibility of doctrinal discourse. *[See also* Madhyamika *and the biography of Nagarjuna.]*

Yogacara Philosophy

The critical Yogacara philosophy of Asanga and Vasubandhu (fourth century) attempted to ground Nagarjuna's teaching of emptiness within a critical understanding of the consciousness that generates all meaning. [*See* Vijnana.] Their intent was not only to maintain the teachings of the Prajnaparamita scriptures and the basic themes of Madhyamika, but also to allow scope for theoretical thinking within the context of the identity of emptiness with dependent co-arising. The contribution of Asanga and Vasubandhu to Buddhist philosophy lies principally in their understanding of emptiness and dependent co-arising within a critical understanding of consciousness. They carried out their project under the themes of the development of consciousness into illusion *(vijnanaparinama)* and the three patterns of consciousness *(trilaksana).*

Asanga summarizes his thinking in three points. The first is his presentation of dependent co-arising, which grounds the meaning of emptiness within consciousness by identifying the imagined pattern of clinging to unreal essences as empty. This illusory, imagined pattern *(parikalpita-laksana)* results from the development of words and images clung to as if they represented real "common mark" *(samanya-laksana).* Logic is developed as the correct procedure for such inference and serves to safeguard the constructed truth of reasoning about the "common marks" of things. Just as for Asanga and Vasubandhu consciousness was structured as the synergistic interplay between preverbal experience stored in the container consciousness and the mental constructs of the active consciousnesses of thinking and imagining, so here consciousness is a synergy between preverbal, pure experience and verbal thinking.

The same epistemological understanding is seen in Dignaga's understanding of the structure of consciousness. The image aspect *(nimitta-bhaga) is* the presence of sensed images as objects for understanding. The insight aspect *(darsana-bhaga) is* the understanding of the meaning of those images. The awareness aspect *(svasamvitti-bhaga) is* the awareness of the knower implicit in such acts of insight into image. Later, the Yogacarin Dharmapala (530-561) added a fourth aspect of reflexive awareness *(svasamvitti-samvitti-bhaga)* as the critical understanding that one is indeed understanding through insight into image.

Dharmakirti furthered Dignaga's pioneering work and constructed a vast epistemological system that was transmitted to and studied in Tibet. However, the Chinese, although they translated some of Dignaga's works, showed scant interest in epistemological and logical questions and did not devote much attention to this aspect of Buddhist thinking. *[See the biographies of Dignaga. Dharmakirti, and Dharmapala.]*

Later Buddhist Thought

The themes of emptiness, dependent co-arising, and double truth, and of their interpretation through the Yogacara notion of the three patterns of consciousness and the Tathagatagarbha notion of the original Buddha nature, form the bedrock philosophical themes that reappear throughout the subsequent centuries in Mahayana Buddhist thinking.

The identity of emptiness and dependent co-arising appears clearly in the philosophy of the Chinese T'ient'ai school. Its principal thinker Chih-i (538-597 CE) describes the "middle" *(chung)* path as including within itself an awareness of emptiness *(k'ung)* and of the temporary and provisional *(chia),* thus repeating Nagarjuna's notion of the Middle Path as the identity of emptiness and dependent co-arising. Chih-i also seems to have been influenced by the Yogacara notion of the three patterns of consciousness, where the other-dependent pattern includes both the perfected pattern of emptiness and the imagined pattern of transient being. *[See* T'ien-t'ai *and the biography of Chih-i.]*

Chinese Hua-yen philosophy begins its analysis with the distinction between truth (*li*) and phenomena *(shih),* reflecting the notion of the double truth. It then moves to a third step, which gains insight into the interpenetration of truth and phenomena, reflecting Nagarjuna's identification of emptiness and dependent co-arising. The fourth Hua-yen step, the interpenetration of phenomena and phenomena, seems to hark back to the Yogacara theme that to the awakened one all things are merely conscious constructs infused with the wisdom of perfection. [*See* Hua-yen.]

The Tantric schools in both Tibet and China were direct outgrowths of the Madhyamika and, especially in China and Japan, were also heavily influenced by Yogacara. The basic theme of the two *mandalas* of the womb *(garbha)* as truth and the lightning bolt *(vajra)* as the seeker after truth reflects the structure of the double truth as the attempt to embody the ineffable within worldly experience. [*See* Buddhism, Schools of, *article on* Esoteric Buddhism.]

Of course, the Madhyamika school itself continued into China in the San-lun school, although this school seems to have concentrated its attention on refutation and emptiness. The entire Tibetan tradition takes its stand upon Madhyamika thinking and develops it within its Tantric thrust. Yogacara also had its successor in the Fa-hsiang school in China, but in the absence of the Indian concerns over the value of theory and its critical grounding within consciousness, it seems to have followed along more narrow scholastic channels.

Chinese Ch'an and Japanese Zen were heavily influenced not only by the Prajnaparamita teaching of emptiness, but also by the notion of the Buddha nature, especially Rinzai Zen, with its paradoxical invitation to discover "one's original face." This theme was also treated by Chinese and Japanese Buddhists of many schools and reinterpreted to indicate the dependent co-arising of the already existing potential for awakening within all sentient beings. It influenced the teaching of the One Vehicle *(ekayana)* for all beings, which was common to most Chinese schools. [*See* Ch'an *and* Zen.]

The same themes continue into the present, as seen in the philosophy of the Kyoto school founded on the work of Nishida Kitaro (1870-1945). Nishida, Nishitani Keiji, and Takeuchi Yoshinori attempt in their philosophizing to synthesize modern Western philosophical understandings within the Mahayana theme of emptiness or "nothingness." [*See the biography of Nishida Kitaro.*]

Of all these various developments in Buddhist thinking, each attempted to bring the Buddha Dharma to speech and relate it to contemporary concerns and issues. Later Buddhists did not merely repeat Indian themes but evolved creative understandings of Buddhism for their times. Yet the basic themes remained as the parameters for Buddhist thinking [*See also* Indian Philosophies; Nirvana; Soul; *article on* Buddhist Concepts; Buddhist Ethics; *and* Soteriology, *article on* Buddhist Soteriology. *For further discussion of the notion of "two truths" in Buddhist thought, see* Language, *article on* Buddhist Views of Language, *and* Buddhist Literature, *article on* Exegesis and Hermeneutics.]

References

1. Ambedkar, B.R.: *The Untouchables,* p. 301.
2. Sattar, S. Abul: *Dr. Ambedkar's Contribution to Buddhism* (In Ambedkar and Social Justice, Vol. II).
3. Benz, E.: *Buddhism or Communism,* pp. 109-110.
4. Thapar, R.: *Ashoka and the Decline of the Mauryas,* p. 141.
5. Dr. Baba Saheb Ambedkar Writings and Speeches, Vol. 7, p. 10.
6. Jiloha, R.C.: *The Native Indians: in Search of Identity,* p. 53.
7. Dutt, R.C.: *Later Hindu Civilisation,* Calcutta.
8. Jiloha, *op. cit.,* p. 53.
9. *Ibid.,* p. 53.
10. Majumdar, R.C.: *Ancient India,* p. 128.
11. Biswas, S.K.: *Buddhism—the Religion of Mohen-jo-daro and Harappa Cities,* p. 194.
12. Nehru, Jawaharlal: *Discovery of India,* p. 110.
13. *Ibid.,* p. 111.
14. *Ibid.*
15. *Ibid.*
16. *Ibid.*
17. Chanchreek, K.L.: *Gautama Buddha—Life and Philosophy,* pp. 6-16.
18. Nehru, *op. cit.,* p. 120.
19. Chanchreek, *op. cit.,* p. 18.
20. Nehru, *op. cit.,* p. 120.
21. Chanchreek, K.L.: *Buddha: Life and Philosophy,* pp. 40-45.
22. *Ibid.,* pp. 46-50.
23. Rao, R. Samgeetha: *Ambedkar and his Political Thought,* p. 42.
24. Jatava, D.R.: *Evolution of Indian Social Thought,* pp. 45-46.
25. *Ibid.,* p. 46.
26. Bishras, p. 23.
27. Chanchreek, K.L.: *Gautama Buddha—Life and Philosophy,* pp. 35 50.
28. See Sagar, S.L.: Hindu Culture and Caste System in India, pp. 24-25.

29. Matanga Jataka, Vol. 4, p. 300.
30. See Sagar, *op. cit.*, pp. 25-26.
31. Pandey, G.C.: *Studies in the Origins of Buddhism,* p. 332.
32. Jatava, D.R. *op. cit.*, p. 49.
33. For detail see B.C. Laws, *Tribes in Ancient India* (Bhandarkar Oriental Series, 4)
34. See Chanchreek's *Bhagwan Gautam Buddha and Koli Jati ka Itihas* (University Publication, New Delhi) for detailed and authentic study.

The best single source for works by both Eastern and Western scholars on the basic philosophic themes of Indian Buddhism is Nakamura Hajime's *Indian Buddhism: A Survey with Bibliographical Notes* (Hirakata, 1980). On pre-Mahayana Buddhism the standard study is Etienne Lamotte's *Histoire du bouddhisme indien: Des origines a l'ere Saka* (Louvain, 1976). The entire history of Indian Buddhism is covered in A.K. Warder's *Indian Buddhism* (Delhi, 1970). More popular in style is the often reprinted *The History of Buddhist Thought* (1933; 2d ed., New York, 1951) by Edward J. Thomas and *Buddhism: Its Essence and Development* (1951; reprint, New York, 1959) by Edward Conze, although this last work reflects the strong preference of its author for the Prajnaparamita negation of all philosophic theory.

Walpola Rahula's What *the Buddha Taught* (1959; 2d ed., Bedford, 1967) is a concise and clear statement of the early teaching. For a scholarly Abhidharma translation, see Louis de La Vallee Poussin's six-volume translation, *L'Abhidharmakosa de Vasubandhu* (1923-1931; reprint, Brussels, 1971). Herbert V. Guenther's *Philosophy and Psychology in the Abhidharma* (Lucknow, 1957) is a readable and informative introduction to Abhidharma. Kimura Taiken's, *Abhidatsumaron no kenkyu* (Tokyo, 1937) is a pioneering study on the developmental stages of Abhidharma thinking.

An excellent study of Madhyamika thought is Frederick J. Streng's *Emptiness: A Study in Religious Meaning* (New York, 1967), which examines the meaning of Nagarjuna's use of the theme of emptiness. Richard H. Robinson's *Early Madhyamika in India and China* (Delhi, 1976) focuses attention upon the transmission of Madhyamika in China. Mervyn Sprung's *Lucid Exposition of the Middle Way* (Boulder, 1979) not only presents an exceptionally good translation of the main sections from Candrakirti's *Prasannapada,* but also offers a particularly insightful introduction to Madhyamika thinking. Nagao Gadjin's *Chukan tetsugaku no komponteki tachiba* (Tokyo, 1976; English translation in preparation), is a classic work on the philosophical issues in both Madhyamika and Yogacara and has served as the source for much of the above treatment of these schools.

The most comprehensive work on the Tathagatagarbha tradition is Takasaki Jikido's *Nyoraizo shiso no keisei* (Tokyo, 1974), which traces the development of Tathagatagarbha thought from its beginning in the *Tathagatagarbha Sutra* to the *Ratnagotravibhaga Sastra.* David Seyfort Ruegg's *La theorie de Tathagatagarbha et du Gotra* (Paris, 1969) examines the same tradition as it moves from the *Ratnagotravibhaga Sastra to* later Tibetan texts. Also to be noted is *The Lion's Roar of Queen Srimala,* translated by Alex Wayman and Hideko Wayman (New York, 1974), which presents a clear introductory essay on Tathagatagarbha and a translation of the above scripture.

There are no comprehensive studies on Yogacara in any Western language, although Japanese scholars have long studied this foundational school of Mahayana. Of particular note is Nagao Gadjin's *Chukan to yuishiki* (Tokyo, 1978). However, translations and studies of particular texts have been made by Louis de La Vallee Poussin, *Vijnaptimatratasiddhi: La Siddhi de Hiuan-tsang* (Paris, 1928-1929); Etienne Lamotte, *Samdhinirmocana Sutra: L'explication des mysteres* (Louvain, 1935); John P. Keenan, *The Scripture on Explicating Underlying Meaning* (Tokyo, 1986); Etienne Lamotte, *La somme du Grand Vehiçule d'Asanga (Mahayanasamgraha)* (1938-1939; Louvain, 1973); John P. Keenan, *The Interpretation of the Buddha Land* (Tokyo, forthcoming); and Janice Dean Willis, *On Knowing Reality: The Tattvartha Chapter of Asanga's Bodhisattvabhumi* (New York, 1979), which also contains valuable notes and interpretations.

On Buddhist epistemology and logic Theodore Stcherbatsky's *Buddhist Logic* (1930-1932; reprint, New York, 1962), although now dated, is still the only comprehensive treatment. Hattori Masaaki's *Dignaga on Perception* (Cambridge, Mass., 1968) sets the standard for scholarship on these difficult issues. Also see Kajiyama Yuichi's "Later Madhyamikans," in *Mahayana Buddhist Meditation: Theory and Practice,* edited by Minoru Kiyota (Honolulu, 1978), for a treatment of later controversies on the need for images in understanding.

On the overall Chinese domestication of Indian Buddhist thought, Erik Zurcher's *The Buddhist Conquest of China* (1959; reprint, Leiden, 1972) remains a classic study of the early period up until 400 CE. There are many excellent studies of the individual schools, but to date no satisfactory doctrinal history of Chinese Buddhism has appeared. For Japanese Buddhism, the two-volume *Foundations of Japanese Buddhism (Los Angeles* and Tokyo, 1974-1976) by Daigan and Alicia Matsunaga is the standard resource. Tibetan Buddhism is discussed in Giuseppe Tucci's *The Religions of Tibet,* translated by Geoffrey Samuel (Berkeley, 1980).

On the Kyoto School, the works of Nishida Kitar still available in English are *Art and Morality,* translated by David A. Dilworth and Valdo H. Viglielmo (Honolulu, 1973), and *Fundamental Problems of Philosophy: The World of Action and the Dialectical World,* translated bv David A. Dilworth (Tokyo, 1970). See also Nishitani Keiji's *Religion and Nothingness,* translated by Jan van Bragt (Berkeley, 1982): Takeuchi Yoshinori's *The Heart of Buddhism* (New York, 1983); Hans Waldenfels' *Absolute Nothingness: Foundations for a Buddhist-Christian Dialogue,* translated by James W. Heisig (New York, 1980); *The Buddha Eye,* edited by Frederick Franck (New York, 1982); and Tanabe Hajime's *Philosophy as Metanoetics* (Berkeley, 1986).

6

The Age of Foreign Invasions

The decline and fall of the Maurya dynasty (324-187) brought an end to an age of assured support for Buddhist monastic institutions. Political circumstances unfavourable to Buddhism began with persecution under Pusyamitra Sunga (r. about 187-151). The Sunga dynasty would see the construction of some of the most important Buddhist sites of India: Bharhut, Sanchi, and Amaravati. But it also foreshadowed the beginning of Hindu dominance. The rising cult of Visnu seemed better equipped to assimilate the religion of the people and win the support of the ruling classes. Although Buddhism served better as a universal religion that could unite Indians and foreign invaders, the latter did not always choose to become Buddhists. A series of non-Indian rulers—Greek, Parthian, Scythian (Saka), Kushan—would hesitate in their religious allegiances.

Among the Greek kings, the Buddhist traditions claims Menandros (Milinda, c. 150 BCE) as one of its converts. The Scythian tribe of the Sakas, who invaded Bactriana around 130 BCE, roughly contemporaneous with the Yueh-chih conquest of the Tokharians, would become stable supporters of Buddhism in the subcontinent. [*See* Inner Asian Religions.] Their rivals in South India, the Tamil dynasty of the Satavahana (220 BCE–236 CE), sponsored in Andhra the construction of major centres of worship at Amaravati and Nagarjunikonda. The Yueh-chih (Kushans) also supported Buddhism, though perhaps less consistently. The most famous of their rulers, Kaniska, is represented by the literature as a pious patron of Buddhism (his dates are uncertain; proposed accession in 78 or 125 CE). During the Kushan period (c. 50-320 CE) the great schools of Gandhara and Mathura revolutionized Indian, especially Buddhist, art. Both the northern styles of Gandhara and Mathura and the southern school of Andhra combined iconic and aniconic symbolization of Buddha: the first

Buddha images appeared around the third century of the common era, apparently independently and simultaneously in all three schools.

The Appearance of Schools and Denominations

Any understanding of the history of composition of the canons, or of their significance in the history of the religion, is dependent on our knowledge of the geographic distribution, history, and doctrine of the various sects. Unfortunately, our knowledge in this regard is also very limited.

Developments in Doctrine and in Scholastic Speculation. As the original community of wandering mendicants settled in monasteries, a new type of religion arose, concerned with the preservation of a tradition and the justification of its institutions. Although the "forest dweller" continued as an ideal and a practice—some were still dedicated primarily to a life of solitude and meditation—the dominant figure became that of the monk-scholar. This new type of religious specialist pursued the study of the early tradition and moved its doctrinal systems in new directions. On the one hand, the old doctrines were classified, defined, and expanded. On the other hand, there was a growing awareness of the gap that separated the new developments from the transmitted creeds and codes. A set of basic or "original" teachings had to be defined, and the practice of exegesis had to be formalized. In fact, the fluidity and uncertainty of the earlier scriptural tradition may be one of the causes for the development of Buddhist scholasticism. By the time the canons were closed the degree of diversity and conflict among the schools was such, and the tradition was overall so fluid, that it was difficult to establish orthodoxy even when there was agreement on the basic content of the canons. In response to these problems Buddhists soon developed complicated scholastic studies.

At least some of the techniques and problems of this early scholasticism must go back to the early redactions of the Sutra section of the canon, if not to a pre-canonical stage. The genre of the *matrka,* or doctrinal "matrices," is not an uncommon form of Sutra literature. It is suggested in the redaction of certain sections of the Pali and Sarvastivadin canons, is found in early Chinese translations (e.g., the *Dharmasariraka Sutra* and the *Dasottara Sutra),* and continues in Mahayana Sutra literature. It is a literary form that probably represents not only an exegetic device but an early technique of doctrinal redaction—a hermeneutic that also served as the basis for the redaction of earlier strata of the oral transmission.

The Early Sects

Given the geographical and linguistic diversity of India and the lack of a central authority in the Buddhist community one can safely speculate that Buddhist sects arose early in the history of the religion. Tradition speaks of a first, but major, schism occurring at (or shortly after) the Second Council in Vaishali, one hundred years after the death of the founder. Whether the details are true or not, it is suggestive that this first split was between the Sthaviras and the Mahasamghikas, the prototypes of the two major divisions of Buddhism: "Hinayana" and Mahayana.

After this schism new subdivisions arose, reaching by the beginning of the common era a total of approximately thirty different denominations or schools and subschools. Tradition refers to this state of sectarian division as the period of the "Eighteen Schools," since some of the early sources count eighteen groups. It is not clear when these arose. *Faut de mieux,* most Western scholars go along with classical Indian sources, albeit with a mild skepticism, and try to sort out a consistent narrative from contradictory sources. Thus, we can only say that if we are to believe the Pali tradition, the Eighteen Schools must have been in existence already in the third century BCE, when a legendary Moggaliputtatissa compiled the *Kathavatthu.* But such an early dating raises manv problems.

In the same vein, we tend to accept the account of the Second Council that sees it as the beginning of a major split. In this version the main points of contention were monastic issues—the exact content and interpretation of the code. But doctrinal, ritual, and scholastic issues must have played a major role in the formation of separate schools. Many of the main points of controversy, for instance, centred on the question of the nature of the state of liberation and the status of the liberated person. Is the liberated human *(arhat)* free from all moral and karmic taint? Is the state of liberation *(nirvana)* a condition of being or nonbeing? Can there be at the same time more than one fully awakened person *(samyaksambuddha)* in one world system? Are persons already on their way to full awakening, the *bodhisattvas* or future Buddhas, deserving of worship? Do they have the ability to descend to the hells to help other sentient beings?

Among these doctrinal disputes one emerges as emblematic of the most important fissure in the Buddhist community. This was the polemic surrounding the exalted state of the *arhat* (Pali, *arahant).* Most of the Buddhist schools believed that only a few human beings could aspire to become fully awakened beings *(samyaksambuddha),* others had to content themselves with the hope of becoming free from the burden of past *karman* and attaining liberation in *nirvana,* without the extraordinary wisdom and virtue of Buddhahood. But the attainment of liberation was in itself a great achievement, and a person who was assured of an end to rebirth at the end of the present life was considered the most saintly, deserving of the highest respect, a "worthy" *(arhat).* Some of the schools even attributed to the *arhat* omniscience and total freedom from moral taint. Objections were raised against those who believed in the faultless wisdom of the *arhat,* including obvious limitations in their knowledge of everyday, worldly affairs. Some of these objections were formalized in the "Five Points" of Mahadeva, after its purported proponent. These criticisms can be interpreted either as a challenge to the belief in the superhuman perfection of the *arhat* or as a plea for the acceptance of their humanity. Traditionally, Western scholars have opted for the first of these interpretations.

The controversies among the Eighteen Schools identified each group doctrinally, but it seems unlikely that in the early stages these differences lead to major rifts in the community, with the exception of the schism between the two trunk schools of the Sthavira and the Mahasamghika; and even then, there is evidence that monks of both schools often lived together in a single monastic community. Among the doctrinal differences, however, we can find the seeds of future dissension, especially in the controversies relating to ritual. The Mahisasakas, for instance, claimed that there is more merit in worshiping and making offerings to the *samgha* than in worshiping a stupa, as the latter merely contains the remains of a member of the *samgha* who is no more. The Dharmaguptakas replied that there is more merit in worshiping a stupa, because the Buddha's path and his present state (in *nirvana)* are far superior to that of any living monk. Here we have a fundamental difference with both social and religious consequences, for the choice is between two types of communal hierarchies as well as between two types of spiritual orders.

Developments in the Scriptural Tradition

Apart from the Theravada recension of the Pali canon and some fragments of the Sarvastivadin Sanskrit canon nothing survives of what must have been a vast and diverse body of literature. For most of the collections we only have the memory preserved in inscriptions referring to *pitakas* and *nikayas* and an occasional reference in the extant literature.

According to the Pali tradition of Sri Lanka, the three parts of the Tripitaka were compiled in the language of the Buddha at the First Council. The Second Council introduced minor revisions in the Vinaya, and the Third Council added Moggaliputtatissa's *Kathavatthu.* A few years later the canon resulting from this council, and a number of extracanonical commentaries, were transmitted to Sri Lanka by Mahinda. The texts were transmitted orally *(mukhapathena)* for the next two centuries, but after difficult years of civil war and famine, King Vattagamani of Sri Lanka ordered the texts written down. This task was carried out between 35 and 32 BCE. In this way, it is said, the canon was preserved in the original language. Although the commentaries were by that time extant only in Sinhala, they continued to be transmitted in written form until they were retranslated into Pali in the fifth century CE.

Modern scholarship, however, questions the accuracy of several points in this account. Pali appears to be a literary language originating in Avanti, western India; it seems unlikely that it could be the vernacular of a man who had lived in eastern India all his life or, for that matter, the lingua franca of the early Magadhan kingdom. The Pali texts as they are preserved today show clear signs of the work of editors and redactors. Although much in them still has the ring of oral transmission, it is a formalized or ritualized oral tradition, far from the spontaneous preaching of a living teacher. Different strata of language, history, and doctrine can be recognized easily in these texts. There is abundant evidence that already at the stage of oral transmission the tradition was fragmented, different schools of "reciters" *(bhanaka)* preserving not only different corpuses (the eventual main categories of the canons) but also different recensions of the same corpus of literature. Finally, we have no way of knowing if the canon written down at the time of Vattagamani was the Tripitaka as we know it today. There is evidence to the contrary, for we are told that the great South Indian scholar Buddhaghosa revised the canon in the fifth century when he also edited the commentaries preserved in Sinhala and translated them into Pali, which suggests that Pali literature in general had gone through a period of deterioration before his time.

Most scholars, however, accept the tradition that would have the Pali canon belong to a date earlier than the fifth century; even the commentaries must represent an earlier stratum. However late may be its final recension, the Pali canon preserves much from earlier stages in the development of the religion.

Developments in Practice

The cult at this stage was still dominated by the practice of pilgrimage and by the cult of the *caitya,* as described above. However, we can imagine an intensification of the devotional aspect of ritual and a greater degree of systematization as folk belief and "high tradition" continued to interact. Sectarian differences probably began to affect the nature of the liturgies, as a body of liturgical texts became part of the common or the specific property of different groups of Buddhists. Among the earliest liturgical texts were the hymns in praise of the Buddha, especially the ones singing the many epithets of the Awakened One. Their use probably goes back to the earliest stages in the history of monastic ritual and may be closely connected with the practice of *buddhanusmrti,* or meditation on the attributes of the Buddha.

Pilgrimage Sites and Stupas

Many Buddhist practices and institutions remain apparently stable in the subcontinent until the beginnings of the common era. The monuments of Bharhut and Sanci, for example, where we find the earliest examples of aniconic symbolism, represent a conservative Buddhism. Other signs of conservatism, however, confirm a continuous nonliterary cult. The oldest section at Sanci, the east gateway, dating from perhaps 90 to 80 BCE, preserves, next to the illustrated Jatakas, the woman and tree motifs, *yaksas* and *yaksis* (with the implied popular cult of male and female fertility deities), and the aniconic representations of the wheel, the footprint, the throne, and the tree.

The most advanced or innovative trait is the increasing iconographic importance of the previous lives of the Buddha, represented in the reliefs of Jatakas. These indicate a developed legend of the Buddha's past lives, a feature of the period that suggests the importance of past lives in the cult and in the future development of Mahayana. The most important cultic development of the pre-Mahayana period, however, was the shift from the commemorative ritual associated with the stupa and the aniconic symbol to the ritual of worship and devotion associated with the Buddha image.

After the beginning of the Christian era major developments in practice reflect outside influence as well as new internal developments. This is the time when the sects were beginning to commit to writing their sacred literature, but it is also the time of foreign invasions. These may have played a major role in the development of the Buddha image. Modern scholarship has debated the place of origin of this important cultic element and the causal factors that brought it about. Some, following Foucher, proposed a northwestern origin, and saw the Buddhas and *bodhisattvas* created under the influence of Greco-Roman art in Gandhara (Kushan period) as the first images. Others, following Coomaraswamy, believed the first images were created in Andhra, as part of the natural development of a South Indian cult of the *yaksas,* and in the north central region of Mathura. Be that as it may, the Buddha image dominates Buddhist iconography after the second century CE; Stupas and Jataka representations remain but play a secondary role.

As a balance to the growing importance of the past lives of the Buddha, the process of redacting the scriptures also brought about the necessity of formulating a biography of the Buddha. The first "biographies" appear at the beginning of the common era, perhaps as late as the second century CE. Partial biographies appear in the literature of the Sarvastivadins *(Lalitavistara)* and Lokottaravadins *(Mahavastu)*. The first complete biography is a cultured poem in the *kavya* style, the *Buddhacarita of* Msvaghosa.

This is also a time when noncanonical literature flourished. Poets wrote Buddhist dramas and poetical recastings of canonical parables and legends. Asvaghosa, for instance, wrote a drama on the life of Sariputra, and a poem narrating the conversion of Nanda *(Saundarananda)*. Developments in the literary tradition perhaps should be seen as reflecting other strata of the living tradition. Thus, the vitality of the Jataka tradition is seen in its appearance as a literary genre in the *Jatakamala* of Aryasura (fl. c. 150 CE). This classical poet is sometimes identified with Matrceta, who in his works (e.g., *Satapafncagatka)* gives us a highly cultured reflection of the hymns of praise *(stotras)* that must have been a regular part of the Buddhist cult of the day. In these hymns we already see the apotheosis of the Buddha figure, side by side with the newly redefined *bodhisattva* ideal.

Mystics and Intellectuals. The development of devotional Buddhism did not obscure the ascetic and contemplative dimensions of the religion. The system of meditation contained in the Nikayas probably achieved its final form during this period. Diverse techniques for the development of enstasy and insight were conflated first in the canonical Sutra literature, then in the Abhidharmic texts.

Side by side with the development of popular and monastic cults, a new elite of religious specialists appeared, seeking to follow the Buddha's path through systematic study into the scriptures. They belonged to the tradition of the *matrkas* and composed treatises purporting to treat the "higher" Dharma *(abhidharma)—or,* what is perhaps the more correct etymology, treatises "on the Dharma." Although the analysis of meditational categories was an important aspect of these traditions, the scholar-monks were not always dedicated meditators. In fact, many of them must have made scholarship the prime objective of their religious life, leaving the practice of meditation to the forest monks. For the scholars, the goal was to account for the whole of Buddhism, in particular, the plethora of ancient doctrines and practices found in the canon. Above all, they sought to define and explain the ultimately real components of reality, the *dharmas,* into which one could analyze or explode the false conception of the self.

This critique was not without soteriological implications. The goal was conceived at times as ineffable, beyond the ken of human conception. Thus canonical literature describes the liberated person, the *arhat,* as follows:

> When bright sparks fly
> as the smith beats red-hot iron,
> and fade away,
> one cannot tell where they have gone.
> In the same way, there is no way of knowing
> the final destination of those who are truly free,
> who have crossed beyond the flood, bondage, and desire,
> obtaining unshakable bliss. (*Udana*, p. 93)

Canonical notions of levels or hierarchies in the path to liberation became the focus of much scholastic speculation—in fact, the presence of these categories in the canons may be a sign of scholastic influence on the redaction of the scriptures. The construction of complex systems of soteriology, conceived as maps or detailed descriptions of the path, that integrated the description and analysis of ethical and contemplative practices with philosophical argumentation, characterized the Abhidharmic schools. This activity contributed to the definition of the doctrinal parameters of the sects; but it also set the tone for much of future Buddhist dogmatics. The concerns of the Abhidharmists, ranging from the analysis of ecstasy and the contemplative stages to the rational critique of philosophical views of reality, had a number of significant doctrinal consequences: (1) scholars began devising "maps of the path," or theoretical blueprints of the stages from the condition of a common human being *(prthag-jana)* to the exalted state of a fully awakened being *(samyaksambuddha); (2)* Buddhist scholars engaged other Indian intellectuals in the discussion of broad philosophical issues; (3) various orthodox apologetics were developed, with the consequent freezing of a technical terminology common to most Buddhists; (4) the rigidity of their systems set the stage for a reaction that would lead to the creation of new forms of Buddhism.

The Sects and the Appearance of Mahayana

Most of the developments mentioned above overlap with the growth of a new spirit that changed the religion and eventually created a distinct form of Buddhist belief and practice. The new movement referred to itself as the "Great Vehicle" (Mahayana) to distinguish itself from other styles of Buddhism that the followers of the movement considered forms of a "Lesser Vehicle" (Hinayana). [*See* Buddhism, Schools of, *article on* Mahayana Buddhism.]

The Early Schools Outside India

If we accept the general custom of using the reign of Asoka as the landmark for the beginning of the missionary spread of Buddhism, we may say that Buddhism reached the frontiers of India by the middle of the second century BCE. By the beginning of the common era it had spread beyond. In the early centuries of the era Mahayana and Hinayana spread in every direction; eventually certain areas would become predominantly Mahayana, others, predominantly Hinayana.

Mahayana came to dominate in East and Central Asia—with the exception of Turkistan, where Sarvastivadin monasteries flourished until the Muslim invasion and conversion of the region. Hinayana was slower to spread, and in some foreign lands had to displace Mahayana. It lives on in a school that refers to itself as the Theravada, a Sinhala derivative of the Sthavira school. It spread throughout Southeast Asia where it continues to this day.

The Great Vehicle

The encounter of Buddhism with extra-Indian ethnic groups and the increasing influence of the laity gradually transformed the monastic child of shramanic Buddhism into a universal religion. This occurred in two ways. On the one hand, monasticism adapted to the changing circumstances, strengthened its ties to the laity and secular authorities, established a satisfactory mode of coexistence with nonliterary, regional forms of worship. Both Mahayana and Hinayana schools participated in this aspect of the process of adaptation. But Buddhism also redefined its goals and renovated its symbols to create a new synthesis that in some ways may be considered a new religion. The new style, the Mahayana, claimed to be a path for the many, the vehicle for the salvation of all sentient beings (hence its name, "The Great Vehicle"). Its distinctive features are: a tilt toward world affirmation, a laicized conception of the human ideal, a new ritual of devotion, and new definitions of the metaphysical and contemplative ideals.

The Origins of Mahayana. The followers of Mahayana claim the highest antiquity for its teachings. Their own myths of origin, however, belie this claim. Mahayana recognizes the fact that its teachings were not known in the early days of Buddhism by asserting that Sakyamuni revealed the Mahayana only to select *bodhisattvas* or heavenly beings who kept the texts hidden for centuries. One legend recounts that the philosopher Nagarjuna had to descend to the underworld to obtain the Mahayana texts known as the "Perfection of Wisdom" (Prajnaparamita).

Western scholars are divided on the question of the dates and location of the origins of Mahayana. Some favour an early (beginning of the common era) origin among Mahasamghika communities in the southeastern region of Andhra. Others propose a northwestern origin, among the Sarvastivadins, close to the second and third centuries CE. It may be, however, that Mahayana arose by a gradual and complex process involving more than one region of India. It is clear that Mahayana was partly a reform movement, partly the natural development of pre-Mahayana Buddhism; still in another sense, it was the result of new social forces shaping the Indian subcontinent.

The theory of a southern origin assumes that the Mahasamghika monastic centres of Andhra continued to develop some of the more radical ideals of the school, until some of these communities saw themselves as a movement completely distinct from other, so-called Hinayana schools. This theory also recognizes external influences: the Iranian invaders as well as the non-Aryan substratum of southern India, the first affecting the mythology of the celestial *bodhisattvas,* the second incorporating non-Aryan concepts of the role of women into the mainstream of Buddhist religious ideals.

Doctrinal factors were primarily the development of the myth of the former lives of Sakyamuni and the cult of former Buddhas, both of which contributed to a critique of the *arhat* ideal. The mythology of the Buddha's former lives as a *bodhisattva* led to the exaltation of the *bodhisattva* ideal over that of the *arhat.* The vows of the *bodhisattva* began to take the central role, especially as they were seen as an integral part of a developing liturgy at the centre of which the dedication of merit was transformed as part of the exalted *bodhisattva* ideal.

It seems likely, furthermore, that visionaries and inspired believers had continued to compose *sutras.* Some of these, through a gradual process we can no longer retrace, began to move away from the general direction of the older scholastic traditions and canonical redactors. Thus it happened that approximately at the time when the older schools were closing their canons, the Mahayana was composing a set of texts that would place it in a position of disagreement with, if not frank opposition to, the older schools.

At the same time, the High Tradition began to accept Mahayana and therefore argue for its superiority; thus, a Mahayana *sastra* tradition began to develop almost at the same time as the great Sarvastivadin synthesis was completed.

In the West, the gap between Mahayana and Hinayana is sometimes exaggerated. It is customary to envision Mahayana as a revolutionary movement through which the aspirations of a restless laity managed to overcome an oppressive, conservative monastic establishment. Recent research suggests that the opposition between the laity and the religious specialists was not as sharp as had hitherto been proposed. Furthermore, it has become apparent that the monastic establishment continued to be a powerful force in Indian Mahayana. It seems more likely that Mahayana arose gradually and in different forms in various points of the subcontinent. A single name and a more or less unified ideology may have arisen after certain common aspirations were recognized. Be that as it may, it seems evident that the immediate causes for the arising of this new form of Buddhism were the appearance of new cultic forms and widespread dissatisfaction with the scholastic tradition.

Merit, bodhisattvas, and the Pure Land. Inscriptional evidence shows that the doctrine of merit transference had an important role in the culture even before the appearance of Mahayana. Although all Buddhists believe that virtuous thoughts and actions generate merit, which leads to a good rebirth, it appears that early Buddhists believed that individuals could generate merit only for themselves, and that merit could only lead to a better rebirth, not to liberation from the cycle of rebirth. By the beginning of the common era, however, some Buddhists had adopted a different conception of merit. They believed that merit could be shared or transferred, and that it was a factor in the attainment of liberation—so much so that they were offering their own merit for the salvation of their dead relatives.

Dedication of merit appears as one of the pivotal doctrines of the new Buddhism. Evidently, it served a social function: it made participation in Buddhist ritual a social encounter rather than a private experience. It also contributed to the development of a Buddhist high liturgy, an important factor in the survival of Buddhism and its assimilation of foreign elements, both in and outside India.

This practice and belief interacted with the cult of former Buddhas and the mythology of the former lives to create a Buddhist system of beliefs in which the primary goal was to imitate the virtue of Sakyamuni's former lives, when he was a *bodhisattva* dedicated to the liberation of others rather than himself. To achieve this goal the believer sought to imitate Sakyamuni not as he appeared in his last life or after his enlightenment, when he sought and attained *nirvana,* but by adopting a vow similar to Sakyamuni's former vow to seek awakening *(bodhi)* for the sake of all sentient beings. On the one hand, this shift put the emphasis on insight into the world, rather than escape from it. On the other hand, it also created a new form of ideal being and object of worship, the *bodhisattva.*

Contemporary developments in Hindu devotionalism *(bhakti)* probably played an important role in the development of Buddhist liturgies of worship *(puja),* but it would be a mistake to assume that the beginnings of Mahayana faith and ritual can be explained adequately by attributing them merely to external theistic influences. For instance, the growth of a faith in rebirth in "purified Buddha fields," realms of the cosmos in which the merit and power of Buddhas and *bodhisattvas* create an environment where birth without suffering is possible, can be seen as primarily a Buddhist development. The new faith, generalized in India through the concept of the "Land of Bliss" (the "Pure Land" of East Asian Buddhism), hinged on faith in the vows of former *bodhisattvas* who chose to transfer or dedicate their merit to the purification of a special "field" or "realm." The influence of Iranian religious conceptions seems likely, however, and one may have to seek some of the roots of this belief among Central Asian converts.

Formation of a New Scriptural Tradition. With the new cult and the new ideology came a new body of scriptures. Mahayana sutras began to be composed probably around the beginning of the Christian era, and continued to be composed and redacted until at least the fifth or sixth century CE. Unlike the canons of the earlier schools, the Mahayana scriptures do not seem to have been collected into formal, closed canons in the land of their origin—even the collections edited in China and Tibet were never closed canons.

In its inception Mahayana literature is indistinguishable from the literature of some of the earlier schools. The *Prajnaparamita* text attributed to the Purvasailas is probably an earlier version of one of the Mahayana texts of the same title; the *Ratnakuta* probably began as part of a Mahasamghika canon; and the now lost *Dharani Pitaka* of the Dharmaguptaka school probably contained prototypes of the *dharani-sutras* of the Mahayana tradition. The Mahayanist monks never gave up the pre-Mahayana Vinaya. Many followed the Dharmaguptaka version, some the Mahasamghika. Even the Vinaya of a school that fell squarely into the Hinayana camp, the Sarvastivida, was used as the basis for Mahayana monastic rule.

Still, the focus of much Mahayana rhetoric, especially in the earlier strata of the literature, is the critique of non-Mahayana forms of Buddhism, especially the ideal of the *arhat.* This is one of the leading themes of a work now believed to represent an early stage in the development of Mahayana, the *Rastrapalapariprccha,* a text of the *Ratnakuta* class. In this text, the monastic life is still exalted above all other forms of spiritual life, but the *bodhisattva* vows are presented for the first time as superior to the mere monastic vows.

It is difficult, if not impossible, to establish with any degree of certainty the early history of Mahayana literature. It seems, however, that the earliest extant Mahayana *sutra is* the *Astasahasrikaprajnaparamita,* or its verse rendering, the *Ratnagunasamcayagatha.* Both reflect a polemic within Buddhism, centering on a critique of the "low aspirations" of those Buddhists who chose not to take the vows of the *bodhisattvas.* The *Ratnaguna* defines the virtues of the *bodhisattva,* emphasizing the transcendental insight or "perfect wisdom" *(prajnaparamita)* that frees him from all forms of attachment and preconceived notions—including notions of purity and world renunciation. An important aspect or complement of this wisdom is skill in means *(upayakausalya)*—defined here as the capacity to adapt thought, speech, and action to circumstances and to the ultimate purpose of Buddhist practice, freedom from attachment. This virtue allows the *bodhisattva to* remain in the world while being perfectly free from the world.

The *Astasahasrika* treats these same concepts, but also expands the concept of merit in at least two directions: (1) dedication of merit to awakening means here seeing through the illusion of merit as well as applying merit to the path of liberation, and (2) dedication of merit is an act of devotion to insight (wisdom, prajna). As the goal and ground of all perfections *(paramita),* Perfection of Wisdom is personified as the Mother of All Buddhas. She gives birth to the mind of awakening, but she is present in concrete form in the Sacred Book itself. Thus, the *Astasahasrikaprajnaparamita Sutra is* at the same time the medium expressing a sophisticated doctrine of salvation by insight and skill in means, the rationalization of a ritual system, and the object of worship.

Another early Mahayana text, the *Saddharmapundarika* (Lotus Sutra), also attacks the *arhat* ideal. This Sutra is considered the paradigmatic text on the developed Buddhology of the Mahayana: Buddha is presented as a supernatural being, eternal, unchanging; at the same time he is Buddha by virtue of the fact that he has become free from all conceptions of being and nonbeing. Buddha never attained awakening or *nirvana* because he is Buddhahood, and has been in awakening and *nirvana* since eternity, but also because there is no Buddhahood or *nirvana* to be attained.

Γhe attitude of early Mahayana *sutras* to laity and to women is relatively inconsistent. Thus, the *Ugradattapariprccha* and the *Upasakasila,* while pretending to preach a lay morality, use monastic models for the householder's life. But compared to the earlier tradition, the Mahayana represents a significant move in the direction of a religion that is less ascetic and monastic in tone and intent. Some Mahayana *sutras* of the early period place laypersons in a central role. The main character in the *Gandavyuha,* for instance, is a young lay pilgrim who visits a number of *bodhisattvas* in search of the teaching. Among his teachers we find laymen and laywomen, as well as female night spirits and celestial *bodhisattvas.* The *Vimalakirtinirdesa is* more down-to-earth in its exaltation of the lay ideal. Although not without its miraculous events, it represents the demythologizing tendencies of Mahayana, which are often carried out to the extreme of affirming that the metaphoric meaning of one doctrine is exactly its opposite.

The Development of Mahayana

Although Buddhism flourished during the classical age of the Guptas, the cultural splendor in which it grew was also the harbinger of Hindu dominance. Sanskrit returned as the lingua franca of the subcontinent, and Hindu devotionalism began to displace the ideals of the Indic period. Mahayana must have been a divided movement even in its inception. Some of the divisions found in the Hinayana or pre-Mahayana schools from which Mahayana originated must have carried through into Mahayana itself. Unfortunately, we know much less of the early sectarian divisions in the movement than we know of the Eighteen Schools. It is clear, for instance, that the conception of the *bodhisattva* found among the Mahasamghikas is different from that of the Sarvastivadins. It appears also that the Prajnaptivadins conceived of the unconditioned *dharmas* in a manner different from other early schools. However, though we may speculate that some of these differences influenced the development of Mahayana, we have no solid evidence.

As pre-Mahayana Buddhism had developed a scholastic system to bolster its ideological position, Mahayana developed special forms of scholarly investigation. A new synthesis, in many ways far removed from the visionary faith underlying the religious aspects of Mahayana, grew in the established monasteries partly as a critique of earlier scholastic formulations, partly due to the need to explain and justify the new faith. Through this intellectual function the monastery reasserted its institutional position. Both monk and layman participated in giving birth to Mahayana and maintaining its social and liturgical life, but the intellectual leadership remained monastic and conservative. Therefore, Mahayana reform brought with it an element of continuity—monastic institutions and codes—that could be at the same time a cause for fossilization and stagnation. The monasteries would eventually grow to the point where they became a burden on society, at the same time that, as institutions of conservatism, they failed to adapt to a changing society.

Still, from the beginning of the Gupta dynasty to the earlier part of the Pala dynasty the monasteries were centres of intellectual creativity. They continued to be supported under the Guptas, especially Kumara Gupta I (414-455), who endowed a major monastery in a site in Bihar originally consecrated to Sariputra. This monastic establishment, called Nalanda after the name of a local genie, probably had been active as a centre of learning for several decades before Kumara Gupta decided to give it special recognition. It would become the leading institution of higher learning in the Buddhist world for almost a thousand years. Together with the university of Valabhi in western India, Nalanda represents the scholastic side of Mahayana, which coexisted with a nonintellectual (not necessarily "popular") dimension, the outlines of which appear through archaeological remains, certain aspects of the Sutra literature, and the accounts of Chinese pilgrims.

Some texts suggest a conflict between forest and city dwellers that may in fact reflect the expected tension between the ascetic and the intellectual, or the meditator and the religious politician. But, lest this simple schema obliterate important aspects of Buddhist religious life, one must note that there is plentiful evidence of intense and constant interaction between the philosopher, the meditator, and the devotee—often all three functions coinciding in one person. Furthermore, the writings of great philosophical minds like Asanga, Santideva, and Aryadeva suggest an active involvement of the monk-*bodhisattva* in the social life of the community. The nonintellectual dimensions of the religion, therefore, must be seen as one aspect of a dialectic that resolved itself in synthesis as much as rivalry, tension, or dissonance.

Mahayana faith and devotion, moreover, was in itself a complex phenomenon, incorporating a liturgy of the High Tradition (e.g., the *Hymn to the Three Bodies of the Buddha,* attributed to Asvaghosa) with elements of the nonliterary and non-Buddhist religion (e.g., pilgrimage cycles and the cult of local spirits, respectively), as well as generalized beliefs such as the dedication of merit and the hope of rebirth in a purified

Buddha Land.

Developments in Doctrine

In explaining the appearance of Mahayana, two extremes should be avoided carefully. On the one hand, one can exaggerate the points of continuity that link Mahayana with pre-Mahayana Buddhism; on the other, one can make a distinction so sharp that Mahayana appears as a radical break with the past, rather than a gradual process of growth. The truth lies somewhere between these two extremes: although Mahayana can be understood as a logical expansion of earlier Buddhist doctrine and practice, it is difficult to see how the phenomenon could be explained without assuming major changes in the social fabric of the Indian communities that provided the base for the religion. These changes, furthermore, are suggested by historical evidence.

The key innovations in doctrine can be divided into those that are primarily critiques of early scholastic constructs and those that reflect new developments in practice. In both types, of course, one should not ignore the influence of visionary or contemplative experience; but this aspect of the religion, unfortunately, cannot always be documented adequately. The most important doctrine of practical consequence was the *bodhisattva* doctrine; the most important theoretical development was the doctrine of emptiness *Sunyata).* The first can be understood also as the result of a certain vision of the concrete manifestation of the sacred; the second, as the expression of a new type of mystical or contemplative experience.

The Bodhisattva

In pre-Mahayana Buddhism the term *bodhisattva* referred primarily to the figure of a Buddha from the time of his adoption of the vow to attain enlightenment to the point at which he attained Buddhahood. Even when used as an abstract designation of an ideal of perfection, the value of the ideal was determined by the goal: liberation from suffering. In the teachings of some of the Hinayana schools, however, the *bodhisattva* became an ideal with intrinsic value: to be a *bodhisattva* meant to adopt the vow *(pranidhana)* of seeking perfect awakening for the sake of living beings; that is, to follow the example set by the altruistic dedication of the Buddha in his former lives, when he was a *bodhisattva,* and not to aspire merely to individual liberation, as the *arhats* were supposed to have done. The Mahayana made this critique its own, and the *bodhisattva* ideal its central religious goal.

This doctrinal stance accompanied a shift in mythology that has been outlined above: the belief in multiple *bodhisattvas* and the development of a complex legend of the former lives of the Buddha. There was likewise a change in ritual centred around the cult of the *bodhisattva,* especially of mythical *bodhisattvas* who were believed to be engaged in the pursuit of awakening primarily, if not exclusively, for the sake of assisting beings in need or distress. Closely allied with this was the increasing popularity of the recitation of *bodhisattva* vows.

Whereas the *bodhisattva* of early Buddhism stood for a human being on his way to become a liberated being, the *bodhisattva* that appears in the Mahayana reflects the culmination of a process of change that began when some of the Hinavana schools extended the apotheosis of the Buddha Sakyamuni to the *bodhisattva*—that is, when they idealized both the Buddha and the spiritual career outlined by the myth of his previous lives. Mahayana then extended the same religious revaluation to numerous mythical beings believed to be far advanced in the path of awakening. Accordingly, in its mythology Mahayana has more than one object of veneration. Especially in contrast to the more conservative Hinayana schools (the Sarvastivada and the Theravada, for instance), Mahayana is the Buddhism of multiple Buddhas and *bodhisattvas,* residing in multiple realms, where they assist numberless beings on their way to awakening.

Accordingly, the early ideal of the *bodhisattva* as future Buddha is not discarded; rather it is redefined and expanded. As a theory of liberation, the characteristic position of Mahayana can be summarized by saying that it emphasizes *bodhi* and relegates *nirvana* to a secondary position. Strictly speaking, this may represent an early split within the community rather than a shift in doctrine. One could speculate that it goes back to conflicting notions of means to liberation found among the shramanic religions: the conflict between ecstasy and insight as means of liberation. But this analysis must be qualified by noting that the revaluation of *bodhi* must be seen in the context of the *bodhisattva* vow. The unique aspiration of the *bodhisattva* defines awakening as "awakening for the sake of all sentient beings." This is a concept that cannot be understood properly in the context of disputes regarding the relative importance of insight.

As noted above, in the early conception a *bodhisattva* is a real human being. This aspect of the doctrine is not lost in Mahayana, but preserved in the belief that the aspiration to perfect awakening (the *bodhicitta)* and the *bodhisatva* vow should be adopted by all believers. By taking up the vow—by conversion or by ritual repetition—the Mahayana Buddhist, monk or layperson, actualizes the *bodhicitta* and progresses toward the goal of becoming a *bodhisattva.* Also uniquely Mahayana is the belief that these human aspirants to awakening are not alone—they are accompanied and protected by "celestial *bodhisattvas,*" powerful beings far advanced in the path, so perfect that they are free from both rebirth and liberation, and can now choose freely if, when, and where they are to be reborn. They engage freely in the process of rebirth only to save living beings.

What transforms the human and ethical ideal into a religious ideal, and into the object of religious awe, is the scale in which the *bodhisattva* path is conceived. From the first aspiration to awakening *(bodhicitta)* and the affirmation of the vow to the attainment of final enlightenment and liberation, countless lives intervene. The *bodhisattva* has to traverse ten stages *(bhumi),* beginning with the intense practice of the virtue of generosity (primarily a lay virtue), passing through morality in the second stage, patience in the third, then fortitude, meditation, insight, skill in means, vows, powers, and the highest knowledge of a Buddha. The stages, therefore, correspond with the ten perfections *(paramita).* Although all perfections are practiced in every stage, they are mastered in the order in which they are listed in the scheme of the stages, suggesting at one end of the spectrum a simple and accessible practice for the majority of believers, the human *bodhisattva,* and at the other end a stage clearly unattainable in the realm of normal human circumstances, reserved for semidivine Buddhas and *bodhisattvas,* the object of worship. Although some exceptional human beings may qualify for the status of advanced *bodhisattvas,* most of these ideal beings are the mythic objects of religious fervor and imagination.

Among the mythic or celestial *bodhisattvas* the figure of Maitreya—destined to be the next Buddha of this world system after Sakyamuni—clearly represents the earliest stage of the myth. His cult is especially important in East Asian Buddhism. Other celestial *bodhisattvas* include Manjusri, the *bodhisattva* of wisdom, the patron of scripture, obviously less important in the general cultus but an important *bodhisattva* in monastic devotion. The most important liturgical role is reserved for Avalokitesvara, the *bodhisattva* of compassion' whose central role in worship is attested by archaeology.

Emptiness

The doctrine of emptiness *(sunyata)* represents a refinement of the ancient doctrine of no-self. In some ways it is merely an extension of the earlier doctrine: the denial of the substantial reality of the self and what belongs to the self, as a means to effect a breaking of the bonds of attachment. The notion of emptiness, however, expresses a critique of our common notions of reality that is much more radical than the critique implicit in the doctrine of no-self. The Mahayana critique is in fact unacceptable to other Buddhists, for it is in a manner of speaking a critique of Buddhism. Emptiness of all things implies the groundlessness of all ideas and conceptions, including, ultimately, Buddhist doctrines themselves.

The doctrine of emptiness was developed by the philosophical schools, but clearly inspired by the tradition of the Mahayana *sutras.* Thus we read: "Even *nirvana* is like a magical creation, like a dream, how much more any other object or idea *(dharma)*. . . ? Even a Perfect Buddha is like a magical creation, like a dream. . ." (*Astasahasrika,* p. 40). The practical correlate of the doctrine of emptiness is the concept of "skill in means" *(upaya):* Buddhist teachings are not absolute statements about reality, they are means to a higher goal beyond all views. In their cultural context these two doctrines probably served as a way of making Buddhist doctrine malleable to diverse populations. By placing the truth of Buddhism beyond the specific content of its religious practices, these two doctrines justified adaptation to changing circumstances and the adoption of new religious customs.

But emptiness, like the *bodhisattva* vows, also reflects the Mahayana understanding of the ultimate experience of Buddhism—understood both as a dialectic and a meditational process. This experience can be described as an awareness that nothing is self-existent. Dialectically, this means that there is no way that the mind can consistently think of any thing as having an existence of its own. All concepts of substance and existence vanish when they are examined closely and rationally. As a religious experience the term *emptiness* refers to a direct perception of this absence of self-existence, a perception that is only possible through mental cultivation, and which is a liberating experience. Liberation, in fact, has been redefined in a way reminiscent of early texts such as the *Suttanipata.* Liberation is now the freedom resulting from the negation of all assumptions about reality, even Buddhist assumptions.

> The cessation of grasping and reifying,
> calming the plural mind—this is bliss.
> The Buddha never taught any thing/doctrine *[dharma]*
> to anyone anywhere. (*Madhyamakakarika,* 25.24)

Finally, emptiness is also an affirmation of the immanence of the sacred. Applied to the turmoil of the sphere of rebirth *(samsara),* it points to the relative value and reality of the world and at the same time transforms it into the sacred, the experience of awakening. Applied to the sphere of liberation *(nirvana),* emptiness is a critique of the conception of liberation as a religious goal outside the world of impermanence and suffering.

Other Views of the Absolute. Mahayana developed early notions of the supernatural and the sacred that guaranteed an exalted status to the symbols of its mystical and ethical ideals. Its notion of extraordinary beings populating supernal Buddha fields and coming to the aid of suffering sentient beings necessitated a metaphysic and cosmology that could offer concrete images of a transcendent sacred. Accordingly, the abstract, apophatic concept of emptiness was often qualified by, or even rejected in favour of, positive statements and concrete images.

Pre-Mahayana traditions had emphasized impermanence and no-self: to imagine that there is permanence in the impermanent is the most noxious error. Mahayana introduced the notion of emptiness, urging us to give up the notion of permanence, but to give up the notion of impermanence as well. Within the Mahayana camp others proposed that there was something permanent within the impermanent. Texts like the *[Mahayana] Mahaparinirvana Sutra* asserted that the Buddha himself had taught a doctrine of permanence: the seed of Buddhahood, innate enlightenment, is permanent, blissful, pure—indeed, it is the true self, present in the impermanent mind and body of sentient beings.

The Tathagata as object of worship was associated with "suchness" *(tathata),* his saving actions were seen as taking effect in a world formed in the image of the Dharma and its ultimate truth *(dharmadhatu),* and his form as repository of all goodness and virtue represented his highest form.

A doctrine common to all Mahayanists sought to establish a link between the absolute and common human beings. The Tathagata was conceived of as having several aspects to his person: the human Buddha or "Body of Magical Apparition" *(nirmanakaya),* that is, the historical persons of Buddhas; the transcendent sacred, the Buddha of the paradises and Buddha fields, who is also the form that is the object of worship *(sambhogakaya);* and the Buddha as Suchness, as nonduality, the Tathagata as embodiment of the *dharmadhatu,* called the "Dharma Body" *(dharmakaya).*

Developments In Practice

The practice of meditation was for the Mahayanist part of a ritual process beginning with the first feelings of compassion for other sentient beings, formulating the vow, including the expression of a strong desire to save all sentient beings and share one's merit with them, followed by the cultivation of the analysis of all existents, reaching a pinnacle in the experience of emptiness but culminating in the dedication of these efforts to the salvation of others.

Worship and Ritual

The uniquely Mahayana aspect of the ritual is the threefold service *(triskandhaka)*. Variously defined, this bare outline of the essential Mahayana ritual is explained by the seventh-century poet Śantideva as consisting of a confession of sins, formal rejoicing at the merit of others, and a request to all Buddhas that they remain in the world for the sake of suffering sentient beings. A pious Buddhist was expected to perform this threefold ritual three times in the day and three times in the night.

A text known as the *Triskandhaka,* forming part of the *Upalipariprccha,* proves the central role of confession and dedication of merit. The act of confession is clearly a continuation of the ancient Pratimoksa ritual. Other elements of continuity include a link with early nonliterary tradition (now integrated into scripture) in the role of the dedication of merit, and a link with the general Buddhist tradition of the Three Refuges.

More complicated liturgies were in use. Several versions remain in the extant literature. Although many of them are said to be "the sevenfold service" *(saptavidhanuttarapuja),* the number seven is to be taken as an abstract number. The most important elements of the longer liturgies are the salutation to the Buddhas and *bodhisattvas,* the act of worship, the act of contrition, delight in the merit of others, and the dedication of merit. Hsiuan-tsang, the seventh-century Chinese pilgrim to India, describes, albeit cursorily, some of the liturgies in use in the Indian monasteries of his time.

Most common forms of ritual, however, must have been less formalized and less monkish. The common rite is best represented by the litany of Avalokitesvara, preserved in the literature and the monuments. In its literary form it is a solemn statement of the *bodhisattva's* capacity to save from peril those who call on his name. But in actual practice, one can surmise, the cult of Avalokitesvara included then, as it does today in East Asia, prayers of petition and apotropaic invocations.

The basic liturgical order of the literary tradition was embellished with elements from general Indian religious custom, especially from the styles of worship called *puja.* These included practices such as bathing the sacred image, carrying it in procession, offering cloth, perfume, and music to the icon, and so forth.

Ritual practices were also expanded in the monastic tradition. For instance, another text also going by the title *Triskandhaka* (but preserved only in Tibetan translation) shows an intimate connection between ritual and meditation, as it integrates—like many monastic manuals of meditation—the typical daily ritual cycle with a meditation session.

Meditation

The practice of meditation was as important in the Mahayana tradition as it had been before. The maps of the path and the meditation manuals of Mahayana Buddhists give us accounts, if somewhat idealized ones, of the process of meditation. Although no systematic history of Mahayana meditation has been attempted yet, it is obvious that there are important synchronic and diachronic differences among Mahayana Buddhists in India. Considering, nevertheless, only those elements that are common to the various systems, one must note first an element of continuity with the past in the use of a terminology very similar to that of the Mahisasakas and the Sarvastivada, and in the acceptance, with little change, of traditional lists of objects and states of contemplation.

The interpretation of the process, however, and the definition of the higher stages of contemplation differed radically from that of the Hinayana schools. The principal shift is in the definition of the goal as a state in which the object of contemplation *(alambana)* is no longer present to the mind *(niralambana).* All the mental images (or "marks," *nimitta, samjna)* that form the basis for conceptual thought and attachment must be abandoned through a process of mental calm and analysis, until the contemplative reaches a state of peaceful concentration free of mental marks *(animitta),* free of conceptualizations *(nirvikalpa-samadhi).*

These changes in contemplative theory are closely connected to the abandonment of the *dharma* theory and the doctrine of no-self as the theoretical focus of speculative mysticism. One may say that the leading theme of Mahayana contemplative life is the meditation on emptiness. But one must add that the scholastic traditions are very careful to define the goal as constituted by both emptiness and compassion *(karund).* The higher state of freedom from conceptions (the "supramundane knowledge") must be followed by return to the world to fulfill the vows of the *bodhisattva*—the highest contemplative stage is, at least in theory, a preparation for the practice of compassion.

The New Ethics

The *bodhisattva* ideal also implied new ethical notions. Two themes prevail in Mahayana ethical speculation: the altruistic vow and life in the world. Both themes reflect changes in the social context of Buddhism: a greater concern, if not a stronger role for, lay life and its needs and aspirations and a cultural context requiring universal social values. The altruistic ideal is embodied in the *bodhisattva* vows and in the creation of a new set of ethical rules, commonly known as the "Bodhisattva Vinaya." A number of Mahayana texts are said to represent this new "Vinaya." Among these, the *Bodhisattvapratimoksa* was especially important in India. It prescribes a liturgy for the ritual adoption of the *bodhisattva* vows, which is clearly based on the earlier rites of ordination *(upasampad).* Although the Mahayana Vinaya Sutras never replaced in India the earlier monastic codes, they preserved and transmitted important, and at times obligatory, rites of monastic and lay initiation, and were considered essential supplements to traditional monastic Vinaya.

The High Tradition and the Universities

The most important element in the institutionalization of Mahayana was perhaps the establishment of Buddhist universities. In these centres of learning the elaboration of Buddhist doctrine became the most important goal of Buddhist monastic life. First at Nalanda and Valabhi, then, as the Pala dynasty took control of East Central India (c. 650), at the universities of Vikramasila and Odantapuri, Mahayana scholars trained disciples from different parts of the Buddhist world and elaborated subtle systems of textual interpretation and philosophical speculation.

The Mahayana Synthesis

Although eventually they would not be able to compete with more resilient forms of Buddhism and Hinduism, the Mahayana scholars played a leading role in the creation of a Mahayana synthesis that would satisfy both the intelligentsia and the common believers for at least five hundred years. Devotion, ritual, ethics, metaphysics, and logic formed part of this monument to Indian philosophical acumen. Even as the ruthless Mihirakula, the Ephthalite ("White") Hun, was invading India from the northwest (c. 500-528) and the Chalukya dynasty was contributing to a Hindu renaissance in the southwest (c. 550-753), India allowed for the development of great minds—such distinguished philosophical figures as Dignaga and Sthiramati, who investigated subtle philosophical issues. Persecution by Mihirakula (c. 550) was followed by the reign of one of the great patrons of Buddhism, Harsa

Vardhana (c. 605-647). Once more Buddhism was managing to survive on the seesaw of Indian politics.

Schools

The scholastic tradition of Mahayana can be divided into three schools: Madhyamika (Madhyamaka), Yogacara, and the school of Saramati. The first two dominated the intellectual life of Mahayana in India. The third had a short-lived but important influence on Tibet, and indirectly may be considered an important element in the development of East Asian Buddhism.

Madhyamika. The founder of this school can also be regarded as the father of Mahayana scholasticism and philosophy. Nagarjuna (fl. c. 150 CE) came from South India, possibly from the Amaravati region. Said to have been the advisor to one of the Satavahana monarchs, he became the first major philosopher of Mahayana and a figure whose ideas influenced all its schools. The central theme of his philosophy is emptiness (*sunyata*) understood as a corollary of the pre-Mahayana theory of dependent origination. Emptiness is the Middle Way between affirmations of being and nonbeing. The extremes of existence and nonexistence are avoided by recognizing certain causal relations (e.g., the path and liberation) without predicating a self-existence or immutable essence *(svabhàva) to* either cause or effect. To defend his views without establishing a metaphysical thesis, Nagarjuna argues by reducing to the absurd all the alternative philosophical doctrines recognized in his day. For his own "system," Nagarjuna claims to have no thesis to affirm beyond his rejection of the affirmations and negations of all metaphysical systems. Therefore, Nagarjuna's system is "the school of the Middle" *(madhyamaka)* both as an ontology (neither being nor nonbeing) and as a logic (neither affirmation nor negation). In religious terms, Nagarjuna's Middle Way is summarized in his famous statement that samsara and *nirvana* are the same.

Three to four centuries after Nagarjuna the Madhyamika school split into two main branches, called Prasangika and Svatantrika. The first of these, represented by Buddhapalita (c. 500) and Candrakirti (c. 550-600), claimed that in order to be faithful to the teachings of Nagarjuna, philosophers had to confine themselves to the critique of opposing views by *reductio ad absurdum.* The Svatantrikas, on the other hand, claimed that the Madhyamika philosopher had to formulate his own thesis; in particular, he needed his own epistemology. The main exponent of this view was Buddhapalita's great critic Bhavaviveka (c. 500-550). The debate continued for some time but was eclipsed by other philosophical issues;

for the Madhyamika school eventually assimilated elements of other Mahayana traditions, especially those of the logicians and the Yogacarins.

Madhyamika scholars also contributed to the development of religious literature. Several hymns (*stava*) are attributed to Nagarjuna. His disciple Aryadeva discusses the *bodhisattva's* career in his *Bodhisattva yogacara-catuhsataka*, although the work deals mostly with philosophical issues. Two anthological works, one attributed to Nagarjuna, the *Sutrasamuccaya*, and the other to the seventh-century Santideva, the *Siksasamuccaya*, became guides to the ritual and ethical practices of Mahayana. Santideva also wrote a "guide" to the *bodhisattva's* career, the Bodhicaryavatara, a work that gives us a sampling of the ritual and contemplative practices of Madhyamika monks, as well as a classical survey of the philosophical issues that engaged their attention.

Yogacara

Approximately two centuries after Nagarjuna, during the transition period from Kushan to Gupta power, a new school of Mahayana philosophy arose in the northwest. The founders of this school, the brothers Asafiga. (c. 310-390) and Vasubandhu (c. 3204-00), had begun as scholars in the Hinayana schools. Asanga, the elder brother, was trained in the Mahisasaka school. Many important features of the Abhidharma theories of this school remained in Asanga's Mahayana system. Vasubandhu, who converted to Mahayana after his brother had become an established scholar of the school, began as a Sautrantika with an extraordinary command of Sarvastivadin theories. Therefore, when he did become a Mahayanist he too brought with him a Hinayana scholastic grid on which to organize and rationalize Mahayana teachings.

The school founded by the two brothers is known as the Yogacara, perhaps following the title of Asang's major work, the *Yogacarabhumi* (sometimes attributed to Maitreya), but clearly expressing the centrality of the practice of self-cultivation, especially through meditation. In explaining the experiences arising during the practice of yoga, the school proposes the two doctrines that characterize it: (1) the experience of enstasy leads to the conviction that there is nothing but mind (*cittamatrata*), or the world is nothing but a perceptual construct *(vijnaptimatrata)*; (2) the analysis of mind carried out during meditation reveals different levels of perception or awareness, and, in the depths of consciousness, the basis for rebirth and karmic determination, a storehouse consciousness (*alaya-vijnana*) containing the seeds of former actions. Varying emphasis on these two principles characterize different modes of the doctrine. The doctrine of mind-only dominates Vasubandhu's *Vimsatika* and *Trimsika*; the analysis of the *alayavijnana* is more central to Asanga's doctrine. Since both aspects of the doctrine can be understood as theories of consciousness *(vijnana),* the school is sometimes called Vijnanavada.

One of the first important divisions within the Yogacara camp reflected geographical as well as doctrinal differences. The school of Valabhi, following Sthiramati (c. 500-560), opposed the Yogacarins of Nalanda, led by Dharmapala (c. 530-561). The point at issue, whether the pure mind is the same as the storehouse consciousness, illustrates the subtleties of Indian philosophical polemics but also reflects the influence of another school, the school of Saramati, as well as the soteriological concerns underlying the psychological theories of Yogacara. The debate on this point would continue in the Madhyamika school, involving issues of the theory of perception as well as problems in the theory of the liberated mind.

Tathagata-garbha Theory

Another influential school followed the tendency—already expressed in some Mahayana *sutras*—toward a positive definition or description of ultimate reality. The emphasis in this school was on the ontological basis for the experience and virtues of Buddhahood. This basis was found in the underlying or innate Buddhahood of all beings. The school is known under two names; one describes its fundamental doctrine, the theory of *tathagata-garbha* (the presence of the Tathagata in all beings), the other refers to its purported systematizer, Saramati (c. 350-450). The school's emphasis on a positive foundation of being associates it closely with the thought of Maitreyanatha, the teacher of Asanga, to whom is often attributed one of the fundamental texts of the school, the *Ratnagotravibhaga.* It may be that Maitreya's thought gave rise to two lines of interpretation—*tathagata-garbha* and *cittamatrata.*

Saramati wrote a commentary on the *Ratnagotravibhaga* in which he explains the process whereby innate Buddhahood becomes manifest Buddhahood. The work is critical of the theory of emptiness and describes the positive attributes of Buddhahood. The *bodhisattva's* involvement in the world is seen not so much as the abandonment of the bliss of liberation as it is the manifestation of the Absolute *(dharmadhatu)* in the sphere of sentient beings, a concept that can be traced to Mahasamghika doctrines. The *dharmadhatu* is a positive, metaphysical absolute, not only eternal, but pure, the locus of ethical, soteric, and epistemological value. This absolute is also the basis for the *gotra*, or spiritual lineage, which is a metaphor for the relative potential for enlightenment in living beings.

The Logicians

An important development in Buddhist scholarship came about as a result of the concern of scholastics with the rules of debate and their engagement in philosophical controversies with Hindu logicians of the Nyaya school. Nagarjuna and Vasubandhu wrote short treatises on logic, but a creative and uniquely Buddhist logic and epistemology did not arise until the time of Dignaga (c. 480—540), a scholar who claimed allegiance to Yogacara but adopted a number of Sautrantika doctrines. The crowning achievement of Buddhist logic was the work of Dharmakirti (c. 600–650), whose *Pramanavarttika* and its *Vrtti* revised critically the whole field. Although his work seems on the surface not relevant for the history of religion, it is emblematic of the direction of much of the intellectual effort of Mahayana scholars after the fifth century.

Yogacara-Madhyamika Philosophers

As India moved away from the security of the Gupta period, Mahayana Buddhist philosophy gradually moved in the direction of eclecticism. By the time the university at Vikramasila was founded in the eighth century the dominant philosophy at Nalanda was a combination of Madhyamika and Yogacara, with the latter as the qualifying term and Madhyamika as the core of the philosophy. This movement had roots in the earlier Svatantrika Madhyamika and like its predecessor favored the formulation of ontological and epistemological theses in defense of Nagarjuna's fundamental doctrine of emptiness. The most distinguished exponent of this school was Santiraksita (c. 680-740); but some of his theories were challenged from within the movement by his contemporary Jnanagarbha (c. 700-760). The greatest contribution to religious thought, however, came from their successors. Kamalasila (c. 740-790), a disciple of Santiraksita who continued the latter's mission in Tibet, wrote a number of brilliant works on diverse aspects of philosophy. He traveled to Tibet, where he wrote three treatises on meditation and the *bodhisattva* path, each called *Bhavanakrama*' which must be counted among the jewels of Indian religious thought.

New Scriptures

The philosophers found their main source of inspiration in the Mahayana sutras, most of which did not advocate clearly defined philosophical theories. Some sutras, however, do express positions that can be associated with the doctrines of particular schools. Although scholars agree that these compositions are later than texts without a clear doctrinal affiliation, the connection between the sutras and the schools they represent is not always clear.

For instance, some of the characteristic elements of the school of Saramati are clearly pre-Mahayanic, and can also be found in a number of *sutras* from the *Avatamsaka* and *Ratnakuta* collections. However, Saramati appealed to a select number of Mahayana *sutras* that clustered around the basic themes of the school. Perhaps the most famous is the *Srimaladevisimhanada*, but equally important are the *[Mahayana] Mahaparinirvana Sutra*, the *Anunatvapurnatvanirdesa*, and the *Dharaniraja*.

A number of Mahayana sutras of late composition were closely associated with the Yogacara school. Although they were known already at the time of Asanga and Vasubandhu, in their present form they reflect a polemic that presupposes some form of proto-Yogacara theory. Among these the *Lankavatara* and the *Samdhi nirmocana* are the most important from a philosophical point of view. The first contains an early form of the theory of levels of *vijnana*.

Decline of Mahayana

It is difficult to assess the nature and causes of the decay of Mahayana in India. Although it is possible to argue that the early success of Mahayana led to a tendency to look inward, that philosophers spent their time debating subtle metaphysical, logical, or even grammatical points, the truth is that even during the period of technical scholasticism, constructive religious thought was not dormant. But it may be that as Mahayana became more established and conventional, the natural need for religious revival found expression in other vehicles. Most likely Mahayana thinkers participated in the search for new forms of expression, appealing once more to visionary, revolutionary, and charismatic leaders. But the new life gradually would adopt an identity of its own, first as Tantric Buddhism, eventually as Hinduism. For, in adopting Tantric practices and symbols, Mahayana Buddhists appealed to a symbolic and ritual world that fit naturally with a religious substratum that was about to become the province of Hinduism.

The gradual shift from Mahayana to Tantra seems to have gained momentum precisely at the time when Mahayana philosophy was beginning to lose its creative energy. We know of Tantric practices at Nalanda in the seventh century. These practices were criticized by the Nalanda scholar Dharmakirti but apparently were accepted by most distinguished scholars of the same institution during the following century. As Tantra gained respectability, the Pala monarchs established new centers of learning, rivaling Nalanda. We may say that the death of its great patron, King Harsa, in 657 signals the decline of Mahayana, whereas the construction of the University of Vikramasila under Dharmapala about the year 800 marks the beginning of the Tantric period.

Tantric Innovations

As with Mahayana, we must assume that Tantra reflects social as well as religious changes. Because of the uncertainties of the date of its origin, however, few scholars have ventured any explanation for the arising of Tantra. Some advocate an early origin for Tantra, suggesting that the literature existed as an esoteric practice for many centuries before it ever came to the surface. If this were the case, then Tantra must have existed as some kind of underground movement long before the sixth century. But this theory must still explain the sudden appearance of Tantrism as a mainstream religion.

In its beginnings, Buddhist Tantra may have been a minority religion, essentially a private cult incorporating elements from the substratum frowned upon by the Buddhist establishment. It echoed ancient practices such as the critical rites of the *Atharvaveda* tradition, and the initiatory ceremonies, Aryan and non-Aryan, known to us from other Brahmanic sources. Starting as a marginal phenomenon, it eventually gained momentum, assuming the same role Mahayana had assumed earlier; a force of innovation and a vehicle for the expression of dissatisfaction with organized religion. The followers of Tantra became the new critics of the establishment. Some asserted the superiority of techniques of ritual and meditation that would lead to a direct, spontaneous realization of Buddhahood in this life. As wandering saints called *siddhas* ("possessed of *siddhi,*" i.e., realization or magical power), they assumed the demeanor of madmen, and abandoned the rules of the monastic code. [*See* Mahasiddhas.] Others saw Tantra as the culmination of Mahayana and chose to integrate it with earlier teachings, following established monastic practices even as they adopted beliefs that challenged the traditional assumptions of Buddhist monasticism.

The documented history of Tantra, naturally, reveals more about the second group. It is now impossible to establish with all certainty how the substratum affected Buddhist Tantra—whether, for instance, the metaphoric use of sexual practices preceded their explicit use, or *vice versa*. But it seems clear that the new wandering ascetics and their ideology submitted to the religious establishment even as they changed it. Tantra followed the pattern of cooperation with established religious institutions set by Mahayana in its relationship to the early scholastic establishment. Tantric monks would take the *bodhisattva* vows and receive monastic ordination under the pre-Mahayana code. Practitioners of Tantra would live in the same monastery with non-Tantric Mahayana monks. Thus Tantric Buddhism became integrated into the Buddhist high tradition even as the *siddhas* continued to challenge the values of Buddhist monasticism.

Although it seems likely that Tantric Buddhism existed as a minority, esoteric practice among Mahayana Buddhists before it made its appearance on the centre stage of Indian religion, it is now impossible to know for how long and in what form it existed before the seventh century. The latter date alone is certain because the transmission of Tantra to China is marked by the arrival in the Chinese capitals of Tantric masters like Subhakarasimha (arrives in Ch'ang-an 716) and Vajrabodhi (arrives in Lo-yang 720), and we can safely assume that the exportation of Tantra beyond the Indian border could not have been possible without a flourishing activity in India. Evidence for an earlier origin is found in the occasional reference, critical or laudatory, to *mantras* and *dharanis* in the literature of the seventh century (Dharmakirti, Santideva) and the presence of proto-Tantric elements in Mahayana *sutras* that must date from at least the fourth century *(Gandavyuha, Vimalakirtinirdesa, Saddharmapundarika).*

Tantra in general makes use of ritual, symbolic, and doctrinal elements of earlier form of Buddhism. Especially the apotropaic and mystical formulas called *mantras* and *dharanis* gain a central role in Tantrayana. The *Mahamayuri,* a proto-Tantric text of the third or fourth century, collects apotropaic formulas associated with local deities in different parts of India. Some of these formulas seem to go back to *parittas* similar to those in the Pali canonical text *Atanatiya Suttanta (Digha Nikaya* no. 32). Although one should not identify the relatively early, and pan-Buddhist, genre of the *dharani* and *paritta* with the Tantrayana, the increased use of these formulas in most existing forms of Buddhism, and the appearance of *dharani-sutras* in late Mahayana literature perhaps marks a shift towards greater emphasis on the magical dimension of Buddhist faith. The Mahayana *sutras* also foreshadow Tantra with their doctrine of the identity of the awakened and the afflicted minds *(Dharmasangiti, Vimalakirtinirdesa),* and innate Buddhahood (Tathagata-garbha *sutras).*

Varieties of Tantra

Whatever may have been its prehistory, as esoteric or exoteric practice, the new movement—sometimes called the third *yana,* Tantrayana—was as complex and fragmented as earlier forms of Buddhism. A somewhat artificial, but useful classification distinguishes three main types of Tantra: Vajrayana, Sahajayana, and Kalacakra Tantra. The first established the symbolic terminology and the liturgy that would characterize all forms of the tradition. Many of these iconographic and ritual forms are described in the *Manjusrimulakalpa* (finished in its extant form c. 750), the *Mahavairocana Satra,* and the *Vajrasekhara* (or *Tattvasamgraha) Sutra,* which some would, following East Asian traditions, classify under a different, more primitive branch of Tantra called "Mantrayana." The Sahajayana was dominated by long-haired, wandering *siddhas,* who openly challenged and ridiculed the Buddhist establishment. They referred to the object of their religious experience as "the whore," both as a reference to the sexual symbolism of ritual Tantra and as a challenge to monastic conceptions of spiritual purity, but also as a metaphor for the universal accessibility of enlightenment. The Kalacakra tradition is the farthest removed from earlier Buddhist traditions, and shows a stronger influence from the substratum. It incorporates concepts of messianism and astrology not attested elsewhere in Buddhist literature.

Unfortunately, the history of all three of these movements is clouded in legend. Tibetan tradition considers the Mantrayana a third "turning of the wheel [of the Dharma]" (with Mahayana as the second), taking place in Dhanyakataka (Andhra) sixteen years after the enlightenment. But this is patently absurd. As a working hypothesis, we can propose that there was an early stage of Mantrayana beginning in the fourth century. The term *Vajrayana* could be used then to describe the early documented manifestations of Tantric practice, especially in the high tradition of the Ganges River valley after the seventh century.

Sahajayana is supposed to have originated with the Kashmirian yogin Lui-pa (c. 750-800). The earliest documented Sahajayanists are from Bengal, but probably from the beginning of the ninth century. Regarding the Kalacakra, Western scholarship would not accept traditional views of its ancient origins in the mythic land of Shambhala. It must be dated not earlier than the tenth century, probably to the beginning of the reign of King Mahipala (c. 974-1026). Its roots have been sought in the North as well as in the South.

The Vajrayana

The Vajrayana derives its name from the centrality of the concept of *vajra* in its symbolism. The word *vajra* means both "diamond" and "cudgel." It is therefore a metaphor for hardness and destructiveness. Spiritually, it represents the eternal, innate state of Buddhahood possessed by all beings, as well as the cutting edge of wisdom. The personification of this condition and power is Vajrasattva, a deity and an abstract principle, which is defined as follows:

By vajra is meant emptiness;
sattva means pure cognition.
The identity of these two is known
as the essence of Vajrasattva.
(Advayavajra Samgraha, p. 24*)*

Behind this definition is clearly the metaphysics of Yogacara-Madhyamika thought. Vajrasattva stands for the nondual experience that transcends both emptiness and pure mind. In religious terms this principle represents a homology between the human person and the essence of *vajra*: in the human body, in this life, relative and absolute meet.

The innate quality of the nondual is also represented by the concept of the "thought of awakening" *(bodhicitta).* But innate awakening in Vajrayana becomes the goal: enlightenment is present in its totality and perfection in this human body; the thought of awakening is awakening:

The Thought of Awakening is known to be
Without beginning or end, quiescent,
Free from being and nonbeing, powerful,
Undivided in emptiness and compassion.

(*Guhyasamaja* 18.37)

This identity is established symbolically and ritually by a series of homologies. For instance, the six elements of the human body are identified with different aspects of the body of Mahavairocana, the five constituents of the human personality *(skandhas)* are identified with the five forms of Buddha knowledge.

But the most characteristic aspect of Tantric Buddhism generally is the extension of these homologies to sexual symbolism. The "thought of awakening" is identified with semen, dormant wisdom with a woman waiting to be inseminated. Therefore, wisdom *(prajna) is* conceived as a female deity. She is a mother *(janani),* as in the Prajnaparamita literature; she is the female *yogi* (*yogini*); but she is also a low-caste whore *(dombi candali).* Skillful means *(upaya)* are visualized as her male consort. The perfect union of these two *(prajnopaya-yuganaddha)* is the union of the nondual. Behind the Buddhist interpretation, of course, one discovers the non-Aryan substratum, with its emphasis on fertility and the symbolism of the mother goddess. But one may also see this radical departure from Buddhist monkish prudery as an attempt to shock the establishment out of self-righteous complacency.

Because the sexual symbolism can be understood metaphorically, most forms of Buddhist Tantra were antinomian only in principle. Thus, Vajrayana was not without its vows and rules. As *upaya,* the symbols of ritual had as their goal the integration of the Absolute and the relative, not the abrogation of the latter. Tantric vows included traditional monastic rules, the *bodhisattva* vows, and special Tantric rules—some of which are contained in texts such as the *Vinayasutra* and the *Bodhicittasiladanakalpa.*

The practice of the higher mysteries was reserved for those who had mastered the more elementary Mahayana and Tantra practices. The hierarchy of practice was established in systems such as the "five steps" of the *Pancakrama* (by the Tantric Nagarjuna). Generally, the order of study protected the higher mysteries, establishing the dividing line between esoteric and exoteric. Another common classification of the types of Tantra distinguished external daily rituals (Kriya Tantra), special rituals serving as preparation for meditation,' (Carya Tantra), basic meditation practices (Yoga Tantra), and the highest, or advanced meditation Tantras (Anuttarayoga Tantra). This hermeneutic of sorts served both as an apologetic and a doctrinal classification of Tantric practice by distinguishing the audience for which each type of Tantra was best suited: respectively *Sravakas, pratyekabuddhas,* Yogacarins, and Madhyamikas.

Elements of Tathagata-garbha theory seem to have been combined with early totemic beliefs to establish a system of Tathagata families or clans that also served to define the proper audience for a variety of teachings. Persons afflicted by delusion, for instance, belonged to Mahavairocana's clan, and should cultivate the homologies and visualizations associated with this Buddha, who, not coincidentally, represents the highest awakening. This system extends the homologies of *skandhas,* levels of knowledge, and so forth, to personality types. This can be understood as a practical psychology that forms part of the Tantric quest for the immanence of the sacred.

The Sahaja (or Sahajiya) Movement

Although traditional Sahaja master-to-disciple lineages present it as a movement of great antiquity, the languages used in extant Sahaja literature belong to an advanced stage in the development of New Indic. These works were written mostly in Apabhramsa (the *Dohakosa)* and early Bengali (the *Caryagiti).* Thus, although their dates are uncertain, they cannot go as far back as suggested by tradition. Scholars generally agree on a conjectural dating of perhaps eighth to tenth century.

Works attributed to Sahaja masters are preserved not only in New Indian languages (Saraha, c. 750-800, Kanha, c. 800-850, Ti-lo-pa, c. 950-1000); a few commentaries exist in Sanskrit. The latter attest to the influence of the early wandering *siddhas* on the Buddhist establishment.

The basic doctrinal stance of the Sahaja movement is no different from that of Vajrayana: *sahaja* is the innate principle of enlightenment, the *bodhicitta,* to be realized in the union of wisdom and skillful means. The main difference between the two types of Tantra is in the life-style of the adept. The Sahajiya was a movement that represented a clear challenge to the Buddhist establishment: the ideal person was a homeless mad man wandering about with his female consort, or a householder-sorcerer—either of which would claim to practice union with his consort as the actualization of what the high tradition practiced only in symbolic or mystical form. The Vajrayana soon became integrated into the curriculum of the universities, controlled by the Vinaya and philosophical analysis. It was incorporated into the ordered program of spiritual cultivation accepted in the monasteries, which corresponded to the desired social and political stability of the academic institutions and their sponsors. The iconoclastic saints of the Sahaja, on the other hand, sought spontaneity, and saw monastic life as an obstacle to true realization. The force of their challenge is seen in quasi-mythic form in the legend that tells of the bizarre tests to which the *siddha* Ti-lo-pa submitted the great scholar Na-ro-pa when the latter left his post at Vikramasila to follow the half-naked madman Ti-lo-pa.

This particular Tantric tradition, therefore, best embodied the iconoclastic tendencies found in all of Tantra. It challenged the establishment in the social as well as the religious sphere, for it incorporated freely practices from the substratum and placed women and sexuality on the level of the sacred. In opposition to the bland and ascetic paradises of Mahayana—where there were no women or sexual intercourse—Tantrism identifies the bliss of enlightenment with the great bliss *(mahasukha)* of sexual union.

The Kalacakra Tantra

This text has several features that separate it from other works of the Buddhist tradition: an obvious political message, suggesting an alliance to stop the Muslim advance in India, and astrological symbolism and teachings, among others. In this work also we meet the concept of "Adibuddha," the primordial Buddha, whence arises everything in the universe.

The high tradition, however, sees the text as remaining within the main line of Buddhist Tantrism. Its main argument is that all phenomena, including the rituals of Tantra, are contained within the initiate's body, and all aspects of time are also contained in this body. The concept of time *(kala)* is introduced and discussed and its symbolism explained as a means to give the devotee control over time and therefore over the impermanent world. The *Sekoddesatika,* a commentary on part of the *Kalacakra* attributed to Na-ro-pa (Nadapada, tenth century), explains that the time *(kala)* of the *Kalacakra is* the same as the unchanging *dharmadhatu,* whereas the wheel *(cakra)* means the manifestations of time. In *Kalacakra* the two, absolute and relative, *prajna* and *upaya,* are united. In this sense, therefore, in spite of its concessions to the substratum and to the rising tide of Hinduism, the *Kalacakra* was also integrated with mainline Buddhism.

Tantric Literature

The word *tantra* means "thread" or "weft" and, by extension, "text." The sacred texts produced as the new dispensation, esoteric or exoteric, were called Tantras, and formed indeed a literary thread interwoven with the secret transmission from master to disciple. Some of the most difficult and profound Tantras were produced in the early period (before the eighth century); the *Mahavairocana, Guhyasamaja,* the earlier parts of the *Manjusrimalakalpa,* and the *Hevajra.* By the time Tantra became the dominant system and, therefore, part of the establishment, a series of commentaries and authored works had appeared. Nagarjuna's *Pancakrama* is among the earliest. The Tantric Candrakirti (ninth century) wrote a commentary on the *Guhyasamaja,* and Buddhaguhya (eighth century) discussed the *Mahavairocana.* Sanskrit commentaries eventually were written to fossilize even the spontaneous poems of the Sahaja saints.

Tantra and the High Tradition

Thus, Tantra too, like its predecessors, eventually became institutionalized. What arose as an esoteric, intensely private, visionary and iconoclastic movement, became a literary tradition, ritualized, often exoteric and speculative.

We have abundant evidence of a flourishing Tantric circle at Nalanda, for instance, at least since the late seventh century. Tantric masters were by that time established members of the faculty. Especially during the Pala dynasty, Tantric practices and speculation played a central role in Buddhist universities. This was clearly the period of institutionalization, a period when Tantra became part of the mainstream of Buddhism.

With this transformation the magical origins of Tantra were partly disguised by a high Tantric liturgy and a theory of Tantric meditation paralleling earlier, Mahayana theories of the path. Still, Tantric ritual and meditation retained an identity of their own. Magic formulas, gestures, and circles appeared transformed, respectively, into the mystical words of the Buddhas, the secret gestures of the Buddhas, and charts *(mandalas)* of the human psyche and the path.

The mystical diagram *(mandala)* illustrates the complexity of this symbolism. It is at the same time a chart of the human person as it is now, a plan for liberation, and a representation of the transfigured body, the structure of Buddhahood itself. As a magic circle it is the sphere in which spiritual forces are evoked and controlled, as religious symbol it is the sphere of religious progress, experience, and action. The primitive functions remain: the *mandala* is still a circle of power, with apotropaic functions. For each divinity there is an assigned meaning, a sacred syllable, a colour, and a position within the *mandala*. Spiritual forces can thus be evoked without danger. The sacred syllable is still a charm. The visualization of Buddhas is often inseparable from the evocation of demons and spirits. New beings populate the Buddhist pantheon. The Buddhas and *bodhisattvas* are accompanied by female consorts—these spiritual sexual partners can be found in explicit carnal iconographic representations.

Worship and Ritual

Whereas the esoteric ritual incorporated elements of the substratum into a Buddhist doctrinal base, the exoteric liturgies of the Tantric high tradition followed ritual models from the Mahayana tradition as well as elements that evince Brahmanic ritual and Hindu worship. The daily ritual of the Tantric Buddhist presents a number of analogies to Brahmanic *puja* that cannot be accidental. But the complete liturgical cycle is still Buddhist. Many examples are preserved, for instance, in the Sanskrit text *Adikarmapradipa*. The ritual incorporates Tantric rites (offering to a *mandala*, recitation of *mantras)* into a structure composed of elements from pre-Mahayana Buddhism (e.g., the Refuges), and Mahayana ritual (e.g., confession, vows, dedication of merit).

More complex liturgies included rites of initiation or consecration *(abhiseka)* and empowerment *(adhisthana)*, rites that may have roots going as far back as the *Atharvaveda*. The burnt-offering rites *(homa)* also have Vedic and Brahmanic counterparts. Elements of the substratum are also evident in the frequent invocation of *yaksas* and *devatas*, the propitiation of spirits, and the underlying sexual and alchemical symbolism.

Meditation

The practice of Tantric visualization *(sadhana)* was even more a part of ritual than the Mahayana meditation session. It was always set in a purely ritual frame similar to the structure of the daily ritual summarized above. A complete *sadhana* would integrate pre-Mahayana and Mahayana liturgical and contemplative processes with Tantric visualization. The meditator would first go through a gradual process of purification (sometimes including ablutions) usually constructed on the model of the Mahayana "sevenfold service." He would then visualize the mystical syllable corresponding to his chosen deity. The syllable would be transformed into a series of images that would lead finally to clear visualization of the deity. Once the deity was visualized clearly, the adept would become one with it. But this oneness was interpreted as the realization of the nondual; therefore, the deity became the adept as much as the adept was turned into a deity. Thus, the transcendent could be actualized in the adept's life beyond meditation in the fulfillment of the *bodhisattva* vows.

Tantric doctrine

Tantric symbolism was interpreted in the context of Mahayana orthodoxy. It is therefore possible to explain Tantric theoretical conceptions as a natural development from Mahayana. The immanence of Buddhahood is explicitly connected with the Mahayana doctrine of the identity of *samsara* and *nirvana* and the teachings of those Yogacarins who believed that consciousness is inherently pure. The magical symbolism of Tantra can be traced—again through explicit references—to the doctrine of the *bodhisattva* as magician: since the world is like a dream, like a magical apparition, one can be free of it by knowing the dream as dream—knowing and controlling the magical illusion as a magician would control it. The *bodhisattva* (and therefore the *siddha)* is able to play the magical trick of the world without deceiving himself into believing it real.

One should not forget, however, that what is distinctively Tantric is not limited to the externals of ritual and symbolism. The special symbolism transforms its Mahayana context because of the specifically Tantric understanding of immanence. The Buddha is present in the human body innately, but the Buddha nature is manifested only when one realizes the "three mysteries," or "three secrets." It is not enough to be free from the illusion of the world; one becomes free by living in illusion in such a way that illusion becomes the manifestation of Buddhahood. Tantra seeks to construct an alternative reality, such that a mentally constructed world reveals the fundamental illusion of the world and manifests the mysterious power of the Buddha through illusion. The human body, the realm of the senses, is to be transformed into the body of a Buddha, the senses of a Buddha.

The body, mind, and speech of the Buddha (the Three Mysteries) have specific characteristics that must be recognized and reproduced. In ritual terms this means that the adept actualizes Buddhahood when he performs prostrations and ritual gestures *(mudras);* he speaks with the voice of the Buddha when he utters *mantras;* his mind is the mind of the Buddha when he visualizes the deity. The magical dimension is evident: the power of the Buddha lives in the formalized "demeanor of a Buddha." But the doctrine also implies transforming the body by a mystical alchemy (rooted in substratum sexual alchemy) from which is derived the soteriological meaning of the doctrine: the ritual changes the human person into a Buddha, all his human functions become sacred. Then this person's mind is the mind of an awakened being, it knows all things; the body assumes the appearance appropriate to save any living being; the voice is able to speak in the language of any living being needing to be saved.

The Decline of Buddhism in India

With Harsa's death Indian Buddhism could depend only on the royal patronage of the Pala dynasty of Bihar and Bengal (c. 650-950), who soon favoured the institutions they had founded—Vikramasila (c. 800), Odantapuri (c. 760). The last shining lights of Nalanda were the Madhyamika masters Santiraksita and Kamalasila, both of whom participated actively in the conversion of Tibet. Then the ancient university was eclipsed by its rival Vikramasila, which saw its final glory in the eleventh century.

Traditionally, the end of Indian Buddhism has been identified with the sack of the two great universities by the troops of the Turk Muhammad Ghuri: Nalanda in 1197 and Vikramasila in 1203. But, although the destruction of Nalanda put an end to its former glory, Nalanda lingered on. When the Tibetan pilgrim Dharmasvamin (1197-1264) visited the site of the ancient university in 1235 he found a few monks teaching in two monasteries remaining among the ruins of eighty-two others. In this way Buddhism would stay on in India for a brief time, but under circumstances well illustrated by the decay witnessed by Dharmasvamin—even as he was there, the Turks mounted another raid to further ransack what was left of Nalanda.

For a long time scholars have debated the causes for the decline of Buddhism in India. Although there is little chance of agreement on a problem so complex—and on which we have precious little evidence—some of the reasons adduced early are no longer widely accepted. For instance, the notion that Tantric Buddhism was a "degenerate form" of Buddhism that contributed to or brought about the disappearance of Buddhism is no longer entertained by the scholarly community. The image of a defenceless, pacifist Buddhist community annihilated by invading hordes of Muslim warriors is perhaps also a simplification. Though the Turkish conquerors of India were far from benevolent, the Arabs who occupied Sindh in 711 seem to have accepted a state of peaceful coexistence with the local population. Furthermore, one must still understand why Jainism and Hinduism survived the Muslim invasion while Buddhism did not.

Buddhist relations with Hindu and Jain monarchs were not always peaceful—witness the conquest of Bihar by the Bengali Saiva king Sasinka (c. 618). Even without the intervention of intolerance, the growth of Hinduism, with its firm roots in Indian society and freedom from the costly institution of the monastery, offered a colossal challenge to Buddhism. The eventual triumph of Hinduism can be followed by a number of landmarks often associated with opposition to Buddhism: the spread of Vaisnavism (in which the Buddha appears as a deceptive *avatara* of Visnu); the great Vaisnava and Saiva saints of the South, the Alvars and Nayanars, respectively, whose Hindu patrons were openly hostile to Buddhism and Jainism; the ministry of Sankara in Mysore (788-850), a critic of Buddhism who was himself accused of being a "crypto-Buddhist"; and the triumph of Saivism in Kashmir (c. 800).

But the causes for the disappearance of Buddhism were subtle: the assimilation of Buddhist ideas and practices into Hinduism and the inverse process of the Hinduization of Buddhism, with the advantage of Hinduism as a religion of the land and the locality. More important than these were perhaps the internal causes for the decline: dependence on monastic institutions that did not have broad popular support but relied exclusively on royal patronage; and isolation of monasteries from the life of the village community, owing to the tendency of the monasteries to look inward and to lose interest in proselytizing and serving the surrounding communities.

The disappearance of Buddhism in India may have been precipitated by the Muslim invasion, but it was caused primarily by internal factors, the most important of which seems to have been the gradual assimilation of Buddhism into Hinduism. The Muslim invasion, especially the Turkish conquest of the Ganges Valley, was the *coup de grace;* we may consider it the dividing line between two eras, but it was not the primary cause for the disappearance of Buddhism from India.

Buddhist Remnants and Revivals in the Subcontinent

After the last days of the great monastic institutions (twelfth and thirteenth centuries) Indian Buddhism lingered on in isolated pockets in the subcontinent. During the period of Muslim and British conquest (thirteenth to nineteenth century) it was almost completely absorbed by Hinduism and Islam, and gave no sign of creative life until modern attempts at restoration (nineteenth and twentieth centuries). Therefore, a hiatus of roughly six hundred years separates the creative period of Indian Buddhism from its modern manifestations.

Buddhism of the Frontier

As the Turk occupation of India advanced, the last great scholars of India escaped from Kashmir and Bihar to Tibet and Nepal. But the flight of Buddhist talent also responded to the attraction of royal patronage and popular support in other lands. The career of Atisa (Dipankara Srijnana, 982-1054), who emigrated to Tibet in 1042, is emblematic of the great loss incurred by Indian Buddhism in losing its monk-scholars. He combined extensive studies in Mahayana philosophy and Tantra in India with a sojourn in Sumatra under the tutorship of Dharmakirti. He had studied with Bodhibhadra (the successor of Na-ro-pa when the latter left Vikramasila to become a wandering ascetic), and was head master *(upadhyaya)* of Vikramasila and Odantapuri at the time of King Bheyapala. He left for Tibet at the invitation of Byan-chub-'od, apparently attracted by a large monetary offer.

The migration of the Indian scholars, and a steady stream of Tibetan students, made possible the exportation of Buddhist academic institutions and traditions to Tibet, where they were preserved until the Chinese suppression of 1959. The most learned monks were pushed out to the Himalayan and Bengali frontiers in part because the Indian communities were no longer willing to support the monasteries. Certain forms of Tantra, dependent only on householder priests, could survive, mostly in Bengal and in the Himalayan foothills. But some Theravadin Buddhists also survived in East Bengal—most of them taking refuge in India after the partition, some remaining in Bangladesh and Assam.

Himalayan Buddhism of direct Indian ancestry remains only in Nepal, where it can be observed even today in suspended animation, partly fused with local Hinduism, as it must have been in the Gangetic plain during the twelfth century. Nepalese Buddhists produced what may very well be considered the last major Buddhist scripture composed in the subcontinent, the *Svayambhu Purana (c.* fifteenth century). This text is an open window into the last days of Indian Buddhism. It reveals the close connection between Buddhist piety and non-Buddhist sacred localities, the formation of a Buddhist cosmogonic ontology (the Adibuddha), and the role of Tantric ritual in the incorporation of religious elements from the substratum. Nepalese Buddhism survives under the tutelage of married Tantric priests, called *vajracaryas.* It is therefore sometimes referred to as "Vajracarya Buddhism."

Buddhism of Tibetan origin survives in the subcontinent mostly in Ladakh, Sikkim, and Bhutan, but also in Nepal. Perhaps the most significant presence in modern India, however, is that of the Tibetan refugee communities. The Tibetan diaspora includes about eighty thousand persons, among which are several thousand monks. Some have retained their monastic robes and have reconstructed in India their ancient Buddhist academic curricula, returning to the land of origin the disciplines of the classical universities. So far their impact on Indian society at large has been insignificant and their hope of returning to Tibet dwindles with the passing of time. But the preservation, on Indian soil, of the classical traditions of Nalanda and Vikramasila is hardly a trivial accomplishment.

Attempted Revival: The Mahabodhi Society

Attempts to revive Buddhism in the land of its origin began with the Theosophical Society, founded in Colombo, Sri Lanka in 1875 by the American Henry S. Olcott. Although the society eventually became the vehicle for broader and less defined speculative goals, it inspired new pride in Buddhists after years of colonial oppression. The Sinhala monk Anagarika Dharmapala (1864-1933; born David Hewavitarane) set out to modernize Buddhist education. He also worked untiringly to restore the main pilgrimage sites of India, especially the temple of Bodh Gaya, which had fallen in disrepair and had been under Hindu administration for several centuries. To this end he founded in 1891 the Mahabodhi Society, still a major presence in Indian Buddhism.

Ambedkar and "Neo-Buddhism."

The most significant Buddhist mass revival of the new age was led by Dr. Bhimrao Ramji Ambedkar (1891-1956). He saw Buddhism as the gospel for India's oppressed and read in the Buddhist scriptures ideals of equality and justice. After many years of spiritual search, he became convinced that Buddhism was the only ideology that could effect the eventual liberation of Indian outcastes. On 14 October 1956 he performed a mass "consecration" of Buddhists in Nagpur, Maharashtra. The new converts were mostly from the "scheduled caste" of the *mahars.* Although his gospel is in some way on the fringes of Buddhist orthodoxy, Buddhist monks from other parts of Asia have ministered to the spiritual needs of his converts, and inspired Indian Buddhists refer to him as "Bodhisattva Ambedkar." [*See Marathi Religions and the Biography of Ambedkar.]*

Other Aspects of Modern Buddhism

The most fruitful and persistent effort in the rediscovery of Indian Buddhism has been in the West, primarily among Western scholars. The achievements of European scholars include a modern critical edition of the complete Pali canon, published by the Pali Text Society (founded in London in 1881), and the recovery of original texts of parts of the canon of the Sarvastivada. The combined effort of Indian, North American and European historians, archaeologists, and art historians has placed Indian Buddhism in a historical and social context, which, though still only understood in its rough outlines, allows us to see Buddhism in its historical evolution.

Japanese scholarship has also made great strides since the beginning of the twentieth century. The publication in Japan of three different editions of the Chinese canon between 1880 and 1929 may be seen as the symbolic beginning of a century of productive critical scholarship that has placed Japan at the head of modern research into Indian Buddhism.

Another interesting phenomenon of the contemporary world is the appearance of "neo-Buddhists" in Europe and North America. Although most of these groups have adopted extra-Indian forms of Buddhism, their interest in the scriptural traditions of India has created an audience and a demand for research into India's Buddhist past. The Buddhist Society, founded in London in 1926, and the Amis du Bouddhisme, founded in Paris in 1928, both supported scholarship and encouraged the Buddhist revival in India.

In spite of the revived interest in India of the last century, the prospects of an effective Buddhist revival in the land of Sakyamuni seem remote. It is difficult to imagine a successful living Buddhism in India today or in the near future. The possibility of the religion coming back to life may depend on the reimportation of the Dharma into India from another land. It remains to be seen if Ambedkar and Anagarika Dharmapala had good reasons for hope in a Buddhist revival, or if in fact the necessary social conditions for the existence of Indian Buddhism disappeared with the last monarchs of the Pala dynasty.

References

Bareau, Andre. "Le bouddhisme indien." In *Les religions de l'Inde,* Vol. 3, pp. 1-246. Paris, 1966. In addition to this useful survey, see Bareau's "Le bouddhisme indien," in *Histoire des religions,* edited by Henri-Charles

Puech Vol. 1, (Paris, 1970), pp. 1146-1215. Bareau has written the classical work on the question of the dating of the Buddha's life, "La date du Nirvana," *Journal asiatique* 241 (1953): 27-62. He surveys and interprets classical documents on the Hinayana schools in "Les sectes bouddhiques du Petit Vehicule et leurs Abhidharmapitaka." *Bulletin de l'Ecole Francaise d'Extreme-Orient* 50 (1952): 1-11; "Trois traites sur les sectes bouddhiques dus a Vasumitra, Bhavya et Vinitadeva," *Journal asiatique* 242-244 (1954-1956); *Les premiers conciles bouddhiques* (Paris, 1955); *Les sectes bouddhiques de Petit Vehicule* (Saigon, 1955); "Les controverses relatives a la nature de l'arhant dans le bouddhisme ancien," *Indo-Iranian Journal* 1 (1957): 241-250. Bareau has also worked extensively on the "biography" of the Buddha: *Recherches sur la biographie du Bouddha,* 3 Vols. (Paris, 1970-1983); "Le parinirvana du Bouddha et la naissance de la religion bouddhique," *Bulletin de l'Ecole Francaise d'Extreme-Orient* 61 (1974): 275-300; and, on a more popular but still scholarly bent, *Le Bouddha* (Paris, 1962).

Basham, A.L. *The Wonder That Was India.* London, 1954. This is the most accessible and readable cultural history of pre-Muslim India. A more technical study on the religious movements at the time of the Buddha is Basham's *History and Doctrine of* the *Ajivikas* (London, 1951).

Beal, Samuel. *Travels of Fa-hian and Sung-Yun, Buddhist Pilgrims from China to India (400 A.D. and 518 A.D.).* London, 1869. The travel records of two early pilgrims. See also Beal's *Si-yu-ki: Buddhist Records of the Western World,* 2 Vols. (London, 1884). Translation of Hsuan-tsang's accounts of his travels to India.

Bechert, Heinz. "Zur Fruhgeschichte des Mahayana-Buddhismus." *Zeitschrift der Deutschen Morgenlandischen Gesellschaft* 113 (1963): 530-535. Summary discussion of the Hinayana roots of Mahayana. On the same topic, see also "Notes on the Formation of Buddhist Sects and the Origins of Mahayana," in *German Scholars on India,* Vol. I (Varanasi, 1973), pp. 6-18; "The Date of the Buddha Reconsidered," *Indologica Taurinensia* 10 (1982): 29-36; "The Importance of Asoka's So-called Schism Edict," in *Indological and Buddhist Studies in Honour of Prof. J.W. de Jong* (Canberra, 1982), pp. 61-68; and "The Beginnings of Buddhist Historiography," in *Religion and Legitimation of Power in Sri Lanka,* edited by Bardwell L. Smith (Chambersburg, Pa., 1978), pp. 1-12. Bechert is also the editor of the most recent contribution to the question of the language of Buddha and early Buddhism, *Die Sprache der altesten buddhistischen Uberlieferung/ The Language of the Earliest Buddhist Tradition* (Gottingen, 1980).

Bechert, Heinz, and Georg von Simson, eds. *Einfuhrung in die Indologie: Stand, Methoden, Aufgaben.* Darmstadt, 1979. A general introduction to Indology, containing abundant materials on Indian history and religion, including Buddhism.

Bechert, Heinz, and Richard Gombrich, eds. *The World of Buddhism.* London,

1984. This is by far the most scholarly and comprehensive survey of Buddhism for the general reader. Indian Buddhism is treated on pages 15-132 and 277-278.

Demieville, Paul. "L'origine des sectes bouddhiques d'apres Paramartha." In *Melanges chinois et bouddhiques,* Vol. 1, pp. 14-64. Brussels, 1931-1932.

Demieville, Paul. "A propos du Concile de Vaisali." *T'oung pao* 40 (1951): 239-296.

Dutt, Nalinaksha. *Aspects of Mahayana Buddhism and Its Relation to Hinayana.* London, 1930. Although Dutt's work on the development of the Buddhist sects is now largely superseded, there are no comprehensive expositions to replace his surveys. His *Mahayana Buddhism* (Calcutta, 1973) is sometimes presented as a revision of *Aspects,* but the earlier work is quite different and far superior. Most of Dutt's earlier work on the sects, found hidden in various journals, was compiled in *Buddhist Sects in India* (Calcutta, 1970). See also his *Early Monastic Buddhism,* rev. ed. (Calcutta, 1960).

Dutt, Sukumar. *The Buddha and Five After-Centuries.* London, 1957. Other useful, although dated, surveys include *Early Buddhist Monachism* (1924; new ed., Delhi, 1960) and *Buddhist Monks and Monasteries in India* (London, 1962).

Fick, R. *The Social Organization in Northeast India in the Buddha's Time.* Calcutta, 1920.

Frauwallner, Erich. "Die buddhistische Konzile." *Zeitschrift der Deutschen Morgenlandischen Gesellschaft* 102 (1952): 240-261.

Frauwallner, Erich. *The Earliest Vinaya and the Beginnings of Buddhist Literature.* Rome, 1956.

Frauwallner, Erich. "The Historical Data We Possess on the Person and Doctrine of the Buddha." *East and West* 7 (1956): 309-312.

Fujita Kotatsu. *Genshi jodoshiso no kenkyu.* Tokyo, 1970. The standard book on early Sukhavati beliefs.

Glasenapp, Helmuth von. "Zur Geschichte der buddhistischen Dharma Theorie." *Zeitschrift der Deutschen Morgenlandischen Gesellschaft* 92 (1938): 383-420.

Glasenapp, Helmuth von. "Der Ursprung der buddhistischen Dharma-Theorie." *Wiener Zeitschrift fur die Kunde des Morgenlandes* 46 (1939): 242-266.

Glasenapp, Helmuth von. *Buddhistische Mysterien.* Stuttgart, 1940. Discusses most of the theories on early Brahmanic influence on Buddhist doctrine.

Glasenapp, Helmuth von. *Buddhismus und Gottesidee.* Mainz, 1954.

Gokhale, Balkrishna Govind. *Buddhism and Asoka.* Baroda, 1948. Other of this author's extensive writings on the social and political contexts of early Buddhism include "The Early Buddhist Elite," *Journal of Indian History* 43 (1965): 391-402; "Early Buddhist View of the State," *Journal of the American Oriental Society* 89 (1969): 731-738; "Theravada Buddhism in Western India," *Journal of the American Oriental Society* 92 (1972): 230-236; and "Early Buddhism and the Brahmanas," in *Studies in History of Buddhism,* edited by A.K. Narain (Delhi, 1980).

Gomez, Luis O. "Proto-Madhyamika in the Pali Canon." *Philosophy East and West* 26 (1976): 137-165. This paper argues that the older portions of *Suttanipata* preserve a stratum of the tradition that differs radically from the dominant themes expressed in the rest of the Pali canon, especially in its Theravada interpretation. The question of dedication of merit in the Mahayana is discussed in "Paradigm Shift and Paradigm Translation: The Case of Merit and Grace in Buddhism," in *Buddhist-Christian Dialogue* (Honolulu, forthcoming). On Mahayana doctrine and myth, see also my "Buddhism as a Religion of Hope: Polarities in the Myth of Dharmakara," *Journal of the Institute for Integral Shin Studies* (Kyoto, in press).

Grousset, Rene. *The Civilizations of the East,* Vol. 2, *India.* London, 1931. One of the best surveys of Indian history. See also his *Sur les traces du Bouddha* (Paris, 1957) for a modern expansion and retelling of Hsuan-tsang's travels.

Hirakawa Akira. *Indo bukkyoshi.* 2 Vols. Tokyo, 1974-1979. A valuable survey of Indian Buddhism from the perspective of Japanese scholarship (English translation forthcoming from the University Press of Hawaii). The development of the earliest Vinaya is discussed in *Ritsuzo no kenkyu* (Tokyo, 1960) and in *Shoki daijo bukkyo no kenkyu* (Tokyo, 1969). The author's "The Rise of Mahayana Buddhism and Its Relationship to the Worship of Stupas," *Memoirs of the Research Department of the Toyo Bunko* 22 (1963): 57-106, is better known in the West and summarizes some of the conclusions of his Japanese writings.

Horner, I.B. *Early Buddhist Theory of Man Perfected.* London, 1936. A study of the *arhat* ideal in the Pali canon. See also Horner's translation of the dialogues between King Menander and Nagasena, *Milinda's Questions* (London, 1964), and *Women under Primitive Buddhism* (1930; reprint, Delhi, 1975).

Horsch, P. "Der Hinduismus und die Religionen der primitivstamme Indiens." *Asiatische Studien/Etudes asiatiques* 22 (1968): 115-136.

Horsch, P. "Vorstufen der Indischen Seelenwanderungslehre." *Asiatische Studien/Etudes asiatiques* 25 (1971): 98-157.

Jayatilleke, K.N. *Early Buddhist Theory of Knowledge.* London, 1963. Discusses the relationship between early Buddhist ideas and sramanic and Upanisadic doctrines.

Jong, J.W. de. "A Brief History of Buddhist Studies in Europe and America." *Eastern Buddhist* 7 (May 1974): 55-106, (October 1974): 49-82. For the most part these bibliographic surveys, along with the author's "Recent Buddhist Studies in Europe and America: 1973-1983," *Eastern Buddhist* 17 (1984): 79-107, treat only the philological study of Indian Buddhism. The author also tends to omit certain major figures who are not in his own school of Buddhology. These articles are nonetheless the most scholarly surveys available on the field, and put forth truly excellent models of scholarly rigor.

Joshi, Lal Mani. *Studies in the Buddhistic Culture of India.* Delhi, 1967. Indian Buddhism during the middle and late Mahayana periods.

Kajiyama Yuichi. "Women in Buddhism." *Eastern Buddhist* 15 (1982): 53-70.

Kajiyama Yuichi. "Stupas, the Mother of Buddhas, and Dharma-body." In *New Paths in Buddhist Research,* edited by A.K. Warder, pp. 9-16. Delhi, 1985.

Kimura Taiken. *Abidammaron no kenkyu.* Tokyo, 1937. A survey of Sarvastivada Abhidharma, especially valuable for its analysis of the *Mahavibhasa.*

Lamotte, Etienne. "Buddhist Controversy over the Five Propositions." *Indian Historical Quarterly* 32 (1956). The material collected in this article is also found, slightly augmented, in Lamotte's *magnum opus, Histoire du bouddhisme indien des origines a l'ere Saka* (Louvain, 1958), pp. 300-319, 542-543, 575-606, 690-695. This erudite work is still the standard reference tool on the history of early Indian Buddhism (to circa 200 C.E.). Unfortunately, Lamotte did not attempt a history of Indian Buddhism for the middle and late periods. He did, however, write an article on the origins of Mahayana titled "Sur la formation du Mahayana," in *Asiatica: Festschrift Friedrich Weller* (Leipzig, 1954), pp. 381-386; this is the definitive statement on the northern origin of Mahayana. See also *Der Verfasser des Upadesa und seine Quellen* (Gottingen, 1973). On early Buddhism, see "La legende du Buddha," *Revue de l'histoire des religions* 134 (1947-1948): 37-71; *Le bouddhisme de Sakyamuni* (Gottingen, 1983); and *The Spirit of Ancient Buddhism* (Venice, 1961). Lamotte also translated a vast amount of Mahayana literature, including *Le traite de la grande vertu de sagesse,* 5 Vols. (Louvain, 1944-1980); *La somme du Grand Vehicule d'Asanga,* 2 Vols. (Louvain, 1938); and *L'enseignement de Vimalakirti* (Louvain, 1962), containing a long note on the concept of Buddha field (pp. 395-404).

La Vallee Poussin, Louis de. *Bouddhisme: Etudes et materiaux.* London, 1898. One of the most productive and seminal Western scholars of Buddhism, La Vallee Poussin contributed to historical studies in this and other works, as *Bouddhisme: Opinions sur l'histoire de la dogmatique* (Paris, 1909), *L'Inde aux temps des Mauryas* (Paris, 1930), and *Dynasties et histoire de l'Inde depuis Kanishka jusqu'aux invasions musulmanes* (Paris, 1935). Contributions on doctrine include *The Way to Nirvana* (London, 1917); Nirvana (Paris, 1925); "La controverse du temps et du pudgala dans la *Vijuzanakaya,*" in *Etudes asiatiques, publices a l'occasion du vingt-cinquieme anniversaire de l'Ecole Francaise d'Extreme-Orient,* Vol. I (Paris, 1925), pp. 358-376; *La morale bouddhique* (Paris, 1927); and *Le dogme et la philosophie du bouddhism* (Paris, 1930). On Abhidharma, see "Documents d'Abhidharma," in *Melanges chinois et bouddhiques,* Vol. I (Brussels, 1931-1932), pp. 65-109. The Belgian scholar also translated the most influential work of Abhidharma, *L'Abhidharmakosa de Vasubandhu,* 6 Vols. (1923-1931; reprint, Brussels, 1971). His articles in the *Encyclopaedia of Religion and Ethics,* edited by James Hastings, are still of value. Especially useful are "Bodhisattva (In Sanskrit Literature)," Vol. 2 (Edinburgh, 1909), pp. 739-753; "Mahayana," Vol. 8 (1915), pp. 330-336; and "Councils and Synods (Buddhist)," Vol. 7 (1914), pp. 179-185.

Law, B.C. *Historical Gleanings.* Calcutta, 1922. Other of his numerous contributions to the early history of Buddhism include *Some Ksatriya Tribes of Ancient India* (Calcutta, 1924), *Tribes in Ancient India* (Poona, 1943), and *The Magadhas in Ancient India* (London, 1946).

Law, B.C., ed. *Buddhistic Studies.* Calcutta, 1931, A collection of seminal essays on the history and doctrines of Indian Buddhism.

Legge, James. *A Record of Buddhist Kingdoms.* Oxford, 1886, English translation of Fa-hsien's accounts.

Majumdar, R.C., ed. *History and Culture of the Indian People,* Vols. 2-5. London, 1951. A major survey of the periods of Indian history when Buddhism flourished.

Masson, Joseph. *La religion populaire dans le canon bouddhique Pali.* Louvain, 1942. The standard study on the interactions of high tradition Buddhism with the substratum, not superseded yet.

Masuda Jiryo. "Origins and Doctrines of Early Indian Buddhist Schools." *Asia Major* 2 (1925): 1-78. English translation of Vasumitra's classical account of the Eighteen Schools.

May, Jacques. "La philosophie bouddhique de la vacuite." *Studia Philosophica* 18 (1958): 123-137. Discusses philosophical issues; for historical survey, see "Chugan," in *Hobogirin*, Vol. 5 (Paris and Tokyo, 1979), pp. 470-493, and the article co-authored with Mimaki (below). May's treatment of the Yogicara schools (including the school of Saramati), on the other hand, is both historical and doctrinal; see "La philosophie bouddhique idealiste," *Asiatische Studien/Etuder asiatiques* 25 (1971): 265-323.

Mimaki Katsumi and Jacques May. "Chudo." In *Hobogirin*, Vol. 5, pp. 456-470. Paris and Tokyo, 1979.

Mitra, Debala. *Buddhist Monuments.* Calcutta, 1971. A handy survey of the Buddhist archaeological sites of India.

Mitra, R.C. *The Decline of Buddhism in India.* Calcutta, 1954.

Nagao Gadjin. "The Architectural Tradition in Buddhist Monasticism." In *Studies in History of Buddhism,* edited by A.K. Narain, pp. 189-208. Delhi, 1980.

Nakamura Hajime. *Indian Buddhism: A Survey with Bibliographical Notes.* Tokyo, 1980. Disorganized and poorly edited, but contains useful information on Japanese scholarship on the development of Indian Buddhism.

Nilakanta Sastri, K.A. *Age of the Nandas and Mauryas.* Varanasi, 1952. See also his *A History of South India from Prehistoric Times to the Fall of Vijayanagar* (Madras, 1955) and *Development of Religion in South India* (Bombay, 1963).

Oldenberg, Hermann. *Buddha, sein Leben, seine Lehre, seine Gemeinde* (1881). Revised and edited by Helmuth von Glasenapp. Stuttgart, 1959. The first German edition was translated by W. Hoey as *Buddha, His Life, His Doctrine, His Order* (London, 1882).

Paul, Diana. *The Buddhist Feminine Ideal: Queen Srimala and the Tathagatagarbha.* Missoula, Mont., 1980. See also her *Women in Buddhism* (Berkeley, 1980).

Prebish, Charles S. "A Review of Scholarship on the Buddhist Councils." *Journal of Asian Studies* 33 (February 1974): 239-254. Treats the problem of the early schools and the history and significance of their Vinaya. Other works on this topic include Prebish's "The Pratimoksa Puzzle: Facts Versus Fantasy," *Journal of the American Oriental Society* 94 (April-June 1974): 168-176; and *Buddhist Monastic Discipline: The Sanskrit Pratimoksa Satras of the Mahasanghikas and the Mulasarvastivadins* (University Park, Pa., 1975).

Prebish, Charles S., and Janice J. Nattier. "Mahasanghika Origins: The Beginning of Buddhist Sectarianism." *History of Religions* 16 (1977): 237-272. An original and convincing argument against the conception of the Mahasamghika as "liberals."

Rhys Davids, T.W. *Buddhist India.* London, 1903. A classic, although its methodology is questionable. Also of some use, in spite of its date, is his "Sects (Buddhist)," in the *Encyclopaedia of Religion and Ethics,* edited by James Hastings, Vol. II (Edinburgh, 1920), pp. 307-309.

Robinson, Richard H. "Classical Indian Philosophy." In *Chapters in Indian Civilization,* edited by Joseph Elder. Vol. 1, pp. 127-227. Dubuque, 1970. A bit idiosyncratic, but valuable in its attempt to understand Buddhist philosophy as part of general Indian currents and patterns of speculative thought. Robinson's "The Religion of the Householder Bodhisattva," *Bharati* (1966): 31-55, challenges the notion of Mahayana as a lay movement.

Robinson, Richard H., and Willard L. Johnson. *The Buddhist Religion: A Historical Introduction.* 3d rev. ed. Belmont, Calif., 1982. A great improvement over earlier editions, this book is now a useful manual, with a good bibliography for the English reader.

Ruegg, David S. *The Study of Indian and Tibetan Thought.* Leiden, 1967. The most valuable survey of the main issues of modern scholarship on Ind4n Buddhism, especially on the early period. The author has also written the definitive study of the Tathagata-garbha doctrines in *La theorie du tathagatagarbha et du gotra* (Paris, 1969). See also on the Madhyamika school his "Towards a Chronology of the Madhyamaka School," in *Indological and Buddhist Studies in Honour of J.W. de Jong* (Canberra, 1982), pp. 505-530, and *The Literature of the Madhyamaka School of Philosophy in India* (Wiesbaden, 1981).

Schayer, Stanislaus. "Precanonical Buddhism." *Acta Orientalia* 7 (1935): 121-132. Posits an early Buddhism not found explicitly in the canon; attempts to reconstruct the doctrines of Buddhism antedating the canon.

Schopen, Gregory. "The Phrase '*sa prithivipradesas caityabhuto bhavet*' in the *Vajracchedika: Notes* on the Cult of the Book in Mahayana." *Indo-Iranian Journal* 17 (1975): 147-181. Schopen's work has opened new perspectives on the early history of Mahayana, emphasizing its religious rather than philosophical character and revealing generalized beliefs and practices rather than the speculations of the elite. See also "Sukhavati as a Generalized Religious Goal in Sanskrit Mahayana Sutra Literature," *Indo-Iranian Journal* 19 (1977): 177-210; "Mahayana in Indian Inscriptions," *Indo-Iranian*

Journal 21 (1979): 1-19; and "Two Problems in the History of Indian Buddhism: The Layman/Monk Distinction and the Doctrines of the Transference of Merit," *Studien zur Indologie und Iranistik* 10 (1985): 9-47.

Schlingloff, Dieter. *Die Religion des Buddhismus.* 2 Vols. Berlin, 1963. An insightful exposition of Buddhism, mostly from the perspective of canonical Indian documents.

Snellgrove, David L., ed. *Buddhist Himalaya.* Oxford, 1957. Although the context of this study is modern Himalayan Buddhism, it contains useful information on Buddhist Tantra in general. Snellgrove's two-volume *The Hevaira Tantra: A Critical Study* (London, 1959) includes an English translation and study of this major Tantric work. In *The Image of the Buddha (*Tokyo and London, 1978) Snellgrove, in collaboration with other scholars, surveys the history of the iconography of the Buddha image.

Stcherbatsky, Theodore. *The Central Conception of Buddhism and the Meaning of the Word* "Dharma" (1923). Reprint, Delhi, 1970. A classic introduction to Sarvastivadin doctrine. On the Madhyamika, Stcherbatsky wrote *The Conception of Buddhist Nirvana* (Leningrad, 1927). On early Buddhism, see his '.'The Doctrine of the Buddha," *Bulletin of the School of Oriental Studies* 6 (1932): 867-896, and "The 'Dharmas' of the Buddhists and the 'Gunas' of the Samkhyas," *Indian Historical Quarterly* 10 (1934): 737-760. Stcherbatsky categorized the history of Buddhist thought in "Die drei Richtungen in der Philosophie des Buddhismus," *Rocznik O*rientalistyczny 10 (1934): 1-37.

Takasaki Jikido. *Nyoraizo shiso* no *keisei—Indo daijo bukkyo shiso kenkyu.* Tokyo, 1974. A major study of Tathagata-garbha thought in India.

Thapar, Romila. *Asoka and the Decline of the Mauryas.* London, 1961. Controversial study of Asoka's reign. Her conclusions are summarized in her *History of India,* Vol. 1 (Baltimore, 1965). Also relevant for the study of Indian Buddhism are her *Ancient Indian Social History: Some Interpretations* (New Delhi, 1978), *Dissent in the Early Indian Tradition* (Dehradun, 1979), and *From Lineage to State* (Bombay, 1984).

Thomas, Edward J. *The Life of the Buddha as Legend and History* (1927). New York, 1960. Still the only book-length, critical study of the life of Buddha. Less current, but still useful, is the author's 1933 work *The History of Buddhist Thought* (New York, 1975).

Varma, V.P. *Early Buddhism and Its Origins.* New Delhi, 1973. Vetter, Tilmann. "The Most Ancient Form of Buddhism." In his *Buddhism and Its Relation to Other Religions. Kyoto,* 1985.

Warder, A.K. *Indian Buddhism.* 2d rev. ed. Delhi, 1980. One of the few modem surveys of the field, this work includes a bibliography of classical sources (pp. 523-574). Unfortunately, the author does not make use of materials available in Chinese and Tibetan translation.

Watanabe Fumnimaro. *Philosophy and Its Development in the Nikayas and Abhidhamma.* Delhi, 1983. The beginnings of Buddhist scholasticism, especially as seen in the transition from Sutra to Abhidharma literature.

Watters, Thomas. *On Yuan Chwang's Travels in India.* 2 Vols. London, 1904-1905. Extensive study of Hsuan-tsang's travels.

Wayman, Alex. *The Buddhist Tantras: Light on Indo-Tibetan Esotericism.* New York, 1973. Not a survey or introduction to the study of Indian Tantra, but a collection of essays on specific issues and problems. Chapter 1.2 deals with the problem of the early history of Tantra. See also Wayman's *Yoga of the* Guhyasamajatantra: *The Arcane Lore of Forty Verses; A Buddhist Tantra Commentary* (Delhi, 1977). In his "The Mahasamghika and the Tathagatagarbha (Buddhist Doctrinal History, Study I)," *Journal of the International Association of Buddhist Studies* 1 (1978): 35-50, Wayman discusses possible connections between the Mahasamghika subsects of Andhra and the development of Mahayana. His "Meditation in Theravada and Mahisasaka," *Studia Missionalia* 25 (1976): 1-28, is a study of the doctrine of meditation in two of the leading schools of Hinayana.

Winternitz, Moriz. *Geschichte der indischen Literature,* Vol. 2. Leipzig, 1920. Translated as *A History of Indian Literature* (Delhi, 1983). Largely dated but not superseded.

Zelliot, Eleanor. Dr. *Ambedkar and the Mahar Movement.* Philadelphia, 1969.

7

The Untouchables Through the Ages

Caste in Ancient India

Origin of Varnas. The earliest account of the origin of the Varnas is found in the famous Purusha Hymn of the *Rig-Veda* (x. 90. 11-12). The Hymn thus describes the creation of castes:

"When they divided the Purusha, into how many parts did they divide him? What was his mouth? What were his arms? What were his thighs and feet called? The Brahman was his mouth, of his arms the Rajanya was made; the Vaisyas were his thighs; the Sudra sprang from his feet." The Hymn has, however, been held by some Oriental Scholars as a later interpolation. But independently of this there is evidence to believe that in the *Rig-Veda* period the idea of a separate Brahman caste differing from the Warrior and Agricultural castes had already been evolved. Professors Macdonnell and Keith who advance this view hold that "the caste system is one that has progressively developed and it is not legitimate to look in the *Rig-Veda* for the full caste system even of the *Yajur-Veda;* but at the same time it is difficult to doubt that the system was already well on its way to general acceptance". In the *Yajur-Veda* (Taittiriya Samhita, vii. 1.1.4-6) the theory admittedly receives a clearer expression. Here we read "Prajapati desirous of offspring (performed the Agnishtoma Sacrifice) and created Trivrit hymn, God Agni, Gayatri Metre, Rathatara Saman, Brahman among men and goats among brutes from his mouth. As they were created from the mouth therefore they are superior to all others. (He) created Panchadasa hymn, God Indra, Trishtap Metre, Vrihat Saman, Rajanya among men and sheep among brutes from chest and arms. Therefore they are strong because they have been created from strength (Strong Arms). (He) created Saptadasa hymn, Visvadevas among the gods, Jagati Metre, Vacrupa Saman, Vaisya among men and cows among brutes from the belly. As they have been created from the storehouse of food (belly) so they are the food (or intended to be enjoyed by others). Therefore, they (Vaisyas) are more numerous than others (among men) because many gods were created. (He) created Ekavamsa hymn, Anushtap Metre, Vairaja Saman, Sudra among men and horse among brutes from his feet. Therefore the Sudra and the horse are dependent on other (castes). As no god was created from the feet, so the Sudra is not competent to perform sacrifice. As the Sudra and the horse were created from the feet, so they lived by exerting their feet."

The *Brihadaranyaka Upanishad* (I. 4. 10-14) describes the creation of the four Varnas and law in a rather striking manner. In the beginning we are told the Brahman was created, but being one and not strong enough, the most excellent Kshatra was created. Therefore there is nothing beyond the Kshatra and therefore at the Rajasuya the Brahman sits below the Kshatriya. But the Brahman is the birthplace of Kshatra. Therefore though a king exalted. he sits down at the end (of the sacrifice) below the Brahmana as his birthplace. He who wrongs him injures is own birthplace. He becomes worse, because he has injured one better than himself. The Kshatriya was not strong enough. Therefore he created the Vis (people). He was not strong enough. He created the Sudra colour (Varna) as Pushan (Nourisher).

Creation of Castes. We seem to get to a further stage in the writings of Baudhayana (I. 18. 1. 6), Gautama (iv. 24) and Vasishta (II and IV), which can all be referred to the sixth century B.C. They give nearly the same account of the creation of castes and of their different duties. The last of these after starting that "the four castes are distinguished by their origin and by particular sacraments" quotes the texts of the *Rig* and *Yajur-Veda* hymns in support of the statement that "a Sudra shall not receive the sacraments". The reason given is that the Sudra, according to the *Yajur-Veda,* was created "without any metre". It is, perhaps, inferable from this that the Sudras had by Vasishta's time become a distinct caste or representative heads of a caste going under that name. It is significant that the Yajus text says that "they are not competent to perform sacrifice" while Vasistha extends their disability by saying that "they shall not receive the sacraments". All the same he insists that "truthfulness, suppression of anger, liberality, abstention from injuring living beings and the procreation of offspring are duties common to all castes."

When we come to the period of *Bhagawad-Gita,* we find that though the idea of creation still persists, the exaltation of the Dharma is carried still's further. The position taken in the *Brihadaranyaka Upanishad* is emphasized, if not enlarged. The castes have not only their particular qualities but also their particular duties. And then we are told (*Bhagavad-Gita,* III. 35 *et. seq.*) that the performance of one's own duty though imperfect is better than the performance of another's duty though well performed. Death in performing one's own duty is preferable, the performance of the duties of others is dangerous. The theory of creation is referred to in two places (Ch. IV. 13 & Chap. XVIII. 41) and these indicate the position of the *Bhagavad-Gita* in regard to the Caste. In the first Sri Krishna says: "The four-fold division of castes was created by me according to the apportionment of qualities and duties." In the second he adds:—"The duties of Brahmanas, Kshatriyas and Vaisyas and of Sudras, too, terror of four foes! are distinguished according to the qualities born of nature. Tranquillity, restraint of senses, penance, purity and forgiveness, straightforwardness, also knowledge, experience and belief (in a future world), this is the natural duty of the Brahmanas. Valour, glory, courage, dexterity, non-shirking from battle, gifts, exercise of bodily power, this is the natural duty of the Kshatriyas. Agriculture, breeding cattle, trade (this) is the natural duty of the Vaisyas. And the natural duty of the Sudras, too, consists in service. (Every) man intent on his own respective duties obtains perfection. Listen, now, how one intent on one's own duty obtains perfection. Worshipping, by (the performance of) his own duty, him from whom all things proceed, and by whom all this is permeated, a man obtains perfection. One's duty, though defective, is better than another's duty well performed. Performing the duty prescribed by nature one does not incur sin."

Buddha's Attitude

Buddha's attitude towards caste is well brought by his definition of an outcaste, which is illustrated by the story of Chandala who was reborn in the Brahman world. In the *Sutta Nipata*, in which the story is told, we read : "Not by birth does one become an outcaste, not by birth does one become a Brahman; by deeds one becomes an outcaste, and by deeds one becomes a Brahmana. Buddha himself is neither a Brahman, nor a king's son, nor a Vessa (Vaisya), but a wandering Mendicant".

Views of Jains

The Jain attitude is equally clear. In the *Jaina Sutras* the story is told of the monk Harikesa Bala, born in the family of Svapakesa —the lowest of lowly castes—converting a Brahmana. The self-same *Sutras* state that a Brahmana, Kshatriya, an Ugra or a Lichchavi, when entering the order is not stuck up on account of his Gotra. Their reasoning is direct and simple. If there were only one soul, these could not be of Brahmanas, Kshatriyas, Vaisyas and Sudras.

Kautilya's Arthasastra

Kautilya's *Arthasastra,* though a work of much later date than the

Bhagavad-Gita, which, according to Telang, "must be earlier than the third century B.C., though it is impossible to say at present, how much earlier", takes a view of castes which is in some respects in keeping with it. The duties it assigns to the four castes greatly overlap and the functions of the Vaisyas and Sudras are enlarged to an extent unknown before. It says:—"The duty of the Brahman is study, teaching, performance of sacrifice, officiating in other's sacrificial performance and the giving and receiving of gifts. That of a Kshatriya is study, performance of sacrifice, military occupation and protection of life. That of a Vaisya is study, peformance of sacrifice, giving gifts, agriculture, cattle breeding and trade. That of a Sudra is the serving of twice-born, agriculture and cattle-breeding and trade, profession of artisans and court-bards."

Laws of Manu. In the *Laws of Manu,* which in its present form probably dates from 200 A.D., we have the old theory of the creation of the four castes set down in the traditional manner, but there is a still (Books I to XI) further enlargement in the duties assigned to each of them. Thus the Brahman's duties include study, teaching, sacrifice, officiating at another's sacrifices, making and receiving gifts, living by inheritance, occupancy, lawful gleaning, and gathering or receipt of what is given unasked. In default he may become a soldier, or till the ground or breed cattle. The Kshatriya is to govern, and fight and make conquests, to learn the management of chariots and the use of the bow, to stand firm in battle and not to turn back, to protect the people, to abstain from sensual pleasures, and to pay obedience to Brahmans. The Vaisyas are to tend cattle, to lend money, to trade and to cultivate the land. The Sudra is to serve the three other castes. Comparing these duties with those assigned to the same castes in the *Arthasastra,* we find that within the four centuries which lie between it and the *Laws of Manu,* we find that the Brahman's duties are enlarged in a variety of ways, including agriculture, soldiering, and living a life of ease on patrimony or bounty, the Kshatriya is confined to his royal duties, the Vaisya likewise has no sacrifices to offer and is no more than a mere trader or cultivator and the Sudra is to rest content with serving the three others. This enlargement and contraction of duties is probably based on the actual condition of the age. Undoubtedly the mixed castes bulk large in the pages of Manu.

Manu's theory of the origin of caste, as will readily be seen, is no new thing. In essence it is the same, which we find given expression to in the early writers we have quoted above. The theory as attributed to him has been described by some as fantastic and grotesque. But as Sir Henry Risley points out there is an element of historic truth in it : it shows us that at the time Manu's treatise was compiled, about the 2nd century A.D., there must have existed an elaborate and highly developed social system, including tribal, national and functional groups. Assuming that this was so, and that society then was, as now, a medley of divers and heterogeneous groups apparently not so strictly and uniformly endogamous as the castes of to-day but containing within themselves the germs out of which the modern system has developed by natural and insensible stages, the question is from what source is the theory of the four castes derived? Sir Herbert Risley thinks it possible that it "may be nothing more than modified version of the division of society into four classes—priests, warriors, cultivators and artisans—which appears in the sacerdotal literature of ancient Persia."

Means of Livelihood

It is said that the influence of British civilisation is tending to break down the barriers of caste. With the advent of railways, the growth of trade, and the introduction of machinery, the old social organisation has become unsuitable to modern conditions. Many of the old village industries have become unprofitable, while a great and growing demand has sprung up for labour in mines and mills and workshops of all kinds.

High castes and law are necessarily thrown together in railway carriages, and in the crowded streets of big towns. It is impossible for a man of high caste on a journey to preserve that aloofness which he maintains in his own village, or to purify himself every time he comes in contact with men of low caste, or to be as particular as he should be in regard to what he eats and drinks. Consequently, on journeys and in towns the old rules are no longer rigidly observed. But there is no sign of any such relaxation amongst the masses in their ordinary village life. Amongst the higher and better educated classes there is, no doubt, a general feeling that many of the restrictions of the caste system are absurd. Away from home they will often indulge in food cooked by Muhammadans in the European style, including even beef; and the more advanced will not hesitate to sit down to table, not only with Hindus of other castes, but also with Europeans and Muhammadans, although in their own homes the fear of giving offence to their more orthodox caste-fellows leads them to observe the established rules and properties.

Female Members

The strongest restraining influence has been that of the female members of the family. Brought up in seclusion and without much education, and seldom leaving home, the women of the family are tenacious of the old observances and restrictions, and regard any departure from them with the greatest disfavour. There have recently, however, been signs of a great change in the treatment of Hindu ladies of high caste. Following the example of the Brahmos, Hindu gentlemen are now becoming keen to give their daughters a good education. They are also beginning to perceive the *parda* system, which the Hindus adopted from the Muhammadans. The more advanced among them no longer hesitate to let their wives go unweiled when away from home, or when taking an evening drive. It is now only a matter of time for females of the educated classes to appear freely in public; and when they do so, the restrictions of the caste system amongst the educated classes, so far as ordinary social intercourse is concerned, are doomed. The uneducated masses, however, are far more conservative than the educated few, and it may be doubted whether they will quickly imitate their example in these matters. It is true that girls of the higher castes, in many cases, are no longer given in marriage at so early an age as formerly, but the improvement in this respect is perhaps due quite as much to the difficulty and expense of obtaining suitable bridegrooms as to a growing sense of the evils arising from child marriage. The most noticeable of the efforts yet made to break down injurious rules is in connexion with child widows. In early times, young girls who had lost their husbands prior to cohabitation were allowed to marry again. Subsequently, however, they were forbidden to do so. The result is that all over India large numbers of child widows are condemned to a life of celibacy and austerity. Educated opinion is beginning to recognize the folly and injustice of this rule, and cases sometimes occur in which virgin widows are allowed by their parents to marry again. The opposition to such marriages is still very strong, and comparatively few men have hitherto ventured to face it.

Status of converts. Converts to Christianity or Muhammadanism are freely admitted to the society of persons professing those religions, but hitherto they have been unable to resume their place amongst the Hindus, however much they might wish to do so. Educated Hindus have of late become very much alive to the fact that other communities are growing at their expense, and a movement is in progress to enable persons who have left their ranks to return, and even to encourage them to do so.

At Etawah, in the United Provinces, nearly four hundred Rajputs, whose ancestors became Muhammadans in the time of Aurangzeb, were recently taken back into caste, after an interesting ceremony of purification.

Effect of Western Education. The spread of Western education has disseminated ideas of equality, and men are no longer prepared to admit the superiority of their neighbours merely because they belong to a caste which is supposed to stand on a higher level. The higher castes no more enjoy special privileges or immunity from the ordinary tribunals. In the eye of the law all men are equal. The man of low caste is no longer compelled to leave the road when a man of high caste passes, or to shout out when walking at night to give warning of his approach, or, as was sometimes the case formerly, to paint on his forehead the emblem of his degrading occupation. Education is no longer confined to the higher castes; nor is there anything to prevent a man of low caste from becoming a schoolmaster, a pleader, or even a magistrate.

The *Sastras,* which were once the monopoly of the Brahmans, are no longer sealed books to the lower castes, many of whose members are quite competent to study them for themselves.

Caste and Religion. Although no one who is not a Hindu can belong to a Hindu caste, the fact remains. He must submit to various rules and restrictions, and perform various ceremonies. The fact is that caste is a social rather than a religious institution. It has grown up amongst the Hindus; and so much is said abut it in Hindu religious books that it is often very difficult to say where caste begins and and religion ends. Hence has arisen the common, but mistaken, idea that caste is an invention of the Brahmans, and the still more common, but equally erroneous, belief that the Brahmans have taken the leading part in its evolution and in the elaboration of caste rules and restrictions. The Brahmans have undoubtedly always done their utmost to advance their own interests and to make the supremacy of the hierarchy sure and undisputed.

Jains in South India

Jains. Amongst the Jains, caste follows much the same lines as amongst the Hindus. There are, indeed, certain castes, such as the Agarwals and Oswals, some of whose members are Hindus, while others are Jains. This difference of religion does not operate as a bar to marriage; a Hindu Oswal, for instance, may marry one who is a Jain. In parts of Southern India the Jains appear to form a separate community of the nature of an ordinary caste. The number of these Jains is, however, very small.

Christians. The Roman Catholic Missions allow their converts to retain their original caste distinctions, but this is forbidden by the Anglican and other Protestant Missions. The latter, however, have not always succeeded in wholly obliterating the distinctions of caste, and converts from the higher ranks of Hinduism are sometimes reluctant to eat with or marry persons of inferior origin, especially in places where large numbers of converts were made at one time, as in Nadia during the famine of 1838.

Muhammadans. The conventional division of Indian Muhammadans is into four groups : Shaikh, Saiad, Mughal and Pathan. Persons who, at the present day, describe themselves as Mughals and Pathans are usually descended, at least on the male side, from immigrants belonging to these races, but no such inference can be drawn from the use of the words Saiad and Shaikh. The real meaning of *Saiad* is a descendant of 'Ali, Muhammad's son-in-law, by his wife Fatima, and a *Shaikh* is an Arab.

Social Status

This is especially the case in Bengal. In Northern India conversion to Islam does not so much affect a man's social status, and many castes, such as Rajput, Gujar, and Jat, are divided into two sections, one consisting of Muhammadans and the other of Hindus. The so-called Shaikhs are for the most part cultivators. Many oi those who claim the title are known to others by less complimentary names, such as Nao-Muslim or Nasya.

The Muhammadans recognise two main social divisions: Ashraf, or noble, including all undoubted descendants of foreigners and converts from the higher Hindu castes, and Ajlaf, or common people. The latter term comprises all local converts of low origin, including most of the Shaikhs and the various functional groups, such as Jolaha, or weaver; Dhunia, or cotton-carder; Khulu, or oil-presser; Darzi or tailor; Hajjam or barber; Kunjra or greengrocer; and many others. These functional groups have *panchayats* who manage their affairs, and who, in many parts, exercise almost as rigorous a control as the managing body of a Hindu caste. Amongst the social offences of which they take cognizance are the eating of forbidden food, adultery, divorcing a wife without due cause, making a false accusation against a caste-fellow, and marrying persons not belonging to the group.

Such persons not only remain in their original social group, but also preserve most of the restrictions on social intercourse, inter-marriage, and the like, which they observed when still Hindus. Except in Upper India, the Muhammadans who do not belong to the above-mentioned functional groups, i.e., the Ashraf and the cultivating Shaikhs, have usually no *panchayats.* They are thus more free to follow their own inclinations, and there are, therefore, fewer restrictions on marriage. The pride of blood amongst those of foreign descent is, however, considerable. They keep a careful record of their traditions and family connexions, and it is the general practice for a Saiad to marry a Saiad, a Pathan a Pathan, and so forth. But so long as both parties belong to the Ashraf community, no slur attaches to mixed marriages.

There are fewer restrictions on eating with members of other groups than there are amongst the Hindus; but the rule that a man may not marry outside the limits of his own group or pass from one group to another is equally rigid. There is, however, this marked difference, that although a Darzi cannot become a Dhunia, or a Dhunia a Jolaha, there is no great difficulty in the way of a member of any of these groups who rises in life joining the ranks of the Shaikhs or even of the Ashraf. There is a well-known proverb, 'Last year I was a Jolaha, this year I am a Shaikh; next year, if prices rise, I shall be a Saiad.' A well-to-do man of a functional group will often drop the functional designation, call himself Shaikh, and, by dint of hospitality, secure for himself a circle of friends from the poorer members of the Ashraf community. He will then marry into an Ashraf family, possibly of doubtful status, and his son may hope to be recognized as a true Ashraf.

It may be said that, though caste is unknown to the Muhammadan religion, it exists in full force amongst many of the Muhammadans of Upper India, and in all parts of the country amongst the functional groups that form the lower strata of the community. The other Indian Muhammadans, though they do not recognize caste, have, nevertheless, been so far influenced by the example of their Hindu neighbours that they have, become far more particular about their matrimonial alliances than are their co-religionists elsewhere.

Female Member, Status of Converts, Effect of Western Education, Jains in South India, Social Status, Social Divisions

Gurus on Caste System. The Sikh Gurus condemned caste and caste ideology. Guru Nanak called caste ideology as perverse. The motivative power behind the caste system was the upholding of the caste-status of the Brahmin and other high castes. The Guru preached: "O unwise, be not proud of thy caste. For, a myriad error flow out of this pride."

Bhai Gurdas writes that Guru Nanak "made the Dharma perfect by blending the four castes into one. To treat the King and the pauper on equal footing, and while greeting to touch the feet of the other (i.e., regard oneself humble as compared to others) was made the rule of conduct. Thus Guru Nanak did away with not caste-status consciousness but also with the status-consciousness gap between the rich and the poor. For, far from observing pollution and untouchability, everyone actually touched the feet of everyone else while greeting him. Again, "The four castes were made into one, and castes (Varn) and out-castes (Avarn) regarded as noble. The twelve sects were obliterated and the noble glorious Panth (created)." Here the abolition of caste and sects is linked with the creation of the Sikh Panth. In order to emphasize its significance, Bhai Gurdas repeatedly mentions this achievement.

Writing about Guru Gobind Singh, Dr. Narang says: 'Of the five who offered their heads, one was a Khatri, all the rest being so-called Sudras. But the Guru called them Panj Pyaras, or the Beloved Five, and baptised them after the manner he had introduced for initiation into his brotherhood. He enjoined the same duties upon them, gave them the same privileges, and as a token of newly acquired brotherhood, all of them dined together.'

"The Guru's views of democratic equality were much more advanced than the mere equality among his followers could satisfy. In his system, there was no place even for the privileges of the chief or the leader. No leader, he believed, could be fit to lead unless he was elected or accepted by the followers. History shows that individuals or classes enjoying a religious or sacerdotal superiority have been only too loth to forego even a particle of their privileges. But the Guru, though regarded by his faithful followers as the greatest of prophets, was made of a different stuff, and had too much political insight to stand on an exclusive eminence apart from his followers. Therefore, when he initiated his first five disciples, his Beloved Five, he was initiated by them in turn, taking the same vows as they had done, and claiming no higher privileges than those he allowed them. Soon after he called a meeting of all his followers and announced his new doctrine to them."

Equality and Brotherhood

The significance of equality, brotherhood and fraternization achieved by the Sikh movement can be realized only if it is contrasted with the caste background in which the change was brought about. Bougle observes: 'The spirit of caste unites these three tendencies, repulsion, hierarchy and hereditary specialisation... We say that a society is characterised by such a system if it is divided into a large number of mutually opposed groups which are hereditary specialised and hierarchically arranged—if, on principle, it tolerates neither the parvenu, nor miscegenation, nor a change of profession. From the social and political point of view, caste is division, hatred, jealousy and distrust between neighbour. Nesafield also comes to the conclusion that the caste system leads to a degree of social disunion to which no parallel can be found in human history. All authorities on caste are agreed that mutual repulsion and disunity, besides inequality and hierarchism, are the in-built constituents of the caste system.

Scriptural Sanction. By repudiating the Brahmanical scriptures, Sikhism and the Sikh Panth cut itself away from his perennial source and sanction of caste ideology. "The drum of the Vedas loudly resoundeth for many a faction. Remember god, Name, Nanak; there is none but Him." Since I have embraced Thy feet I have paid regard to none besides. The Purans of Ram (the God of the Hindus) and Quran of Rahim (the God of the Musalmans) express various opinions, but I accept none of them. The Smritis, the Shastras, and the Vedas all expound many different doctrines, but I accept none of them. Since Guru Arjan established *Guru Granth* as the Sikh scripture, the Sikhs have never, not even during darkest hour, owned by other.

The main plank of Sikhism is uncompromising monotheism and the methodology of Name as the sole means of achieving His Grace and God realisation. Excepting these two fundamentals, Sikhism is not wedded to any particular dogma or philosophy. All other beliefs and practices attributable to Sikhism are only subsidiary or contributory. The belief in one universal God is shared by the mystics the world over. There is nothing peculiarly sectarian (i.e. Hindu or Muslim) about it. If anything, this concept of one universal God, and the passionate devotion towards Him as a means of mystic realisation, came to be emphasized much earlier in Christianity and Islam than in India. And the emotional heights that his devotional approach reached among the Muslim saints is hardly to be matched elsewhere.

The Sikh Gurus' stand on this issue is clear from their hymns given below:

"If the ideas of impurity be admitted, there is impurity in everything.
There are worms in cow-dung and in wood;
There is no grain of corn without life.
In the first place, there is life in water by which everything is made green.

How shall we avoid impurity? It falleth on our kitchens. Saith Nanak, impurity is not thus washed away; it is washed away by divine knowledge...

All impurity consisteth in superstition and attachment to worldly things. The eating and drinking which god sent us for sustenance is pure."

"They eat he-goats killed with unspeakable words,
And allow no one to enter their cooking squares.
Having smeared a space they draw lines around it,
And sit within, false that they are,
Saying, 'Touch not ! O touch not I.'
'Or this food of ours will be defiled.'
But their bodies are defiled; what they do is defiled;
Their hearts are false while they perform ablutions after their meals."

Views of Guru Angad. There was no place in Guru Angad's congregation for any one who observed caste. All the castes were treated as equals. Only those who were not afraid of caste injunctions came to his congregations; others did not. At the Langar (free kitchen) all ate at the same platform and took the same food. Guru Amar Das went a step further. No one who had not partaken food at his Langar could see him. In his Langar there were no distinctions of caste. Lines of noble *Gurbhais* (disciples of same Guru) partook food sitting together at the same place. Guru Gobind Singh himself drank Amrit, prepared at the baptism ceremony by the five Beloved ones, of whom four were Sudras. Koer Singh, a near contemporary, of the Guru, records that the Guru 'has made the four castes into a single one, and made the Sudra, Vaish, Khatri and Brahmin take meals at the same place. All the members of the Khalsa Dal, who were drawn from all castes including the Rangrettas dined together.

The process of founding a separate society (the Sikh Panth) started with Guru Nanak himself. He began his career as a teacher of men with the significance utterance. "There is no Hindu, no Musalman." He was asked : "There is one path of the Hindus, and the other that of Musalmans, which path do you follow ?" He replied, "I follow God's path. God is neither Hindu nor Musalman." Guru Nanak's reply clearly indicates his complete break with his Hindu past. Further, Guru Nanak too clear organisational steps in shaping a Sikh society on separate ideological lines. He established Dharamsalas in far-flung places inside the country and outside it. These Dharamsalas became the centres where his followers could meet together, practise the Dharam of his concept, and spread his message to others. In addition, he appointed select persons (Manjis) for the purpose of furthering his mission. In his lifetime, his followers came to be known as Nanak-panthies, and they had their own separate way of saluting each other (Sat Kartar). The greatest single organisational step that Guru Nanak took was to select, by a system of tests, a worthy successor whom he instructed to lead and continue his mission. Guru Nanak's successors consistently worked to establish the separate identity of the Sikh Church and the Sikh Panth. They consolidated and extended the institutions of Dharamsala (religious centres), Sangat (congregation of Sikhs), Langar (common kitchen) and Manjis (seats of preaching), all started by Guru Nanak. In addition, Guru Angad invented the Gurmukhi script and Guru Arjan compiled the Sikh scripture. With a distinct organisation, separate religious centres, a separate script and a scripture of their own, the Sikhs became an entirely separate church and a new society—the Sikh Panth. The main theme of the Vars of Bhai Gurdas, a contemporary of Guru Arjan and Guru

Hargobind, emphasizes the distinct character of Sikh religion, culture and society as contrasted to other religions and sects. He links, as already seen, the creation of the Panth with the abolition of castes and sects.

Creation of Khalsa

The creation of the Khalsa was the acme of the Sikh movement. The Sikhs were militarized to fight religious and political oppressions. At the time of baptism (Amrit) ceremony, the Guru enjoined on all who had joined the Khalsa that they should consider their previous castes erased and deem themselves all brothers, i.e., of one family. The newswriter of the period sent the Emperor a copy of the Guru's address to his Sikh on that occasion. It is dated the first of Baisakh 1756 (A.D. 1699), and runs as follows: "Let all embrace one creed and obliterate differences of religion. Let the four Hindu castes who have different rules for their guidance abandon them all, adopt the one form of adoration and become brothers. Let no one deem himself superior to others... Let men of the four castes receive my baptism, eat out of one dish, and feel no disgust or contempt for one another."

The Guru said: "Many a Vaish (Vaishya), Sudar (Shudra) and Jat have I incorporated in the Panth and that the Guru 'has made the four castes into a single one, and made the Sudra, Vaish, Khatri and Brahmin take meals at the same place. According to same authority, it was a current topic among the people that the Guru had 'blended the four castes into one", had rejected both the Hindu and Muslim religions and created a new noble Khalsa, wherein Sudra, Vaishya, Khatri and Brahmin eat together.

The idea of equality was inherent in the system of the Gurus and the Sikh movement so long it retained its pristine purity. After he had anointed Angad as his successor, Guru Nanak bowed at his feet in salutation. The same custom was followed by the later Gurus.

As there was no difference between the Guru and the Sikh the devotion to the Guru was easily channelized into the service of the Sikhs. 'God-orientated service is the service of the Guru's Sikhs, who should be regarded as one's dearest kith and kin.' 'The Guru's Sikhs should serve the other Sikhs.' One of Guru Gobind Singh's own hymns is :

> "To serve them (The Khalsa) pleaseth my heart; no other service is dear to my soul.
> All the wealth of my house with my soul and body is for them."

Abolition of Caste

The Chuhras are the 'out-caste, par-excellence of the Punjab, whose name is popularly supposed to be corruption of Sudra.' As such, they were about the most despised caste in the Punjab; mere bodily contact with whom defiled a person of a higher caste. On conversion to Sikhism, persons from this caste were given the honorific title of Rangretta in order to raise them in public estimation, much in the same way as depressed classes are nowadays called Harijans. A rhyme, 'Rangretta, Guru Ka Beta', meaning 'Rangretta is the son of the guru', current in the Punjab, is an indication of the status to which the Sikh movement sought to raise them. We have seen how Rangrettas (whose touch, had they remained in the caste society, defiled not only the person but also the food he carried) were coequal members of the Khalsa Dal, where they dined and fraternized, without discrimination, with other Dal members drawn from Brahmins, Khatris, Jats and others. When the Taruna Dal (the Youth wing of the Khalsa Dal) was reorganized into five divisions, one of these was under the leadership of Bir Singh Rangretta. It was bestowed a standard flag (Jhanda) from the Akal Takht in the same manner as was done in the case of the other four divisions. It was thus given an equal status with them.

8

The Bhakti Movement: A Voice of Revolt: History and Tradition

The Bhakti movement has a pretty long history of social equality and awakening. In the beginning it was purely a peoples religious movement. In the medieval age with the emergence of Kabir and Nanak it became a movement of social change. In Bhakti cult religious devotion and dedication to God was always present, but side by side, it revolted against social evils, caste system, untouchability and other social barriers.

Early Bhakti Cult

The earliest Bhakti-cult has its deep root and origin in the Mohenjodaro and Harappan culture which has added a new chapter to the history of India. Referring to the excavations carried out at these places, Sir John Marshall opined: "They exhibit the Indus people of the fourth and third millennia B.C. in possession of a highly developed culture in which no vestige of Indo-Aryan influence is to be found."[1]

"Many traits of Harappan culture appear to anticipate features of the religion of Vedic times or later Hinduism. Motifs like the 'pipal' leaf or the 'Svastika' were already of religious significance for the Harappans.

According to the Bridget and Raymand Allchin: "There is a suggestion of a religion dominated by one great God, who convincingly shares many of the traits of the later Siva being a Yogi, a Lord of Beasts, whose cult was associated with *fertility* and the *Lingam* and who in later times had the epithet Maha-deva (Great God) and by a great Mother who equally shares traits of Parvati, the spouse of Siva known also as Mother and Devi, the Goddess..., we cannot fail to see in them much that continues in subsequent Hinduism."[2]

In some primitive tribes and wandering races, the worship of primitive deities and ancient gods and goddesses is still prevalent. These people have their own rituals and *mantras* which are in their dialects. In village untouchables and Sudras worship a number of deities even now.

Further research is going on to reveal the culture of the ancient Vedic river Saraswati, which has vanished from this land and has references in Rigveda and several scriptural works, which inspired the Bhakti-cult as people still chants songs in praise of river Sarswati.

In Rig-Vedic *mantras* there are several references to Indra, Varuna and other gods. They are divine giver of gifts. From Vedic times still today Hindus have great faith in Vedic gods. They are worshipped as protectors.[3]

According to Dr. S. Radhakrishnan "if Bhakti means faith in personal god, love for him, dedication of everything to his service and attainment of *moksha* or freedom by personal devotion, surely we have all these elements in Varuna worship."[4]

Similarly Indra is worshipped as a rain-god. He is also the protector of Aryan race and destroyer of forts and cities of the non-Aryans, the Dasyus.

Svetasvatara Upanishad,[5] refers to Bhakti, which was composed during the post-Buddha period. In the older Upanishads much stress is laid on knowledge (*Jnana*) for which faith (*Sraddha*) is an essential basis. Upanishads also called Aranyakas stated that self cannot be gained by the Veda, or by understanding or by much knowledge. 'He whom the self chooses, by him the self cannot be gained.[6] The doctrine of grace (*prasada*) gains prominence. This is bhakti or pious faith.

In Vishnu Purana,[7] Krishna is said to be the greatest *bhakta* (devotee) of Vishnu. It recommends *samadhi* for attainment of salvation (*moksha*), prescribes *bhakti* as an alternative for devotees of lower order and womenfolk. Vishnu purifies the hearts of devotees and forgives for their sins due to *bhakti*. Bhakti was treated as shakti (strength) in Puranic literature.

In Bhagvata Purana, Krishna is a complete incarnation (*purna avatar*). There is great stress on *bhakti* in Vishnu and Bhagavata Purana. The devotees are given *prasada* (grace) by the Gods. While ascetics receive spiritual strength the householders get prosperity and wealth and even long life, due to *bhakti*. The great *tapasvis* (*siddhas*) are bestowed with miraculous power. For saints guidance of Guru is essential. The God comes in the form of a man to solve the problems of the householders, the difficulties of the devotees. Here *bhakti* is spiritual medium to obtain blessings from God.

While Vedas and *Dharma shastras* (scriptures) were meant for the highly learned priestly class, the *bhakti* marga (path of *bhakti*) is open to all irrespective of caste. It was thus a great revolt, both social and religious. Though some people said that after the doctrine of Buddhism, the Puranic literature attracted the masses through mythology and *bhakti* cult as it wanted a personal god in their daily routine life, not only for worship but also for solving their problems and spiritual progress.

In the Mahabharata,[8] Narayana is supreme deity. He is all powerful and recognised as a founder of *bhakti* cult. He is identified as Vishnu, Vasudeva and Bhagavan (Bhagavat).

In *Gita* Lord Krishna is supreme deity and recognised as God, the creator. He is the fountain head of *bhakti* and his devotees get salvation (*moksha*). The householders are blessed with spiritual progress. He is not only supreme but incarnation of God. There is no end of praises and even literature on Lord Krishna. It is said the Bhakti-cult or Vaishnavism took birth during the age of the Guptas. Vaishnaism is connected with Vedic tradition, in a purified way. In Harivansha Purana and Mahabharata Vishnu is a great deity.

Throughout India there is a very large chain of temples of Vishnu and Krishna, which strengthen the *bhakti* cult. The role of saints and Sikh tradition is worth mentioning in strengthening the worship of Hindu gods and spreading the *bhakti* cult.

According to Banerjee the "literary and philosophical tradition ascribes the foundation of this Dharma to Krishna-Vasudeva. Whether he is a historical personality is a controversial issue and it is not possible to place him in any chronological issue."[9]

"But in whole of northern India the Rama and Krishna *bhakti* cult has a very strong base in lower classes. *Ramayana* of Tulsi Das and poets of 'Ashta Chchap' have made Rama and Krishna as supreme deities. Their devotional *bhakti* songs are immortal."[10]

According to Puranic myth in the Kali age (machinery and nuclear age) only the *namjap* and the *bhagvad bhakti* will give mental peace to an individual. From materialism people turn up towards *bhakti* and spiritualism.

Bhakti Cult in South: Alvars and Adyars

The *Bhakti* cult has its root in the Dravidadesa (the South). The people of South have a flourished culture and rich language. They needed a personal God, assurance of immortality and call to prayer, as well as worship which was met by Alvars and Adyars through *bhakti*.

These Alvar poets and saints through their devotional songs spread the message of love, unity, and pure *bhakti* since the beginning of the 1st century A.D. They attracted the rich and the poor, throughout South and kindled new hopes in ordinary *Sudras*, untouchables and poor people who were denied knowledge of scriptures and even entry into temp'

Sudras were not allowed to hear the teachings of holy books. The Alvars and Adyars who were mostly from backward and *Sudra* communities also spread the message of social reforms and rejected the deep-rooted caste system.

The 'Jnana marg' and 'Karma marg' were for the rich and elite class, but the *Bhakti marg* was meant for the lowest class, the common ordinary people. For nearly six-seven centuries these saint poets of South raised their voice against orthodoxy, Varna system and transformed the social-structure of the society through their songs.

According to the poet and writer R.S. Dinkar: "The great religious movement known as *Bhakti* cult, which gradually spread over the whole of India, during the medieval period, exercised a powerful influence on cultural, spiritual and social life of the people and had its origin in the South."[11]

According to Senart *Bhakti* cult which spread over in North India was a liberal movement of worship which attracted more and more people through devotional songs, full of moral values. The Saint-poets freed the religion from orthodoxy, discouraged caste system in *bhakti* and gave a message of unity and ethical values. Barth has the some views as Senart.

The *Bhakti* cult was not an ordinary movement. It was a peoples movement, a great silent social revolution. A cultural renaissance, as it was it has its roots in the South.

"During the centuries following the premature death of Sankara three far-reaching changes transformed the religious situation in South India. First, the decay and gradual disappearance of Buddhism and Jainism cleared the ground for the consolidation of religious ideas which could be linked with the Vedic system. Secondly, the emergence of the *bhakti* cult, in a somewhat unorthodox form in the simple vernacular songs of the Tamil saint-poets, and in the orthodox classical form in the majestic Sanskrit verses of the Bhagavata Purana symbolised the vitality of the ancient faith. Thirdly, the steady increase in the numerical strength of Muslim immigrants brought Islam into greater prominence than it had acquired in Sankara's days." Ramanuja (b. 1028) was the greatest philosopher and reformer of South. His philosophical system was influenced by the *Bhakti* cult of the Alvars. He preached that salvation is possible through Bhakti and grace of God (*prasada*), not by *jnana* and *karma*. *Bhakti*, according to Ramanuja means 'man's' reaching out towards a fuller knowledge of God quietly and meditatively. By eleventh century Hinduism could no longer ignore social reforms and abolition of caste system. Alvars had taught that caste system has no meaning in worshipping God. Everyone can know the truth and reach God through *bhakti.* They rejected the rituals and regulations of the scriptures'. Ramanuja offered religions instructions to the *Shudras.* It opened the door for the *Shudras* (*Sudras*)—the Pariahs (outcastes) to acquire knowledge of Brahman, to know the God.

Thus, *Bhakti* became a symbol of social revolt and reforms.

"Advars and Alvars of South India had a pretty long history as devotional saint-poets. "There is epigraphic evidence that *Bhagavata dharma* had found its way into South India sometime before the first century A.D.; but it was through the poet-saints of the Tamil country—the Adyars (followers of Siva) and the Alvars (followers of Vishnu)—that the *bhakti* cult gained a firm footing in that part of the country. Their aim was to wean the people from their faith in Buddhism and Jainism and to attract them to the worship of Siva and Vishnu. They appealed to the heart through devotional songs composed in the language of the people. They assimilated the ethical ideas of the Jains as well the Buddhist views on asceticism and impermanence of the world. They were influenced by the Buddhist and Jain ideas on social equality and relaxation of caste rules."

These poets were respected by the common folk who preached *bhakti* and morality in their own langauge. In those days Jainism was having a strong base in South, specially in Karnataka. Buddhism was also gaining fresh strength. But the masses was in need of a godly figure, who may be having an interaction with them sharing their sorrows and miseries.

"These poet-saints flourished between the seventh and twelfth centurics. "The literature of the Adyars was arranged into eleven groups which were designated as *Tiru-murai* in the tenth century. The hymns of the Alvars were collected and arranged in four parts by Nathamuni in the tenth century. This collection is known as *Nalayira Prabandham.* The third part, the famous *Tiruvaymoyi* of Nammalvar is considered as sacred as the Vedas. It elucidates five principal, topics; the absolute reality, the individual soul, its relation to the Supreme, the destruction of the undesirable, the realisation of the desirable."[12]

For the Saiva poet-saints the supreme deity is Siva, the liberator of the individual soul from bonds which fetter it. They do not treat the world as an illusion. A personal tie binds the individual soul go god; so the individual soul yearns to see God. "Tirruvasagam depicts in beautiful hymns the progress of the soul from the bondage of ignorance and passion into the liberty of light and love, its first awakening, its joy and exaltation waywardness and despondency, struggle and unrest, the peace and joy of union.' The compositions of the Saivas are 'more verile and masculine' than those of the Vaishnavas. There is a growing protest against caste restrictions. The reform movement of Basava in the twelfth century was marked by a revolt against Brahminical supremacy although he himself was a Brahmin. Philosophically the Saivas were guided by their own *Agamas* which, however, had antecedents in the Vedic conception of Rudra and the Rudra-Siva cult of the *Brahmanas*.

Of the Alvars, twelve obtained canonical recognition: four Pallavas (Poygaiar, Pudattar, Peyar, Tirumalisai); three Cholas (Tiruppanar, Tondaradippodi, Tirumangai); one Chera (Kulasekhara); four Pandyas (Periyar, Andal, Nammalvar, Madhurakavi). This list includes a woman (Andal), several *Sudras* and a prince (Kulasekhara). The recognition of a woman and several Sudras as religious teachers was a socio-religious revolution in the Tamil country which was a stronghold of Brahmin ascendancy. Since the days of Alvars, non-Brahmin movement of social awakening in South has gained momentum.

Alongwith the social consciousness amongst the *Sudras* of South, their social status had greatly improved. In the early history of Vaishnavism in South India. Dr. Krishna Swami Ayyanger has mentioned that one of the Alvar saints, Pwai Gai Alvar was born during second century A.D.. Similarly another Alvar saint Kulshekhar was born in sixth century A.D. From first to sixth century A.D. the Alvars did tremendous work of awakening and uniting the *Sudras*.

In the medieval period it was felt by some Acharyas that "the best way to attract the popular mind towards Hinduism was to interpret it in terms understood by the Masses." Due to Muslim invasions and growing cultural impact of Islam on India Masses the necessity of making Hinduism a living active force in the life of the common people was gradually becoming stronger and stronger. Islam had already thrown a powerful challenge to the guardians of Hindu society in India.

Vaishnava Acharyas

Vaishnavism had spread throughout South while Buddhism and Jainism could not gain ground. Though it was Brahmanic revivalism, but it was against caste and practice of untouchability.

"The Alvars was succeeded by *acharyas* or theologians who aimed at establishing a philosophical basis for the worship of a personal god and faith in the saving grace of that god. Among them may be mentioned Nathamuni and Alavandar or Yamunacharya. The former arranged the hymns of the Alvars, as already stated, and the latter defended the Vaishnava *Agamas*, arguing that they had the same purport as the Vedas.

These two *Acharyas* tried to build a bridge between the emotional ardour of the Alvar songs and the philosophical speculations of the past. They prepared the ground for the philosophy of Ramanuja, 'the second founder of Vaishnavism.' His debt to the Alvars is clearly indicated by the links between his *Sribhasya* on the *Vedantasutra* and the *Tiruvaymoyi of* Nammalvar. Indeed, the latter work may be said to have laid the foundation of the *Visistadvaita* doctrine of Ramanuja.

The *Bhagavata Purana,* with its strong emphasis on *bhakti* of an intensely emotional character, and its symbolic representation of the relation of God with the human soul that of man and maid, carried clear traces of Alvar influence.[13] It contains indirect references to the Alvars, showing that it was composed at a time when their message was fairly well-known.[14]

There is little distinction between the Adyars and the Alvars in regard to the central issue, *viz.* the relation between man and his creator, the approach is necessarily dualistic, the only key to liberation is *bhakti*, and the unity of god is a central factor."

We thus see that for the masses and common men, in South India, the Adyars and Alvars responded to the needs of an accepted deity. They also provided an assurance of immortality and a call to prayer in peoples language. The Brahmanical society's spiritual needs were met by Sankar (Shankaracharya) a great philosopher in Indian history. His Advaita system appeals to the intellect, but the masses could not understand his philosophy. Even Buddhism and Jainism could not attract the masses in South. And as a spiritual and religious alternative Alvars and Adyars in South and Kabir and other Saint-poets raised the banner of awakening and refirms humanity and unity amongst the common people.

The teachings of the Sikh gurus had no direct links with those of Shankara. The Guru's precepts are conveyed to the common man through people language—the language of the saints and the bhagats of the medieval times. The Sikh gurus were more conscious to the social problems and spiritual uplift of the Hindu community as a whole including the ignored and isolated Untouchables and the Shudras. Guruvani gave moral strength to the people, when they were being crushed by Islam in Punjab.

Ramananda

The phase of medieval reformation was initiated by Ramananda, a North Indian Brahmin born at Prayag. He belongs to the philosophical school of Ramanuja and lived during the last quarter of the fourteenth and the first half of the fifteenth century. He was strong bridge between *Bhakti* movement of South and the North. He was a reformer and initiated low caste saints in his *Bhakti* cult. Ramananda emphasised the need of *Bhakti* for spiritual development. He avoided jnana marg and karma-marg.

According to Macauliffe "He deemed forms of adoration superfluous, and held that the supreme reward of devotion was to be obtained by incessantly uttering God's name."

In medieval times *nam-jap* (recitation of God's name) was given preference. All saints and poets have emphasised the need of *nam-jap* or singing and remembering God through devotional songs. "What was an essentially radical departure from the system of Ramanuja was considerable relaxation of the rules of castes in religious and social spheres. Ramananda said: "Let no man ask a man's caste or sect. Whoever adores God is God's own.[15] He admitted to his *sampradaya* disciples from all castes, even from the Muslim community, and called them 'the liberated.' His apostolate of twelve included a Brahmin, a barber, a leather-worker, a Rajput and a woman.[16] He relaxed to a great extent the culinary and kindred rules observed by the orthodox Ramanuja *sampradaya*. The popularisation of religion involved another factor: the substitution of Sanskrit, the language of the learned, by the vernacular, the language of the masses. Socially as also linguistically, religion descended to the level of the common people."

"The simplification of worship and the liberalisation of the caste rules were Ramananda's most important contributions to the solution of the socio-religious problems of his age. He made a well-conceived response to the situation created by the entrenched position of Islam in the heartland of India. His reforms ushered in one of the most fruitful religious movements in Indian history. But we must not minimise the strength of the old social pattern and as also of the Macauliffe's economic structure—particularly the agrarian system which kept the vast majority of the people tied to the feudal lords—which stood against the winds of change. Ramananda did not find recognition in the Hindu community as a religious teacher like Ramanuja, nor did he succeed in attracting any recognisable section of the Muslim community to the *bhakti* cult and the Rama-Sita creed. Orthodox Hinduism seems to have gradually engulfed the liberal movement initiated by him. Most of his followers in later centuries observed caste rules with the utmost strictness. As regards their tenets, Macauliffe's writing in the early years of the present century, found them 'hopelessly confused with the Ramanuja's and to differ only in their sectarial marks and their preference for Sita and Rama to Lakshmi and Narayana as subjects of worship."[17]

This unfortunate result seems to have been due to three factors. First, the Hindu society still retained something of its old capacity to win over followers of other faiths as also seceders from its own fold. The virtually complete absorption of the Buddhists in the Hindu society was still a living memory, and the progressive assimilation of the Jains was a continuing process. The Yogis were gradually losing their distinctive identity and sinking into the general pool of Hindu society. Secondly, Ramananda propagated his ideas through oral teaching; he left nothing in writing, although religious songs supposed to have been composed by him enjoyed much popularity among common people in North India and a hymn attributed to him is found in the *Adi Granth*. The absence of a scriptural collection of his religious ideas and injunctions was partly responsible for distortion and oblivion. Thirdly, although he left many disciples—including Kabir, according to one tradition—he did not leave behind him an integrated and enduring sect. His influence survived, but it flowed through different channels and fell—more or less—into the mainstream of Hindu thought. There was neither an organisational compactness such as the Sikhs were able to evolve to preserve their identity, nor a succession of philosophers and poets which provided a continuing identity for the Gaudiya Vaishnavas, i.e., the followers of Chaitanya. The historical importance of Ramananda's role as a religious teacher is indicated by a Hindi couplet saying that *bhakti* was born in the South (the Dravida country), brought to the North by Ramananda, and spread over the seven seas and nine continents by Kabir.[18]

Medieval Period Bhakti Movement

In the medieval period the saints and poets of bhakti cult as said earlier in their devotional songs and other poems preached the gospel of humanity, equality and universal brotherhood, through their verses which were mainly addressed to formless god. Most of these saints and poets were from the backward and lowest strata of society. They never bothered for the caste factor. Both in ideology and practice a saint or *sannyasi* has no caste. He is above these worldly gradations (*jati-pati puchehe nahin koi, hari ko bhaje so Hari ka hoi*). There is no need of caste in the worship of God.

In the medieval period we also see great synthesis between the religious faiths of the Hindus and Muslims. The saints and poets of the *bhakti* school, like Kabir, Ravidas, Sen, Dhanna, Pipa and several others preached this synthesis and influenced the entire society through their songs and poems. Purely devotional in character the vanis and poems of these saint-poets became the voice of the masses, which condemned the prevailing social evils, such as caste system, untouchability, superstitions, myths and beliefs and Brahmanic and Islamic religions practices full of much ritualism and orthodoxy.

The common people were not only inspired spiritually by these songs, but got strength to fight tyranny and injustice. The religion is always a forum for community's unity. The *Bhakti* movement morally and culturally gave a call of unity and strengthened the already much frustrated community through their songs and poems.

The historians, sociologists and literateurs believe that the *Bhakti* cult provided the much needed relief to the Dalits. The simplification of worship and the liberalisation of the traditional caste rules encouraged and united the lower classes the Sudras and the untouchables. No doubt, the saints and the poets of the Bhakti cult from third century AD in South and from eleventh century onwards to the medieval period of Indian history in the North showed the worthlessness of the caste system, much ritualism and preached that God was one and meant for all. After the decline of Buddhism this was the most power ul call of social awakening and religious thought amongst lower strata of society in a caste ridden Brahmanical social order, led by the scriptures.

In due course of time, throughout India, the Bhakti movement basically became a non-Brahmin movement. It was a movement against Brahmanical hold on society, scriptures and language barrier. It inspired the masses—the peasants, the artisans and the common householders towards simplicity, social unity and purity in the innermost heart, with new moral and social values. The love of God, was love of humanity, the service of the poor and the oppressed. They discarded all symbols of Brahmanical worship, as a protest, when Islam posed danger to social life.

Their preachings, *bhajans*, verses and songs created an atmosphere of brotherhood, oneness among the people. They became partners of their miseries and sorrows. We see much how Kabir and Ravidas were subjected to harassment by orthodox Hindus and the Brahman priests.[19]

Jagjivan Ram has observed: "The saint-poets of the *Bhakt*i school during the medieval period of history created awakening amongst the untouchables and the Dalits. In *Bhakti*, as preached by Kabir and Ravidas and other saints and poets, there was no need to visit the temples, one's own pure heart was the temple. There was no need to read the mantras from the scriptures, the devotional songs were enough to worship and remember God. There was no need to follow the rigorous course of rituals, but only two and a half words of love were enough to be a wise or learned man. Bhakti cult was no doubt a great social revolution, a renaissance of Dalit awakening and Kabir and Ravidas were the champions of this social revolt, who were not spared by the Brahmans and harassed in several who sprang chiefly from the lower orders of society—tailors, carpenters potters, gardeners, shop-keepers, barbers, and even *mahars*—more often than Brahmins'. The result was that 'the influence of higher spirituality was not confined to this or that class, but permeated deep through all strata of society, male and female, high and low, literate and illiterate, Hindu and Mahomedan alike.' In the spiritual field, 'the supreme efficacy of devotional love over all other methods of attaining to His knowledge' was fully recognised. The impact of this 'elevated teaching' was felt in the social field. Caste exclusiveness was eliminated from the sphere of religion; it was 'relegated solely to the social concerns of men and even there its restrictiveness was much relaxed' in comparison with the caste prejudices of South Indian Brahmans. Despite its primarily regional association the message of the Pandharpur movement was carried to North India by Namdev probably in the second quarter of the fourteenth century.[34]"

According to Maity, "in the fifteenth century religious and social life in Bengal was stagnant. The rules of caste became more and more stringent... The Gap between man and man was evidenced by caste restrictions. The lower strata of society groaned under the autocracy of the higher, who shut the portals of learning against the inferior classes... the religion of the new school (Puranik) became the monopoly of the Brahmans..." A natural reaction against this system was embodied in the Vaishanavism preached by Sri Chaitanya. This great teacher raised his voice against the rituals... He did not observe caste restrictions in accepting disciplers. Vaishnavism, thus opened a new life of spirituality and knowledge to the lower castes, and new challenge to the caste-ridden society.[35]"

Thus from Punjab to South and Maharashtra and Gujarat to Bengal the saint poets played an important role in social awakening discarding caste system and untouchability and opened the closed doors of knowledge and truth.

Nath Panth and Nath Yogis

There is enough reference to Yoga practices in the poems and songs of poets and Saints of Bhakti cult. Yogis in some quarters were known as having supernatural powers. The influence of Nath panth is seen in Guru Nanak's times.

Guru Nanak refers to six systems (of philosophy) and six teachers. As well as their different teachings.[36]' The six systems are: *Samkhya, Yoga, Nyaya, Vaisesika, Purva, Mimansa, Uttara Mimansa* or *Vedanta*. The names of the six teachers are: Kapila, Patanjali, Gautama, Kanada, Jaimini and Vyasa.

ways. The unity of the Shudras and out castes made their efforts unsuccessful.[20]"

Kabir

There is not much in history books on Kabir, a pioneer of social awakening—among Dalits and the Sudras. However in literary works and later researches he has been given an important place.

"In the medieval times when Islam as religion of the ruling class was threatening Hinduism and the Muslim rulers were in power to support and patronise their religion, Kabir raised his voice of reform and unity. Any nation can be proud to have such social rebel. He is much ahead of his times, as a thinker, radical reformer and mystic poet. As Banerjee observes: of the religious reformers who followed the trail of Ramananda, simplifying and liberalising his teachings and thereby making the movement more meaningful and responsive to social urges, the greatest undoubtedly was Kabir. He was probably the most cosmopolitan of the *bhagats* of medieval India. Macauliffe says: 'Kabir has written works which all religious denominations can accept, and which, if perused without bigotry, are advantageous for the salvation of all persons'. Dedicated to steadfast utterance of God's name, he 'deemed worthless the rules of caste and the Hindu and Muhammadan religious observances.[21]"

Kabir's catholicity may be explained in a large measure by the variety in his social and religious experience. He was probably born in a *julaha* family..., and he seems to have followed his hereditary occupation, i.e., weaving, without adotping the ascetic ways of a *faqir.* But his mind was exposed to Hindu influence from his earliest years; he lived at Benares in a Hindu environment... there are references in his compositions to his association with Muslim saints, indicating his interest in Islam. He seems to have been unfamiliar with the sacred languages and scriptures of either community; but his contact with saints of different religious denominations apparently familiarised him with philosophical ideas and technical terms, some of which he utilised in his verses. (Many scholars and Kabir panthis say that he was a Hindu (Koli) weaver and not muslim. Orthodox Brahmins might have spread this rumour of his being a Muslim Woner.)

"Torn asunder by religious doubts and deep searchings of heart Kabir became a nonconformist; as a result, he became a victim of persecution by the orthodox sections of both Hindus and Muslims. Tradition makes him a disciple of Ramananda to whom he was driven, it is said, by his spiritual unrest. According to his mid-seventeenth century work *Dabistan,* attributed to Mohsin Fani, he was directed by somebody to 'an old man of bright genius, the Brahman Ramananda,' after he had failed 'to find what he sought from the best Hindu and Muslim spiritual guides'. In one of the verses attributed to Kabir he himself acknowledges his debt, saying that he 'was awakened by Ramananda.[22]'

This tradition, however, has been challenged on chronological grounds. Kabir seems to have lived during the reigns of Bahlol Lodi and Sikandar Lodi, the traditional date of his death being 1518. This date is consistent with the traditions relating to his meeting with Guru Nanak and Sikandar Lodi's attempt to persecute him,[23] but it is inconsistent with his contemporancity with Ramananda. The authenticity of the *Bijak* the sacred text of the Kabirpanthis, in which we have Kabir's statement on his awakening by Ramananda, is not beyond question; but most of the verses attributed to Kabir in the *Adi Granth* are also found, though in a different arrangement, in the *Bijak*.

The legendary version of Kabir's first contact with Ramananda is a curious one. It is said that on one occasion Kabir lay down on the steps of a bathing *ghat* at Benares and Ramananda, stepping on him by accident, exclaimed, 'Rama, Rama'. Kabir took this exclamation as his *mantra* and was later accepted as a disciple by Ramananda. It is not quite unlikely that this legend hints at spiritual discipleship through *mantra* without actual physical association with the *guru*. The *guru* and the disciple might not have been contemporaries; they might not have entered into formal relationship even if they were contemporaries. Benares, where Kabir lived, was the centre of Ramananda's missionary work. Here his influence was probably quite strong for many years after his death, which might have occurred not long before Kabir's birth. The name of Rama might have brought to Kabir spiritual satisfaction which he looked for in vain in other *mantras*. The statement in the *Dabistan* is strong evidence of some kind of contact between Kabir and either Ramananda himself or the Ramananda *sampradaya*. The statement that Kabir's references to a guru 'point unmistakably to the *Satguru* within, the voice of God within the human soul.[24] may be accepted as correct, but it does not necessarily exclude the possibility of some kind of guidance by a human *guru*, specially at the initial stage of the spiritual journey."

"It is not easy to determine Kabir's actual debt to Ramananda, but *bhakti* was undoubtedly the prime factor in his strivings, Contemporary conditions and environmental influence probably brought in other elements and gave to his belief and faith a composite character. His mystical love of God might have been influenced by Sufism, although it could easily be connected with the ecstasy of the Tamil saints and the *Bhagvata Purana*. His recognition of duality, which would end in mystical union with God, was a continuation of the Ramanuja tradition. A Nath background' may also be postulated for some of his ideas in view of his frequent use of *hathayoga* terminology. But it is hardly correct to stress any link between this background and the rejection of rituals and caste distinctions, for Ramanuja and Ramananda had already made a beginning in this regard. On the whole, we are hardly justified in saying that the 'basis' of Kabir's belief 'was not Vaishnava *bhakti* or Sufism but tantric *yoga.*[25] The compositions attributed to him appear to indicate that Sufism and Tantric *yoga* were no more than subsidiary elements playing a comparatively minor role in the formulation of his ideas. His conception of God was monotheistic, with touches of immanentism; and it is not difficult to discover its root in the teachings of Ramanuja which were given a popular form by Ramananda. The persistent tradition of Kabir's awakening' by Ramananda seems to be correct in a spiritual sense even if its historicity might remain open to question."

"Kabir was not a philosopher or a theologian; he was primarily a mystic, and his teachings had a large proportion of obscurity and apparent inconsistency which are probably inseparable features of religious mysticism. He recognised to some extent the value of both Hindu and Muslim scriptures. He had no faith in the spiritual value either of external rituals or of caste rules; and he did no favour asceticism although he did not, like the Sikh Gurus, entirely ban it. The Kabirpanthis are permitted to live either as house-holders or as monks attached to a monastery belonging to the order.

Kabir, was a practical reformer in so far as he advocated a *rapprochement* between the Hindus and the Muslims in the sphere of religion. He said: 'The religion of those who understand is one, whether they are Pandits or Shaikhs'. Here we have a direct hint at the divisive role played by the orthodox custodians of Hinduism and Islam. The adherence of the unthinking masses to their guidance led to fratricidal strife: 'Hindus call upon Rama, the Mussalmans on Rahiman, yet both fight and kill each other, and none knows the truth.[26]' This was a cry in the wilderness in the reign of the persecuting Sultan, Sikandar Lodi. 'The seed of the message of the unity of Hari and Allah was not evidently sown on a fertile soil and did not sprout.[27]'

The teaching and message of Kabir is in a very simple people's language, but of mystic character. A common man can understand early, but an intellectual is always baffled. This is the beauty of his language. Incidental to Kabir's role as a religious was his contribution to vernacular literature. Gifted with considerable poetical genius, he explained his views and imparted religious instruction by means of *Ramainis, Sabada* and *Sakhis* which was easily understood by the people and could be sung by them as *bhajans.* Sanskrit was losing its ancient position as the sole vehicle of religious thought."

"Kabir's teachings exercised considerable influence on later generations, as the inclusion of a very large collection of his compositions in *Adi granth* shows, but these did not provide a clear-cut and firm doctrinal background for his followers. This seems to be one of the reasons which prevented the Kabirpanthis from developing into an organised and integrated community like the Sikhs. Another crucial factor leading to the same result was the absence of centralised and continuous leadership to give the new religious community direction and purpose. Kabir nominated no successor, and after his death his son Kamal, approached by his disciples to found a sect, refused to do so on ground that it would be inconsistent with his father's lifelong struggle against sectarianism. The result was the dispersal of Kabir's followers, who formed small sects under different leaders instead of coalescing into a single religious fraternity. Tradition mentions twelve groups of Kabirpanthis; in fact, there are only two main divisions with headquarters at Benares and in the Chattisgarh district in Madhya Pradesh.[28]"

Due to the spread of Sikh religion world wide alongwith a chain of Gurudwaras and Sikh *sangats* abroad, the recitation of devotional songs of Kabir and other *Bhagats* from Guru Granth Saheb, has inspired the people to know the truth and the reality of life. Kabir is thus not an individual in revolt, but a guiding force, a torchbearer and a movement.

In the words of Jagjivan Ram saints like Ramanand, Kabir, Nanak, Ravidas stress the godliness of man and the sinfulness of denying them their status." Nehru remarked the voice of Kabir is voice of revolt against all social odds, untouchability and caste system, prejudices and ritualism. He was indeed a wonderful personality of his age.

Inspite of mysticism, he was a remarkable reformer of his time and still remembered for his strong feelings against casteism, orthodoxy and superstitions. Whatever he preached through, his poems and songs' it reflected in the views of phule, Gandhiji and Dr. Ambedkar.

"Kabir's social reform and spiritual movement was powerful tool to break the priesthy domination. He condemned both Brahmin priests and the Muslim Mullas, responsible for creating differences and divisions among people of different religions and faith.[29]"

Kabir ceaselessly tried to establish unity in diversity by preaching to one and all the eternal noble religion of love. For him the God was one.

Different religions and the so-called priests had created disunity and differences among people. He himself condemned the practice of untouchability and caste system and said a Brahmin and an untouchable *Shudra* both were born from the some womb of a mother. He was undoubtedly a Koli Hindu weaver.

Ravidas a cobbler by profession but a great saint also said the artificial barriers between man to man, have all been created by the Hindu and Muslim priests. He also revolted against the caste system and believed that by doing one's duty in life and having true faith in God one can achieve sainthood. Through true worship of God he united the masses and created social awakening in the depressed and exploited people. His *Bhakti* is a movement of social reforms.[30] It is said Mirabai was has disciple. She was a great devotee of Krishna and still remembered for her devotional songs. There is a large following of Ravidas throughout the country. No doubt, like Kabir, he was also a symbolt of revolt.

Dr. Ambedkar believed Kabir and other saint poets united the masses; the untouchable class, awakened them to use intellect towards social problems, prejudices and disabilities. He was a symbol of social revolt against narrow views of Brahmanic and Muslim theologists. Thus, Kabir has a unique place in the medieval periods of social—Bhakti movement.

Other Bhagats and Saint Poets

Not only in northern India, but also in other parts of the land, saint poets preached equality, and spiritualism together. It is said that the Muslim rule and the spreading Islamic values have made them mystic. They turned to almighty God and tries to unite the people. Awakening them they recite: 'their God is all powerful and eternal and one need not be afraid of any body.'

This tradition "as recorded in Nabhaji's *Bhagat Mal* (Bhakt Mal) gives us the names of some other disciples of Ramananda. It is unlikely that all of them were initiated by him personally; some at least were probably attracted by his teachings after his death. The tradition which groups them together does not necessarily imply regular membership of a *sampradaya*; it is probably a testimony to the influence acquired by Ramananda in the contemporary world of religion.

Some compositions of Pipa, Sain, Dhanna, and Ravidas—all of them associated with the Ramananda tradition—are incorporated in the *Adi Granth*. Others whose compositions have found place in the *Granth* are Jaidev, Namdev, Trilochan, Paramanand, Sadhna, Beni, Mira Bai, Shaikh Farid, Bhikan, and Sur Das. They are collectively known as *bhagats* (devotees), and they 'preceded Guru Nanak as the dawn before sunrise.' They belonged to different territorial regions and castes, representing different stages of the social hierarchy. For instance, Jaidev was a Brahman of Bengal, Pipa was the ruler of a small State called Gagaraungarh, Dhanna was a Jat of Rajasthan. Sain was a barber in Rewa, Ravidas was a shoemaker at Benares, and Namdev was the son of a tailor in Maharashtra. Collectively, these *bhagats* represented the all-India character of the *bhakti* cult. The general uniformity of their views on spiritual and social problems leaves no room for doubt that the basic principle of their faith was the same, although personal factors, coupled with regional differences in religious and social practices, sooner or later canalised in into different streams. None of them founded a *sampradaya,* but their compositions were preserved by their followers.[31]

Some of the *bhagats* are associated by some modern writers with 'the Sant tradition of Northern India' which is described as 'essentially a ... compound of elements drawn mainly from Vaishnava *bhakti* and the *hatha-yoga* of the Nath yogis, with a marginal contribution of Sufism.[32]' Namdev, Ravidas and Kabir are specifically included in this group. But the extent of Nath and Sufi influence could hardly have been considerable, even in the case of Kabir, it was more or less local or personal, and to universalise it would be unwarranted. In the case of Namdev, who belonged to the Varkari sect of Pandharpur and is said to have visited the Punjab in old age, the dedication to the *bhakti* cult is too prominent to be missed in his compositions.[33] The Sants' love, it has been argued, 'was offered not to an avatar, but directed to the supreme God Himself.' But Namdev speaks of the sport of Krishna and Narayana in Brindaban. It was customary to identify one of the *avataras* with the Supreme Beings; for example, the followers of Chaitanya identify Krashna with God Himself."

Here one can argue and say that influence of Kabir was not local, today it is universal. Even all the *bhagats* and saint poets occupy an important place in country's social cultural life.

"Even before the advent of Ramananda the *bhakti* cult had begun to assume a new complexion in Maharashtra through the Varkari sect which centred round the shrine of Vithoba or Vitthal (Krishna) at Pandharpur. The Vithoba cult reflected the principal features of the traditional *bhakti* approach to salvation through the emotional adoration of God. Three names stand pre-eminent in the history of the Pandharpur movement: Jnanesvar (thirteenth century); Namdev (1270-1350), and the Tukaram (seventeenth century). At the head of a remarkable religious revival in Maharashtra there were 'saints and prophets, poets and philosophers,

Banerjee observes: "The teachings of Patanjali, propounded about the second century B.C., which provide the basis of the *Yoga* system, constitute 'a manual of psychological ethics intended for developing the powers of the mind.' The word *yoga* literally means 'connection' or 'union'. Its philosophical meaning is 'union' with the Supreme Spirit, although the Supreme Spirit is One, it appears to be Many when seen through the prism of ignorance, and men fell themselves separate from it, as also from one another, and thus see an endless variety of selves without realising their underlying unity. Through *yoga* man can free himself from ignorance, rise above the erroneous concept of selves, and attain 'union' with the One Supreme Spirit.

Different kinds of *yoga* are specified even though these are linked together. Bhaktiyoga is the path which leads to the realisation of God through love and devotion (*bhakti*). For one who chooses this path the first step is prayer; it brings him into touch with the inner force of infinite power which lies hidden in human beings. With prayer is associated *japa, i.e.,* repetition of some sacred words denoting the Godhead; it is a semi-mechanical exercise for controlling the mind. Worship of images, reading of scriptures, association with spiritually advanced persons, pilgrimages to holy places, etc., are auxiliary processes.

Karmayoga is worship through work (*karma*) which must be absolutely unselfish and free from desire for external success. Selfishness creates a barrier between man and Truth; conscious striving for success separates man from god who is the bestower of success. Unselfishness and freedom from egotism clear the grounds for spiritual enlightenment.

Jnanayoga means worship through jnana (knowledge) i.e., rejection of everything that is unreal and absorption in the Reality. The followers of Jnanayoga believe in liberation from the bondage of human existence, control of mind and senses through acquisition of special power, absence of sensual enjoyment and attachments.

Rajayoga demands concentration of mind on the Reality to acquire the capacity of realising the Truth. It teaches the mind to be calm, disciplined, free from purposeless. Eight processes are prescribed for practicing *Rajayoga*: (i) *Yama* (practice of non-injury or love, truthfulness, non-receipt of gifts etc.) (ii) niyama (practice of cleanliness, austerity study of holybooks), (iii) asana (practice of physical postures in which one can sit for long time), (iv) *pranayama* (breathing exercises), (v) pratyahara (practice of sense-control, non-attachment), (vi) *dharana* (steadiness of mind), (vii) *dhyana* (meditation) and (viii) *samadhi* (diving down to the innermost self and realising the truth).

In the days of Guru Nanak, different kinds of *yoga* occupied a more or less prominent place in the religious life of India. Many yogis forgot the spiritual purpose of yoga and tried to impress and mislead the ignorant people of their miraculous activities.

The religious order of *yogis* is popular known as Nath-panth, Kanphatas or Gorakhapanth. The literal meaning of 'Nath' is master. There are nine human 'Naths' and Matsyendranath and Gorakhnath attained immortality and became objects of worship. Most of the Nathpanthis were from the lower order. They spread their message in the masses and the working class.

The Kamphata yogis split the ears and had acquired recognition and spiritual significance among Nath-path. Similarly an 'Aughar' or 'Siddha' was a yogi who had attained a stage of perfection, semi-divine stage. They were known for miracles and extended life. People surrounded them for granting favours. They were popular among common men.

Sikh Tradition

Sikhism is a great socio-religious movement of the eighteenth century. It is a leading religion of India and has recently completed three centuries of its foundation. Sikhism is a revolt against Islamic tyranny and Hindu orthodoxy as well as ritualism. Through bhakti Sikh cult gave a call of unity and nationalism. "Among early British writers mention should be made of Browne, the political representative of the East India Company at the court of the puppet Mughal Emperor Shah Alam II, who incorporated in his *Indian Tracts* (1788) an account of the Sikhs which was compiled on the basis of some Hindu accounts in possession of two learned Hindus of Lahore. Forster, who travelled through the Punjab in 1783-84, incorporated in his *A Journey from Bengal to England* (1798) a short sketch of the Sikhs. He relied upon 'received tradition' and 'legends which have the least exceptionable claims to credit.' The first full-fledged British account of the Sikhs is, as previously stated, Malcolm's *Sketch of the Sikhs* (1812). He collected historical materials, including a copy of the *Adi Granth,* during his stay with the British army in the Punjab in 1805. But what he wrote is scanty so far as information is concerned, and often lacks in authenticity.

On Social Problems

Nanak's watchful eyes notice clear symptoms of the crippling effects of foreign rule on the Hindus. There was a general trend towards slavish imitation of Muslim manners and customs. Even the Kshatriyas, says Nanak, 'have forsaken their religion and adopted the language of the

Malechhas.' These words are uttered with regret, but the Kshatriyas are not urged—directly or indirectly—to revert the ways of their ancestors and to stand against social and political degeneration. There is a general condemnation of all-pervading degeneration which affects the rulers as also the ruled.

In the age of darkness,
Men have become as dogs,
They eat the ill—gotten gains,

And bark out their lies... On this society descended cruel punishment in the form of Babar's invasion. It could not save itself by customary prayer and worship.

For the Muslim woman the hour of prayer is past,
For the Hindu the time of worship is gone.

Nanak's attention is fixed primarily on the moral aspect of the catastrophe. As he says in another context: '... the counterfeit shall not be received in the great God's treasury...[40]'

It seems Nanak and the Sikh-panth was more socially conscious than medieval saint-poets on social issues.

Of the social problems which engaged the attention of all medieval reformers, caste was by far the most important as also the most difficult. In Hindu society caste and religion have been inseparable from time immemorial. But the Alvars of South India, Ramanuja, Ramananda, Kabir and other *bhagats* evolved a new approach, *viz.*, caste was not an inescapable or even a necessary feature of religious life. They released forces of liiberalism which penetrated into the Punjab. That province had known a casteless society—the Muslims—since the early years of the eleventh century. Nanak's sensitive and receptive mind was thus open to two influences leading in the same direction: an internal process of repudiation of caste initiated by the *bhagats,* and an external operating as a challenge. But the importance of this challenge should not be exaggerated; for about five centuries it had been a fact of life in the Punjab, but it had not provoked the Hindu society even to consider the possibility of relaxation of the rigours of caste."

Banerjee further writes: "Nanak was not a social reformer in the ordinary sense of that term. He did not aim directly and specifically at removal of social injustice. His primary purpose was to lay down a wide track for man's spiritual journey. For admission to that track, as also for progress along it, no social qualifications such as high caste or high rank in the social hierarchy would be needed; a personal craving for spiritual bliss would be the only passport. In pursuing that track it would be necessary for man to drop his inherited social prejudices. Such a spiritual venture would in itself be a social revolution. It would necessarily result in considerable erosion—if not total elimination—of the caste system which crippled human dignity and formed a dyke against the spiritual regeneration of the Hindu society.

From this point of view it is easy to understand the well-known remark of Bhai Gurdas: By the Guru's instruction the four castes were blended in one society of saints.[41]' According to Nanak, *Sat Sangat* is the 'society of the holy' where 'the name of the one God is mentioned.[42]' If we take the statement of Bhai Gurdas in a literal sense it would imply the formation of a casteless Sikh society based on removal of traditional caste restrictions such as prohibition of intercaste marriage and intercaste dining. But those statements of Nanak which are usually quoted in support of such wide interpretation clearly imply a religious context. For instance, the statement that 'castes are folly' is followed by another statement: 'It is the reality that is tested.' The 'test' is obviously a spiritual one: it is to be held in the next world where 'caste hath no power' and 'there is a new order of beings.' In that 'new order' a man's place is determined solely by the stage of spiritual progress which he has reached. 'No one calleth clarified butter or silk impure; such is a saint in regard to caste.[43]

"In the light of such passages in Nanak's hymns it would probably be better to take the statement of Bhai Gurdas in a restricted sense. In other words, by 'blending of four castes in one society of saints' he means—not the removal of the traditional social classification or external social distinctions—but the elimination of caste as a factor in spiritual life. According to Ramanuja, the 'Grace' of God is not available for the Sudra in his present life; but by good conduct he may work his way up to birth in a higher caste and then be admitted to the privileged group in social and religious matters. Nanak recognises no such restriction based on birth; in his view even a low-born person can earn God's 'Grace' without waiting for birth in a higher caste through transmigration. Behind his sayings lies the revolutionary principle that the worth of a man in the religious sector of life is to be judged solely by the intensity of his devotion to God; the Creator does not look upon caste as a test of eligibility for His grace. Those who take shelter in God are equals so far as their status as seekers of salvation is concerned.

"Although the application of this principle would be limited in the first instance to the sphere of religion, it could not but have a powerful impact on general social relations and activities. A man who had made considerable progress in his spiritual journey could not be looked upon as a socially degraded person on the ground of his birth in a low caste. Even in orthodox Hindu society nobody raised the question of caste in the case of *sannyasis.* A radical change of social outlook was the necessary consequence of Nanak's approach to the problem of caste. It was extremely difficult to completely eliminate a system which had been the basis of Hindu society for many centuries and was closely linked with its economic organisation; but orthodoxy could hardly resist a breach in the citadel. Thus Nanak prepared the ground for a social revolution even though he did not directly and deliberately initiate it. The seed sown by him developed into a plant in the days of Guru Gobind Sings.[44]"

In the words of Macauliffe as quoted by Banerjee: "The caste-ridden Hindu society did not accord to women the respect which was due to them. The cruel practice of *Sati* (the immolation of widows on their husband's pyres) was prevalent, and Kabir criticised it." Nanak's appreciation of the social importance of women is a pleasant and meaningful deviation from medieval ideas. He recognizes them as playing the most vital role in the preservation of society as also in the proper development of family life as wives mother, and links in the development of 'social ties.' From them 'are born leaders and rulers.' 'It is a woman who is friend and partner of life.' Why, then, asks Nanak, should we consider woman cursed and condemned?' The conception of woman as man's helpmate became one of the distinctive features of Sikh society. This was in complete accord with the position assigned to the house-holder in the Sikh religion. Those men who seek salvation need not keep themselves aloof from women and treat their company as a sinful barrier to spiritual efforts. 'It is a women who keeps the race going', says Nanak, and adds: 'Without woman only the True One existes.[45]' His view on the union of man and woman through marriage transcends the external urges of personal and social life. 'An ideal marriage is a sacrament, a mystical union between two souls, two hearts meeting in a union of love as two lamps blend with each other (*ek jyoti doe murti*).[46] Thus Nanak encouraged a classless and casteless society alongwith dignity of labour and respect to the Womenfolk during religious persuits. Bhai Gurdas says: 'From a temporal and spiritual point of view woman is half man's body and assisteth to a salvation.[47]

Nanak's sympathy for the down-trodden and the oppressed is expressed through condemnation of those who are responsible for injustice and exploitation. 'How can the mind of a person remain unpolluted', he asks, 'if that persons sucks human blood?'

'...Encroachment upon what rightfully belongs to others', the Guru says, 'is forbidden to both Muslims and Hindus, as pork to the former and beef to the latter.[48] The ideal society is to be based on justice, elimination of exploitation, and recognition of the rights of all men irrespective of caste, rank, and wealth.

Nanak's conception of world society was based on the ideal of universal brotherhood. This is evident from his first significant utterance at Sultanpur after his Enlightenment: 'There is no Hindu and no Musalman.' Every individual is primarily a man; he becomes a Hindu or a Muslim by the accident of birth. The accidental difference between Hindus and Muslims does not alter their fundamental position in regard to their Creator, for 'all creatures have one shelter, that of God.[49]'

The new community of disciples which Nanak seeks to create as a unit of this universal brotherhood is necessarily egalitarian. For him all men are 'equal since God's light is contained in the heart of each.[50]' To emphasize the principle of equality of men he calls himself 'lowliest of the low.' He 'identifies himself with the down-trodden and lowly.[51]' If the highborn Khatri and religious teacher who had received Light from God Himself could publicly adopt such an attitude of humility, no other man could claim a higher social status for himself over his fellow men on the ground of birth, wealth or accomplishment.

Nanak's ethical teachings are relevant to an egalitarian society. He connects 'honest labour' with spiritual progress: 'They who eat the fruit of their labour and bestow something recognise the right way.' To live on offerings for performance of religious ceremonies, as the Brahmins do, is to 'take poison.[52]' Accumulation of wealth is harmful. Nanak says: 'What have I to do with upper classes?[53]' This is a condemnation not only of pride of birth but also of pride of wealth. One must 'bestow something' on others to discharge his obligation to society and, when he is rich, to lighten the burden of his wealth. Contributions to the Guru's *langar* were an approved form of sharing one's income with others. Sharing the expenses of the *langar* according to one's ability, and eating with others in violation of caste restrictions, were practical methods of promoting brotherhood and social unity.

Adherence to truth is a highly commended virtue in all religious systems, but truth is often treated as a metaphysical abstraction. Nanak brings truth in close relation with practical life. To know the truth is not enough; it should be made a part of life. He says: 'It is through acting in accordance with truth that one finds release.[54] He establishes a link between truthful living and salvation.

There are five principal vices which should be avoided: *kama* (lust), *krodha* (anger), *lobh* (greed), *moha* (attachment), *ahamkara* (egoism). Here Nanak's thought is very close to the Hindu idea of man's six *ripus* (enemies). The inner struggle between good and evil continues perpetually in the human heart, but 'The five thieves can be destroyed with the sword of the Word.[55]' Kabir and other uystic poets have said the same in their verses.

Nanak did not recognise the authority of the Vedas, he spoke as God had bidden him to speak, the 'divine word' was his Guru. He did not seek scriptural sanction for his teachings. He stressed the futility of ceremonies. There is no place for caste system in the new community. Social equality was its foundation.

Nanak totally rejected the Puranic form of Hinduism. One formless God (*Nirgun/Nirankar*) was worshipped by this new religion, rejecting the worship of numerous gods and goddesses.

He even rejected the Hindu theory of incarnations of God. His teachings gave a new message to the humanity, the message of love, peace, brotherhood, equality, social justice and social thinking. Nanak believes in '*niskama Karma*' (action without expectation of reward). In Brahmanical and Jaina philosophy, doctrines of *Karma* and transmigration have been mentioned prominently. Nanak has faith in both.

In the Opinion of Banerjee: "The *Bhakti* has been an integral element in the Brahminical spiritual tradition since practically the age of the Vedas. Though the non-Brahman Alvars and Adyars gave it an emotional depth and intensity unknown in previous centuries, its new form was introduced into the fold of orthodox Brahmanical philosophy by Ramanuja and found an elaborate classical expression in the *Bhagavata Purana.* From the South it was brought to the North by a Brahman, Ramananda. The teachings of a Brahman, Chaitanya, made it the basis of Bengal Vaishnavism. Although the spread of the *bhakti* cult in North India was due primarily to the teachings of non-Brahman *bhagats* like Kabir, its Brahmanical origin and its primarily Brahmanical orientation—in the recognition of Brahmanical deities as objects of devotion, for instance—could not be overlooked. The most significant difference between the old and new forms of *bhakti* cult lay in the repudiation of caste by the medieval *bhagats.* He brought to it a social and humanistic complexion which was unknown before, but even in this respect Ramanuja was the pioneer although he was a hesitating and cautious innovator.

Nanak and Kabir

Nanak belongs to the *bhakti* school with which Kabir is associated in tradition and legend. The affinity between them is indirectly stressed in the inclusion of a very large number of the latter's compositions in the *Granth.* But they differ in several respects. Kabir is primarily a mystic, expressing his ideas through aphorisms, but incapable of formulating a body of doctrines and organising a new religious community. In Nanak there is a unique combination of the emotions of a mystic with the gift which are needed for the foundation of a religion. Again, tradition recognises Ramananda as Kabir's *guru,* and even though the authenticity of this tradition is open to question, Kabir does not explicitly claim—as Nanak does—that God Himself is his guru and that he carries His message to the world. Furthermore, the Tantric *Yoga* element is strong in Kabir's approach to spiritual problems, but it is practically absent in Nanak's thought. Nanak's travels brought him into contact with different shades of religious views and practices in different parts of the world; but Kabir, cooped up in the narrow world of Banaras, had little opportunity of enriching his ideas through such experience. Perhaps this was one of the factors which made him an introvert and strengthened the mystic element in his spiritual approach. Nanak's scholastic attainments appear to have been much higher than those of Kabir. Although he separated Vedantic philosophy from religion and treated religion as less a matter of intellect than of spirit, the intellectual element in stronger is his writings than in those of Kabir.[56]

It has been said that Nanak's differences with the *bhakti* cult were 'fundamental.[57]' The *bhagats* directed their loving adoration to incarnations of God, particularly Vishnu, while Nanak was a devotee of One Supreme god and recognised no incarnation. But the *bhagats* generally identified the object of their *bhakti* with God Himself; for instance, the philosophy of Bengal Vaishnavism declares that 'Krishna is God Himself', i.e., not an *avataras*—Ram, Krishna—to indicate the formless Supreme being. Again, it is pointed out that, although the *bhagats* look upon the world as *maya* (illusion) in accordance with Sankara's view, Nanak used the same word in a modified sense, arguing that the world, though not permanent, was real as an expression of God's moral law. This difference would have been a metaphysical abstraction but for its practical impact on Nanak's view of life. Asceticism is relevant to a world which is unreal, but it is irrelevant to a world which is real within the limits of time. This explains Nanak's repudiation of asceticism and acceptance of a householder's secular life. But he was not the only *bhagat* who took this view. Kabir followed his hereditary occupation of weaving. Sain worked as a barber, Sadhna as a butcher. The *bhakti* cult in its medieval form had no necessary connection with asceticism." Both Nanak and Kabir revolted against social prejindices and were successful in their life long mission of raising the status of sub-merged sections of society through *bhakti.*

Adi Granth

Adi-Granth is the holy scripture of the Sikhs, compiled by the Fifth Guru, Arjun Das in 1603-04. It contains 974 compositions of Guru Nanak. Most important of the Guru's direct references to contemporary events occurs in the verses known as Babar-Vani and relates to Babar's invasion. It helps to reconstruct the sequence of events in the Guru's life in *Janam-Sakhi.* Contemporary references to social and religions conditions are found in it.

It is thus evident that the teaching of the Sikh Guru's revolutionised the whole social structure of Hindu society.

Guru Nanak Dev: A Reformer and Rebel

Guru Nanak realised that Hindu orthodoxy and caste system were deep rooted and social evils and it was completely difficult to eliminate them because they were linked with economic organisation, social and cultural interactions backed by the religion. Guru Nanak prepared the ground for a social revolution through religion. He advocated to provide equality and social justice to the poor and needy in the society.

His sympathy of the down-trodden and the oppessed is expressed through condemnation of those who are responsible for injustice and exploitation. He believed a person cannot remain unpolluted if he sucks human blood.

Guru says, 'Encroachment upon what rightfully belongs to others is forbidden to both Hindus and Muslims, as beef to the former and pork to the latter."

He says, "The ideal society is to be based on justice, elimination of exploitation, and inequality, and recognition of the right of all men irrespective of caste, rank; and his conception of ideal world order was based on the concepts of universal brotherhood and natural equality. He himself calls as lowliest among low."

Thus the Guru identifies himself with the downtrodden and lowly. Ground of birth and wealth were not the criteria for status, but personal good character and virtues will determine one's social status. He declared accumulation of wealth was good for nothing and what he has to do with the upper classes, if they are not sympethic to the lower classes and poor people.

It is most unfortunate, historians have cared little to see and throw light on popular urge of social transformation, which concerned the social life of the millions of common people, whereas they concentrated only on a handful who were either invaders, and responsible for massacres and large scale looting. After decline of Buddhism the revival of Hinduism, the Bhakti-cult kept alive the feeling of social revolt. It is thus clear that the entire Bhakti-movement from Alvars to Kabir and Nanak was basically a doctrine of social change having democratic roots in humanism and spiritualism. It preached the feeling of social equality and tended to breakdown the social barriers which divided the people in various sects and caste. The mission of Alvars, Adyars, Saints, Ramananda, Kabir, Ravidas, Chaitanya, Nanak, Tuka Ram, Namdev and several other saints, poets and bhagats was to spread the message of human love and unite all castes and creeds. The Brahmanical scriptures never satisfied the common people the working classes, whereas they created difference on the basis of birth and heredity, but the *Bhagats* softened the rigidity in social relations and condemned caste system and practice of untouchability.

In Adigranth, page 15, Guru Nanak Dev ji beautifully defends the status of the lowest caste and condemns those who take advantage of their pitiable plight. He opines, 'Nanak is by their side; He envies not the great of the world! Lord! Thy grace falls on the land where the poor are cherished.'

Sant Ravi Das has shown much concern for suffering and sorrow of the Dalits. He calls all fellow citizens as loving friends.

The name of my city is 'griefless'.
Suffering and sorrow do not abide in it.
There is neither any worry of paying taxes or trade,
Nor any fear of default in one.
And anguish for a decline in other
I have now found a wonderful place in my homeland.
Where there is always peace, my brother;
Its sovereignty is firm and inviolate for ever.
There is no second or third class.
It is ever populous,
And enjoys ever-enduring reputation.
Its residents are prosperous and contended.
They go about as they please.
As they are intimates of the mansion and its Lord.
No one prevents their entry into it.

So says Ravidas, the liberated cobbler,
To whom all fellow citizens are loving friends.

Ravi Das
Adigranth Gauri—p. 345

Sant Kabir does not favour the status of a person simply because he is born in a Brahmin family. He recited verses having deep bearing on social equality in our society. In Adigranth, p. 325, he gives vent to his feelings thus:

"If thou dost claim to be *Brahmin* by birth from a *Brahmin* woman, why was they birth not from a different source?"

How are you *Brahmin* and we Surdas? How are we made of mere blood, and you of milk?

It is evident that the Sikh principle of Meeri-piri could be the starting point of discussion. In 15th and 16th centuries, Sikhism had serious encounters with the Islamic understanding of the society. Undoubtedly Islam inspired Sikhism in many respects, but they had their points of divergence. The Sikh gurus stuck to their principles and preaching in a firm way and did not bow their heads at any cost.

The Social ideal of the Gurus proclaims that authenticity of the world, society and life on earth. In accordance with their philosophy, the world is declared holy and named as a place of righteous deeds. One can quote any number of hymns from Guru Granth Sahib to prove the fact that the Gurus outrightly denounced the caste system. In fact, the theories of *karma,* transmigration and pollution and ritual status attributed to the scriptures recommending and *varuna* system were banished by the Sikh gurus. So far so, the Sikh practices of Pangat and Langar are clearly aimed at breaking the food taboos, which formed the anthropological basis for untouchability and casteism. Hopefully, the Khalsa was envisaged as a necessary form of empowerment of the poor and oppressed. Thus the critique of caste system exposes the essential features of the caste system such as hierarchy, fragmentation and inequality and the Sikh social ideal replaces them with holism and equality.

Guru Teg Bahadur (1621-75) was full of pity for suffering humanity. To him, life was transient and the only abiding thing was the reality of the Name. Just like a bubble of water, the world dissolves away, never to raise again. His hymns are full of devotion and pity for the people, down trodden and victims of caste system. He says in one of his *saloks.*

'Man blinded by the intoxication of Maya pays no heed to the spirit, says Nanak, without devotion to the Lord, Man shall fall into the noose of death.' The Adi Granth is the Sikh Bible. Guru Arjan Dev compiled it and installed it with all reverence and devotion at *Harmandar* at Amritsar in 1604. The Granth contains *Gurbani* or the Guru's teaching. In fact it is the Guru incarnate; Guru Gobind Singh installed Guru Granth as the timeless Guru after him. Thus Guru Granth Sahib is a sort of living Guru in the midst of the Sikhs. It gives light and good counsel.

Apart from the transcendental idea of God, Sikhism lays emphasis on to the immanent natures of God. God, for Sikhism, is a living truth, the creator and the sustainer of the Universe. He is *ik-oam-kar* meaning that God manifests himself as a determinating infinity in the dimension of time and History. He is conceived to be the creator-person (Karta-purakhu).

"God who has created, sustains the creation; He gives sustenance to all . . . thine Benefactor".

The history of Sikhism is indeed a long-drawn history of 'class struggle'. Fought at various levels, viz., political imperialism, economic exploitation, and caste inequality and religious hypocrisy. It has been well said:

"If the mighty molest the mighty no feeling of protest rises in my mind.

But should a ferocious tiger (the greedy caste men attack the feeble herd (Nature, women and the downtrodden).

I would question ever to my Lord (Guru Nanak). For Kabir, in his protest against poverty, says I cannot keep on meditating on a hungry stomach. Here have thy rosary back, my Lord !"

Guru Nanak Dev has rightly said, "Caste is hollow, fame is hollow and the One Saviour protects all fellows." He advises the caste ridden Indian mind not to practise it, and for him, the person who is proud of his caste and practises it, causes pollution for the other. Is the Brahmin really born of Brahma? Is the question to be raised. For the Sikh Gurus, the source of pollution is primarily in the mind of man which is self-centered.

Khalsa, is the congregation, whose members, when initiated into the order, are baptised by Water. Indeed the order of the Khalsa is the first human society in the world history, organised with the deliberate object of and pledged to bring about ecosophical society.

The Guru is a true Yogi who treats all the creations equally, and hence asceticism is discouraged in Sikhism, because detachment from everyday life is just like that of escapism that amounts to the denial of God. Sikhism has thrown a challenge to the efficacy of Manu's philosophy. The Sikh logic is ecological. In fact Sikhism promotes ecological equilibrium and self-righteousness of all beings in the cosmos.

References

1. Marshall, John: *Indus Valley Civilisation.*
2. Khanna, Amarnath: *Archaeology of India,* (1-4).
3. Refer to Rigvedic: *Verses of Indra and Varuna.*
4. Radhakrishnan, S.: *Indian Philosophy,* p. 704 (London, 1927).
5. Svetasvatara Upanishad, VI, 23.
6. Katha (1, 2, 23) and Mundaka Upanishad (III, 2-3).
7. See Vishnu and Narad Purana for details.
8. Mahabharata (XII, 335-52).
9. Bararjee, Anil Chandra: *The Sikh Gurus and Sikh Religion,,* p. 3.
10. Chanchreek, K.L. Brij and Braj Yatra.
11. Dinkar Ramdhari Singh: *Sanskriti ke Char Adhyaya.*
12. Banerjee, Anil Chandra: *The Sikh Gurus and the Sikh Religion,* p. 4.
13. Andal wrote: 'I shall wed, if at all, none other than the Supreme Lord.' Tara Chand, *Influence of Islam on Indian Culture,* p. 94.
14. *Bhagavata Purana,* VIII, 3, 3, 20; XI. 4, 38-40.
15. S. Radhakrishnan, *op. cit.,* p. 7.
16. The traditional list of these twelve disciples is as follows: Anantananda, Kabir, Pipa, Bhavananda, Sukha, Sursura, Padmavati, Narahari, Raidas, Dhana, Saina, Sursura's wife. Tara Chand, *op. cit.,* p. 145.
17. Macauliffe, VI, p. 104.
18. Khushwant Singh: *History of the Sikh,* I, p. 23.
19. Chanchreek, K.L.: *Kabir: Life and Philosophy*, pp. 13-14 *and Ravidas: Life and Philosophy*, pp. 20-98.
20. Jagjivan Ram: *Introduction in Sant Ravidas Aur Unka Karya by Swami Ramananda Shastri,* p. 1.
21. Macauliffe, *op. cit.,* p. 126.
22. Bijak, Ramaini, 77. (p. 17-18)
23. Macauliffe, VI, *op. cit.,* p. 131-134.
24. W.H. Mcleod, *Guru Nanak and the Sikh Religion,* p. 156.
25. *Ibid.*
26. Tara Chand, *op. cit.,* p. 165.
27. R.C. Majumdar ed., *The History and Culture of the Indian People,* VI, *The Delhi, Sultanate,* p. 565.
28. Benerjee, *op. cit.,* p. 21.
29. Chanchreek, K.L.: *Kabir: Life and Philosophy,* pp. 25-74.
30. *Ibid.,*: and Ravidas: *Life and Philosophy,* pp. 20-98.
31. Macauliffe, *op. cit.,* VI, p. 1.
32. W.H. Mcleod, *op. cit.,* p. 152.
33. Macauliffe, VI, *op. cit.,* pp. 40-76.
34. Benerjee, *op. cit.,* p. 22.
35. Maity, S.K.: *Cultural Heritage of India* (Abhinav), 1983, pp. 26-27.
36. Trilochan Singh, *et. al., Selection from the Sacred Writings of the Sikhs,* p. 61.

37. Benerjee, *op. cit.*, p. 67.
38. S.S. Kohli, p. 187.
39. Trilochan Singh, *et. al.*, p. 115.
40. Macauliffe, I, p. 264.
41. *Ibid.*, p. 244.
42. *Ibid.*, I, p. 278.
43. *Ibid.*, I, pp. 278-283.
44. Benerjee, *op. cit.*, pp. 121-2.
45. Trilochan Singh, *et. al.*, p. 93.
46. Trilochan Singh, *The Ethical Philosophy of Guru Nanak*, p. 67.
47. Macauliffe, IV. *op. cit.*, p. 251.
48. Harbans Singh, pp. 148-99.
49. Macauliffe, I, *op. cit.*, pp. 37-278.
50. *Ibid.*, p. 332. (All quoted by A.C. Benerjee, pp. 122-4.
51. Trilochan Singh, *op. cit.* pp. 203.
52. Macauliffe, I, *op. cit.*, p. 45.
53. Trilochan Singh, *op. cit.*, p. 3.
54. Mcleod, *op. cit.*, p. 204.
55. Trilochan Singh, *op. cit.*, p. 56.
56. Benerjee, *op. cit.*, pp. 136-7.
57. Gopal Singh, p. 137.

9

Socio-Economic Problems and New Awakening

With the outbreak of the second global war, on 3 September 1939 the Viceroy, proclaimed India as a belligerant against Germany. But the Congress Working Committee, by its resolution on 14 September 1939, protested against this proclamation, as it had been done without consulting the popular governments in the provinces. This resolution also asked the British government to give freedom to India, if the former wanted the latter's cooperation in the war. The Congress party's demand for Swaraj and its follow-up action was not supported by other parties, such as Muslim League, Hindu Mahasabha and the Depressed Classes.

Future Status

So far as the Depressed Classes were concerned, the question of their future constitutional status was mainly raised by four separatist leaders, B.R. Ambedkar, R. Srinivasan, N. Sivaraj and M.C. Rajah. The first three had always kept aloof from the Congress movement. M.C. Rajah had played an important part in the making of the Poona Pact, and supported the Harijan movement, by the time of the outbreak of the war, he was a bitter critic of the Congress because of his difference with the Congress ministry in Madras on the question of temple entry legislation. While raising the question of the future status of the Depressed Classes, these leaders repudiated the Congress party's claim to represent the whole nation, and particularly, the Depressed Classes, on the questions of war and independence, and extended support to the British Government's war efforts. Ambedkar held that India should support Great Britain in the war against Germany. Simultaneously, he, along with five non-Congress-Muslim League leaders, wrote to the Viceroy not to treat Congress and Muslim League as representing the whole or even the bulk of India'.

At this point of time, Ambedkar raised the issue of the future constitutional status of the Depressed Classes in his meeting with the

Viceroy on 9 October 1939. He complained that the Poona Pact had been far from satisfactory from the standpoint of the Depressed Classes, and that in the absence of multi-membered constituencies they had not been able to send their real representatives to the legislatures. He made it known that unless some method of securing the real representatives of the Depressed Classes was adopted, he would insist on separate electorates for them.

Views of Congress Party

The Congress party's demand for independence was rejected by the British Government on the plea that there were various 'communities, parties and interests' which did not subscribe to the Congress party's viewpoint on war and independence. So far as the Scheduled Castes were concerned, L.S. Amery, the Secretary of State for India, observed in the House of Commons that "in spite of Mr. Gandhi's earnest endeavours on their behalf as a community they stand outside the Hindu community which is represented by the Congress. The Congress party regarded the British Government's stand as 'an unequivocal reiteration of the old imperialist policy' of blocking the country's advance towards independence on the pretext of minorities' interests. Protesting against the British stand on independence, all the Congress ministries in the provinces resigned by 15 November 1939, and the Congress thereafter moved towards non-cooperation and a revolutionary course of action.

But the separatist Depressed Class leaders fully welcomed the British Government's stand, and once again assured their cooperation to the war efforts. While supporting the Government stand, the separatist leaders criticized the Congress party's stand. In the Bombay legislature Ambedkar opposed the views of the Congress on war and independence, and described the party's demand for freedom as 'improper and inopportune'. He held that the problems of minorities and particularly Scheduled Castes should be solved before the transfer of power to the Indians. In a statement to the Press on 18 December 1939, Ambedkar bitterly criticized the Congress ministry of Bombay which had already resigned by that time, for the alleged oppression of the Depressed Classes during its regime.

Ambedkar's Criticism

Ambedkar criticized the Congress party's move for civil disobedience which was being planned in the party's Ramgarh session on 19 March 1940. In a conference of his followers at Mahad, on the same day, he criticized this move, and held that it was entirely wrong to concentrate on the political independence of the country, and forget 'the foremost serious problems of social and economic independence'. The General Secretary of the All-India Congress Committee issued a circular on 29 March 1940 for the guidance of the active *satyagrahis* in the forthcoming civil disobedience movement which was to be launched on 17 October 1940, that untouchability 'in any shape or form' should be discarded at the earliest. On 18 August 1940, Gandhi published a thirteen-point constructive programme in which he stressed the removal of untouchability as a condition for winning 'non-violent *swaraj*'.

The British authorities gave undue weightage to the anti-Congress stand of the separatist Depressed Class leaders, particularly that of Ambedkar, and held that the Depressed Classes as a community were opposed to the Congress. The authorities also enlisted such leaders' cooperation for the war efforts. B.R. Ambedkar and M.C. Rajah were appointed as the members of the National Defence Council which was constituted on 21 July 1941. In the House of Commons, L.S. Amery highly eulogized Ambedkar as the 'unwearied champion of the Scheduled Castes'.

The British view that the Scheduled Castes as a community were opposed to Congress was wrong and obviously based on tactical considerations. As has been pointed out earlier, in the election to provincial legislatures held in 1937, the Congress party had captured 78 out of 151 Scheduled Caste seats, and according to Ambedkar's analysis, in 38 seats the Congress candidates had polled majority of the Scheduled Caste votes. Besides this, All-India Depressed Classes League, a nationalist organisation of the Scheduled Castes endorsed the Congress party's stand on war and independence. The Executive Committee of this association, in its meeting held at Allahabad on 24 October 1939 under the chairmanship of Jagjivan Ram, resolved that Congress was the one single political organisation which had a legitimate right to represent various communities and interests in the country.

The menacing war situation, made the British Government feel the necessity of cooperation from the Indian political leaders, specially those of the Congress, who had been released from jail in the first week of December 1941. To satisfy the Indian political parties, His Majesty's Government sent one of their cabinet ministers, Sir Stafford Cripps, with fresh Constitutional proposal called 'Draft Declaration'. Cripps arrived in Delhi on 22 March 1942 to discuss the said Declaration with the Indian leaders. The Draft Declaration conceded the Indians the right to make their constitution, but the constitution was to be framed at the end of the war by a constituent assembly consisting of representatives elected by the members of the lower houses of the provincial legislatures by the system of proportional representation and the representatives appointed by the Indian states, but in the interim period, while retaining the control and direction of the defence of India as part of their world war effort, the British Government desired and invited 'the immediate and effective participation of the leaders of the principal sections of the Indian people in the counsels of their country'.

On behalf of the Depressed Classes, Ambedkar and M.C. Rajah met Sir Stafford Cripps on 30 March 1942. They pointed out that under the existing system of election, the Depressed Classes would not be able to return their real representatives, as most of their representatives would be the nominees of the Congress whom they were not prepared to recognize as the real representatives of the Depressed Classes. Cripps hoped that Ambedkar and Rajah would not oppose the Draft Declaration, "since there was no other scheme under which they culd get any greater measure of protection. But in their letter to the former, dated 1 April 1942, the latter vehemently opposed the Draft Declaration. They pointed out : 'We are all of us absolutely convinced that the proposals are calculated to do the greatest harm to the Depressed Classes and are sure to place them under an unmitigated system of Hindu rule. Any such result which takes us back to the black days of the ancient past will never be tolerated by us and we are all determined to resist any such catastrophe befalling our people with all the means at our command". They further pointed out that the Depressed Classes would not accept a constitution which did not have their consent and necessary provisions for safeguarding their interests.

In a press statement Ambedkar held that the Depressed Classes had been betrayed in the Draft Declaration. Disappointed with the Draft Declaration, Ambedkar lost enthusiasm for cooperation with the Government's war efforts. He did 'not put his weight' 'overmuch' for the recruitment of Mahars in the army, though he had 'long clamoured for Mahars being taken in combatant units'.

In spite of the bitter reaction of Ambedkar against the Draft Declaration, the Secretary of the State and the Viceroy still counted on his support. Amery held that Ambedkar's criticism might be only 'meant to register a claim and might not preclude his coming in to help'.

Organisation of Depressed Classes. Ambedkar and some other Depressed Class leaders decided to organise an all-India organisation of Depressed Classes so as to give greater weight to their claims in the eyes of the British Government. For this purpose, they organised a conference at Nagpur on 18, 19 and 20 July 1942, which was attended by representative from Bombay, Central Provinces, Bengal, Bihar, Madras and the Punjab. In his address to the conference Ambedkar criticized the Draft Declaration as a 'complete volte-face' on the part of His Majesty's Government. He held that the Depressed Classes were not a 'sub-head' or 'sub-section' of the Hindu society, and that they were 'a separate and distinct element in the national life of India' like the Muslims, and were, like the latter, 'entitled to separate political rights as against the Hindus of India'. He pointed out that the Hindus would keep the Depressed Classes 'submerged', if the latter failed to get recognition 'as a distinct element'. He denounced Gandhi as the 'greatest opponent' of the Depressed Classes, because the latter was 'a determined opponent of the claim of the untouchables for a separate political recognition'.

Quit India Revolt of August 1942 and British Policy towards the Depressed Classes

The Draft Declaration was rejected by the major Indian political parties including the Congress. After this, the Congress party moved towards a further revolutionary course. On 14 July 1942, the Congress Working Committee passed a resolution at Wardha to launch civil disobedience movement for attaining the immediate end of British rule and establishing a provisional Government which would convene a constituent assembly. The resolution also pointed out that communal problem could be solved only after the cessation of the foreign rule. The Congress revolt finally commenced with the passing of the above resolution by the All-India Congress Committee on 8 August 1942 at Bombay.

The British, in the meantime, sought to counter-act the Congress movement by enlisting the support of the non-Congress parties and individuals. As early as 30 May 1942, Amery asked Linlithgow whether it would be possible to take anti-Congress leaders like Ambedkar into the latter's Executive Council and engage them in delivering 'stirring speeches on war effort' so as to 'deflect lime-light' from the Congress spokesmen. On 2 July 1942, it was announced by the Government that Ambedkar would be appointed as the member of the Viceroy's Executive Council. On 20 July, Ambedkar telegraphically took charge of the labour portfolio in it. The Viceroy was very hopeful that Ambedkar 'will do all that he can ... to swing the depressed classes definitely against Congress and to organise such demonstrations or public statements as may be practicable in reasoned condemnation of the line of the main Congress resolution".

In an interview to the Press on 27 July 1942, he denounced the Congress party's move as 'irresponsible and insane'. In the Central Legislative Assembly, he defended the repressive measures taken by the Government for the supression of the Congress party's civil disobedience movement. Like Ambedkar, M.C. Rajah also responded to the official suggestion, and issued a statement on 15 August 1942 criticizing the Congress party's move. He expressed surprise over the agitation of the Congress, because, according to him, the substance of independence had already been promised by the British.

Views of British Government

The British Government also once again sought to justify their opposition to the Congress party's demand for independence and started that the party did not represent such important elements of Indian national life as the Muslims and Scheduled Castes and the States. On 31 July 1942, Winston Churchill wrote to the President of the United States of America, F.D. Roosevelt: "The Congress party in no way represents India, and is strongly opposed by over 90 million Mohammedans, *40 million untouchables,* and the Indian States comprising some 90 millions to whom we are bound by treaty. Congress represents mainly the intelligentzia of non-fighting Hindu elements, and can neither defend India nor raise a revolt. On 10 September 1942, Churchill made a statement in the House of Commons to oppose the Congress party's demand for freedom: "Outside that party (Congress) and fundamentally opposed to it are 90 million Muslims in British India.... *50 million depressed classes or untouchables as they are called because they are supposed to defile their Hindu co-religionists by their presence or by their shadow,* and 95 million subjects of the princes of India with whom we are bound by a treaty".

Thus, treating the Congress as an anti-Congress minority, the British granted them some concessions so as to win them. After being asked and reminded several times by Lord Linlithgow, Ambedkar submitted a memorandum on the grievances of the Scheduled Castes on 29 October 1942 to the frmer whom the latter regarded as 'the benefactor of Scheduled Castes'. The major and political demand, set forth in the memorandum, was the adequate representation of the Scheduled Castes in the Central Legislature as well as the Viceroy's Executive Council in each of which they had only one representative at that time. The other demands were reservation of 13½ per cent of the annual vacancies in the public services, the increase of the maximum age for recruitment, reduction of the examination fees, representation in the Federal Public Service Commission, special facilities of the educational advancement, provision for adequate publicity of the social and political grievances of the Scheduled Castes, and special provision for securing to the Scheduled Castes a footing in the Government contract system in the Public Works Department.

Both the Secretary of State and Viceroy considered it politically expedient to treat the Scheduled Castes as a minority community like the Muslims obviously with a view to counter-acting the Congress. Amery considered it 'well worth-while' to give the Scheduled Castes 'a substantial leg-up', and 'assimilate their position to that of the Muslims'.

On 11 August 1943, the Home Department of the Government of India, in its Resolution on Communal Representation of the Scheduled Castes, extended the following benefits to them in the matter of recruitment to the public services: "(4)8 $\frac{1}{3}$ per cent* of all vacancies to be filled by direct recruitment of all Indians in the Central and Subordinate services to which recruitment is made on an all-India basis will be reserved for Scheduled Caste candidates.

"(7) The maximum age-limit prescribed for appointment to a service or post will be increased by three years in case of candidates belonging to the Scheduled Castes.

"(8) The fees prescribed for admission to any examination or selection will be reduced to one-fourth in the case of candidates belonging to the Scheduled Castes".

Ambedkar's Further Efforts for the Recognition of Scheduled Castes as a Separate Element

While the British sought to bolster the separatist movement among the Scheduled Castes, Ambedkar also tried to establish his claim for their treatment as a separate political element in various ways. To the Depressed Classes Welfare Association at Delhi he announced on 23 August 1942: "I want to put the Depressed Classes on terms of equality with the other communities in India, I want to place the reins of government in your (Depressed Classes') hands. You should share in the political power of the country on terms of equality with the Mussalmans".

In 1942, Ambedkar raised the question of the Depressed Classes in an international conference at Quebec, held under the auspices of the Pacific Relations Committee. He presented a paper to this forum on the problem of Depressed Clases in India. The gist of the paper was that while asking the British Government to give independence, the Congress or Hindu nationalists should ensure justice and fair play for the Depressed Classes. He wrote: The British had declared war against Hitler. Mr. Gandhi had declared war against the British. The British have an Empire. So have the Hindus. For is not Hinduism a form of Imperialism and are not the untouchables a subject race, owing their allegiance and their servitude to their Hindu masters? If Churchill must be asked to declare his war aims, how could anybody avoid asking Mr. Gandhi and the Hindus to declare their war aims? Both say their war is a war for freedom. If that is so, both have a duty to declare what their war aims are. What does Mr. Gandhi propose to do after he gets his victory over the British? Does he propose to use the freedom he hopes to get to make the untouchables free or will be allow the freedom he gets to endow the Hindus with more power than they now possess to hold the untouchables as their bondsmen? Will Mr. Gandhi and the Hindus establish a New Order or will they be content with rehabilitation of the traditional Hindu India, with its castes and its untouchability, with its denial of Liberty, Equality and Fraternity?

In the meantime, the second session of the All-India Scheduled Castes Federation which was held at Cawnpore on 29 and 30 January 1944 under the presidency of N. Sivaraj, once again, passed the resolutions of the Nagpur session of July 1942, and put forth further demand for the special treatment of the Scheduled Castes in the post-war scheme of economic reconstruction. At the end of this session, in response to the welcome given to Ambedkar by three Scheduled Caste Organisations, he made a fiery appeal to his people to unite and 'build up sanction by organisational strength behind' the All-India Scheduled Caste Federation in such a manner that British Government would be obliged to recognise their importance in any future constitution for India. He held that if the Scheduled Castes failed to unite and demonstrate their strength, the Congress and Muslim League would reach an accord, leaving the Scheduled Castes in the lurch. He further pointed out that 'freedom of the Scheduled Castes' was more important than the liberation of the country from British rule.

Gandhi's Demand

Gandhi was released from jail on 6 May 1944, Gandhi started negotiation with Lord Wavell, and the Muslim League leader, M.A. Jinnah. To the Viceroy Gandhi offered to withdraw the civil disobedience, if the Government issued 'a declaration of immediate Indian independence', and formed a national government responsible to the Central Legislature. The Viceroy, in his reply, ruled out the possibility of national government during the war, and as regards the freedom by the British after the war was 'conditional upon the framing of a constitution by the main elements of India's national life, which were to include 'the racial and religious minorities' and 'the Depressed Classes'. In the nationalist circles, the 'dragging' of the 'Depressed Classes' in Lord Wavell's reply to Gandhi was regarded as 'a mere matter of tactics adopted to postpone transfer of power,' and encourage the separatist section among them 'to obstruct a settlement'. But the Working Committee of the All-India Scheduled Castes Federation, in its meeting at Madras on 23 September 1944, regarded the specific reference of Lord Wavell to the 'Depressed Classes' as one of the main elements whose claims must be satisfied before the transfer of power.

The Madras meeting of the Working Committee of Scheduled Castes Federation, while reiterating the resolutions passed in its Nagpur and Cawnpore sessions, also drafted the following scheme for the effective representation of the minorities including Scheduled Castes in Central and provincial executives :

1. The executive should consist of a Prime Minister and other ministers drawn from the general community and minority communities in proportion to be specified in the constitution.

2. The Prime Minister and ministers drawn from the general community shall be elected to the executive by the whole House by single transferable vote.

3. The ministers representing the minority communities shall be chosen by the members representing the different communities by single transferable vote.

4. The members of the executive shall be members of the legislature, shall answer questions, vote and take part in debates.

Ambedkar and Congress

In June 1945, Ambedkar published his famous work, *What Congress and Gandhi Have Done to the Untouchables.* The book was an indictment of the attitude of Gandhi and Congress towards the Scheduled Castes, and a plea for the political and constitutional recognition of the spirit of separatism, inherent in the social status of the Scheduled Castes.

What else is there in Gandhism which the untouchables can accept as opening a way for their ultimate salvation? Barring this illusory campaign against untouchability Gandhism is simply another form of Sanatanism which is the ancient name for militant orthodox Hinduism. What is there in Gandhism which is not to be found in orthodox Hinduism? There is caste in Hinduism, there is caste in Gandhism. Hinduism believes in the law of hereditary profession, so does Gandhism... Hinduism upholds the law of *karma,* pre-destination of man's condition in this world, so does Gandhism... What hope can Gandhism offer to the untouchables? To the untouchables Hinduism is a veritable chamber of horrors. The sanctity and infallibility of the *Vedas, Smritis* and *Shastras,* the iron law of castes, the heartless law of *karma* and the senseless law of status by birth are to the untouchables veritable instruments of torture which Hinduism has forged against the untouchables. These very instruments which have mutilated, blasted, and blighted the life of the untouchables are to be found intact and untarnished in the bosom of Gandhism. How can the untouchables say that Gandhism is a heaven and not a chamber of horrors as Hinduism has been? The only reaction and a very natural reaction of the untouchables would be to run away from Gandhism.

Ambedkar's criticism of Gandhian approach to the problem of untouchability showed the vehemence of an aggressive and extremist champion of the Scheduled Castes, but to many it would appear to be devoid of proper understanding of Gandhi's work for their cause. Gandhi's earnest endeavours for their cause were appreciated by the impartial external observers. Though it is true that some of his followers took up Harijan work out of political motives, he himself decried such motives, and his turning to this work at the cost of the Civil Disobedience was criticized in the Congress camp. The strong orthodox opposition which had been roused by his Harijan movement would prove that he was undermining the unjust and oppressive features of the traditional social order instead of upholding it. It would not, however, be inappropriate to appreciate the underlying reason or motive behind Ambedkar's criticism of Gandhian approach, because the former stood for an all-out rejection of Hinduism which he considered as beyond repair, while the latter had profound faith in the innate vitality of Hinduism and sought to reform and revitalize it.

His opinion for the treatment of the Scheduled Castes as a separate and distinct element in the future constitution of India was challenged in the nationalist circles. In his booklet *Ambedkar Refuted,* Chakravarty Rajagopalachari propounded that as the Scheduled Castes were 'evenly distributed all over India', 'in every village, in every town, in every district, and in every province, and were about ten per cent of the population', they 'have to be part of the general population and cannot isolate themselves into a separate democracy'.

Sapru Committees Report: The Sapru Committee's Recommendations and Ambedkar's Reaction

The Sapru Committee whose constitutional proposals were ready by 8 April 1945 made the following recommendations relating to the Scheduled Castes :

1. They should be given 20 seats in a constituent assembly of 160 members which was to be constituted according to the provision of the Draft Declaration,

2. The Committee considered their representation in the Government

of India Act, 1935 as inadequate, and held that "the quantum of increased representation to be given to them should be left to the constitution-making body".

3. The method of election devised in the Poona Pact should continue for another ten years "subject to the proviso that in the primary election for the panel no candidate shall be deemed to be elected unless he secures 20 per cent of the votes polled".

4. Their representation in the Central and provincial executives and public services should be in proportion to their population,

5. Legal protection should be given to them to ensure equality of treatment to them, and

6. Special measures should be adopted for their educational and economic advancement.

Wavell's Plan

Early in June 1945, the Viceroy, Lord Wavell, made a plan for reconstituting his Executive Council. According to this plan which was officially announced on 14 June 1945, the Viceroy's Executive Council was to consist of fifteen members—the Viceroy, Commander-in-Chief and thirteen representatives of Indian political parties.

Gandhi took exception to the use of the expression 'caste Hindu' in the speeches of the Secretary of States and the Viceroy, because he claimed "that there is no such person, speaking politically, as a caste Hindu". In his interview with the Viceroy on 24 June 1945, Gandhi indicated that "it would be open to Congress to put forward the names of Muslims or Scheduled Castes for the Executive Council. While agreeing to this, the Viceroy sought to remove Gandhi's reservation about the use of the expression 'caste Hindus' by pointing out that the purpose of using it was to ensure parity between Muslims and Hindus other than Scheduled Castes

The Secretary of State received several telegrams from Depressed Class organisations, demanding three seats in the Viceroy's Executive Counil. Sympathetic to this demand, the Secretary of State felt inclined to give the Scheduled Castes two seats, but in view of Gandhi's recent objection to use of term 'caste Hindu' and his strenuous opposition to the separate electorate at the time of the Communal Award, he did not think it wise to give 'any separate representation for the Depressed Classes as a community'.

In response to the Viceroy's request to the political parties in the Simla Conference to recommend names for the new Executive Council, the All-India Scheduled Castes Federation gave four names, i.e. B.R. Ambedkar,

N. Sivaraj, Mandal (M.L.A. Bengal) and Ram Prasad Tamta (U.P.) and the Congress party, in its list, recommended names of two Scheduled Caste leaders, i.e. V.I. Muniswamy Pillay, ex-minister of agriculture, excise and forest, Madras and Vice-President of All-India Scheduled Classes League and Radhanath Das, M.L.A. (Bengal), Vice-President of All-India Scheduled Classes League.

Results of Elections

The results of 1946 election further prove that while in 1937 election there was a reluctance on the part of caste Hindu voters in many cases to use their franchise for the Scheduled Caste candidates, Congress or non-Congress, in 1946 election the caste Hindu voters in many cases exercised their franchise in favour of the Congress Scheduled Caste candidates, because otherwise the Congress could not have, in all probability, won majority of Scheduled Caste seats while winning minority of popular votes in the primary elections. The Congress not only captured an overwhelming majority of the Scheduled Caste seats but also of the general non-Muhammadan seats. On the other hand, the Muslim League captured overwhelming majority of Muhammadan seats. The election, therefore, confirmed by the British policy of arriving at a settlement on the basis of agreement between Congress and Muslim League. The Labour Government now fully discarded the war Cabinet's policy of insisting on the settlement of minorities' claims as a condition for the transfer of power. Prime Minister, Attlee, firmly declared in the Commons: "We can not allow a minority to place a veto on the advance of the majority". He renounced the idea of British trusteeship for the Indian minorities which had particularly been professed by his predecessor, Churchill, and held that the settlement of the minorities problem was the responsibility of Indian political leaders.

Role of AISC Federation

At this stage, on 2 April 1946, the Working Committee of the All-India Scheduled Castes Federation, in its meeting at Delhi, resolved that the future constitution of India must include proper safeguards for the protection of the Scheduled Castes' rights and interests as determined by the Scheduled Castes themselves of whom the All-India Scheduled Castes Federation was claimed to be the sole representative body. It reiterated all its earlier demands, such as separate electorate, proper representation of the Scheduled Castes in the legislatures, executive and services, separate village settlements etc. Of all the demands the separate electorate was emphasized most in view of the party's debacle in the election which was attributed to the system of joint electorate devised by the Poona Pact. The

Working Committee wanted the above safeguards to be embodied in the constitution and not in the treaty between His Majesty's Government and independent India. The Working Committee also voiced its opposition to the idea of constituent assembly as it had done earlier, and wanted the above constitutional safeguards to be guaranteed by the British Government. He presented the above demands in the form of a memorandum to the Cabinet Mission during his interview with the latter on 5 April 1946. During discussion he laid special stress on separate electorates. He held that because of the double election system devised by the Poona Pact the caste Hindus could nullify the result of the primary elections in which the Scheduled Castes were the only voters. He showed how because of this election system the candidates of the All-India Scheduled Castes Federation who had topped the polls in the primary election were defeated in the final election. He also told the cabinet delegation that before the British left India, they must ensure that the new constitution of India contained the necessary safeguards for the Scheduled Castes, particularly separate electorate. He warned that if India became independent without the necessary constitutional safeguards for the Scheduled Castes, it would be one of the greatest disasters for them.

The Cabinet Mission, in its statement of 16 May 1916, which was immediately endorsed by His Majesty's Government, sought to protect the interests of minorities in two ways. First, in the constituent assembly whose members were to be elected by the provincial legislatures by means of proportional representation the Mission reserved for the Muslims and Sikhs. Secondly, the constituent assembly would set up an influential Advisory Committee with 'due representation of the interests affected', which would prepare and recommend the list of fundamental rights, minority protection clauses and the proposals for the administration of tribal and excluded areas.

Reaction to Cabinet Mission

The Cabinet Mission's disowning of responsibility for the protection of Scheduled Castes' interests in the future constitution of India was regarded by the Working Committee of the All-India Scheduled Castes Federation as the violation of the past pledge of His Majesty's Government that "no constitution which had not the consent of the Scheduled Castes would be imposed upon them". The Working Committee also criticized the Cabinet Mission for its future to make provision for the reservation of seats for the Scheduled Castes in the constituent assembly as had been done in the case of the Muslims and the Sikhs as well as to ensure their representation in the Advisory Commission. While accusing the Cabinet Mission of 'the gravest act of treachery', the Working Committee resolved that if His Majesty's Government and the Labour party in England failed to take up the cause of the Scheduled Castes 'in right earnest', the Scheduled Castes Federation would take resort to direct action 'to save the Scheduled Castes from the impending catastrophe'.

The Scheduled Castes Federation not only asked the British Government to rectify the alleged wrong done to the Scheduled Castes by the Cabinet Mission, but also simultaneously sought clarification from the Congress leader, Gandhi, as to what would be the status of Scheduled Castes in the constitution of independent India. The Scheduled Castes Federation asked the Congress to accord the Scheduled Castes the status and safeguards of a minority community in the future constitution of India. Among the safeguards, separate electorate was specially emphasised by it on the ground that the Scheduled Castes Federation candidates who topped the polls in the primary election were defeated in the final election by the Congress candidates on account of the proponderant majority of the caste Hindu votes cast in favour of the Congress.

On 15 July 1946, the Scheduled Castes Federation started its *satyagraha* at Poona against the Congress which was alleged to have deprived the Scheduled Castes of their representation as well as against the British Government which was alleged to have ignored their legitimate claims. Twenty demonstrators were arrested because of their attempts to enter the Council Hall of Poona where the session of the Bombay Legislative Assembly had begun. Traffic in the Poona Station Road was held up because of the sitting of 1,000 demonstrations in row.

Ambedkar in England

On 14 October 1946, Ambedkar went to England to present the viewpoint of his party before the British. On 22 October, in an exclusive interview inside the Parliament, he accused the Cabinet Mission and the Labour Government of having let down the Scheduled Castes in their constitutional negotiations. In a memorandum, which he submitted to the Prime Minister, the Conservative Party leader, Churchill, and the Secretary of State for India, Lord Pethick Lawrence, he recalled the previous declarations of His Majesty's Government recognising the Scheduled Castes as a separate element. The memorandum raised the question, "why the Cabinet Mission recognises the Muslims and Sikhs as separate elements and why they refused to give the Scheduled Castes the same status". In a pamphlet addressed to the Parliament, Ambedkar requested its members to press upon His Majesty's Government to declare the Scheduled Castes as a minority, to institute a machinery to examine whether the safeguards framed by the Constituent Assembly for the protection of minorities were 'adequate and real' and to see that the future constitution of India contained the provisions 'circumscribing the power of the future Indian Legislature to do away with minority safeguards by majority'. He held that such a check upon the work of the Constituent Assembly was necessary in the interest of the Scheduled Castes, as majority of the members in this body were caste Hindus and the Scheduled Castes members who had been elected to it 'by the good will of the Congress' were 'but the creatures of the Hindus'. He further pointed out that the device of Advisory Committee was a hoax which could not be relied upon to counteract the mischief of the Hindu majority.

On returning from England, on 20 November 1946, in an exclusive interview to the *Globe,* Ambedkar held that a settlement between the Scheduled Castes (obviously meaning his own party) and the Congress would be possible, if the Congress party agreed to the separate electorate for the Scheduled Castes. He further held that the Muslim League had no objection to the proposal of separate electorates for them.

Plan for Interim Government

In the meantime, Lord Wavell was planning to form the interim Government on the basis of the electoral verdict expressed through the election to the provincial assemblies. The formula, put forward by him on the eve of Simla Conference of June 1945, sought to give the Scheduled Caste seat in the Viceroy's Executive Council to Ambedkar. In the Simla Conference also Sivaraj had opposed the Congress Party's claim to represent the Scheduled Castes. But, now, in view of the swamping victory of the Congress in the Scheduled Caste seats, its claim was accepted by Lord Wavell. On 2 September 1946, on behalf of the Congress party, Jagjivan Ram, the nationalist Scheduled Caste leader, joined the Viceroy's Executive Council as the Labour Member. On 15 October 1946, another Scheduled Caste repesentative, Jogendra Nath Mandal, joined the Executive Council on behalf of the Muslim League. Mandal, a member of the Working Committee of All-India Scheduled Castes Federation, was nominated by the Muslim League in protest against the nomination of a nationalist Muslim member by the Congress. Gandhi objected to the nomination of a Scheduled Caste member by the League on the ground that it represented the Muslims only.

In its Advisory Committee consisting of 72 members the Constituent

Assembly drafted 7 Scheduled Caste members, and Ambedkar was one of them as the representative of the non-Congress Scheduled Caste opinion. On 29 April 1947, the Constituent Assembly passed the following resolution as part of the draft Constitution, moved by Sardar Vallabhbhai Patel: "Untouchability in any form is abolished and the imposition of any disability on that account shall be an offence". The passing of this resolution did not result in the abolition of untouchability root and branch, because sanction behind the practice of untouchability was social, not legal. But in the legal sense this measure constituted a radical departure from the past policy of the British Government which not only hesitated to declare untouchability illegal but also extended legal support to it.

10

Conclusion

I

The social plight of Dalits in the Indian sub-continent had been most deplorable for several centuries. Broadly speaking, our society was divided into four varnas as explained in the text. Whereas the elite or the upper class people had complete dominance in all socio-economic matters, the lowest class suffered perpetually and miserably and they were devoid of any hope for their better future. Thus they were always at the beck and call of the elite class and were found readily available for service even at odd hours.

Undoubtedly, their dwellings were far away from the village so that their shadow could not be visible to other communities. Their services were commissioned even for the meanest jobs. The element of reluctance or avoidance was never found on their lips. They were used as bonded labourers; very young children were employed to rear animals, and perform several other functions whether their physique permitted them or not. Very often they were victims of deadly diseases on account of pressure of work.

There were castes which were looked down upon by the higher sections of society either due to their ethnic origin or on account of their following low professions. The *Chandalas,* the *Venas,* the *Nishadas,* the *Rathakaras,* and the *Pukusas* appears as low castes. Among the despised castes, the *Chandalas* were the most unfortunate. He was the lowest and the meanest on the earth, and the *Sigala Oataka* compares a jackal, low and wretched among animals, with a *Chandala.* The *Chandalas* were not only untouchable but also unseeable. The daughter of the *Sethi* and wealthy merchant washed her eyes when she saw the *Chandala* at the city gate. Food was polluted at the sight of a *Chandala.* Sixteen thousand Brahmanas were once ostracized because they committed thesin of eating the food served by a *Chandala.* One Brahmana was starved to death because of the same sin. The wind, that had touched the body of a *Chandala,* was considered impure. So far so the *Chandalas* lived outside the city gates. Their dialect was different and showed their ethnic difference. They were often engaged as carriers of corpses and as slaughterers of criminals condemned to death by the king. But we also come across some *Chandalas* who were respected in the society. Harikeshabala, born in the family of *Chandalas,* became a monk possessing some of the highest virtues. He subdued his senses and observed the rules of walking, begging, speaking etc. He was well-disciplined and was always attentive to his duty. He protected his thoughts, speech and body from sins.

Along with the *Chandalas,* there were *Nishadas, Pukkusas,* and a few others. The *Nishadas* were generally hunters and foresters. The *Pukkusas* used to pluck flowers and lived generally by hunting and only occasionally by dirty work like cleaning temples and palaces of the rulers. There were carpenters, basket-makers, flute-makers, weavers, and barbers whose professions were considered to be low.

There was a steady increase in the mixed castes during this period, and there are found mentioned in the *Dharamsutras.* These mixed castes across not only as a result of the prohibited *pratiloma* marriages (where the husband's castes was lower than that of the wife).

At this point of time, slavery was quite common in the society, and both male and female slaves (*dasas* and *dasis*) were employed for doing all sorts of household work. Not only kings and wealthy people, but even ordinary families could keep slaves. It was not restricted to a particular *Varna,* but even Kshatriyas, Brahmanas, and men belonging to the upper strata of society were reduced to slavery. It is said that Purana Kassapa and Ajita Kesakambali had been slaves in their previous lives.

There were different categories of slaves. Slaves born of slave mothers were known. That slaves were bought and sold is mentioned in the Jaina, Buddhist and *dharmasastra* literatures. According to *Nanda Jataka,* seven hundred *panas* were enough for the purchase of a slave. The physical fitness of a male slave and the beauty of a female one might have been responsible for a higher price. Slaves were also given in gift. The *Digha* and *Anguttara Nikayas* say that the Buddha had prohibited the *Bhikshus* from accepting the gifts of slaves, either male or female. According to a *Jataka,* a Brahmana demanded a hundred slave girls from a king along with other requisites as his gift, and his demands were fulfilled.

Very often war-captives, were either sold or given in gifts to others by their masters. Chandana, the first female disciple of Mahavira, was a slave of this type. Some people became slaves for paying off their debts. A widow who purchased two *palis* of oil from a grocer on credit, had, when unable to pay off the debt, to serve him as a slave girl. Slaves were made during famine for want of food. The *Vidhura-pandita-Jataka* refers to those men who were driven to slavery mainly on account of fear. Some were also condemned to slavery as a punishment for their crimes.

The nature of the work of a slave depended upon his own ability as well as the social and financial status of the master. In the case of rich masters, the qualified slaves could be kept as treasurers, store-keepers, and even private secretaries. Thus, from the *Nanda-Jataka,* it is known that the master showed his full faith in his slave by giving the latter all sorts of information relating to his treasure. In spite of all the commendable jobs given to slaves, there is no doubt that most of them were employed to perform ordinary household duties. U.N. Ghoshal observes, A slave was engaged in cooking, fetching water, pounding and drying rice, carrying food and watching the field, giving alms, handling the plates and dishes, bringing the spitoon and fetching the fans during meals, sweeping the yards and stables and other such duties.

As regards the treatment meted out to the slaves, it depended upon the temperament of the master. There are conflicting statements on this subject. Generally masters harassed their slaves but in a few cases, they showed kindness towards them. Slaves were punished for their acts of commission and omission. Sometimes they were ill-treated by their masters when the latter chose, in a wanton mood, to do so. One *Jataka* informs that the wanton daughter for a high treasurer used to revile and beat her slaves and servants. According to the *Namasiddhi Jataka,* the master of the slave girl Dhanapali used to beat her. She was also sent on her hire to work for others. Slaves were given thrashing and kept in fatters by their masters.

There are some instances to prove that some slaves received good treatment from their masters. They were given opportunities to learn reading, writing nd handicrafts alongwith their masters' sons. Sometimes, the daughters of the masters fell in love with their slaves. In the *Katahaka* and *Kalanduka Jatakas,* girls of some reputed families are found marrying their slaves and eloping with them. Certain methods of liberating the slaves prevailed in the society. War-captives made slaves could get emancipation if the vanquished party subsequently regained its strength and conquered the enemy. Slaves could also be liberated either by accepting *Sannyasa* (monkhood) or by the will of the masters or by paying them a ransom for their emancipation.

The caste system indeed was a slur on the fair name of our society. Whereas Brahmins, Kshatriyas and Vaishyas enjoyed socio-eccnomic status, the Sudras later on known as Dalits were left far behind. Their children could not receive education even upto primary standard and, even if, a few could reach the school, the management, the teachers and the fellow-students despised them and gave them no encouragement to mix with them. This fact has been adequately explained by eminent social reformers like Mahatma Gandhi, B.R. Ambedkar, Sant Kabir, Sant Ravi Das, Guru Nanak Dev and others.

If we browse through the pages of history of our sub-continent having deep bearing on ancient, medieval and British period, we are at once caught in the complex cobweb pertaining to the general status of the Dalits. It is evident that the Sudra caste is divided into most sub-castes. It is a common saying that there are eighteen chief sub-castes which are again split into 108 lesser divisions.

The awakening among Dalits is a glaring phenomenon through the efforts of several social reformers. Buddhism proved as a crusade against caste prejudices and a revolt against Brahmanism. In fact, it was a movement against superstitions, social discrimination including untouchability and all sorts of cruelty and exploitation. Buddha was critical of the Vedic literature which preached caste system and human exploitation in the name of divinely order of Varna system. In fact the society was guided by the Vedic traditions and Sudras were exploited by the *Trivarnic* social order and Hindu aristocracy. In such an atmosphere, Buddha opined, "No caste, no Brahmin inequality, no superiority, all are equal." Indeed the social distinctions and caste barriers were all abolished with the spread of Buddhism in several regions of our sub-continent and abroad. His philosophy of life, comprehensively based on reason and logic, proved himself to be the first teacher, who showed a path to humanity and opposed caste-system.

II

Throughout India, there is a large number of temples of Vishnu and Krishna which have deep bearing on *bhakti* cult. The role of saints and emergence of such tradition afforded much strength to the worship of Hindu gods and spreading the *bhakti* cult in several regions. In fact, the *bhakti* cult has its roots in the Dravida desa, the southern region of India. They needed a personal God, devotion for immortality and call to prayer, as well as worship which was supported by Alvars and Adyars through the strength gained by *bhakti.* Indeed, these Alvar poets and saints, through their devotional songs, spread the message of love, unity and pure *bhakti* since the commencement of the 1st century A.D. So far so, they attracted the elite class as well as the poor, throughout south and kindled a new ray of hope among Sudras, untouchables and economically weaker sections, who were deprived of the knowledge of scriptures and even entry into temples. The *Sudras* were not permitted to hear the teachings of holy books. However, the efforts of Alvars and Alyars, in this direction, were quite sincere and fruitful when they could spread the message of social reforms and rejected the deep-rooted caste system.

Thus, for nearly seven centuries these saint poets of the Southern region raised their voice against orthodoxy, the varna system, and brought about a rich transformation in socio-economic structure of our society through their religious songs. Even in the North, as Senart has opined, the *bhakti* cult was a liberal movement of worship which attracted more and more people through these devotional songs, indeed full of moral values. As a result of their sincere efforts, these saint-poets freed the religion from the cob-web and intricacies of orthodoxy by giving a clear message of love, unity and ethical values. Even a well-known scholar, Barth, holds the similar views, it is therefore quite evident that the *bhakti* cult was not an ordinary movement. It was a peoples movement, indeed a great silent social resolution. A cultural renaissance as it was, it has its roots in the southern region of India.

The common folk showed much respect for these saint-poets who preached *bhakti* and morality in their own language. In those Jainism was having a strong base in Karnataka. Buddhism was also gaining fresh strength. But the masses were in need of a godly figure who may be having an interaction with them, sharing their complex problems mixed with several kinds of miseries and sorrows.

III

In medieval times, *nam-jap* (recitation of God's name) was accorded preferential attitude. In fact all saints and poets laid emphasis on the need of *nam-jap* or singing and remembering God through devotional songs. Ramananda stated, "Let no man ask a man's caste or sect. Whoever adores God is God's own." He showed quite liberalism in admitting to his *sampradaya* disciples from all castes, even from the Muslim community and called them 'the liberated'. So far so his apostolate had a liberal admission into well-known 'twelve' which included a Brahmin, a barber, a leather-worker, a Rajput and a woman. Moreover, the slightly difficult language of Sanskrit was replaced by the vernacular to suit the level of the common people. Thus one could say while assessing the philosophy of Ramananda that 'the simplification of worship and the liberalisation of the caste rules were Ramanandas' most important contributions to the solution of the socio-religious problems of his age. His reforms ushered in one of the most fruitful religious movements in Indian history.'

We may mention here the name of well-known saint Kabir who was a pioneer of social awakening among Dalits and Sudras. In fact, he had to face a complex situation during the time of Muslim rulers. The ruling class was threatening Hinduism and Muslim rulers were in power to support and patronise their religion. Kabir strongly raised his voice through his writings. He was probably the most cosmopolitan of the bhagats of medieval India. Indeed dedicated to steadfast utterance of God's name, he deemed worthless the rules of caste and the Hindu and Muhammadan religious observances. Due to the spread of Sikh religion in India and abroad, the recitation of devotional songs of Kabir in the chain of Gurudwaras has inspired the common people to know the truth having bearing on humanity and morality. He was a wonderful personality of his age. Pandit Nehru remarked, that the voice of Kabir is voice of revolt against all social odds, untouchability and caste system, prejudices and ritualism. In the words of Jagjivan Ram, saints like Ramanand, Kabir, Guru Nanak Dev and Sant Ravidas stress the godliness of man and sinfulness of denying them their due status in Indian society.

The contribution of Ravidas in Dalit awakening is significant. Born in a humble-family, he reached the stature of a great saint. He opined that the artificial barriers between man and man have all been created by the Hindu and Muslim priests. He revolted against the caste system and believed that by doing one's duty in life and having true faith in God one is capable of achieving sainthood. In fact he united the masses and created social awakening in the depressed and exploited people. It is said that Mirabai was the disciple. There is a large following of Saint Ravidas throughout the Indian sub-continent. We should call him a true, sincere and disciplined symbol of social revolt against tyranny and exploitation of Dalits.

V

If we browse through the pages of history of eighteenth century, we come across Sikhism as a great socio-religious movement. It is a revolt against Islamic tyranny. Indeed through *bhakti* supported by Guru Nanak Dev and other Gurus, Sikh cult gave a call of unity and nationalism. It seems Guru Nanak and the Sikh-panth were more socially conscious than medieval saint poets on social issues. The Guru's sympathy for the down-trodden and the oppressed is expressed through condemnation of those who are responsible for injustice and exploitation. He opined, indeed in the name of humanity, 'How can the mind of a person remain unpolluted if that person sucks human blood ?' He further observed that the ideal society is to be based on justice, elimination of exploitation and recognition of the rights of all men irrespective of caste, creed, rank and wealth.

For him all men are equal since God's light is contained in the heart of each. To emphasise the principle of equality of men he calls himself lowliest of the low. He in fact identifies himself with the downtrodden and lowly. He establishes a link between truthful living and salvation. There is no place for caste system in the new community. Indeed, social equality is its foundation. He further stated, 'Caste is hollow, fame is hollow and the One saviour protects all fellows'. He advises the caste ridden Indian mind not to practise it, and for him, the person who is proved of his caste and practises it, causes pollution for the other.

VI

The theme, well-weaved into ten chapters along with a Bibliography, has dealt with the important sections of Indian society whose socio-economic problems and status are well-analysed since the days of yore. Their sufferings had been unending and a continuous process. They had to bear them with a degree of patience without generating the spirit of revolt in their mind and heart. Thus, they passed their time without any kind of 'good hope or future' in the long journey of life.

Their problems were seriously realised by numerous social reformers, saints and poets who dealt with the socio-economic condition of the Dalits. They did not favour the caste system, rather opposed it tooth and nail and comprehensively recommended a casteless society. Such a theme, including views of social reformers is enriched by their subsequent writings and preaching from place to place. As a result of their sincere efforts some of their problems have been solved and they are being brought in the streamline of our society. We indeed find a significant change in their social status in socio-economic, political, cultural and educational fields. This is the result of the new awakening among them.

Bibliography

Primary Sources

Home political (National Archives of India, New Delhi)

AICC Papers

The Collected Works of Mahatma Gandhi.

Reports of the Sessions of the Indian National Congress.

Selected Works of Jawaharlal Nehru, S. Gopal, (ed.).

Indian Annual Register, edt. by H.N. Mitra and N.N. Mitra relevant volumes

Private Papers

Halifax Papers

Nehru Papers

Gandhi Papers

Motilal Nehru Papers, edt. by H.N. Mitra

Dr. Rajendra Prasad Papers edt. by Valmiki Chaudhry

Reading Papers

Lineith gon Papers

Newspapers and Periodicals

The Amrita Bazar Patrika

Bengal Past and Present

The Bombay Chronicle

The Harijan

The Hindu

The Hindustan Times

The Hitavada

Journal of Indian History

Indian Review

The Leader

Modern Review

National Herald

The Pioneer

Proceedings of Indian History Congress

Punjab Past and Present

The Searchlight

The Statesman

The Times of India

The Tribune

Young Indiaj

Oral History Interviews

These recorded interviews are available in Nehru Memorial Museum

Transcripts of Chhabil Das

Transcripts of Durga Das Khanna

Transcripts of Feroze Chand

Transcripts of Jai Dev Gupta

Transcripts of Manmathnath Gupta

Secondary Works

Ali, Mohamed, *My Life a Fragment,* Lahore, 1944.

Ambedkar, B.R., Published workers, Speeches and Writings, Bakshi, S.R.; Gandhi and Harijans, Bakshi, S.R. and Sangh Mittra, Saints of India, (Encyclopaedia) Delhi, 2003

Bipan Chandra, *Rise and Growth of Economic Natiionalism in India,* New Delhi, 1966.

—; *Nationalism and Colonialism in Modern India,* New Delhi, 1979.

Bandopadhyaya, Jayantanuja, *Indian Nationalism versus International Communism,* Calcutta, 1966.

Besant Annie, India: Bond or Free, Adyar, 1939.

Caveeshar, S.S., *India's Fight for Freedom,* Lahore, 1936.

Chakravarty, Chandra, *New India,* Calcutta, 1951.

Chatterjee, Jogesh, *The Search of Freedom,* Calcutta, 1967.

Chintamani, C.Y., *Indian Politics since the Mutiny,* Allahabad, 1947.

Chirol, Valentine, *Indian Unrest,* London, 1910.

Coupland, R., *The Constitutional Problem of India,* Madras, 1934.

Craddock, Reginald, *The Delimma in India,* London, 1929.

Das, C.R., *India for Indians,* Madras, 1921.

Fischer, Louis, *The Soviets in World Affairs,* London, 1930.

Fraser, Andrew, *Among Indian Rajas and Ryots,* London, 1911.

Gandhi, M.K., *Autobiography,* Ahmedabad, 1963.

Gokhale, G.K. *Speeches,* Madras, 1916.

Gopal, S., *Jawaharlal Nehru: A Biography,* Vols. I-III, 1889-1964, London, 1975.

Halifax, the Earl of, Fullness of Days, London, 1957.
Hoyland, John S. *The Case for India,* London 1929.
Hyndman, H.M. *The Awakening of Asia,* London, 1919.
Irwin, Lord, *Indian Problems,* London, 1932.
Iyer, C.S. Ranga, *India in the Crucible,* London, 1928.
Jagjivan Ram, *Caste Challenge in India.*
Jatava, D.R.; *Evolution of Indian Social Thought.*
Maity, S.K; Cultural Heritage of India.
Majumdar, R.C., *History of the Freedom Movement in India,* Vol. II, Calcutta, 1963.
Manu's Writings and *Ancient India.*
Mehrotra, S.R., *India and the Commonwealth, 1885-1929,* London, 1965.
—Meston, Lord, *India and the Empire,* London, 1924.
Moraes, Frank, *Jawaharlal Nehru,* Bombay, 1957.
Nehru, Jawaharlal, *An Autobiography,* Delhi, 1962.
Pal, B.C., *Nationality and Empire,* Culcatta, 1916.
Parmanand, Bhai, *The Story of My Life,* Lahore, 1934.
Payne, Robert, *Red Storm Over Asia,* New York, 1951.
Ramesh Chandra, Indian Heritage (in 5 Vols.) Delhi, 2003
Rai, Lajpat, *Young India,* Lahore, 1929.
Riv Veda.
Saints of India, available in Nehru Memorial Museum and Library, New Delhi.
Sarkar, Sumit, *The Swadeshi Movement in Bengal, 1903-08,* New Delhi, 1973.
Sitaramayya, B. Pattabhi, *The History of the Indian National Congress,* Vol. I, Bombay, 1946.
Tara Chand, *History of the Freedom Movement in India,* Vols. II and III, Delhi, 1967, 1972.
Wolpert Stanley, *A New History of India.*
Woodruff, Philip, *The Men who Ruled India,* London, 1954.
Woolacot, J.E., *India on Trial,* London, 1929.

Index

C